ILLUSTRATIONS OF THE STAGE

ILLUSTRATIONS OF THE STAGE AND ACTING IN ENGLAND TO 1580

Clifford Davidson

Early Drama, Art, and Music
Monograph Series, 16

MEDIEVAL INSTITUTE PUBLICATIONS

WESTERN MICHIGAN UNIVERSITY

Kalamazoo, Michigan
1991

ISBN 0-918720-47-8 (casebound)
ISBN 0-918720-48-6 (paperbound)

Printed in the United States of America

for Audrey

CONTENTS

ILLUSTRATIONS

PREFACE

The present book was prepared following encouragement by numerous colleagues who urged the compilation of a collection of illustrations of acting and the stage in England prior to 1580, the date at which R. A. Foakes' *Illustrations of the Stage 1580–1642* (1985) begins its survey. Because I have aimed at more than those rare early drawings which depict the physical stage (e.g., the stage diagrams for *The Castle of Perseverance* and the Cornish *Ordinalia* and *Meriasek*), the material chosen for inclusion had to be selective, especially in categories involving actors and entertainers such as the depiction of fools, wild men, and minstrels. The illustrations in the two illuminated playbooks of the Middle Ages—the St. Albans *Terence* and the Trinity College manuscript of Thomas Chaundler's *Liber Apologeticus*—have been previously published and at least in the case of the latter will be easily accessible; hence here again it has been found appropriate to be selective rather than inclusive. The woodcuts in sixteenth-century playbooks, on the other hand, are more often than not of limited value in the interpretation of drama, and therefore these have been presented only in the case of the most important examples, particularly since these woodcuts have been all published by W. W. Greg in his *Bibliography of the English Printed Drama to the Restoration* (1939).

Continental illustrations of the stage and acting have been omitted here with the hope that these can be treated later in separate volumes in the Early Drama, Art, and Music Monograph Series. To be sure, there is nothing available from England like the Lucerne stage diagrams of the sixteenth century, the well-known Valenciennes illustration, or the scene depicting the martyrdom of St. Apollonia in the *Hours of Etienne Chevalier*, though the assumption that the last of these is a depiction of the performance of a play has been challenged of late. Nevertheless, collectively the English material is of very considerable interest in itself, and this is so even when we are confronted with manuscript illuminations that may be subject to the artist's fancy.

I have begun with the Romano-British theater, of which some physical examples are known to us through the excavations of archaeologists. The use of theater masks, evidenced not only in the remains of actual Roman masks but also in the illuminations in the St. Albans *Terence*, was continued in medieval drama, as the dramatic records from Beverley, York, and other locations indicate. Traditions that helped to inform the practices of medieval entertainers in some instances had been passed down ultimately from Roman times.

With the Christian ceremonies of a quasi-dramatic character and with such liturgical dramas as the *Visitatio Sepulchri* the drama was allegedly reborn from the ruins of the ancient theater. Potted theater histories tend to distort the significance of the little drama so often presented on Easter morning across Europe, but the vitality of the *Visitatio* has been demonstrated in recent performances of variant examples of the play from widely different geographical locales. It was most often associated with monastic, particularly Benedictine, establishments and cathedral practice, yet it nevertheless appeared in a parish church in the case of the Church of Mary Magdalene, Taunton, in Somerset, for which documentary evidence exists. The earliest text of the *Visitatio* is English and was included in the tenth-century *Regularis Concordia*, which represents the liturgical practices established at Winchester. While, in spite of the rubrics, it is difficult to know precisely how such plays were presented in buildings such as the Anglo-Saxon cathedral at Winchester, their original performances also raise questions of genre. Probably the text and music moved easily back and forth between *drama* and *ritual* in a fluid process described by Cynthia Bourgeault as analogous to breathing ("Liturgical Dramaturgy," *Comparative Drama*, 17 [1983], 124–40). As O. B. Hardison, Jr., pointed out more than two decades ago, there is no evidence that such ecclesiastical spectacles *evolved* into the vernacular drama in spite of connections that may be observed between the Latin rites and plays in English or in other vernaculars.

The famed pageant wagons on which vernacular drama was staged fail to come down to us in a single reliable illustration. The engraving by David Jee showing a pageant wagon in Thomas Sharp's *Dissertation on the Pageants, or Dramatic Mysteries, Anciently Performed at Coventry* (1825) is frequently repeated by theater historians but is based on an unsympathetic seventeenth-century account that seems to have been faulty and was in fact written after the suppression of the plays. For the structure of the pageant wagons themselves we would be better advised to depend at least a little on the actual seventeenth-century pageant wagons which survived for the inauguration of the Lord Mayor in London. Early fixed stages, in contrast, are shown only in the diagrams which are subject to even greater interpretation and controversy.

Fools, acrobats, minstrels, and other entertainers are encountered in numerous media in the visual arts. In spite of the hostility that emerged in the Roman empire toward the theater—a factor which, it has been suggested, might have spelled the end for the theater at Verulamium when the structure became a dumping ground for garbage while the town remained prosperous—certain categories of musicians remained acceptable, and these categories tended to be broadened as time progressed. Hence while the harp and other instruments in the court of King David in illuminations of the psalms were accepted, secular music and its traditions as well as secular dance remained under considerable suspicion. Fools, though privileged, were likewise understood in terms of a double role, including behavior which tended (foolishly, to be sure) to deny God. Here we have biblical and liturgical influences, since the fifty-second psalm with its *Dixit insipiens in corde suo: Non est Deus* was a division point in the text of the psalms that required a marker, often in the form of a historiated initial.

Illustrations which do not verifiably show some aspect of the theater, acting, or entertainment, though they might stand in some relation to the iconography of the early English stage, have been in every case omitted. Hence the figure of St. Denys in painted glass from the York church dedicated to this saint was not eligible for inclusion in spite of its date and location, both of which argue for its potential relationship to the York saint play of *St. Denys*. Nor did the principles of selection allow the inclusion of the wall painting of the Nativity at St. John's Church, Chester, where this illustration has associations with the same guild that was responsible for a play on the subject in the Chester cycle.

In other cases I have had to pass over entire categories. For instance, with the exception of the illumination in the Harley Psalter which shows a bearward along with other entertainers, animal acts have been excluded, though of course a study of such acts would be very welcome, especially when one considers the delightful example of the man with his acrobatic monkey in the Luttrell Psalter (fol. 73).

Something perhaps needs to be said about the inclusion of photographs of places for playing as these exist in modern times. While no apology should be necessary for the Roman theater at Verulamium, the publishing of a photograph of the interior of the Church of Mary Magdalene at Taunton may be another matter. This church has been changed radically upon at least two occasions, and yet the photograph can be defended since from it we can still learn something about the acoustical and physical layout of the building which held liturgical drama prior to the Reformation. Properties such as the Norwich Snap Dragon additionally provide useful information in spite of the fact that these might have undergone changes between their early recorded use in pageants or processions and the construction of the examples that remain on display in the Castle Museum in Norwich.

In one entire section of this book the cutoff date of 1580 has been deliberately set aside. My appendix on the Rose Theater is admittedly an afterthought, but it appears that this archaeological find is the most important theatrical excavation of the century. Unfortunately, the discovery was at the center of a political storm, and the resolution of the controversy—to build new construction over the site—will seem satisfactory only to the developer and the present Conservative government in Britain. I arrived in England in the summer of 1989 almost at the very moment that the foundations of the Rose were covered over with sand, and hence was denied a personal view of the site. But the findings at the location of this theater were sufficiently remarkable to demand attention and at least a summary of the information gleaned about the Elizabethan theater.

I am grateful to the numerous colleagues and friends who assisted in various ways by making suggestions or by giving valuable advice during the preparation of this book. Likewise, without the help and cooperation of many librarians, archivists, and museum curators, I would not have been able to complete this project. I am particularly grateful to Ian Lancashire for his *Dramatic Texts and Records of Britain* (1984), especially his Appendix III ("An Index of Playing Places and Buildings to 1558"), and to Sarah Brown and the National Monuments Record.

Research was begun in the libraries of Western Michigan University and the University of Michigan—work made more efficient by the check list prepared for the Early Drama, Art, and Music project over the years. Interlibrary loan services at the former library provided access to a great many articles and books not otherwise available. The library of the Society of Antiquaries as well as the photographic collections of the Warburg Institute and the Courtauld Institute's Conway Library proved to be most valuable indeed, and the incredible resources of the British Library and the Bodleian Library were indispensable. The staffs of various other libraries, archives, and museums, both abroad and in the United States, require my gratitute for their kindnesses. Thomas Seiler, Managing Editor of Medieval Institute Publications, encouraged me along the way and insisted that the book should be destined for the Early Drama, Art, and Music Monograph Series. Support for the project was provided through a summer research fellowship and grant from Western Michigan University.

Francis Cheetham, Jeremy Montagu, David O'Connor, and Jennifer Alexander provided photographs that I otherwise would not have been able to obtain, and Gail McMurray Gibson kindly lent her copy of the photograph of W. K. Hardy's painting of Bury St. Edmunds Abbey as it might have appeared before its suppression. Lynette Muir and Canon John White facilitated arrangements for a photograph of a woodcarving at St. George's Chapel, Windsor. B. T. Batsford, Ltd. permitted the use of a drawing showing an organist in painted glass at Merevale, Warwickshire, from J. Charles Cox's *English Church Fittings, Furniture and Accessories*. Alexandra F. Johnston, Elizabeth Chalmers, and Peter Meredith have allowed me to reproduce drawings illustrating two modern reconstructions of the York pageant wagon which had appeared previously in *Leeds Studies in English* and *Medieval English Theatre*. I am grateful to many libraries, archives, museums, churches, and cathedrals for genuinely kind permission to use the photographs in this book.

Finally, Pamela Rups provided the line drawing of the Cowthorpe Easter sepulcher and the diagrams showing various theatrical sites, while Linda K. Judy not only prepared the camera-ready copy of this book for the printer but also designed the cover. And I am grateful to my wife, to whom this book is dedicated, for her tireless devotion to the craft of music and for her encouragement over many long years.

I

THE ROMAN THEATER IN BRITAIN

Tacitus (d. c.117) in his *Annals* (XIV.32) makes mention of a theater in the city of Camulodunum (now Colchester) at the time when it was attacked and pillaged during the bloody rebellion of Boadicea in A.D. 61–62.[1] The entire city apparently was destroyed at this time, and much of it was put to the flames. The existence previously of a theater in this location is proof that the imperial effort to provide theaters and places of entertainment following the arrival of its armies in lands far distant from Rome was applied early to Britain, where the Gallo-Roman type of theater building[2] was apparently established as an architectural feature in major population centers. Vitruvius, interested in town planning, recommended building a theater as soon as the forum had been built, and maintained that the choice of a site should be a primary concern since the effort should be to find a location "as healthy as possible."[3] Also, very sensibly, he argued that the design of the building should be acoustically satisfactory so that "the voice can range in it with the utmost clearness" (V.iii.5).

The location of the theater identified by Tacitus is not necessarily identical to the later city theater that would be erected at Colchester as part of the rebuilding scheme following the Boadicean rebellion.[4] Excavations show that this later theater probably had a diameter of 233 feet and that it was semi-circular in design.[5] One of its walls remains visible under the north wall of St. Helen's church, which was built directly on the diameter of the Roman theater at St. Helen's Lane and Maidenburgh Street.[6] The theater was built during the century between A.D.150 and A.D. 250.

But a more elaborate theater was established outside the city of Colchester at a location now known as Gosbeck's Farm (fig. 1). This theater, in spite of its unusual location outside the city and its small stage, was one of the two largest recorded in Roman Britain. Built around A.D. 100 in the vicinity of a temple to a Romano-Celtic

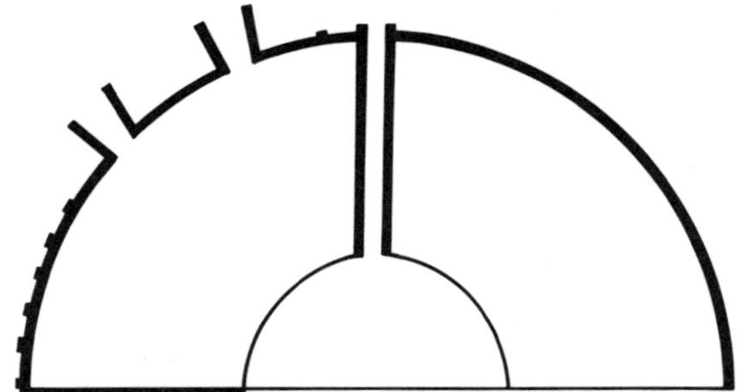

1. Roman Theater at Gosbeck's farm, near Colchester.

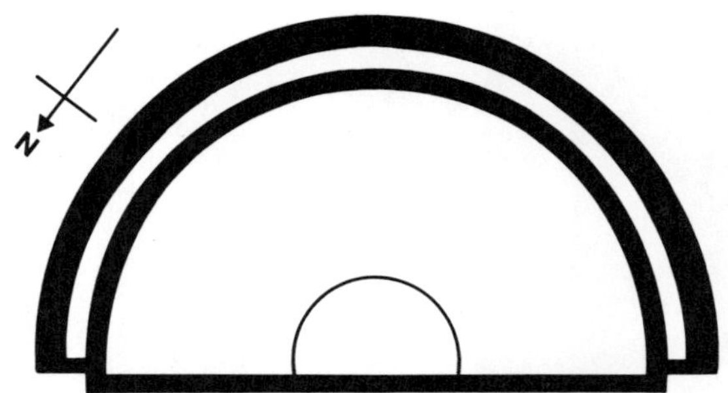

2. Roman Theater at Canterbury (Stage II).

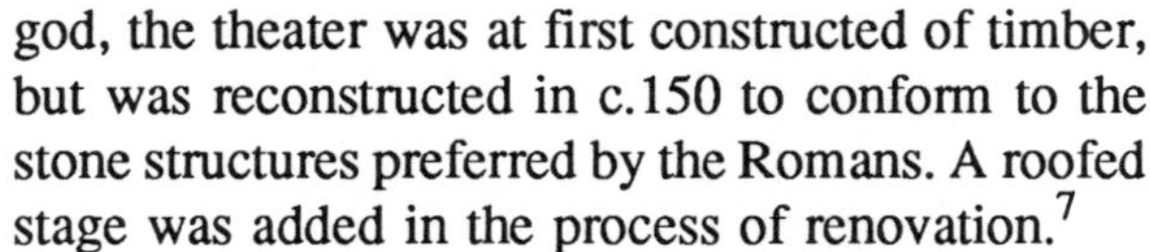

god, the theater was at first constructed of timber, but was reconstructed in c.150 to conform to the stone structures preferred by the Romans. A roofed stage was added in the process of renovation.[7]

A theater in Canterbury, at the intersection of Watling Street and St. Margaret's Street, was built in the first century A.D., apparently at first of the cock-pit variety, useful for various kinds of entertainments including gladiatorial contests as well as stage plays. In the early third century, however, the Canterbury theater was redesigned to bring it more into line with the classical model as defined by Vitruvius (fig. 2). The width, 232 feet, was not enlarged, but the depth was increased so that the structure would hold up to 7000 persons. Also, emphasis was moved from arena staging to more conventional production on the stage itself as opposed to entertainment located in the orchestra. Eventually the theater fell into complete ruin and was built over by the end of the twelfth century. It would be rediscovered only following World War II when sites destroyed by bombing were available for archaeological excavation.[8]

Much more can be ascertained about the Roman theater discovered at St. Albans in the middle of the nineteenth century and involving a site that could be more thoroughly excavated (fig. 3). The Roman city at this location was Verulamium. The theater, located in the northern part of this city with its east façade facing Watling Street, was near a Romano-Celtic temple built in the second century. The remains of the theater itself demonstrate that it went through at least four stages of building and rebuilding between the middle of the second century and A.D. c.300.[9]

In its first stage, the St. Albans theater, which like the example at Canterbury was a cock-pit theater, had a round orchestra of approximately 82 feet in diameter encircled by seating (*cavea*) set upon earthworks built up against a retaining wall (fig. 4). The seating, extending more than three-quarters of the distance around the orchestra, was separated from it by a wall of perhaps four feet in height. The floor of the orchestra was either cement or wood, and in the center was an indentation in the shape of a cross with a space for a post in the middle—was this a post to which beasts might be chained, or was it used for executions? A small stage was placed facing the audience across the orchestra. Its floor was wood, as would have been normal for Roman theaters, and beneath it there was a space of about a foot and a half to allow for resonance.[10]

Changes of a major sort were adopted in A.D. c.155–60 when the stage was enlarged and altered, access to the seating was improved, and the orchestra, now covered with sand, was in part given over to seating accommodation for the audience (fig. 5). The stage (48 feet 6 inches in width) was also extended forward so that its front was now marked by a new (and straight) wall across the orchestra. Its floor was again apparently of wood. Three piers, with columns estimated to have been approximately nineteen feet in height, were added at the back of the stage to bring the stage design into conformity with the usual classical model. The design adopted for the proscenium was the Corinthian order. There seems also to have been a curtain in front of the stage that would have separated it from the orchestra; further, in ex-

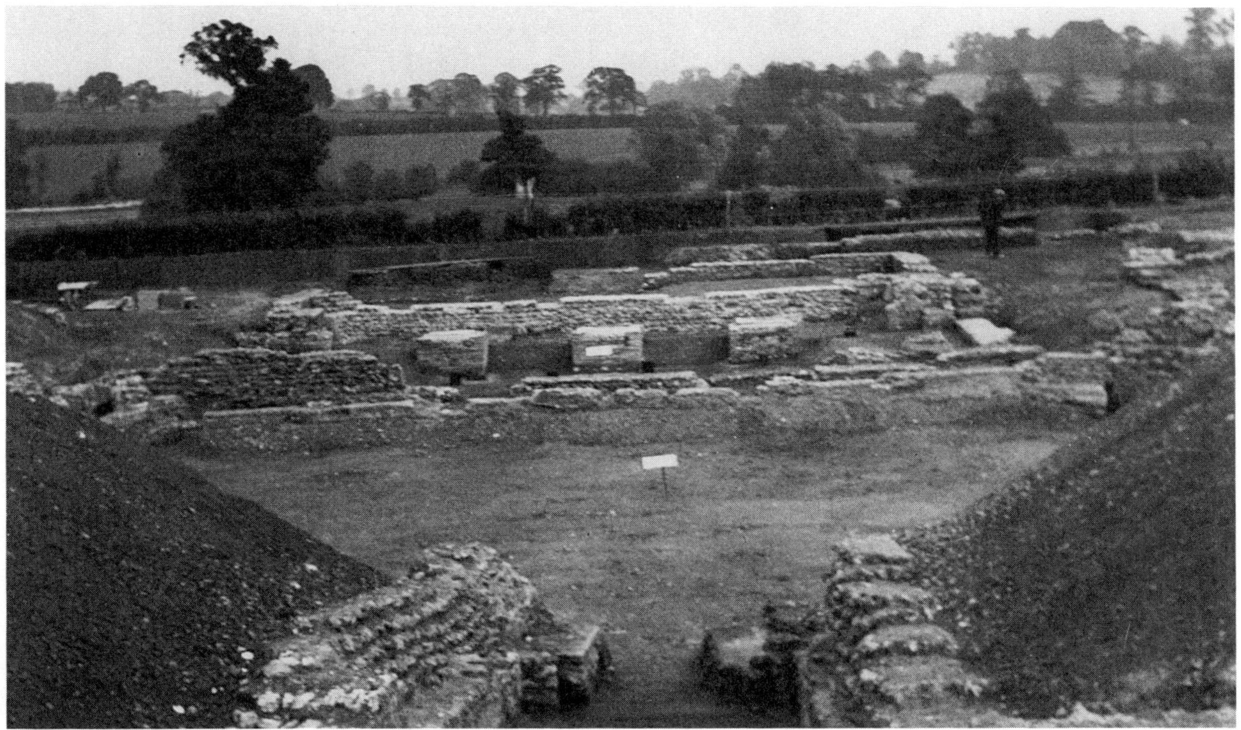

3. Roman Theater at St. Albans (Verulamium) following excavations in 1934. By permission of the Royal Commission on the Historical Monuments of England.

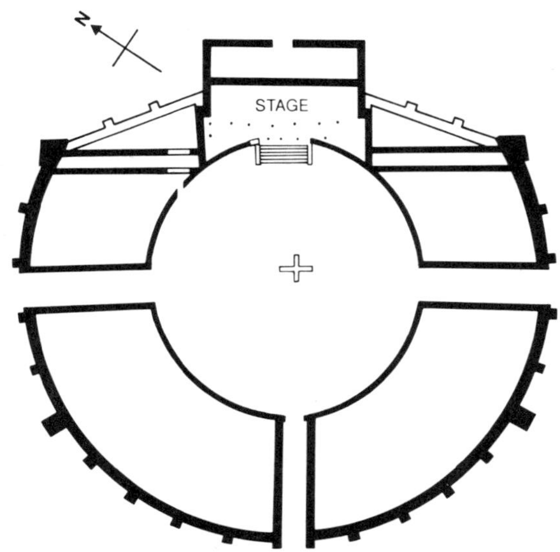

4. Roman Theater at St. Albans (Stage I).

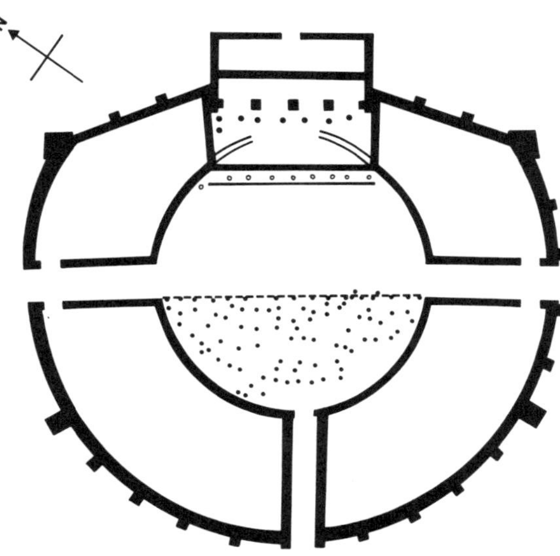

5. Roman Theater at St. Albans (Stage II).

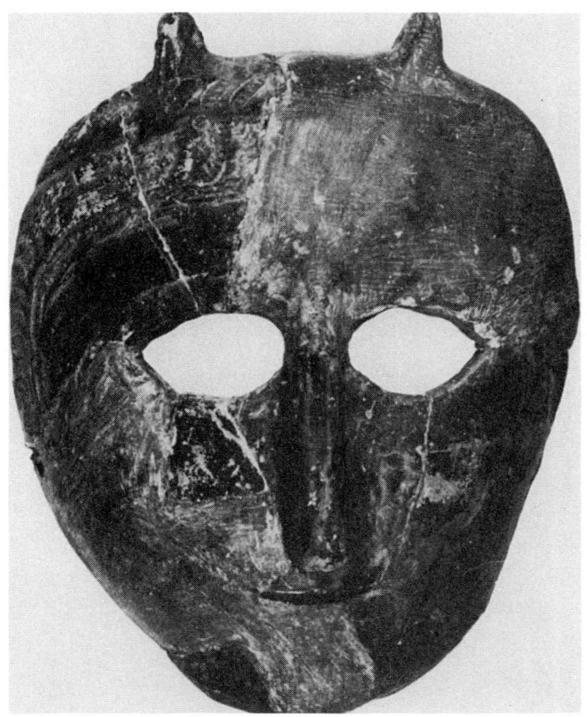

7. Ceremonial mask, probably utilized in processions, from Catterick, Yorkshire. Courtesy of Her Majesty's Stationery Office.

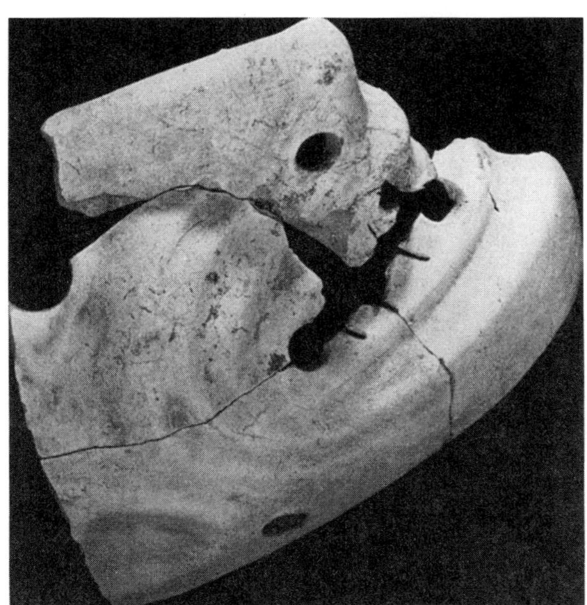

8. Fragment of Romano-British tragic mask from Baldock, Hertfordshire. Courtesy of Her Majesty's Stationery Office.

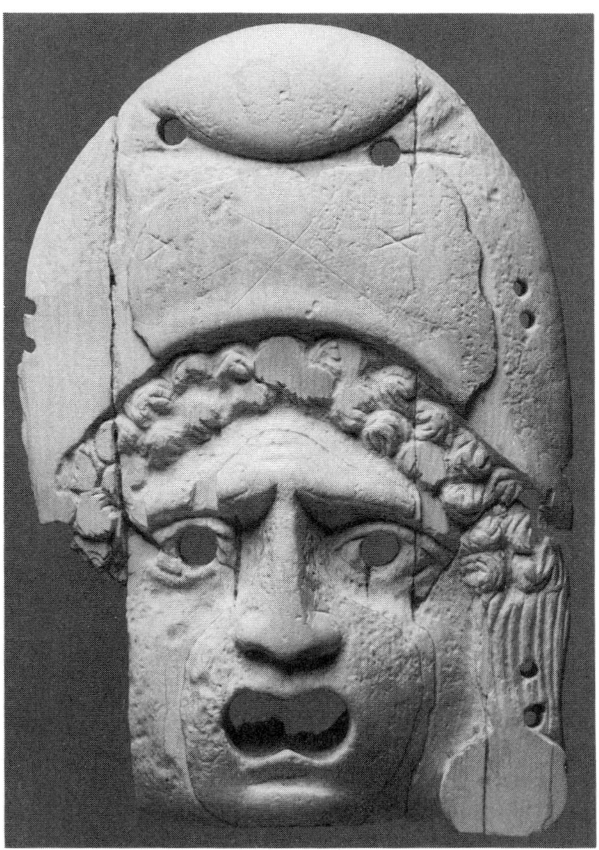

9. Romano-British tragic mask from Caerleon, Monmouthshire. Legionary Museum of Caerleon. Courtesy of the National Museum of Wales.

7).[16] There are large openings for eyes, but none for breathing or speaking. At the top are two protuberances (horns?).

A tragic mask, discovered at Baldock, Hertfordshire, is fragmentary but fitted with openings for mouth and nostrils as well as eyes (fig. 8).[17] Another tragic mask, made of ivory and probably carved on the continent, from Caerleon, Monmouthshire, has been dated in the second or third century (fig. 9).[18] The face is finely formed, with holes for eyes and mouth, the latter formed in a traditional shape for a theater mask. On the head of the figure is a diadem.

Fragments from three masks have also been identified from London, and two of these are now in the Museum of London while the third was excavated by the Department of Urban Archaeology at St. Magnus, the Roman waterfront site, as recently as 1975.[19] As G. D. Marsh indicates concerning these masks, which seem related to continental examples, "it is doubtful if they were used in classical theatre." Instead, "more likely they were worn in semi-religious performances and processions."[20]

Theater masks are in any case rare, very probably, as Marsh suggests, on account of their construction from fragile and biodegradable materials.[21] Yet later documents verify the continued tradition of play-acting by actors with masks, as in the record of a Resurrection play (c.1220) at Beverley in which the players appeared wearing masks "as usual."[22] The extent of medieval knowledge of the design of the Roman theaters and of their production methods has been argued in recent scholarship, but most will now admit some influence to have been present from the practices of classical times in spite of the attempt by the Church to suppress the stage and the total collapse of Romano-British cultural systems after A.D. 410.[23]

II

CEREMONIES AND LITURGICAL PLAYS

The earliest dramatic ceremony for Easter appears in an English manuscript, the *Regularis Concordia* (c.965–75), prepared for use in Benedictine monasteries and associated with the cathedral at Winchester. The ceremony is a *Visitatio Sepulchri*, dramatizing the visit of the Marys to the empty tomb where they are met by an angel who sings the famous words "Quem queritis," unfortunately in the manuscript (British Library MS. Cotton Tiberius A.III, fol. 21^{r}–21^{v}) not followed by the remainder of the speech since only the incipits are included.[1] The liturgical space in which this ceremony was presented can only be conjecturally reconstructed, since the present cathedral at Winchester is vastly different from the building of the tenth century. The tenth-century structure, which was much smaller than the Norman cathedral that would eventually replace it, was to be re-dedicated in 980 after an energetic building program by Ethelwold. Ethelwold's additions to the seventh-century building joined it to a tower to the west. In this cathedral, then, there would be sufficient space for processions, including the procession of the three Marys, impersonated by three brothers vested in copes and carrying incense in thuribles, to the Easter sepulcher placed near the altar. The most likely direction of this procession of the Marys would have been from west to east—i.e., from the westwork to the sepulcher. Based on archaeological evidence, the diagram showing the tenth-century cathedral (fig. 10) gives a good indication of the horizontal design of the building but nothing of its vertical dimensions.[2]

The principal property used in productions of the *Visitatio* was the Easter sepulcher, which was also required for the quasi-dramatic *Depositio* and *Elevatio* ceremonies for Good Friday and very early on Easter morning. The sepulcher at Winchester probably was a temporary tomb, a type which almost does not survive into modern times on account of destruction by iconoclasts at the time of the Reformation. A wooden Easter sepul-

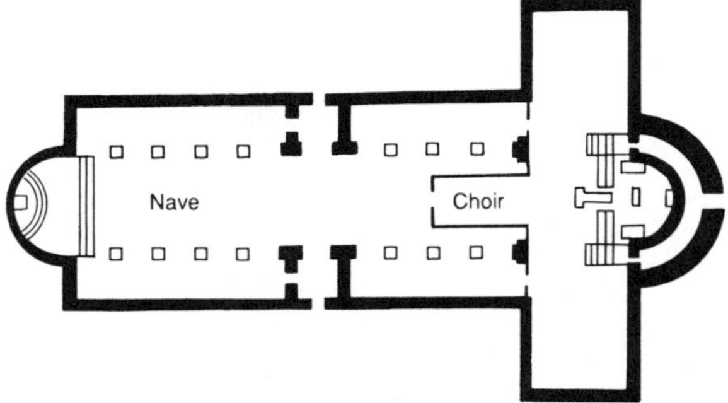

10. Plan of Winchester Cathedral in the tenth century.

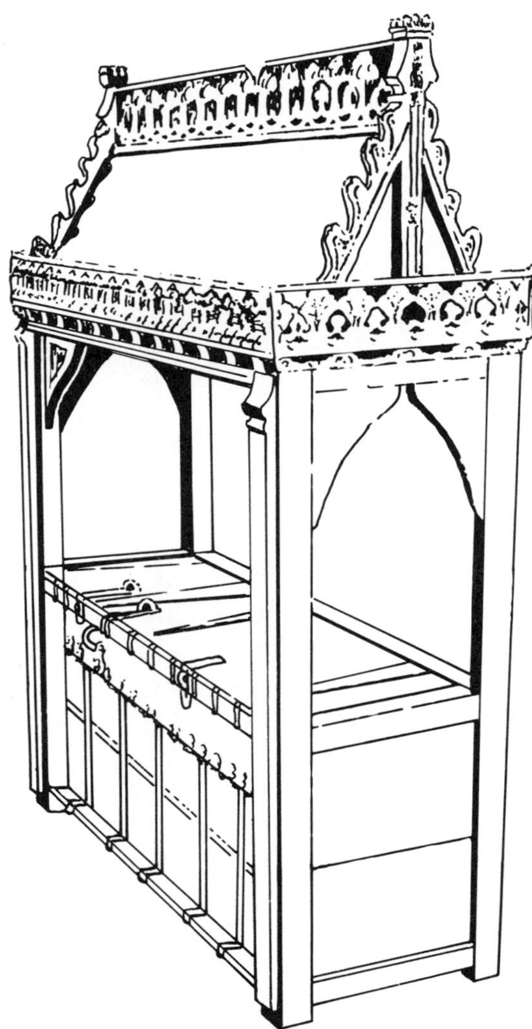

11. Wooden Easter Sepulcher. Cowthorpe, West Yorkshire.

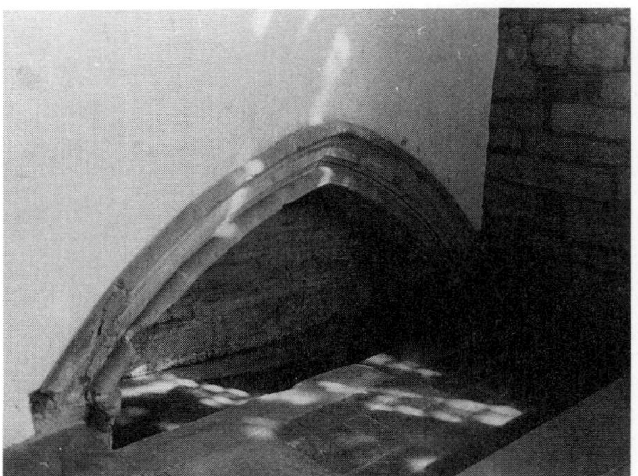

12. Easter Sepulcher. Ratcliffe-on-Soar, Nottinghamshire. Photograph: Jennifer Alexander.

cher does, however, survive at Cowthorpe, Yorkshire,[3] though another example once found in the vicarage at Snitterfield (originally at Kilsby, Northamptonshire) has been missing since the 1920's.[4] The Cowthorpe sepulcher (fig. 11), which was constructed in the fifteenth century, has a gabled canopy on top of a wooden chest.[5]

On the other hand, numerous examples of Easter sepulchers in the north wall of the chancel of churches and cathedrals remain, some of them with identifying sculpture that betrays the use to which they were put in the Middle Ages. While such sepulchers also were likely to have been put to regular use as sacrament houses for the reserved sacrament, on Good Friday they would have received the Host, often placed within a crucifix which was "buried" in the "tomb" (*Depositio*) until removed on Easter morning in another ceremony (*Elevatio*). These sepulchers ranged from the simplest (fig. 12) to the elaborate Easter sepulcher at Lincoln Cathedral (fig. 13) where the structure is an elaborate tomb guarded by three sleeping soldiers. The Easter sepulcher in the latter case is attached to the tomb of Lincoln's founder, Remigius, and consists of three bays at the north side of the high altar.[6] The existence of another sepulcher, a removable tomb with "other Furniture belonging to the same Sepulcre" noted in a Lincoln Cathedral inventory of 1557,[7] may suggest an alternate location for the quasi-dramatic ceremonies

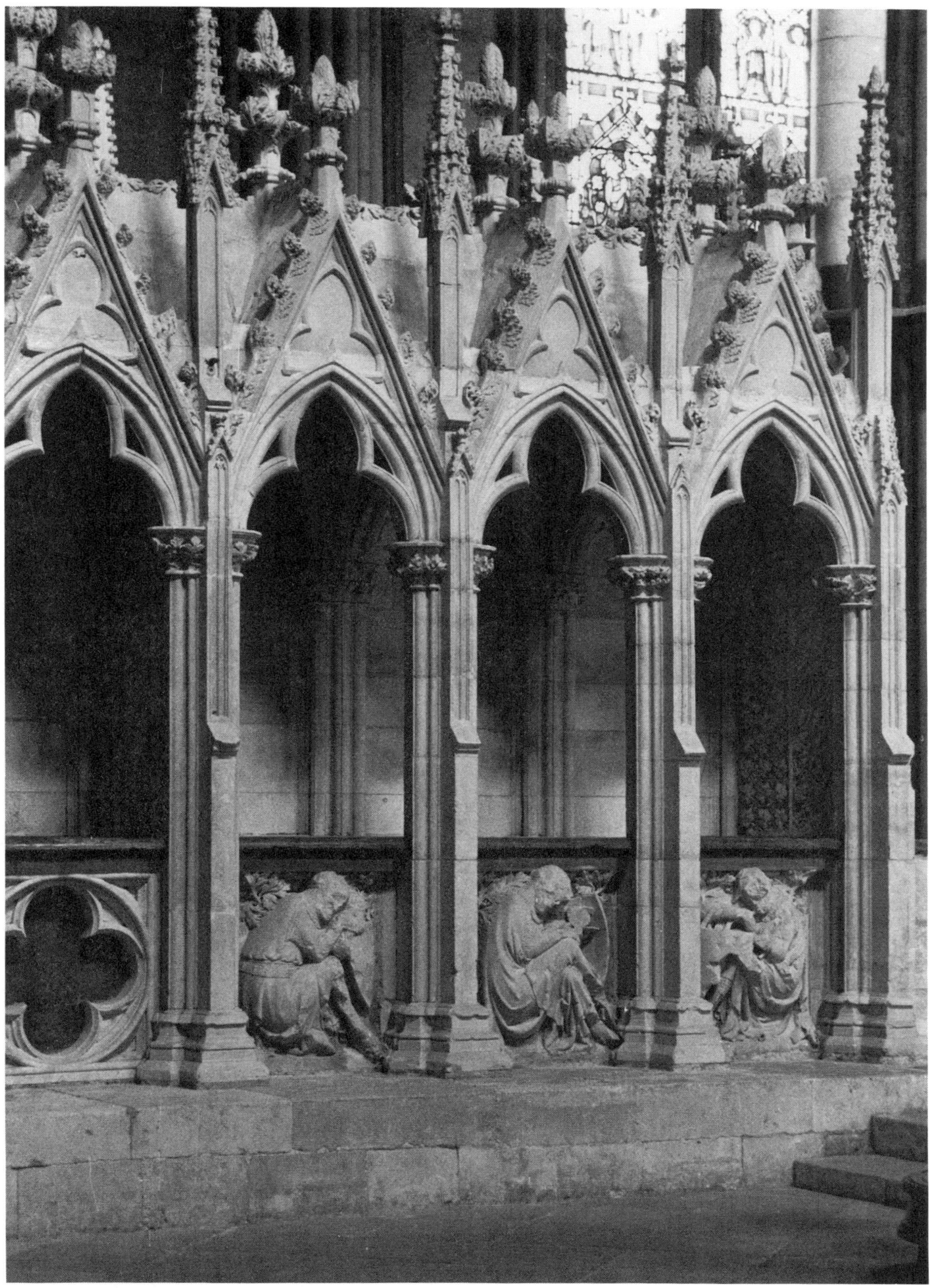

13. Easter Sepulcher. Lincoln Cathedral. Photograph: Jennifer Alexander; reproduced by kind permission of the Dean and Chapter of Lincoln.

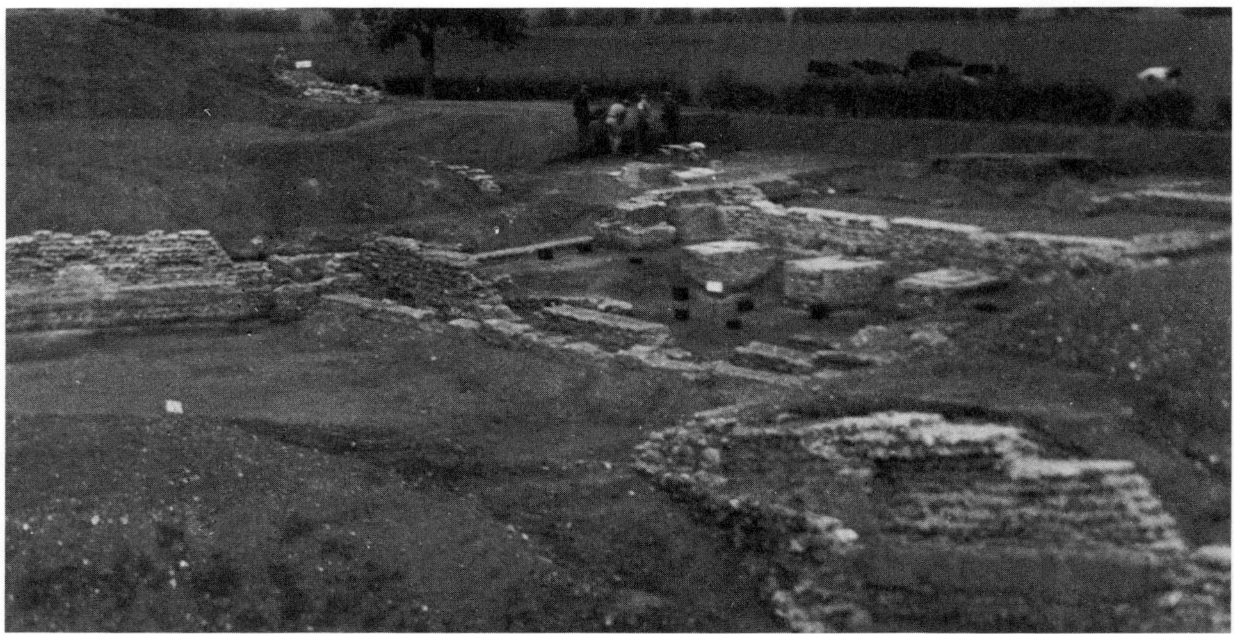

6. The theater at St. Albans. The two walls showing successive additions to the stage indicate where it was expanded into the orchestra in the second and third centuries. By permission of the Royal Commission on the Historical Monuments of England.

cavating the site, archaeologists discovered an iron counterweight which may have been intended to assist in the raising and lowering of the curtain.[11] Such a curtain would have been raised by means of telescoping poles set in slots, which seem to be present in the current site.

In the early third century, the stage front was widened to a width of 72 feet 6 inches, and a new wall of stone was placed in front of the wall previously separating the orchestra from the stage (fig. 6). Some additions were also made to the wings.[12] Complete rebuilding, however, took place in the course of the third century, perhaps in response to the deterioration of the structure. The seating was removed from the orchestra, which was resurfaced with cement. Apparently the theater had been deliberately shifted back from the classical model to a design consistent with the uses to which it had been put in the first stage of its development. Though the stage now remained unchanged, the stage walls were rebuilt at this time, and one of the wings was rebuilt according to a new design. Near this wing (the southeast) there was also constructed across Watling Street a triumphal arch. How long afterward the theater fell into decay we cannot say, but by the fourth quarter of the fourth century the theater was being used as a garbage dump.[13]

In spite of the belief that theaters would have existed at Lincoln and London, there is neither any written record nor archaeological evidence to prove that such structures existed at these cities. However, at Brough-on-Humber in the East Riding of Yorkshire (now in Humberside), an inscription found on a limestone dedication slab indicated that the aedile of the Roman village of Petuaria had given a new "stage" (*proscaenium*) for the theater.[14] Also, in addition to the amphitheater outside the walls at Cirencester, Gloucestershire, there was a theater in the town. The diameter of the building was very likely about 192 feet.[15]

There are, however, some remains of theater masks from the Roman period in Britain, in one case apparently in connection with a small theater. From Catterick in the North Riding of Yorkshire (now North Yorkshire), a fourth-century Romano-Celtic mask, very likely originating in the pottery works near Peterborough, survives (fig.

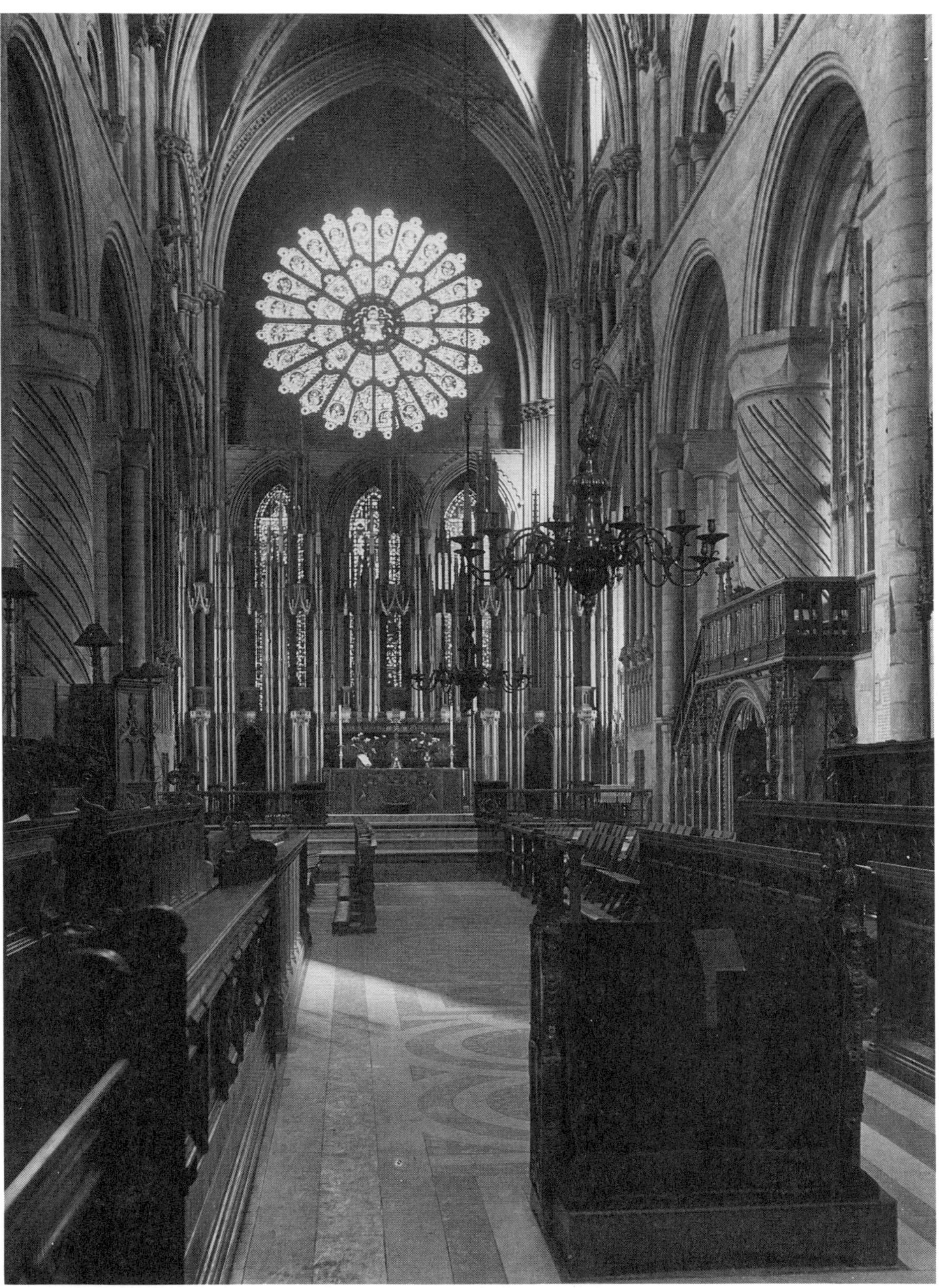

15. Durham Cathedral Choir. By permission of the Royal Commission on the Historical Monuments of England.

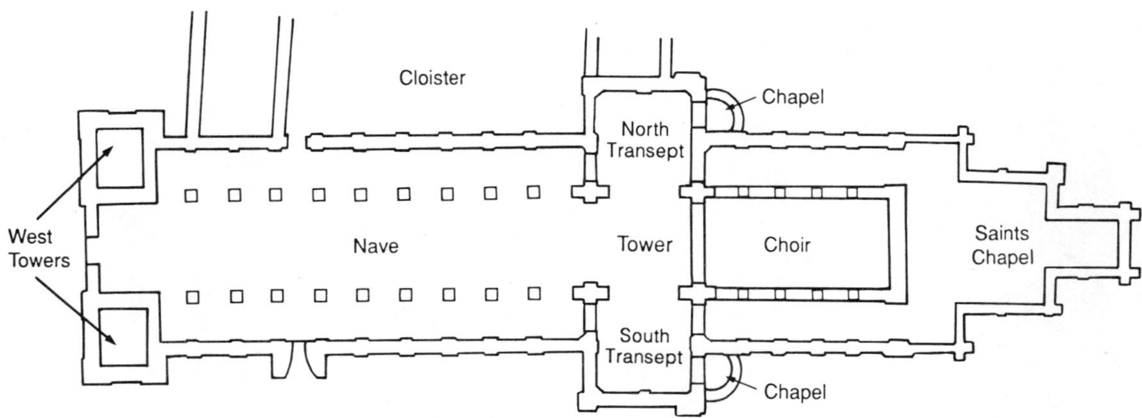

16. Plan of Barking Abbey Church before the Dissolution.

and *Elevatio*, comes from Durham Cathedral, where the quasi-dramatic rites are specifically identified as taking place in the choir (fig. 15). *A Description or Breife Declaration of All the Ancient Monuments, Rites, and Customes Belonginge or Beinge within the Monastical Church of Durham before the Suppression* (1593)[12] explains how, after the Passion was sung and the creeping to the cross completed, the crucifix would be carried by the monks to the sepulcher that had been set up on that morning. In the sepulcher there would also be placed a second crucifix with the Host enclosed in it. All was done "with great reverence," and upon conclusion of the burial ceremony the monks prayed on their knees before the sepulcher "a great space." Two candles were lighted before the sepulcher to burn until Easter morning.[13]

Then, on the morning of Easter day, "two of the oldest Monkes of the Quire came to the Sepulchre, beinge sett upp upon Good Friday, after the Passion, all covered with red velvett and embrodered with gold, and then did sence it, either Monke with a pair of silver sencers sittinge on theire knees before the Sepulchre." Rising, they then "came to the Sepulchre, out of the which, with great devotion and reverence, they tooke a marvelous beautifull IMAGE OF OUR SAVIOUR, representing the resurrection, with a crosse in his hand, in the breast wherof was enclosed in bright christall the holy Sacrament of the Altar, throughe the which christall the Blessed Host was conspicuous to the behoulders." The crucifix was elevated for all to see, and then carried to the high altar as *Christus resurgens* was sung. After this chant was completed, the two monks processed from the high altar to the south choir door, whereupon was commenced a procession of all the monks through the interior of the church. At the conclusion of the procession, the image was placed again on the high altar, where it remained until Ascension Day.[14]

The Durham *Depositio* and *Elevatio* ceremonies were less elaborate than the expanded quasi-dramatic rites at the convent at Barking in Essex (fig. 16) where Katherine de Sutton, abbess from 1358 to 1377,[15] arranged mimetic rituals designed to stimulate the members of the congregation in their spirituality. In the Barking *Depositio*, the corpus was detached from the cross for burial and its wounds were washed.[16] The *Elevatio* on Easter morning was moved from an earlier time in the morning to a point following the third respond of Matins and was expanded to include a representation of the Harrowing of Hell. The nuns, identifying with the souls of the Patriarchs in limbo, were "imprisoned" in the Chapel of St. Mary Magdalene, and the priest, representing the soul of Christ, came to its door from the outside, whereupon he exclaimed three times "Open up, ye gates, that the King of Glory might come in." The souls, holding palms (or, more likely, willow branches, which were frequently substituted for palms in England), then went in procession to the Easter sepulcher from which the Host was to be removed. Finally there would be yet another procession, from the high altar to the Holy Trinity altar, to represent Christ's journey to Galilee after his resurrection.[17] Thereafter on Easter morning the nuns also performed the little drama of the *Visitatio sepulchri* at the sepulcher in which three sisters represented the Marys at the tomb. Holding incense jars (*ampullas*) in their hands, they went in procession out of the chapel, where they had dressed themselves, to the sepulcher. There they met the angels, one of whom was played by a *clericus*, who sang the famous words "Quem queritis in sepulchro, o christicole?" This *Visitatio* is of the most complex category, and hence includes the lament of Mary

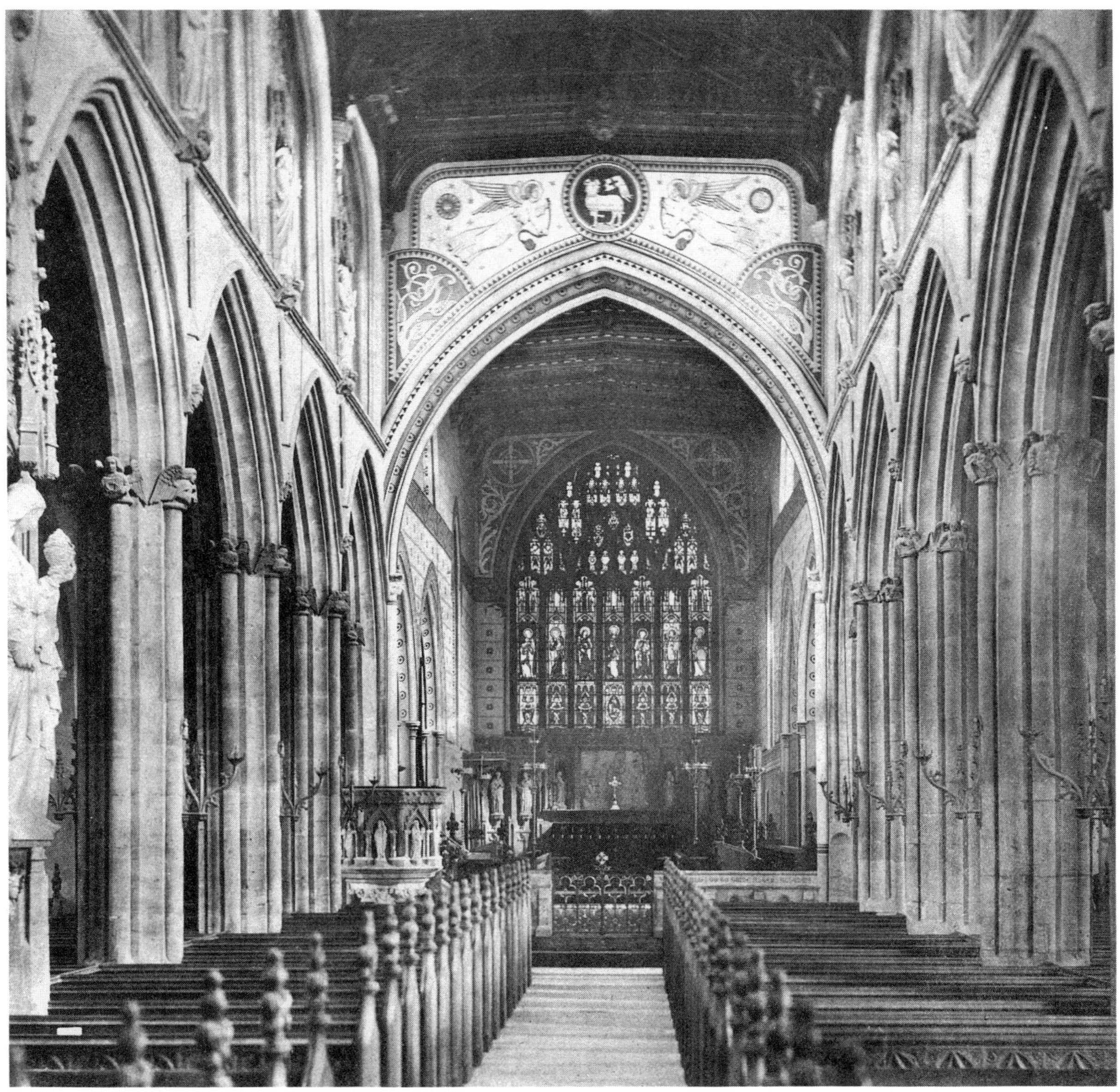

17. The Church of St. Mary Magdalene, Taunton, the site of a *Visitatio Sepulchri*. By permission of the Royal Commission on the Historical Monuments of England.

Magdalene and her meeting with Christ, whom she takes to be the gardener. The entire play ends with the *Te Deum laudamus*.[18] For her efforts in adapting these ceremonies in order to "dispel completely the sluggish indifference of the faithful,"[19] Abbess Katherine has been called the "first English woman playwright,"[20] though there is no proof that the additions to the ceremonies

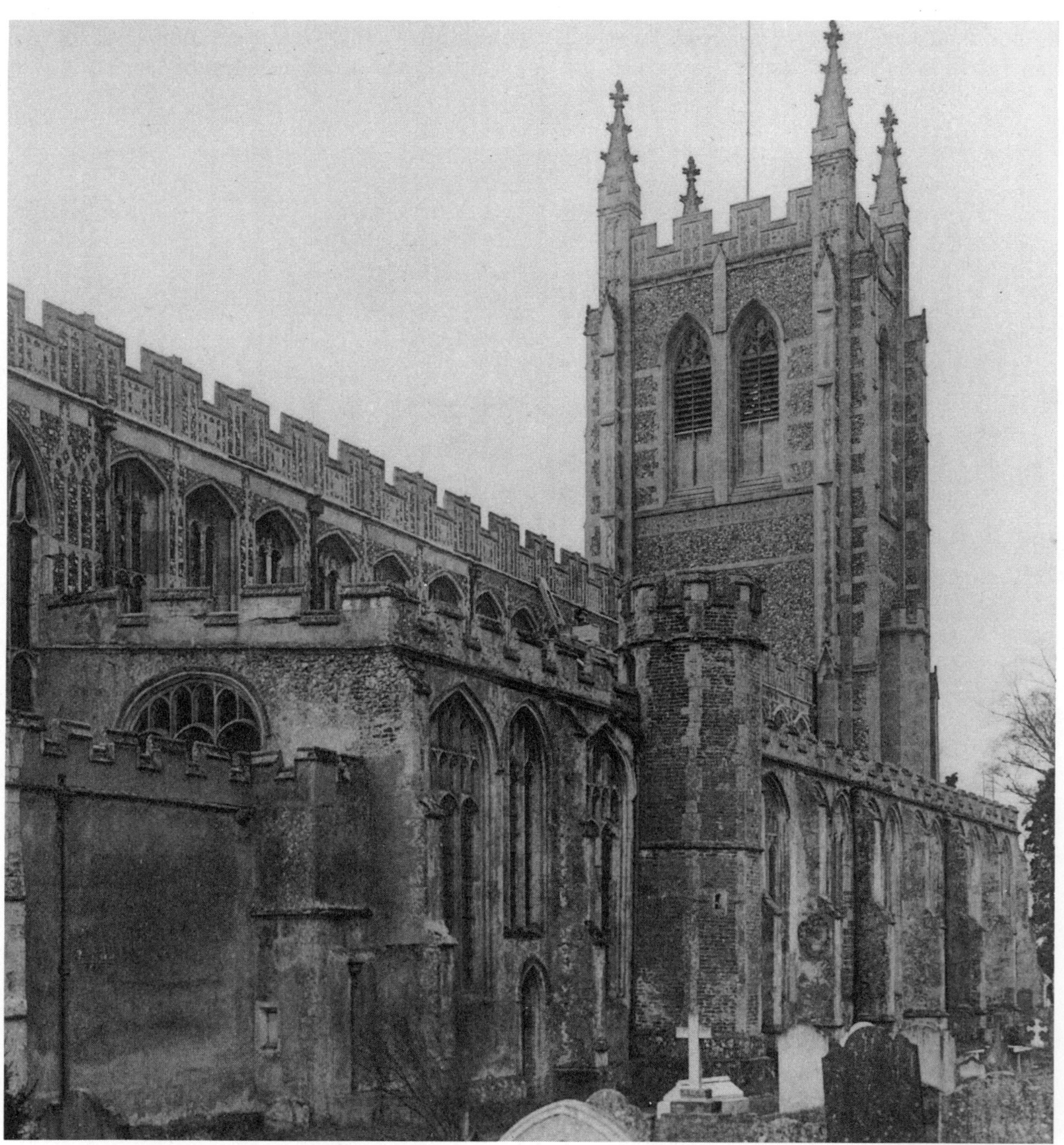

18. Aisle door of Clopton Chapel, Long Melford. From the turret over this door a boy sang the role of a prophet on Palm Sunday. By permission of the Royal Commission on the Historical Monuments of England.

and the *Visitatio* were in fact her own work. Nevertheless, we can be certain that she was indeed the patron and also possibly the dramaturg responsible for expanding the quasi-dramatic rites and the play and for making them much more theatrically vivid. It is thus most unfortunate that the abbey at Barking should have failed to survive the Reformation. The church was the second largest in the county of Essex—337 feet in length—and the third richest in all of England before its destruction in 1541–42.[21]

Another *Visitatio* is recorded at Taunton in Somerset, where reference to it appeared in a will dated 24 January 1503. Dame Agnes Burton contributed in her will to the service of the sepulcher at the church of St. Mary Magdalene at Taunton, and as part of this service she specified the "Mary Magdaleyn play," which would be enriched by her "rede damaske mantell" and her "mentell lyned with sylke."[22] Currently there is a stone chest now in the churchyard that may be the Easter sepulcher, cast out at the Reformation.[23] The interior of this church (fig. 17) went through at least two drastic alterations, the last being in 1843–44 when box pews were removed, benches were replaced in the nave and aisles, and stalls were fitted into the chancel.[24] An early nineteenth-century illustration in the National Monuments Record demonstrates how much was changed by 1845, the date of an engraving in F. T. Dolman's *Some Account of the Church of St. Mary Magdalene.*[25] This engraving must therefore not be regarded as representing the state of the building prior to the suppression of the sepulcher rites and the *Visitatio sepulchri.*

More widespread than the *Visitatio sepulchri* in England were quasi-dramatic ceremonies attached to the Palm Sunday procession. While no processional figure of Christ on an ass fitted with wheels was used, as had been the case in Germany and Poland,[26] there were still some important features that were dramatized on this feast day. Several London churches recorded the appearance of prophets as part of the ritual, and boy choristers commonly took part in the ceremony.[27] At Long Melford a boy, pointing at the sacrament which had been carried in procession, sang the role of the prophet from a turret over the aisle door of the Clopton chapel (fig. 18), and then the people, also in procession and approaching from a separate direction, went to meet the sacrament, whereupon they together went into the church.[28] Sarum manuscripts suggest very elaborate processions not only at Salisbury but wherever the influence of the Sarum rite was felt. Salisbury Cathedral practice involved processions which, beginning with the blessing of the palms,[29] issued forth out of the choir, through the cloister (fig. 19), and around to the north side of the church to the first station at the cross, where the first gospel was read and a boy, "clad like a prophet, standing on some high place," sang the words adapted from *Baruch* 5.5: "Jerusalem, look toward the east and see: lift up thine eyes, Jerusalem, and see the power of the king."[30] At the second station, boys, singing the hymn *Gloria laus et honor* from a point on some sort of platform above the door at the south of the cathedral, threw down flowers and cakes. At Swaffham in Norfolk, payments were recorded in the early sixteenth century "for makyng of the stage of palmesondaye,"[31] presumably because

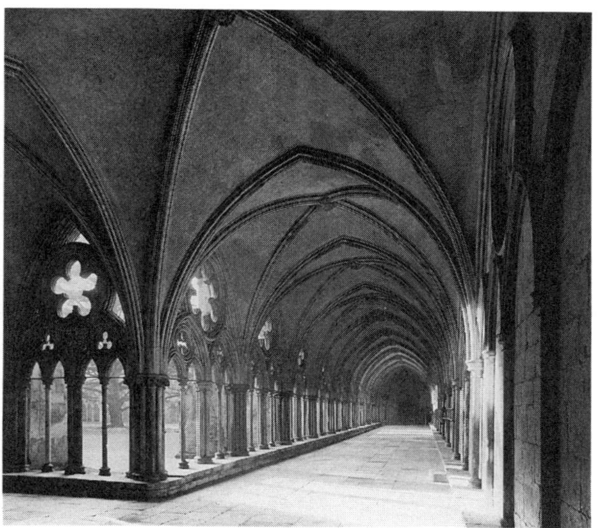

19. Salisbury Cathedral. Cloisters through which the Palm Sunday procession took place. By permission of the Royal Commission on the Historical Monuments of England.

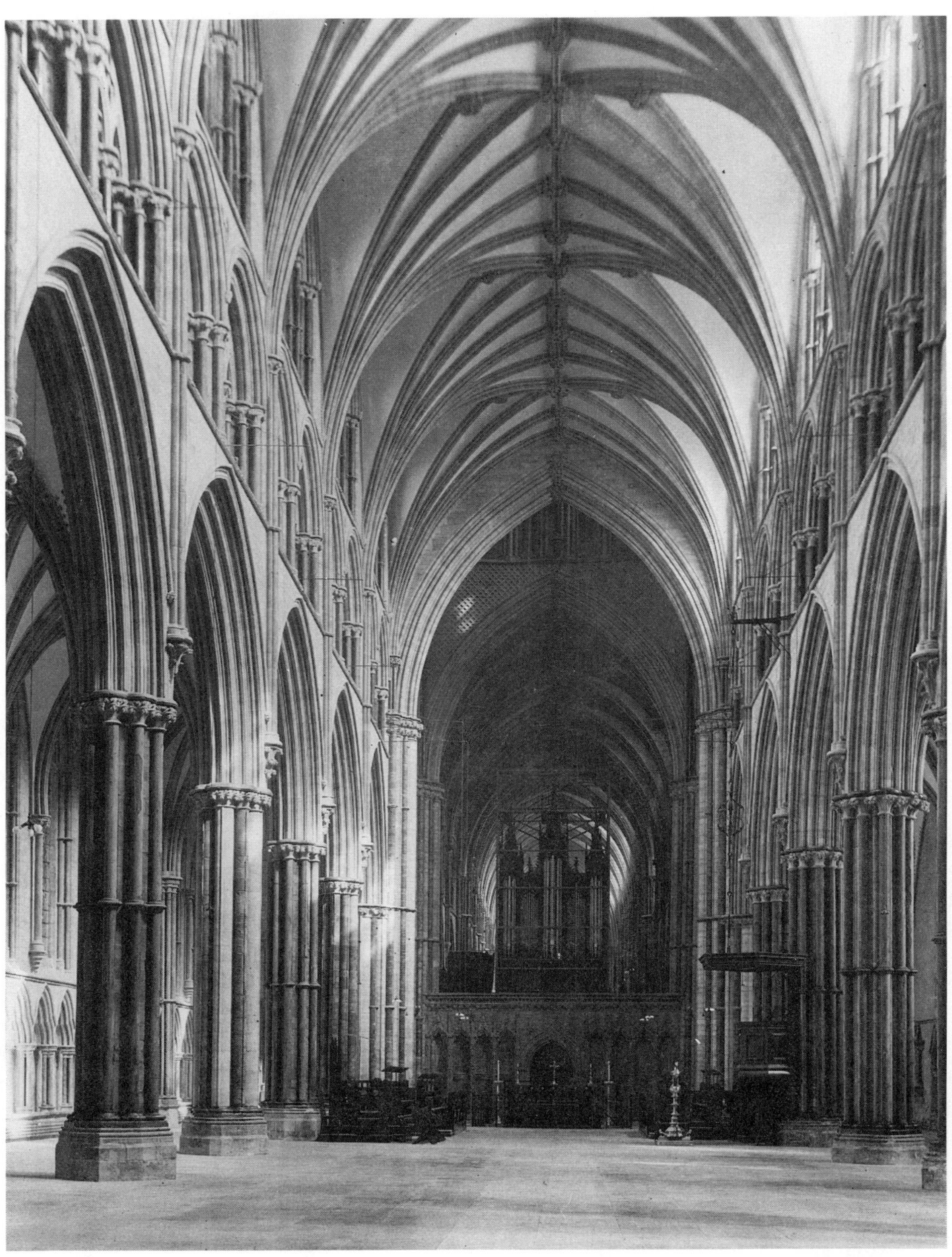

20. Lincoln Cathedral nave. Location of *visus* of Assumption and Coronation of Virgin in the fifteenth century. By permission of the Royal Commission on the Historical Monuments of England.

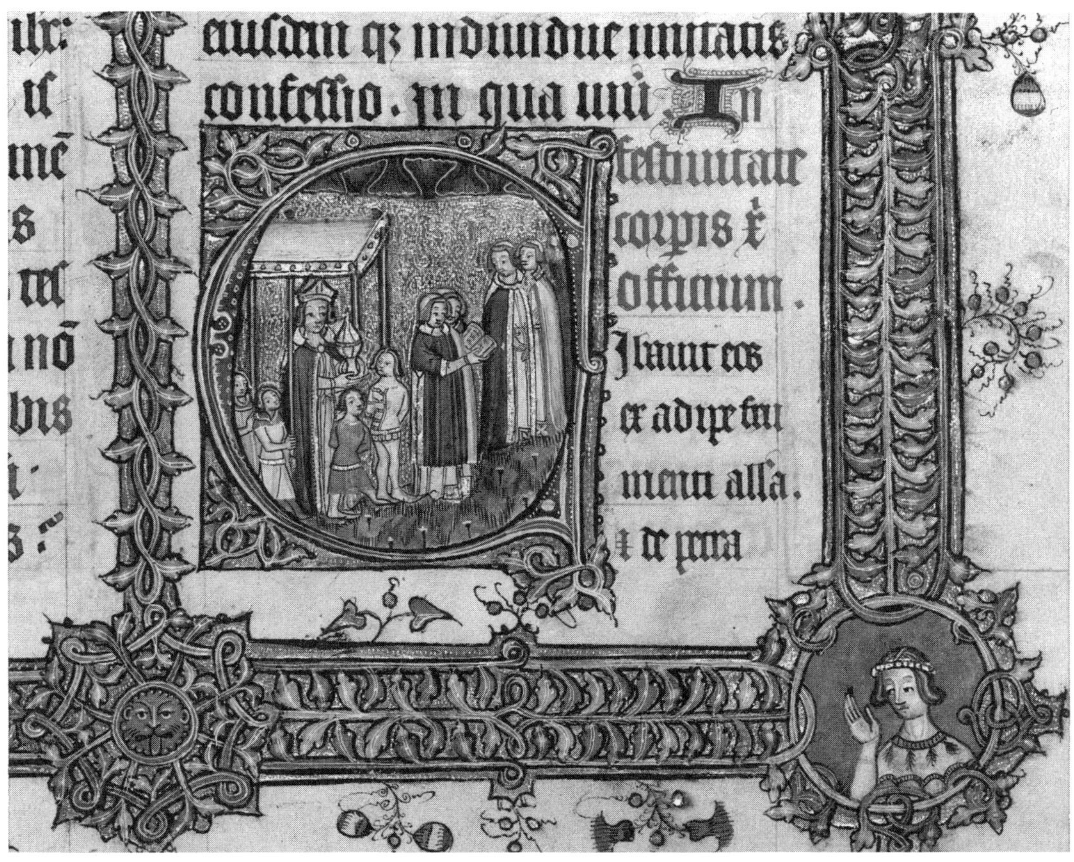

21. Corpus Christi Procession. Litlyngton Missal. Westminster Abbey, MS. 37, fol. 121. c.1383-84. By courtesy of the Dean and Chapter of Westminster.

the architecture of the church did not provide space at a raised level from which the boys might sing. Stages were also recorded in London at St. Peter Cheap, where they were used to raise up persons impersonating the prophets.[32]

Other Church festivals also encouraged similar dramatic and quasi-dramatic production. At York in 1220–25, there were plays or quasi-dramatic ceremonies of the shepherds for Christmas and of the three kings for Epiphany.[33] These were presented in the cathedral, very possibly in the nave, and involved a star. Lincoln had a Christmas play or ceremony involving Mary, the angel Gabriel, and, it would appear, also Elizabeth and prophets in the choir from about 1393 to 1543, and there was a *Stella* play for Epiphany in the fourteenth century. It is not possible to say whether this latter drama or ceremony was in the nave, the location actually specified for a *Ludus de Sancto Thome apostoli*, probably a *Peregrinus* or play about the journey to Emmaus, in 1326–27.[34] The nave at Lincoln (fig. 20) was also the scene of a "visus" of the Assumption and Coronation of the Virgin on the Feast of St. Anne in the fifteenth century.[35] Further, the nave of this cathedral was used for the scene of the descent of the dove on Pentecost, a ceremony that was also performed at St. Paul's in London.[36] This ceremony, as the Lincoln records for 1395–96 indicate, involved both a dove suspended from the ceiling and an angel.[37] Flowers and wafers may have been showered from the roof.

Ceremony can, of course, come in contact with the drama in other ways. At York, the competition between the Corpus Christi procession and the vernacular plays presented along the same route is well documented. In 1426, the friar William Melton suggested separating the plays from the procession, with the play cycle to be postponed until the next day;[38] this, however, did not happen, and eventually the procession and plays were separated, but with the procession transferred to the next day. The plays at York were as intimately connected with the feast day of Corpus Christi as the Corpus Christi procession itself, which is pictured, albeit for a different location, in an illumination in the Litlyngton Missal (fig. 21).

III

PAGEANTS AND PROCESSIONAL STAGING

In productions of vernacular drama in England, no single tradition of staging was adhered to everywhere in the country prior to the Reformation. In East Anglia and the South, place-and-scaffold staging seems to have been the dominant tradition, while in cities in the Midlands and North plays often tended to be performed processionally on pageant wagons. The latter would appear to have been a particularly English manner of play production, though there is evidence that some continental plays drew upon similar practices.[1] On the other hand, there are numerous continental drawings which show pageant wagons used in religious or civic processions, and these would most likely bear some resemblance to those used in the English plays.[2]

Unfortunately, only one manuscript illumination appears to have survived of an English pageant vehicle of any kind (a wheeled dragon in the Luttrell Psalter), and not a single illustration of an English pageant wagon stage is extant from the period prior to 1580. Even the seemingly most detailed description comes from the manuscripts of a person hostile to the early religious drama who never witnessed the actual productions. Archdeacon Rogers, in a version of his *Breviary* dated 1618–19, describes the wagons formerly used at Chester as scaffolds, each of which was like "a high foure square buildinge, with 2 rowmes a higher and alower, the lower hanged aboute richly and closse, into which, none, but the actors came, on the higher they played theire partes beinge all open to the behoulders. . . ."[3] The platform "was sett on 4 wheeles, and soe drawne from streete to street." The first pageant was staged "at the Abbay gates, where when the first pageante was played, it was wheled into an other streete, and the second pagiant came in the place thereof and so till all the pagiantes for the day weare ended, soe into euery streete and, it was soe orderly attended, that before the one Pagiant was played an other came in place to satisfye the beholders in euerye streete at one time."[4]

Rogers' account, however, is complicated

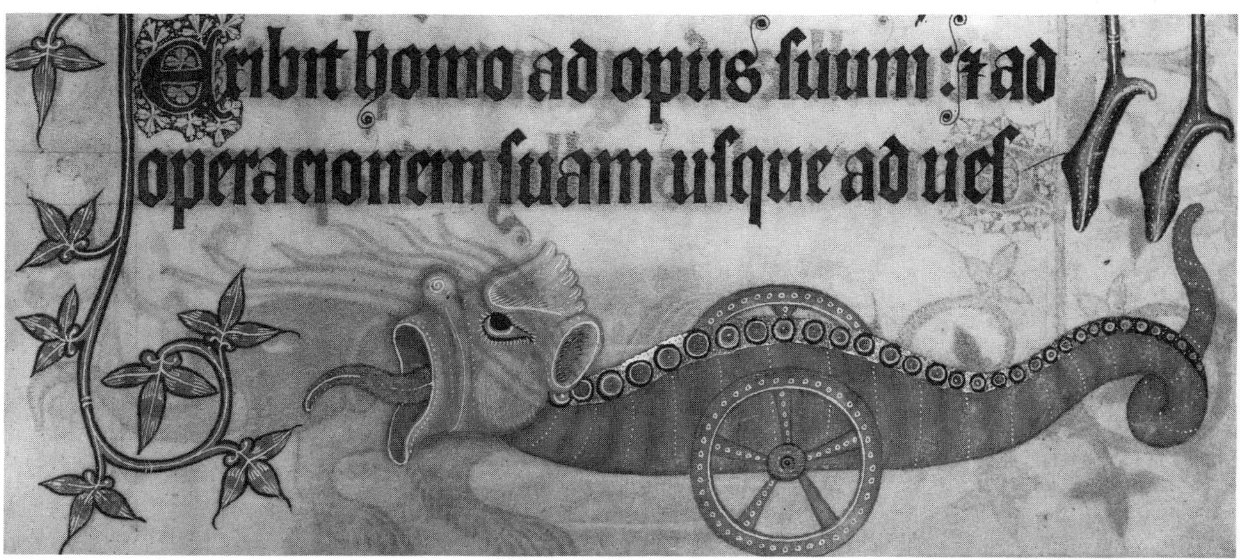

22. Dragon pageant. Luttrell Psalter, British Library, MS. Add. 42,130, fol. 184. By permission of the British Library.

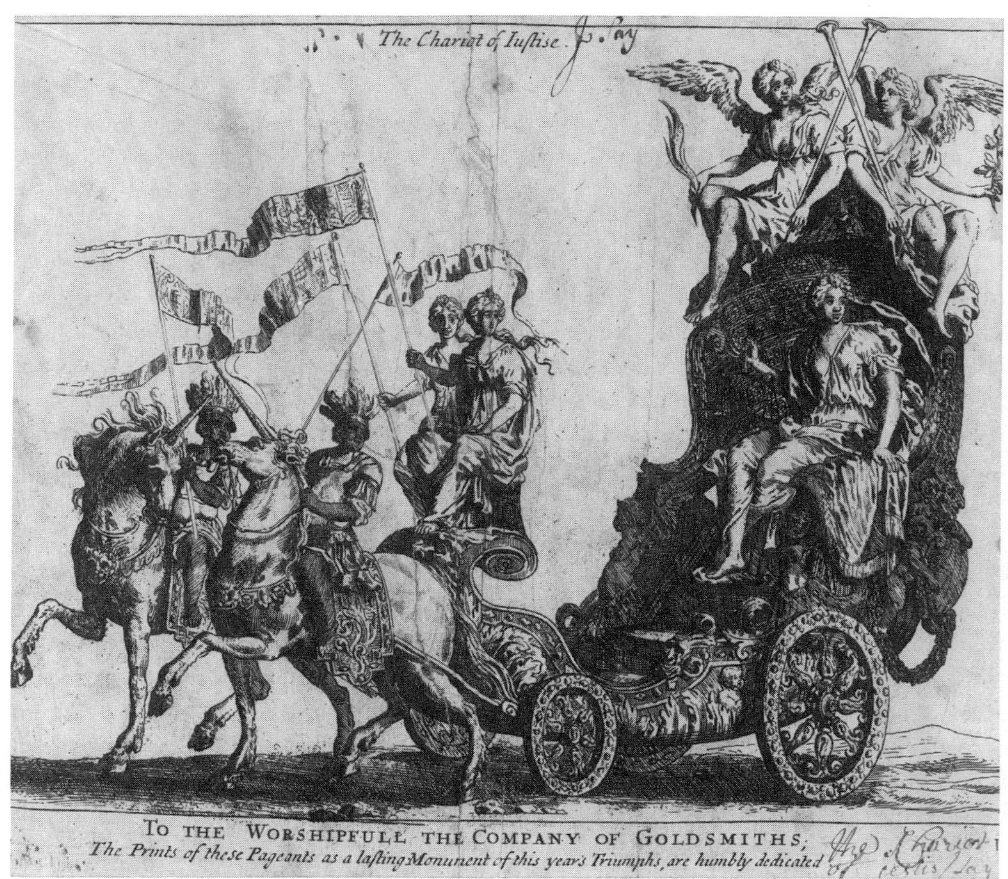

23. Pageant of Chariot of Justice. Elkanah Settle, *Glory's Resurrection: Being the Triumphs of London* (1698). By permission of the British Library.

by an earlier version of the *Breviary* (1608–09) that describes the pageant wagons as having six wheels.[5] The idea of six-wheeled carts of some size and with a dressing room on a lower level was adopted by David Jee in his illustration for Thomas Sharp's *Dissertation on the Pageants, or Dramatic Mysteries Anciently Performed at Coventry* (1825),[6] but seems to argue for larger, more elaborate, and clumsier wagons than could have been accommodated by most medieval streets.[7] Ultimately Rogers' later account, indicating the wagons as having four wheels, most likely needs to be seen as the correct one; nevertheless, it has also been suggested not implausibly that some wagons may have had four wheels and some six wheels.[8] Others, indeed, may have had only two wheels, as in the case of the dragon pageant (fig. 22) illustrated in the Luttrell Psalter, though here the pageant is not designed to be used as a stage upon which the action of the drama is to be presented.[9] In any case, with regard to size, the wagons may have been similar to the pageants utilized later in the seventeenth century in civic pageantry in London. For these wagons we have specific information, since in 1663 John Tatham gave exact measurements for one of them: "fourteen foot long, and eight foot broad."[10] Such dimensions are confirmed by another source, the Goldsmiths' *Court Book*, for 1674,[11] and without question a wagon of this size would have been suited to the winding and narrow streets with the overhanging second stories of buildings jutting

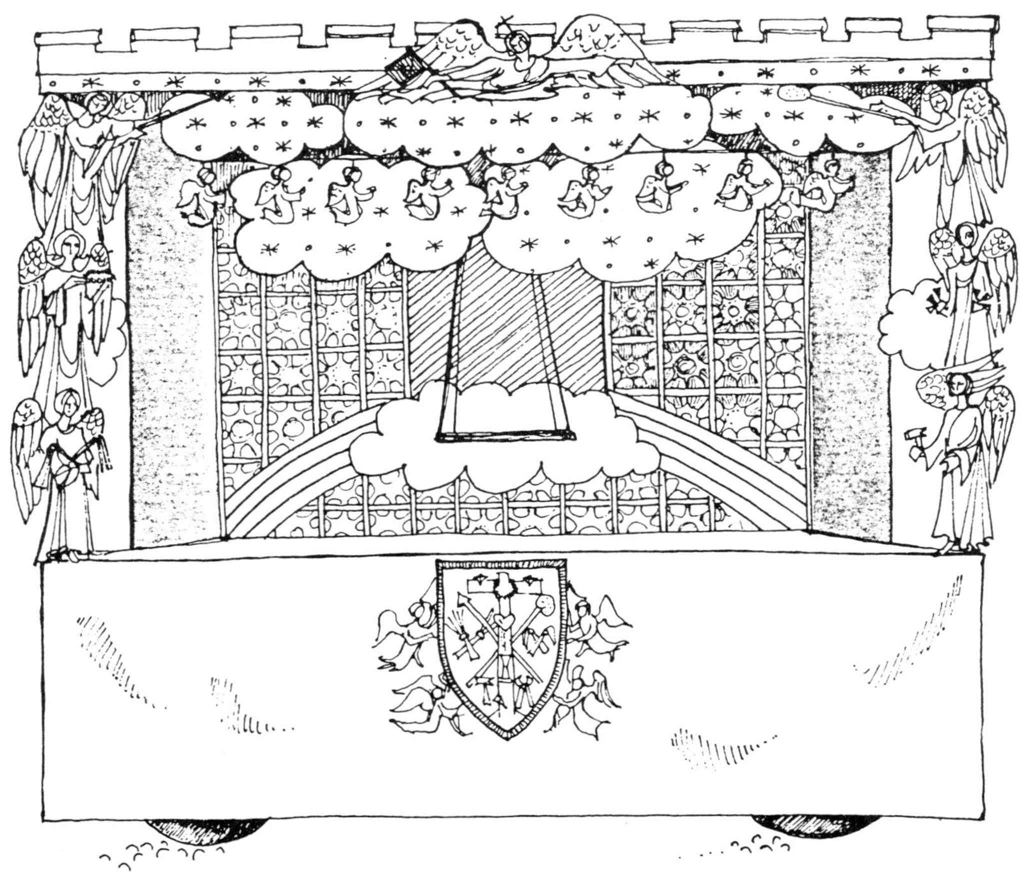

24. York Mercers' Pageant. Reconstruction by Alexandra F. Johnston; illustration by Elizabeth Chalmers. Courtesy of *Leeds Studies in English.*

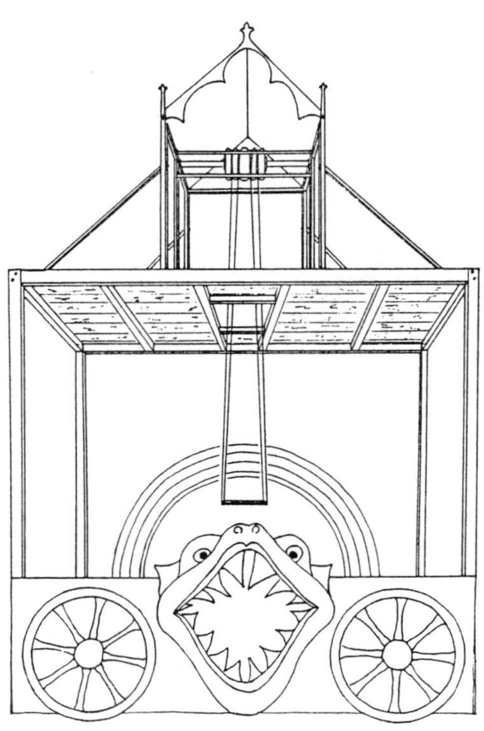

25. York Mercers' Pageant. Reconstruction by Peter Meredith. Courtesy of *Medieval English Theatre*.

out overhead to block any wagon that might be too wide or high.

Although it is quite different in style from the earlier wagons that had been used in the production of the English religious drama at such cities as Chester, Coventry, and York, the pageant of the Chariot of Justice (fig. 23) from Elkanah Settle's *Glory's Resurrection; Being the Triumphs of London* (London, 1698)[12] remains useful in suggesting the kind of wheeled vehicle that was used for drama production. Horses[13] would not normally have been used—the Smiths' horse-drawn pageant at Coventry was an exception[14]—and at least some of the pageant wagons would likely have been designed with the length of vehicle facing the audience. But a vehicle constructed with smaller front wheels and an axel that is capable of turning—in other words, a wagon not so different technologically from nineteenth-century farm wagons—seems plausibly to have been usual as early as the fifteenth century.[15]

The closest thing to a medieval description of a pageant stage has been located in the remarkable indenture of 1433 that describes the properties associated with the Mercers' Doomsday play which concluded the York Corpus Christi cycle. Here we have a vehicle with four wheels, an apparatus for lowering Christ from an upper level representing heaven, a rainbow for him to sit upon, painted cloths to hang about the wagon at the back and sides, and even puppet angels "to renne aboute in the heuen."[16] There was also a hell mouth, which would seem essential to any staging of the Last Judgment, while a generation later a new pageant was added "for ye sallys to ryse owtof."[17]Attempts to reconstruct the Doomsday pageant wagon have tried to solve the technical problems in different ways, but of course can give only a general notion of the actual appearance of the pageant stage. The Toronto reconstruction of Alexandra Johnston seems to be convincing in many respects, though the small puppet angels should most likely circle clockwise around Christ instead of being placed above in a row facing to his left (fig. 24). The technology of the apparatus for lowering Christ, however, is also neglected in this drawing. This aspect of the pageant wagon has been treated by Peter Meredith,[18] whose detailed drawing (fig. 25) nevertheless possibly errs with regard to the placement of the hell mouth, which probably should be at the left of Christ—the conventional location of the place of eternal punishment.

The pageant route taken by the plays on Corpus Christi day at York is easily traced even today in the city, which retains the outline of its medieval streets—and in some instances the actual medieval streets themselves. The medieval city is depicted in John Speed's map of 1611 (fig. 26). The route (see fig. 27) began at Toft Green near the Dominican Friary where the wagons were stored, and moved to the first station at Holy Trinity Priory, where the town clerk positioned

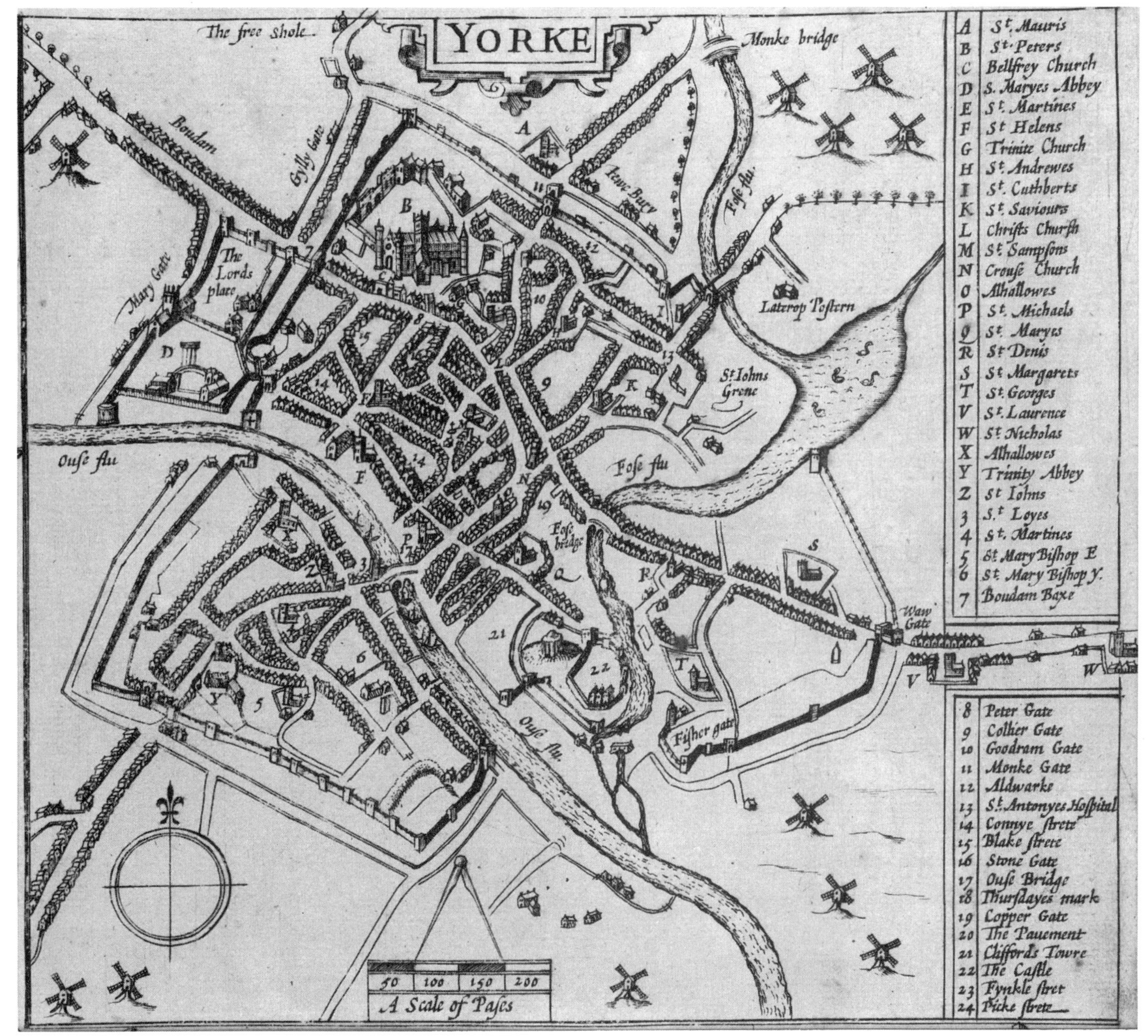

26. York. Map of the city by John Speed. By permission of the British Library.

himself with the Register of the plays in hand to see that quality of production was preserved. Thereafter, the wagons moved up Mickelgate with further stops at St. Martin's Church and St. John's before crossing the Ouse Bridge. At St. Michael Spurriergate, the route would turn up Coney Street. A principal station would be at the gates of the city's common hall. Thereafter the route would take the wagons through St. Helen's Square, into Stonegate (the location of the station at the end of Little Stonegate today perhaps best preserves the medieval character of the York streets), and to the Minster gates, then down Petergate and into the final station at the Pavement near All Saints Church. Here the playing would conclude for the day, though it is difficult to see how the last play of Doomsday could have been presented there before nightfall because of the length of the cycle. The number of stopping places where the plays were performed was twelve in 1399, and in 1569 there were seventeen such stations.[19]

At Coventry the pageants were, according to Dugdale, "very large and high, placed upon wheels, and drawn to all the eminent parts of the

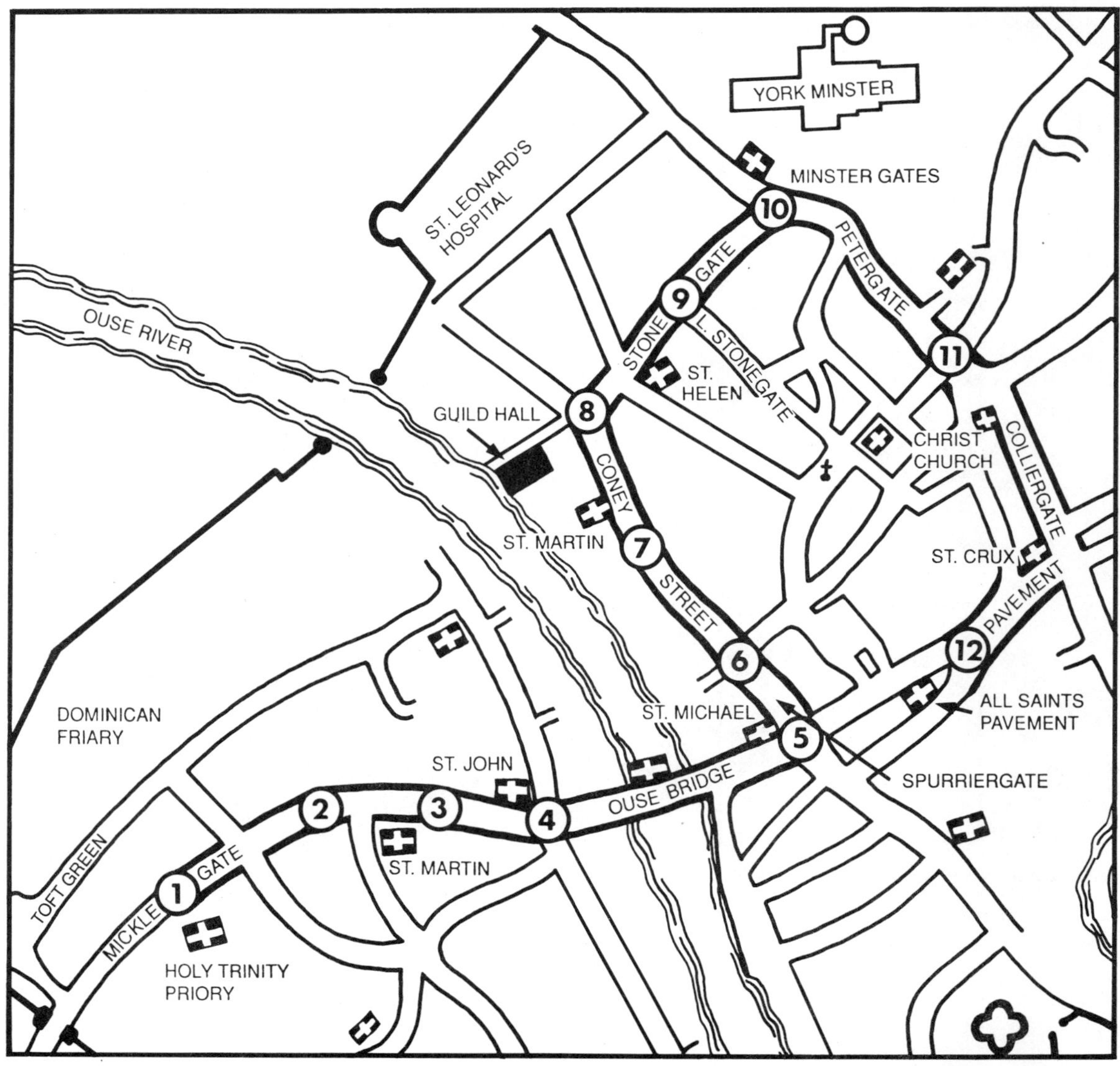

27. The pageant route through the city of York. The twelve stations as designated in 1398 are numbered along the route.

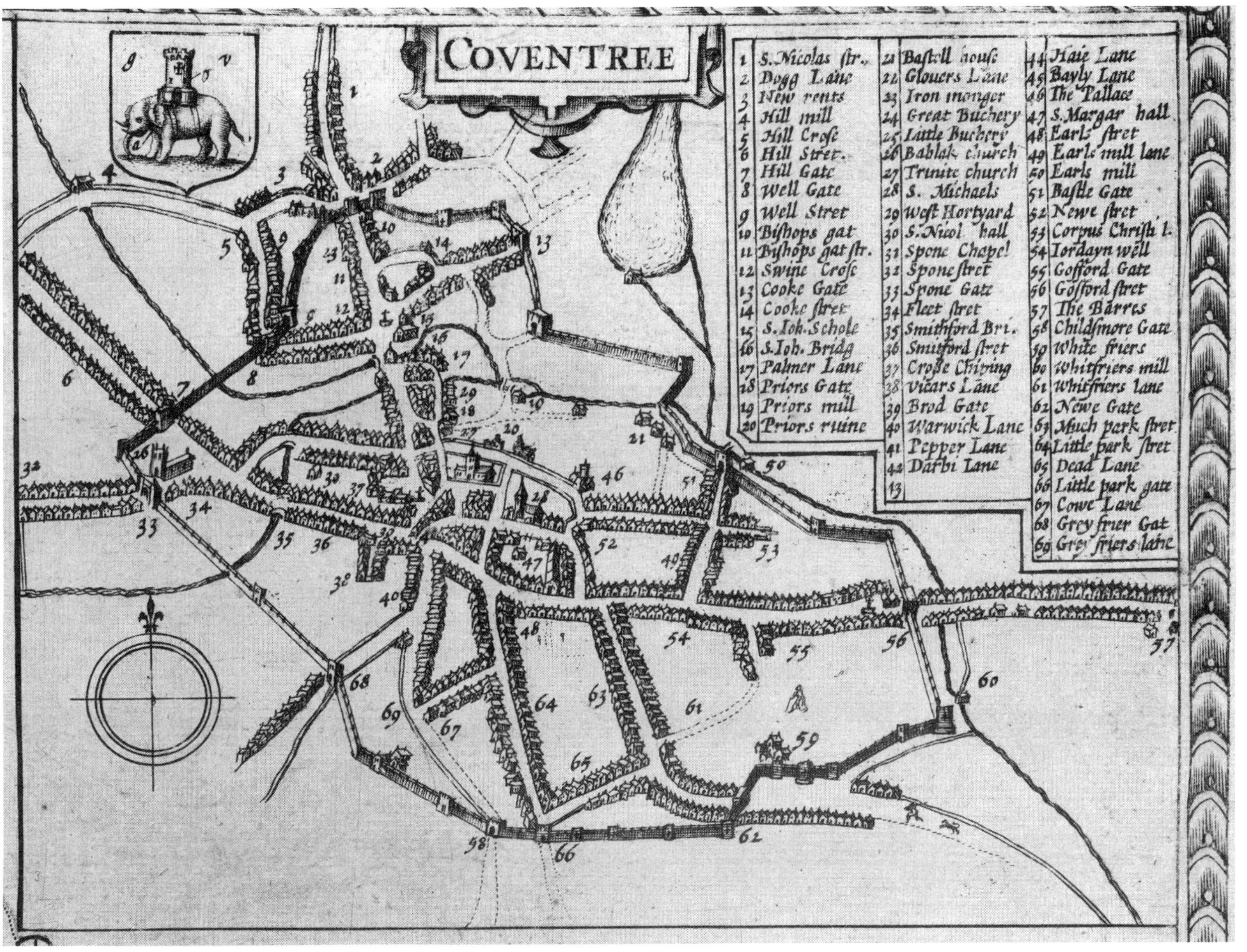

28. Coventry. Map of the city by John Speed. By permission of the British Library.

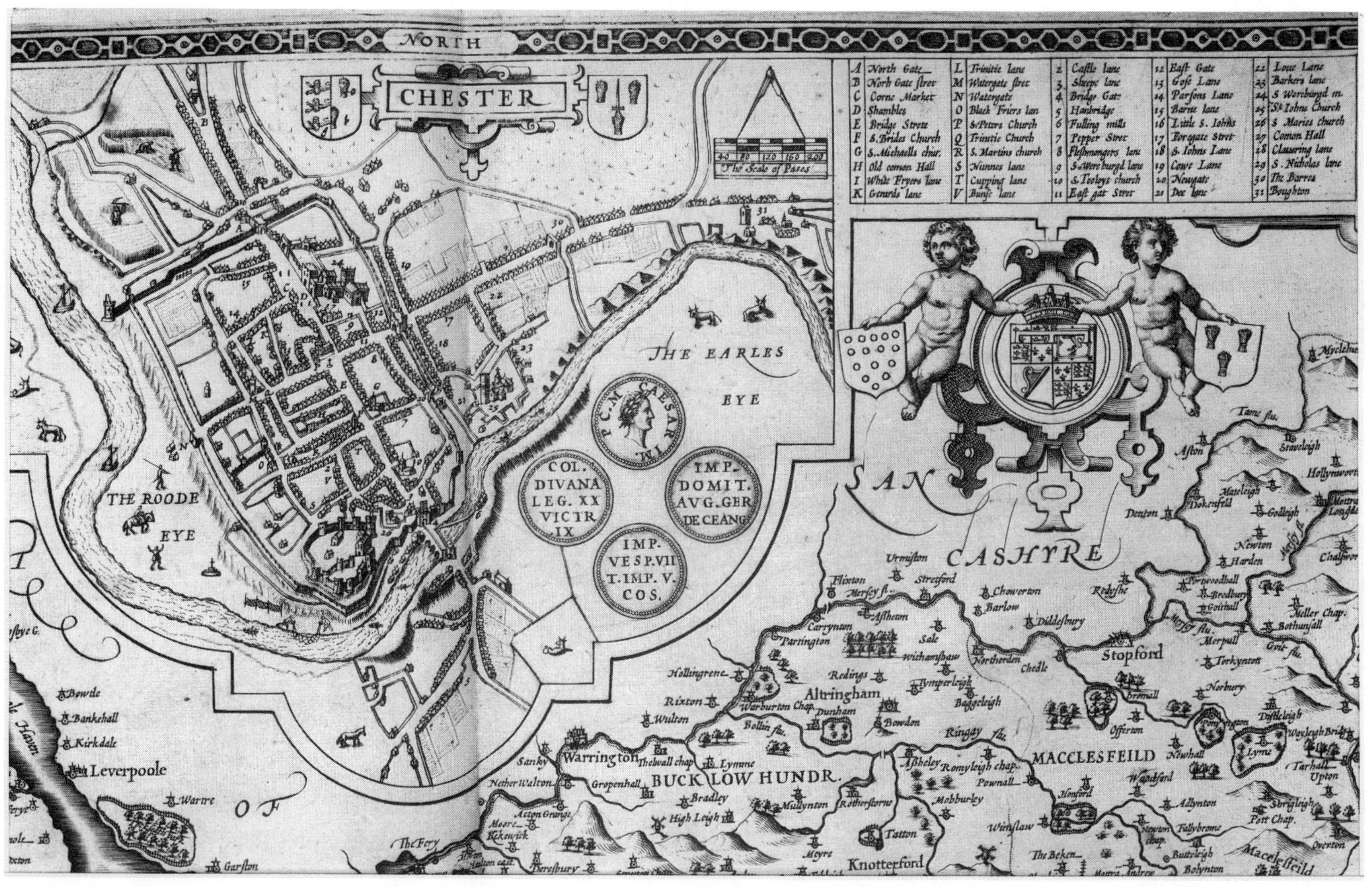

29. Chester. Map of the city by John Speed. By permission of the British Library.

City, for the better advantage of Spectators."[20] The pageant route, including perhaps only three performances but at possibly as many as ten stations, was thus not as fixed as at York.[21] Pageant houses for storage of the wagons seem not to have been located in any one place, and, as we would expect, rehearsals did not require the wagon stages, which were taken out of storage when needed for the actual performances. R. W. Ingram believes that the wagons were assembled at the end of Gosford Street and that the first station was near Earl's Mill Lane.[22] Other places on Speed's map of Coventry (fig. 28) that are most likely to have been chosen for the display of tableaux or full performance include Much Park Street end, Little Park Street end, Bishopsgate, Cross Cheaping, Broadgate, Smithford Street, and Bablake Church.[23]

In the case of Chester we can trace with a little more certainty the route taken by the wagons used in a production of a great cycle of plays, performed in Whitsun week in the sixteenth century. Once again reference may be made to a map by John Speed (fig. 29). The performances, as documents from 1561 help us to determine, began at the Abbey Gates and thereafter continued in front of the Pentice (fig. 30), at the High Cross, in Watergate Street, in Bridge Street, and finally in Eastgate Street.[24] Thus five stations were involved, and each play was presented at every station. The route was chosen, if John Marshall is correct in his interpretation of the documents, in order to avoid unpaved streets and lanes as well as uphill inclines. Even the passage between the final two stations, described by Rogers as "through the lanes"—presumably by way of Fleshmongers' Lane—was paved.[25]

There is no doubt that the processional manner of performance at various stations throughout a city is related to religious and civic pageantry, which itself could be dramatic or semi-dramatic in character. The use of elaborate pageants in such pageantry is well known, and in London during the civic pageantry for Philip of Spain in 1554 the "greate Giauntes" Corineus Britannus and Gogmagog Albinus also performed a function that is related to drama since they involved actors impersonating characters in interaction with an audience.[26] Sometimes quasi-dramatic figures of this sort survived long after the medieval stage had been suppressed. Hence at Salisbury a giant and the hobby horse Hob Nob are separately mentioned in the civic records for the entry of Henry VII in 1496, but exist in later manifestations since they were not put down at the Reformation.[27]

Related to the wheeled dragon in the Luttrell Psalter are numerous dragons without wheels that were operated by men who stood, in leaning-forward position, inside a structure of wood strips and canvas. Such was the Norwich Snap dragon, several late versions of which survive to this day at the Norwich Castle Museum (fig. 31). A Norwich guild record of 1408 tells us, furthermore, that this dragon was part of the Guild

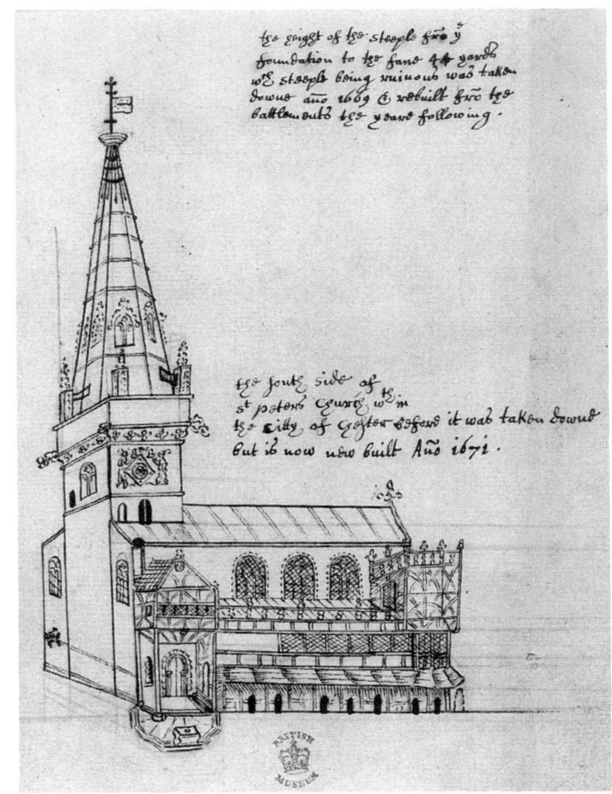

30. The Pentice. South side of St. Peter's Church, Chester. British Library, MS. Harley 2073, fol. 88. By permission of the British Library.

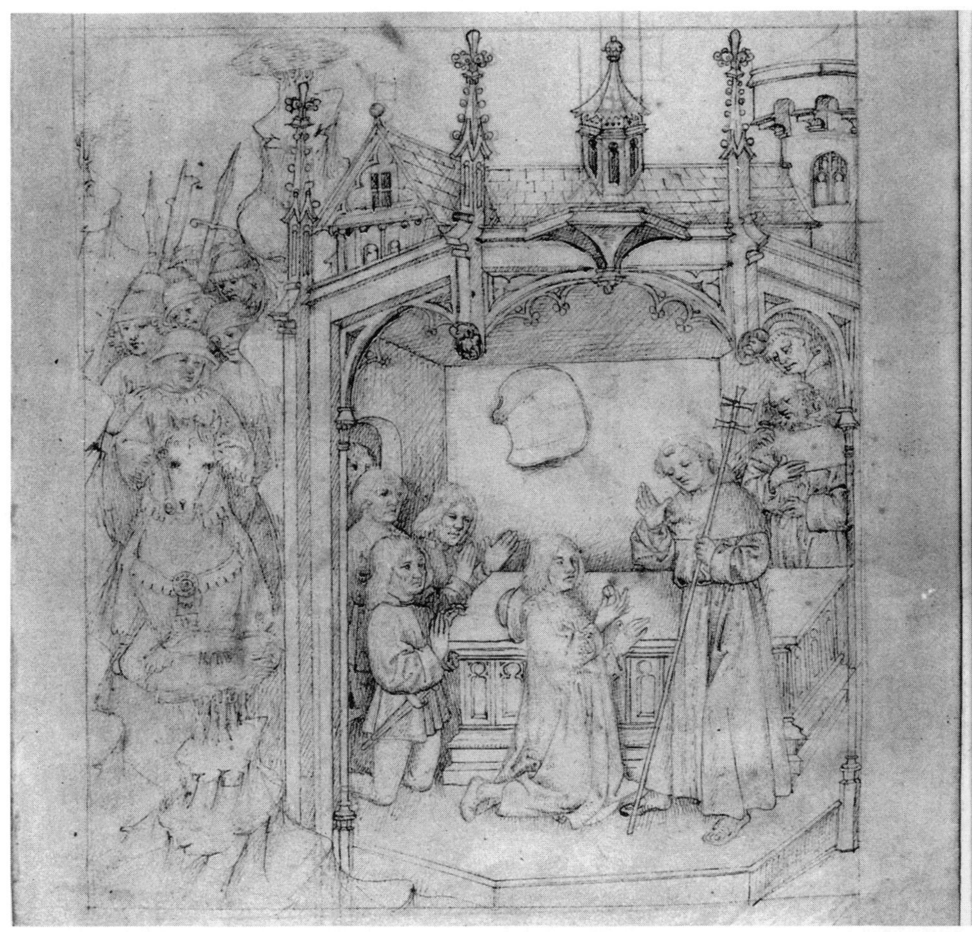

14. Richard Beauchamp, Earl of Warwick, worshipping at the Holy Sepulcher in Jerusalem. British Library, MS. Cotton Julius E.IV, fol. 209. By permission of the British Library.

or plays, which at Lincoln included a *Ludus resurreccionis* in 1384–91.[8]

In some cases, an entire chapel was devoted to the Easter sepulcher. It was understood that the sepulcher of Christ in the Holy Land was enclosed in such a chapel, as in an illumination from British Library MS. Cotton Julius E.IV, fol. 209. Here the sepulcher is a coffer tomb at which pilgrims kneel (fig. 14), and in this illumination it is shown during the visit of Richard Beauchamp, Earl of Warwick, at the site during his pilgrimage to Jerusalem in the first decade of the fifteenth century.[9] Pamela Sheingorn speculates that the Chapel of St. Mary and All Angels, also known as St. Sepulchre's, at York Minster may have served as a sepulcher chapel during Holy Week and at Easter,[10] though during the remainder of the year it was a highly active foundation with other functions until suppressed in the Reformation. The door, which led from the north aisle of the nave of York Minster to this chapel, and a blocked staircase are all that remain of it. But another sepulcher chapel should be of particular interest because of its supposed structural similarity to the model in Jerusalem. The Chapel of the Holy Sepulchre at the Monastery of the Bonhommes at Edington, Wiltshire, was specifically described in the fifteenth century as "made to the lykenes of the sepulkyr of owre Lord at Jerusalem." Unfortunately, this chapel also is no longer extant.[11]

An elaborate description of the Good Friday and Easter morning ceremonies, the *Depositio*

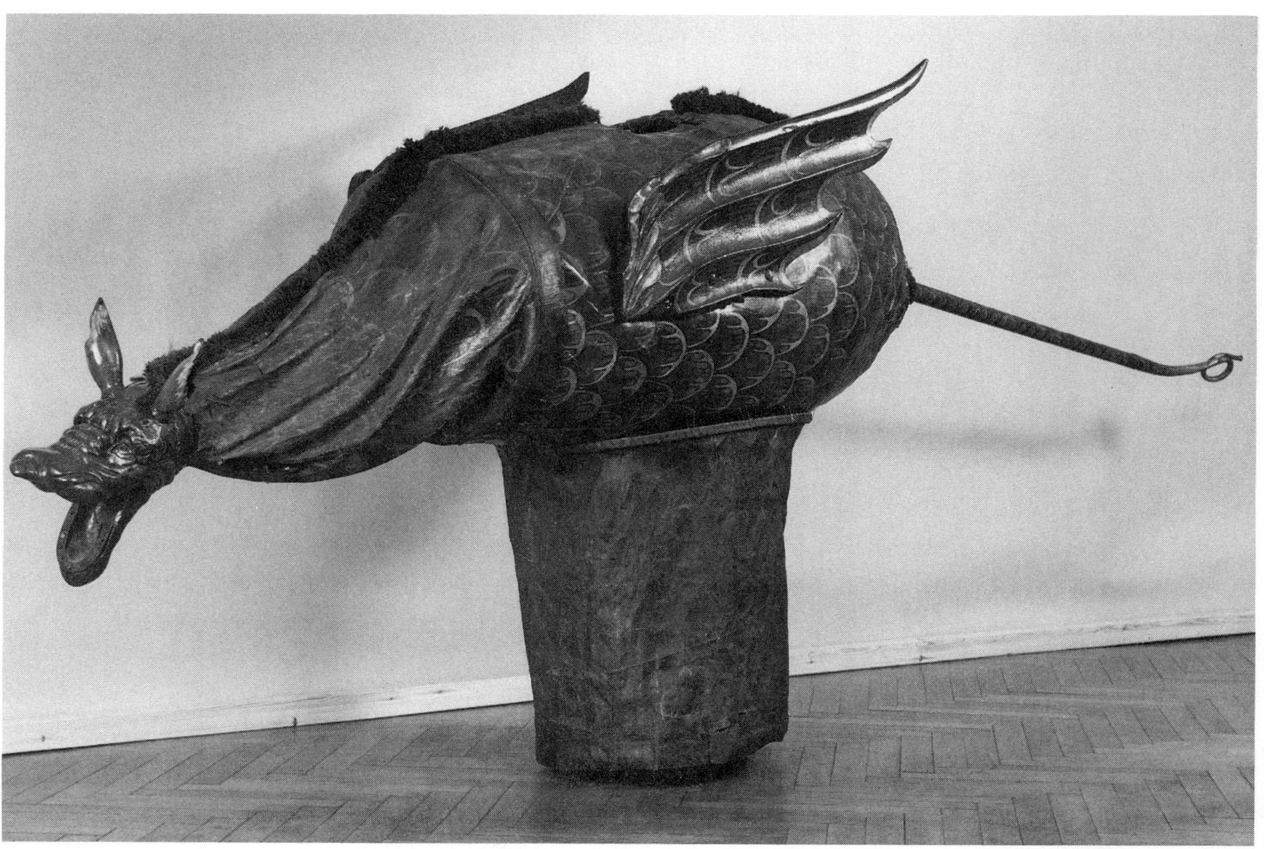

31. Norwich Snap Dragon. Late version of processional dragon, presumably of the type frequently used in the later Middle Ages. Courtesy of the Norfolk Museums Services.

Day procession in which was inserted an actual dramatic skit involving a battle with the knight St. George. The knight inevitably would be the victor in the conflict, whereupon the defeated dragon was given over to the maid Margaret. In 1429, the dragon must have been more realistic than in earlier times, since gunpowder was added as an effect, producing a creature that could breathe forth fire and smoke.[28] At the Reformation it was decreed that "Ther shalbe neyther George nor Margett But for pastyme the dragon to com In and shew hym selff as in other yeares."[29]

IV

PLACES TO SEE THE PLAYS

Fixed stages, especially place-and-scaffold staging, were more widespread than pageant wagon stages in medieval England, and have the advantage of having been often set up in locations which are still extant or of which there remains visual evidence of some sort. It is true that there are some remains of Clerkenwell which, along with Skinners' Well, is identified in the records as standing at the location where plays were performed at London in the fourteenth and fifteenth centuries,[1] but this relic has been moved and is locked away in a basement in Islington.[2] This well, however, tells us nothing about the manner of production of the plays that were presented nearby in medieval times. However, in spite of the existence of numerous playing areas that are not very much changed from the Middle Ages and of some invaluable stage diagrams, much must still remain speculative in any reconstruction of the fixed stage as it existed in the late Middle Ages and early modern period, even after the building of the well-known theaters in the region of London after 1576. The recent discovery of the foundations of Henslowe's Rose Theater, built in 1587 and modified in 1592, has added much to our knowledge of the Renaissance stage, however.[3]

Churchyards, like marketplaces,[4] were an early (and logical) location for drama, and in 1197 the abbot of Bury St. Edmunds specifically prohibited *spectacula* in the monastery's churchyard.[5] Judging from W. K. Hardy's nineteenth-century drawing of the abbey (fig. 32), there would have been a fine space for playing either inside the abbey gate (the only portion of the abbey that is now extant) or, even more satisfactory, in the yard to the south of the church. More explicit concerning the nature of the performance is the record of the Beverley Resurrection play, involving both words and action, in the summer sometime around 1220. This drama, presented by masked actors in the churchyard of St. John's churchyard (now Beverley Minster) (fig. 33) and also thereafter inside the

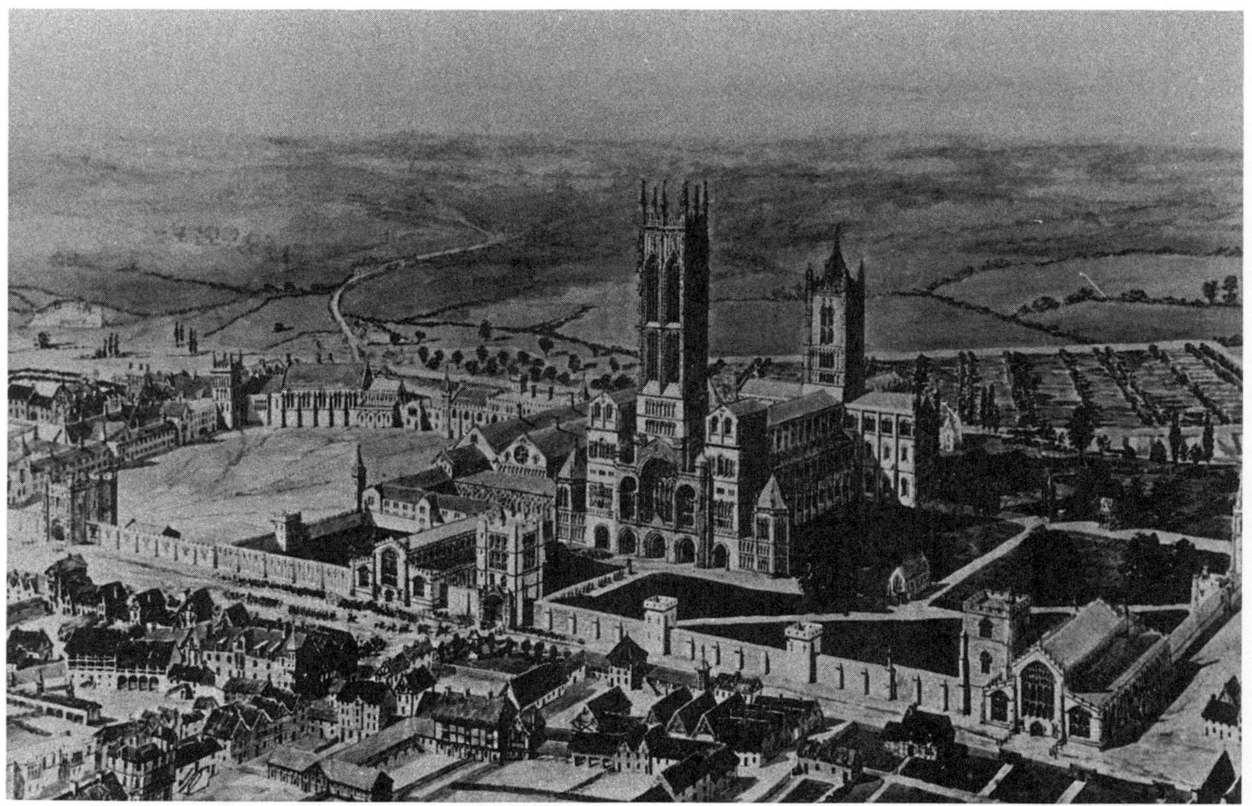

32. Abbey of Bury St. Edmunds before the Reformation (conjectural depiction). Painting by W. K. Hardy. Photograph: O. G. Jarman.

church, was recorded because of an accident that occurred when boys went to the roof to see the play.[6] Presented at a time when it is believed that the nave was under construction, the play was designed for the general public instead of mainly for cloistered monks, and hence presumably differed considerably in its representation of the event of the Resurrection from the quasi-dramatic *Elevatio* ceremony or the *Visitatio Sepulchri*.

At Chester in 1515–16, a Mayors List indicates that the shepherds' play and the Assumption drama were played in the churchyard of St. John's Church (fig. 34),[7] which is still extant though not in its pre-Reformation condition. The plays at this location, however, probably were played from the pageant wagons normally associated with their production rather than from fixed stages. Unfortunately, the exterior of the church was so renewed in the Victorian period that its medieval character is now nearly lost. While it would have been useful to see the building as it was when plays were presented in its churchyard, photographic evidence does not extend beyond the first Victorian building program of 1859–66.[8]

But interior locations must also have lent themselves very early to play production and entertainment. Marianne G. Briscoe has called attention to a papal decree of 1207, issued by Pope Innocent III:

> From time to time theatrical games are produced in certain churches. Not only are imitations of devils introduced in parody; in truth, in certain festivals of the year that immediately follow Christ's birth, deacons, presbyters, and subdeacons in turn present mad parodies with obscene gestures in the sight of the people.

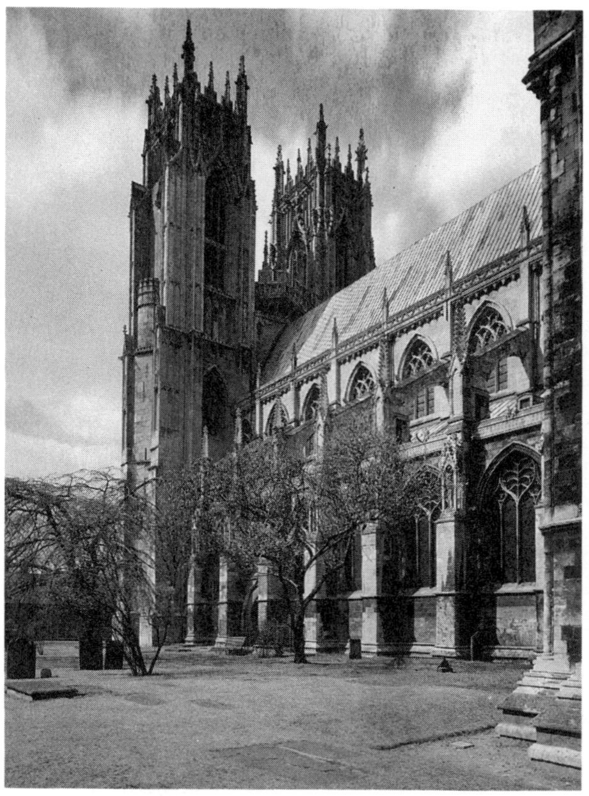

33. Churchyard of Beverley Minster. The scene of a play of the Resurrection in c.1220. By permission of the Royal Commission on the Historical Monuments of England.

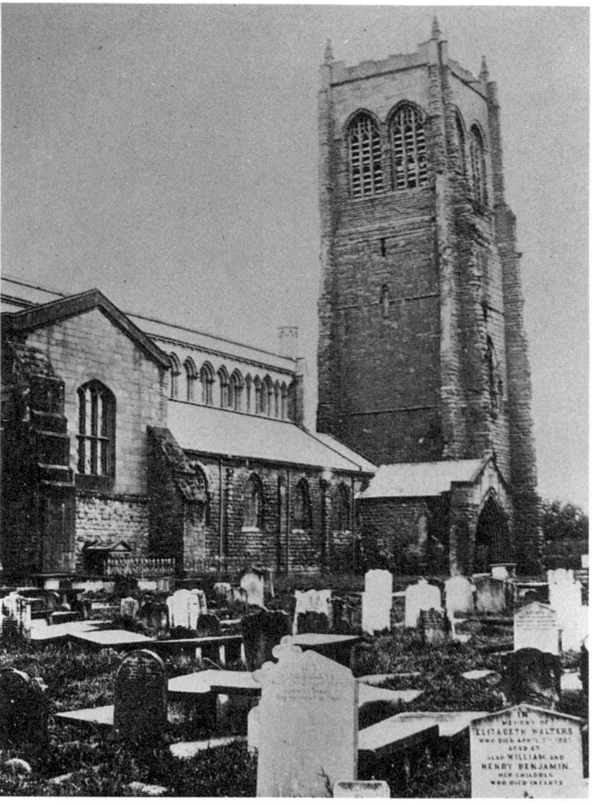

34. Churchyard of St. John's Church, Chester, in c.1860–70. The scene of shepherds' play and a play of the Assumption in early sixteenth century. By permission of the Royal Commission on the Historical Monuments of England.

> They thus tarnish the honor of the clergy who ought better, at that time, to be delighting people by preaching the word of God. The house of God mocks us and the reproaches seem to fall on us. Brothers, we command you to root out these customary parodies and commend the observance of divine and holy orders in your churches. . . .[9]

Such parodies seem to have been viewed as less of a problem on the whole in England, but the use of the church building for plays in this country receives frequent mention in the dramatic records.

The staging normally adopted for indoor production of vernacular drama would probably have been not dissimilar to the place-and-scaffold arrangement in outdoor presentations of plays. In the case of the fifteenth-century Croxton *Play of the Sacrament*, the staging may have been divided between the churchyard, probably with scaffolds set up along the north wall of the church, and then not entirely implausibly the interior of the church itself.[10] If the play was associated with the Norfolk village of Croxton near Thetford, which had a guild capable of presenting plays,[11] the parish church that might have lent its churchyard and nave to the play still exists. Croxton Church is mainly of the thirteenth and fourteenth centuries with an early Tudor clerestory.[12] But other parish churches in which playing of vernacular drama was allowed are also extant. One such church is

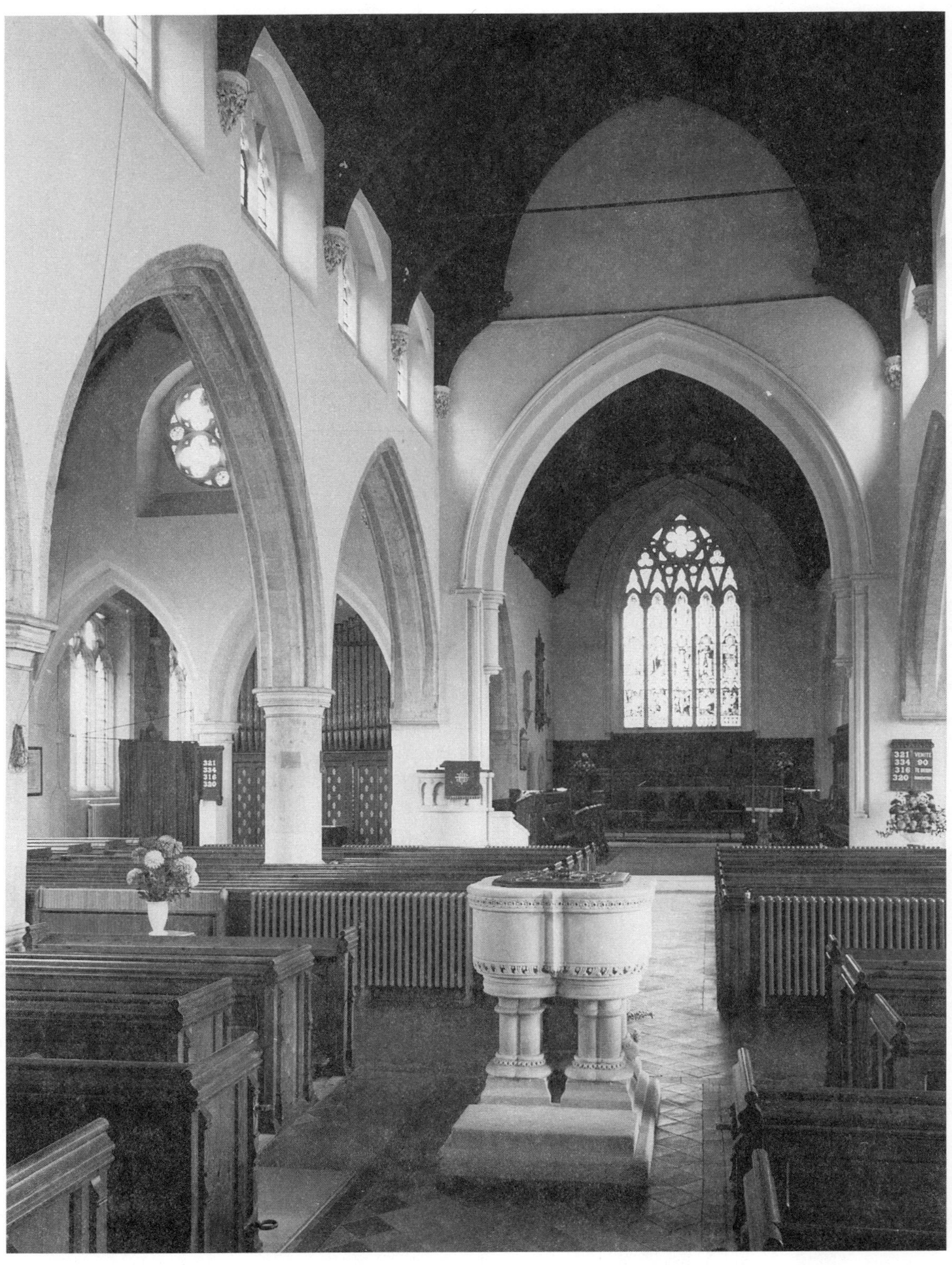

35. Nave of the church at Braintree, Essex, where saint plays were performed in the third and fourth decades of the sixteenth century. By permission of the Royal Commission on the Historical Monuments of England.

that of Braintree, Essex, which, though it has an exterior that now seems thoroughly Victorian, retains a nave (fig. 35) that was used for saint plays dramatizing St. Swithin, St. Andrew, and St. Eustace in 1523–34.[13] Money raised from these plays helped to pay for repairs to the church, and roofs in the north and south chapels remain from this date.[14]

Halls, such as those in palaces, great houses, castles, monasteries, and colleges, appear frequently as locations for playing. Ian Lancashire has called attention to Wressle Castle, a seat of Henry Algernon Percy, fifth earl of Northumberland, in the East Riding of Yorkshire where in the

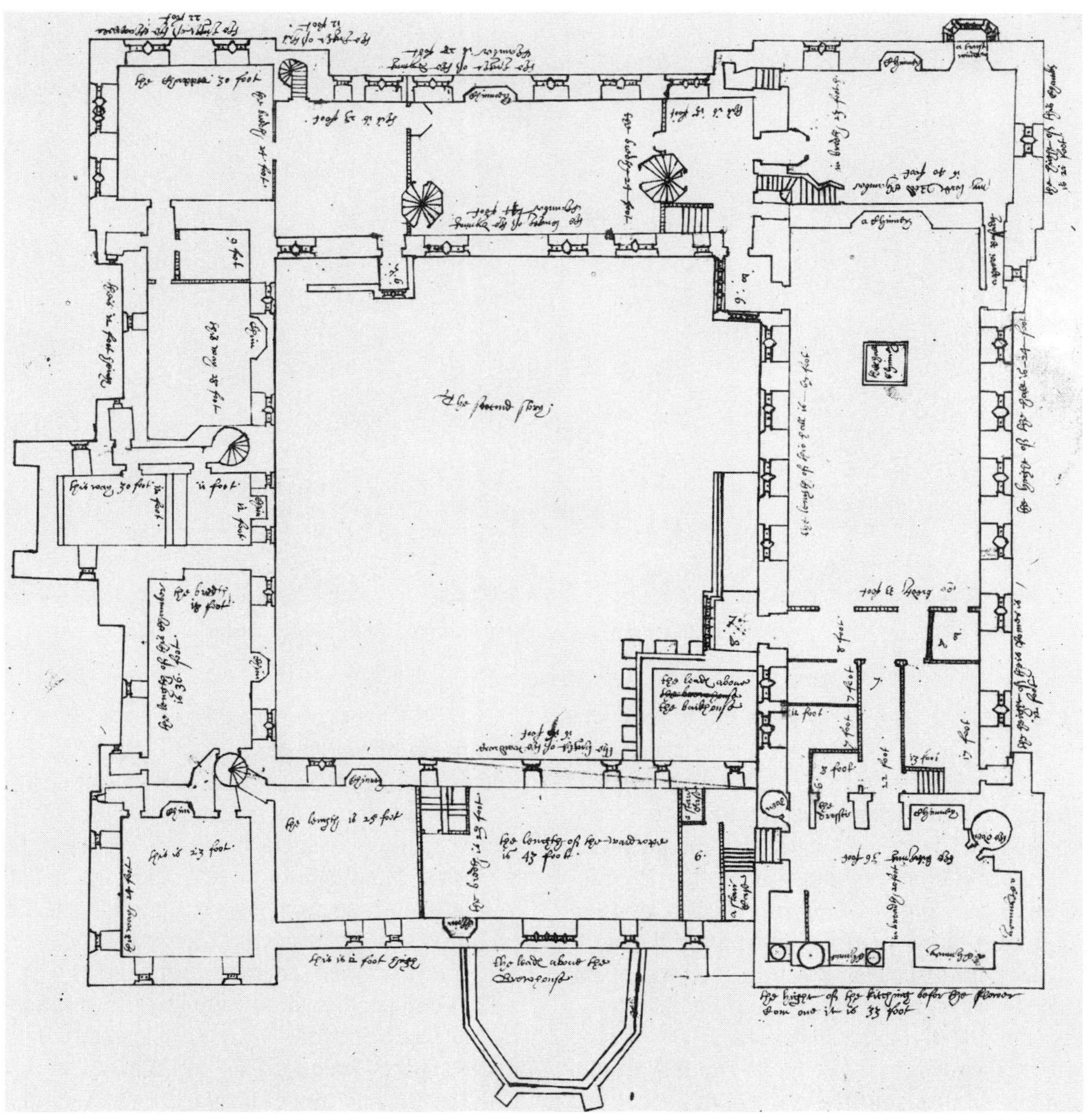

36. Wressle Castle. Second story, showing chapel (above left), great hall (right), dining chamber (top, in the center). West Sussex Record Office, Petworth House Archives 3544. By permission of Lord Egremont.

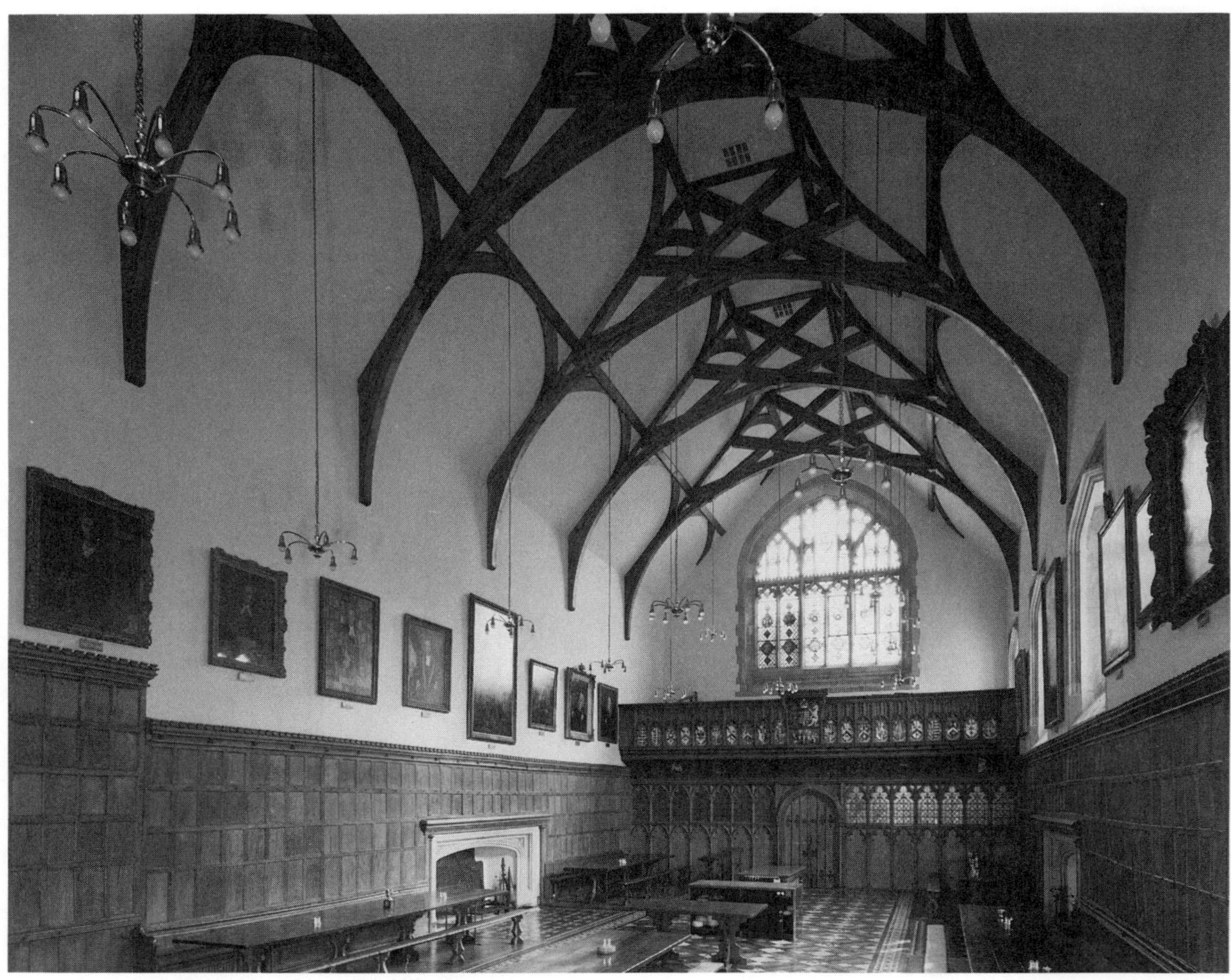

37. Great Hall of Eton College. By permission of the Royal Commission on the Historical Monuments of England.

early sixteenth century not only the chapel was used for such plays as a Nativity drama in which the children sang *Gloria in excelsis* on Christmas morning, the "Play of the Resurrection" on Easter, and a Shrove Tuesday play, but also the great hall during the Christmas season was the scene of interludes, disguisings, and morris dancers who entered from a "towr or thing devisid for theim."[15] Lancashire has called attention to the plan of the second story of this building (fig. 36) which shows the chapel and the great hall as well as a dining chamber that might also have figured in entertainments.[16] Leland described both chapel and great hall as "fair," but gives no further description of them.[17]

Educational institutions had, however, the advantage of young persons who might be called upon to present dramas, usually of a sort designed to teach or inculcate morals. At Eton College, where outdoor production was also recorded, fixed stages or "bouthis" for "enterludes" are noted by William Horman, headmaster from 1495 to 1502, on account of an accident ("The stag*is* of the play fel al downe: and no man hurt that sate in the setis") but whether these were used in an indoor or outdoor performance is not indicated.[18] Nevertheless, plays produced by the schoolmaster and acted by the children of Eton College were recorded in its hall (fig. 37) in 1525–26 and thereafter, and it is also not irrelevant to note that Nicholas

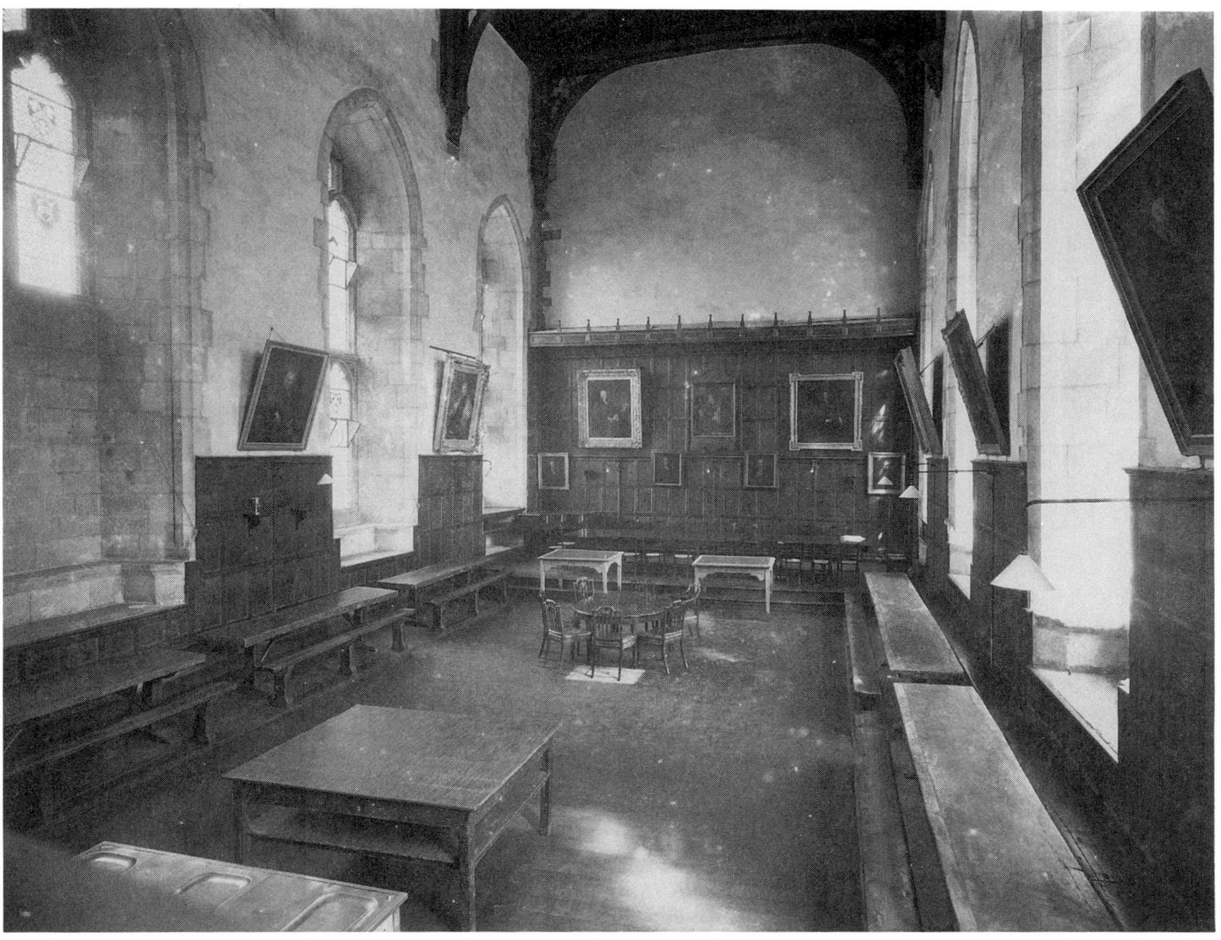

38. Great Hall of Winchester College. By permission of the Royal Commission on the Historical Monuments of England.

Udall, the playwright, was appointed headmaster here in 1534.[19]

At Winchester College, specific interludes are known to have been presented (one was *Occupation and Idleness*[20]) in the fifteenth century,[21] and in 1466–79 players were known to have played in the hall (fig. 38), which also featured visiting players between 1556–57, when the chamberlains' accounts specified "Histrionibus Ludentibus in comon hall," and 1625.[22]

The hall at Queens' College, Cambridge, has been studied by Alan Nelson, whose analysis has led him to the view that the stage area was set up opposite the screen end.[23] Classical drama is known to have been presented as early as 1522–23,[24] and the hall itself was said to have been converted upon occasion into a "theatrum" for plays after 1547–48.[25] This arrangement in fact involved the creation of an elaborate improvised theater, including a platform stage of approximately nine feet in depth and fifteen in width. According to Nelson, "spectator galleries" were "erected around the perimeter of the hall. A triple gallery, with raked seating, was set up behind the stage; double galleries were erected along the East and West walls; another gallery was apparently set against the screens. On either side of the stage were three-storied tiring houses."[26] Records noting a "devils cote" and another for Death in 1546–47 as well as a play requiring a *caelum* in 1551–52[27] suggest a wider repertoire than classical drama for this stage. Unfortunately, the hall

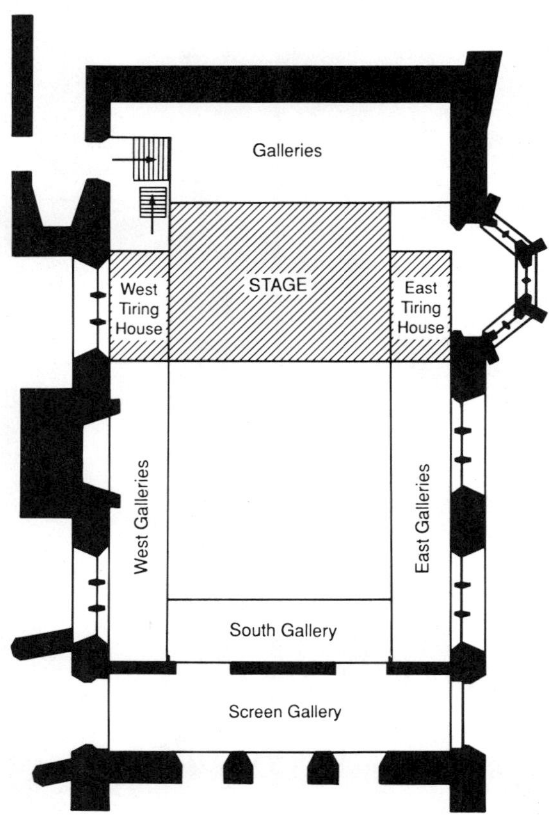

39. Plan of Great Hall Queens' College showing conjectural scaffolding in preparation for a play.

has been much altered since the sixteenth century,[28] and hence requires to be studied for the ground plan of the building in the period before these alterations (fig. 39).[29]

Among the locations used for entertainments and plays at court were the great halls at Windsor Castle and Hampton Court.[30] The latter, 115 feet long and forty feet wide (fig. 40), was extensively used by English monarchs from at least the time of Edward VI; in the first year of Edward's reign, court records report "Sondrye maskyng garmentes" and a moorish mask for revels there, while a Tower of Babylon was also created for use as a stage property.[31] A play at Hampton Court was noted in the Revels accounts in c.1554, and under Queen Elizabeth extensive expenditures were reported for the Shrovetide festivities of 1574 which included both "playes and Maskes."[32] Payments were made to carpenters, tailors, painters, and others involved in preparation for the productions. Artificial lighting was used, for payment was made to the wiredrawer Thomas Leverett for "Plates for the Braunches that bare the lightes in the hall at Hampton Coorte." The plays were reported to have been *Philemon and Phileca*, performed on Monday evening by the Earl of Leicester's Men, and on the next night *Percius and Anthromiris*, presented by the Merchant Taylors' Children.[33] The children were provided with food and lodging at St. John's "whiles they Learned theier partes and Iestures meete for the Mask in which ix of them did serve at hampton Coorte."[34] For the performance they brought their "Masking geare," and apparently they also had masks prepared for them by an old Italian woman.[35]

Public performances in halls are quite a different matter from the private presentations in locations such as those cited above. Nevertheless, there is record of an early London playhouse being set up in Trinity Hall, Aldersgate, at least by 1557 and continuing to 1568. Charles Tyler Prouty has estimated that the documentary evidence, which does not cover every year during this period, suggests more than a hundred performances at this location.[36] Though its paneling had been stripped from inside its walls, the hall was still standing in 1782 when John Carter sketched its interior (fig. 41). Capon's view of the hall from the screen end (fig. 42)—in this case possibly the end where the actors had performed—was executed in 1790 and was apparently sketched as the building was about to be pulled down. It was then a non-conformist chapel, but the presence in the east end of a stained glass window of St. Fabian, previously noted in 1611, and other features indicate little change from the sixteenth century.[37] Prouty's analysis of the evidence suggests that the building was nineteen feet wide and perhaps thirty feet in height, with the interior space of the hall being fifteen feet wide, thirty-five feet long, and seventeen and a half feet high. There was a fireplace on the south wall, and a gallery (with a

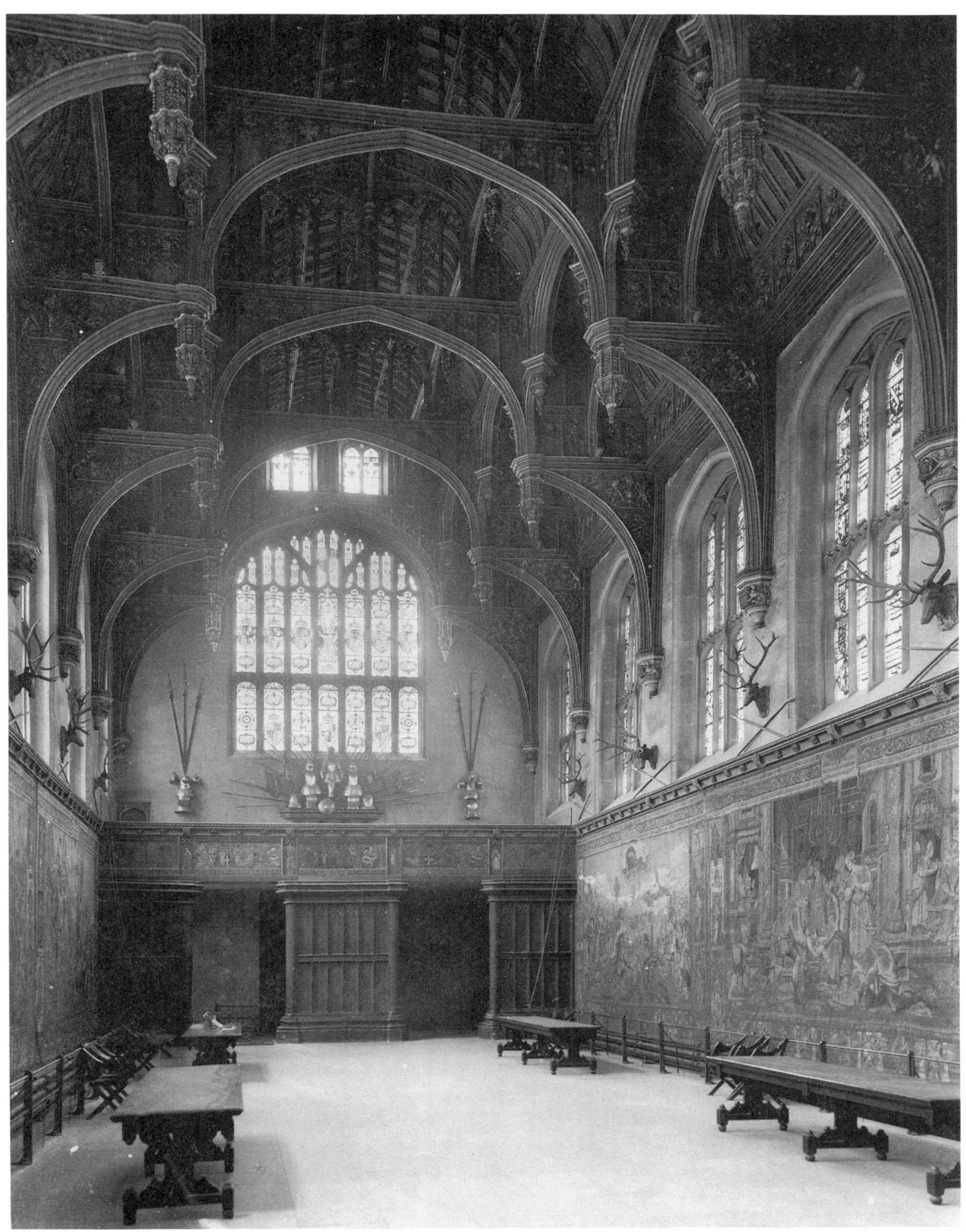

40. Great Hall at Hampton Court. By permission of the Royal Commission on Historical Monuments of England.

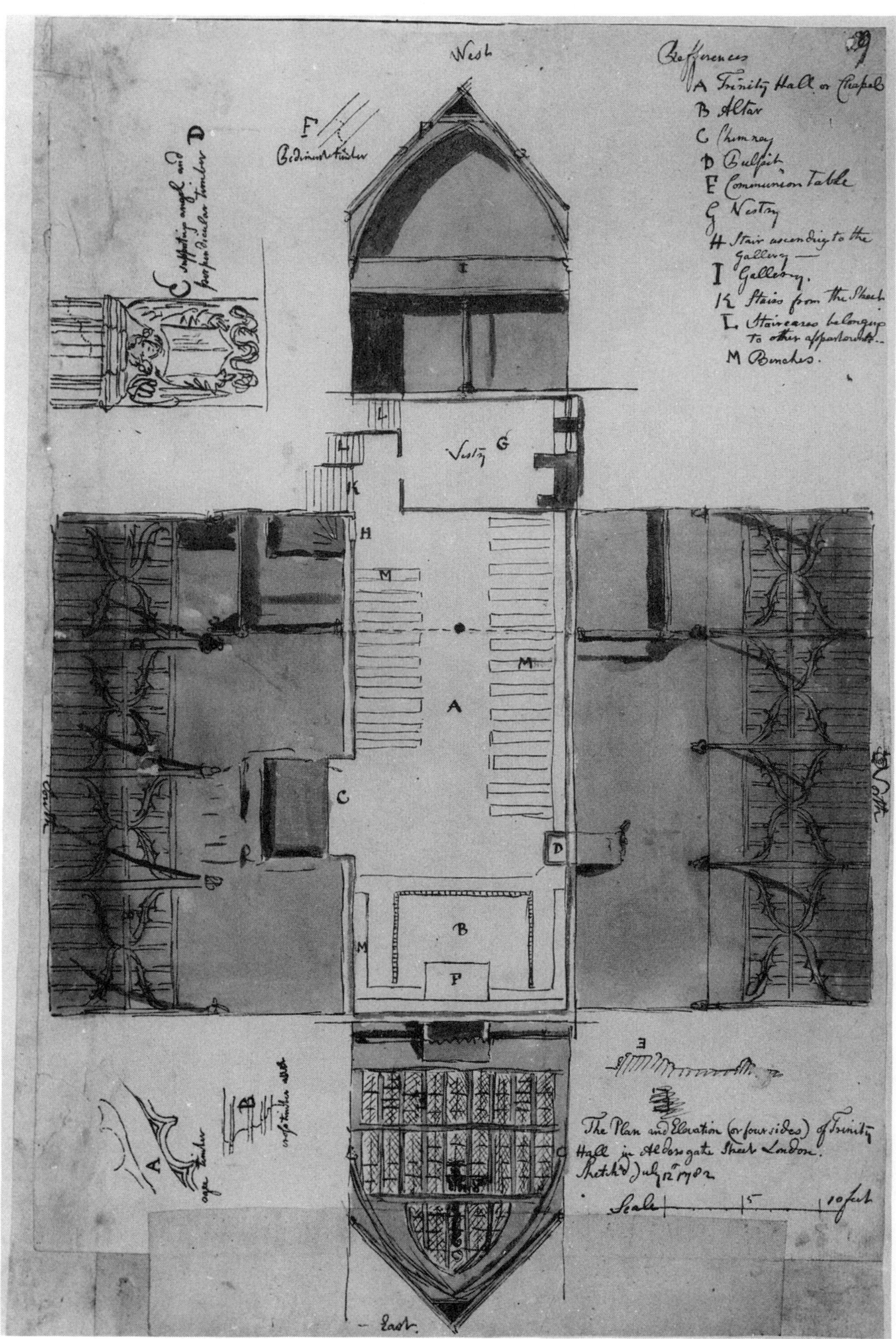

41. Trinity Hall, Aldersgate, London. Interior by John Carter (1782). City of London, Guildhall Library, 591/TRI.

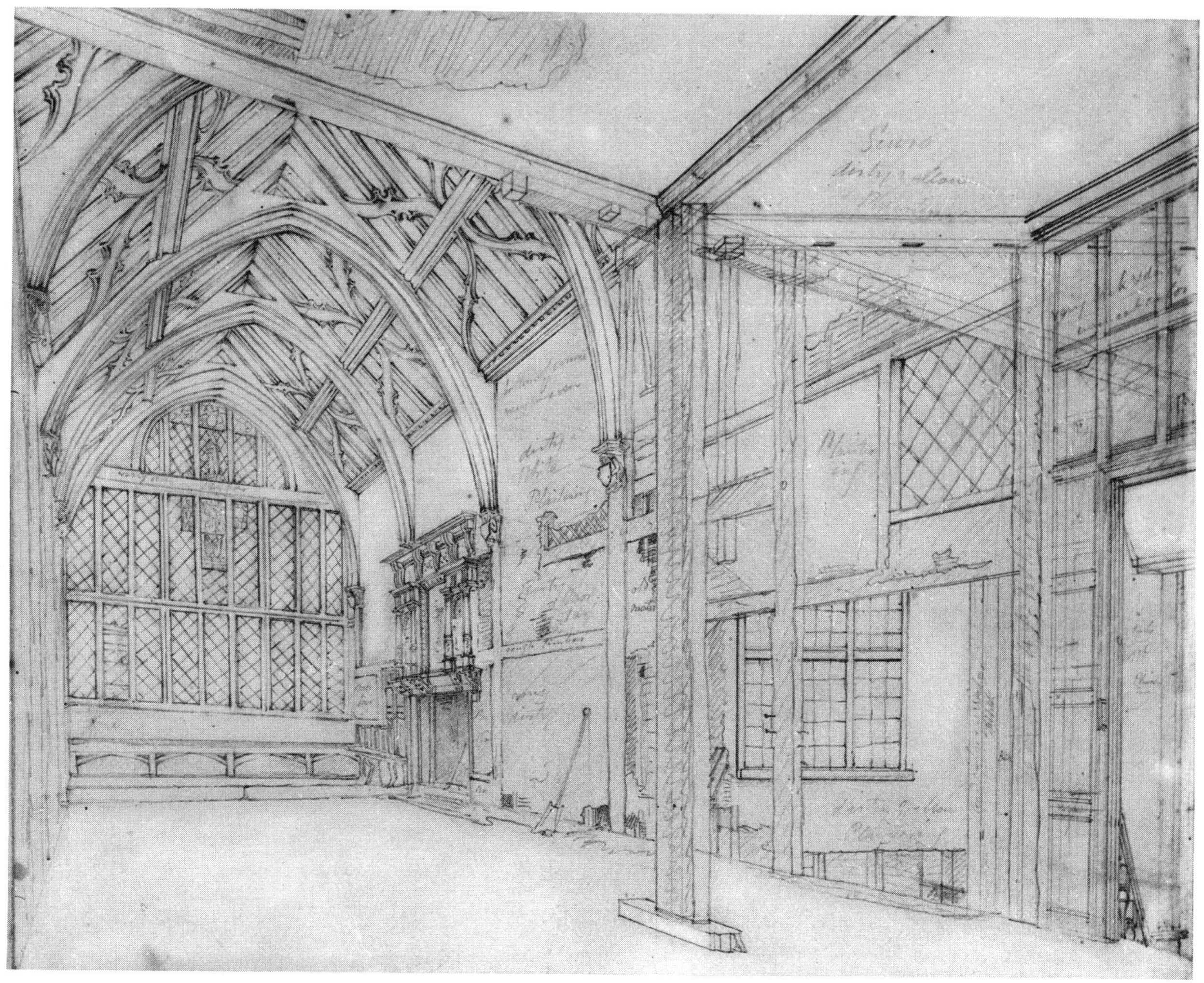

42. Trinity Hall, Aldersgate, London. View from under the gallery by W. Capon (1790). City of London, Guildhall Library, 591/TRI.

central pillar support) at the west. He suggests the use of the western end of the building, including the gallery, for plays.[38] Exits and entrances would be relatively convenient, and there would be the additional advantage of having the gallery as a playing area to supplement the floor level. However, space limitations would not have allowed the construction of a platform, and the playing at this level could therefore not be raised above the spectators. The effect thus would have been perhaps a little like an awkward adaptation of place-and-scaffold staging—or like the pageant wagon and street playing areas in the mystery plays—but would also look forward to the configuration that is found in the later Elizabethan stage as illustrated in the De Witt drawing but without an adequately raised platform stage, which could have been compensated for by raked seating.[39]

Inn yards had been used for stage plays in the London area at least as early as 1557, when a production of a play entitled *Sacke full of Newes* at the Boar's Head without Aldgate was suppressed by the officers of the Lord Mayor and the players arrested because of allegations of lewdness.[40] In perhaps the same year, plays were reported at two inns in Cambridge, the Falcon and the Saracen's Head.[41] The yard of the Falcon, in

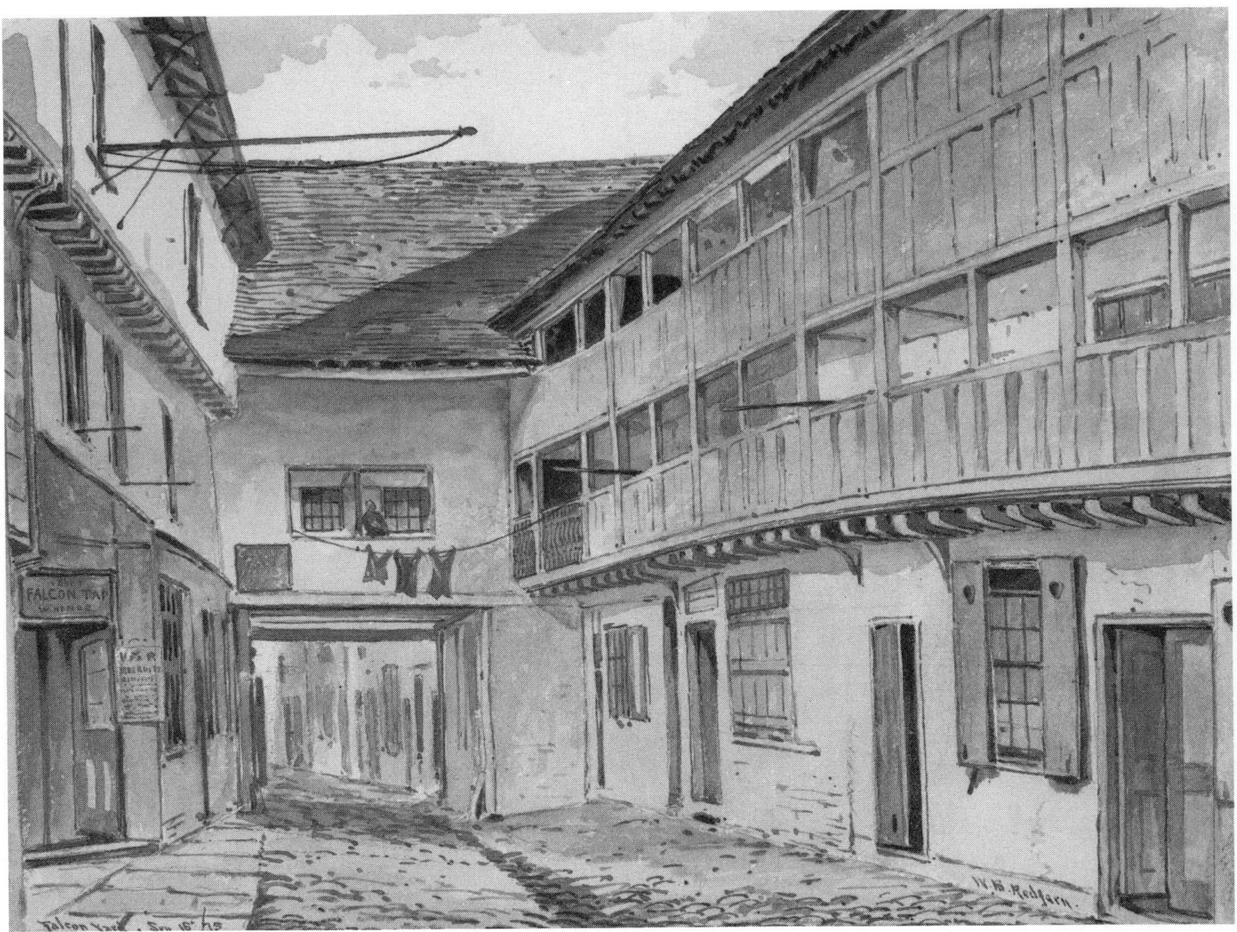

43. Yard of the Falcon Inn, Cambridge. Watercolor by W. H. Redfern. Fitzwilliam Museum, No. 806. Reproduced by permission of the Syndics of the Fitzwilliam Museum, Cambridge.

Petty Curry, remained into modern times, and was shown in a watercolor (fig. 43) by W. H. Redfern dated 1875.[42] That scaffolding would most likely have been used in dramatic productions in such locations might seem to be verified by the dispute about erecting such stages at the Red Lion in Stepney in 1567,[43] but recent research has indicated that this location was a farm rather than an inn.[44]

Stages set up in inn yards in the midsixteenth century would, as Glynne Wickham has argued, have presented serious problems for both the actors and the operation of a busy hostelry,[45] and hence suggest the shortage of playing places in Tudor London in spite of considerable improvisation on the part of theatrical companies. It is not surprising that other locations—permanent theaters—were shortly built to house the players' productions. However, regular playing places had existed previously in England, as even the evidence from small towns and villages will indicate. Kenneth M. Dodd's discovery of a playing place in the village of Walsham-le-Willows, Suffolk, is indicative of the efforts of a local community to have ready a location in which visiting players might perform. A Latin document dated 1581 identifies the place as "le game place," and an English translation of the same identifies it as "a place compassed rownd with a fayer banke cast vp on a good height & havinge many great trees called populers growynge about the same banke, in the myddest a fayre round place of earth wythe a stone wall about the same to the height of the earth made of purpose for the vse of Stage playes."[46] The site of this theater was to be observed in nineteenth-century ordnance survey maps (fig. 44). An open-air theater of this kind, more than 150 feet in diameter, could easily hold several hundred or even a thousand spectators. Such theaters seem to have been not uncommon in England, and probably the type included the remains known as King Arthur's Round Table (fig. 45), near Penrith, Cumbria. This place, noted by William Stukeley as a game place and of a rather large size (capable of holding "at least 10,000 people"), once had a raised embankment on which spectators could stand; further, "the *area* had a circle within, somewhat higher in elevation than the other."[47] John Capgrave of King's Lynn in the mid-fifteenth century had noted places of this type which were called amphitheaters. Capgrave indicates that they were round, and further he identifies *theatra* in which people "stand to se pleyis or wrestilingis."[48]

Reference has frequently been made to the Cornish rounds of the species illustrated by William Borlase in his *Observations on the Antiquities Historical and Monumental, of the County of Cornwall* (1754). Borlase takes note of the theater, semicircular with seating, called "Bryn gwyn, (or Supreme Court), with it's opening to the West" at Angelsea as well as a similar round in the Orkneys.[49] The Cornish theater which he illustrates in this volume, however, is the one which existed at St. Just, Penwith (fig. 46), a round approximately 126 feet in diameter and surrounded by a bank ten feet in height from the bottom of the playing area and seven feet in height when observed from outside the round. In *The Natural History of Cornwall*, published four years later, another round is illustrated: Perran Round (fig. 47), slightly larger in diameter and fitted with an entrenchment known as the "Devil's Spoon,"[50] which may have been used for conveying actors into the playing area without being seen by the audience.

In such "Rounds, or Amphitheatres of stone . . . the Britans did usually assemble to hear plays acted, to see the Sports and Games, which upon particular occasions were intended to amuse

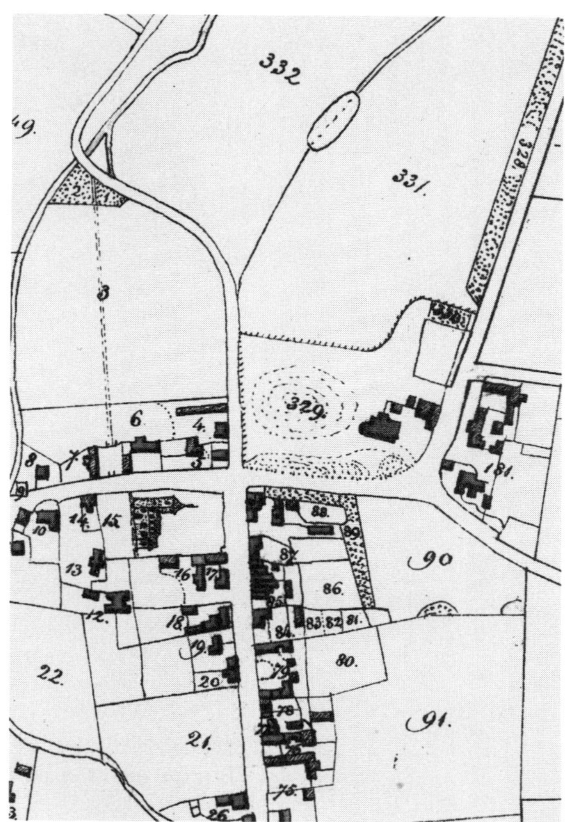

44. Ordnance Survey map showing the location (Plot 329) of the game place or theater at Walsham-le-Willows, Suffolk. Bury St. Edmunds and West Suffolk Record Office EL 159/1/2.1.

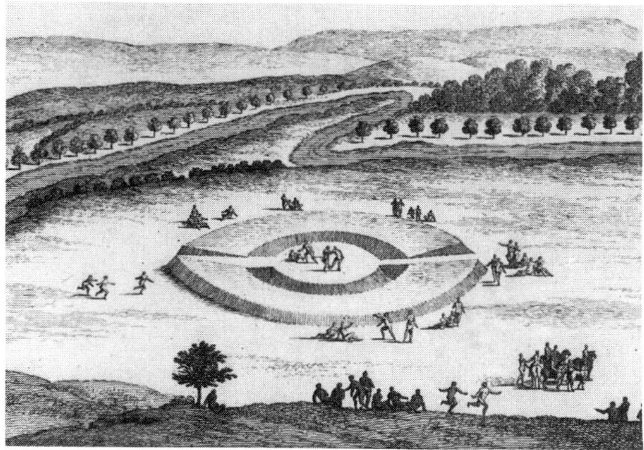
45. King Arthur's Round Table, near Penrith, Cumbria. William Stukeley, *Itinerarium Curiosum* (1776), II, fig. 84. By permission of the British Library.

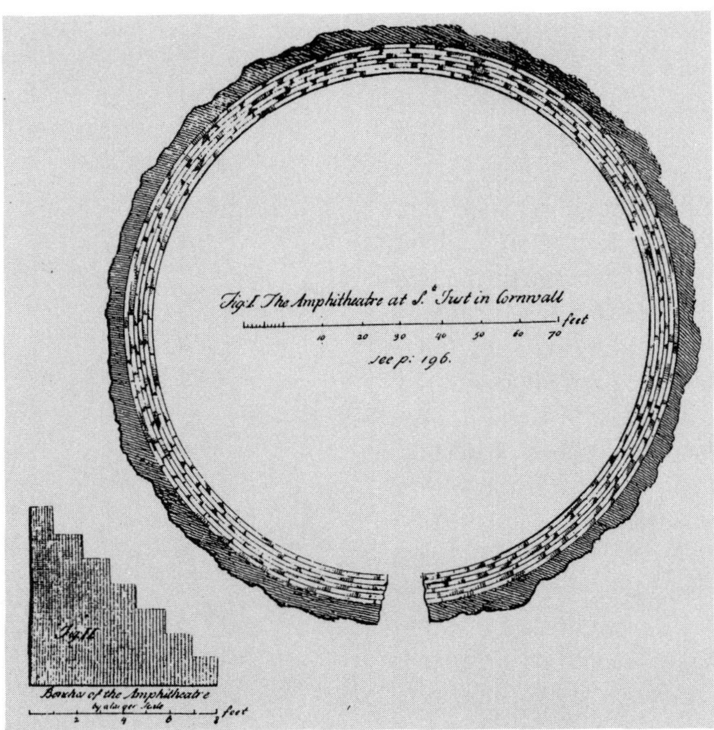

46. Cornish round at St. Just, Penwith. Borlase, *Observations on the Antiquities Historical and Monumental of the County of Cornwall* (1754).

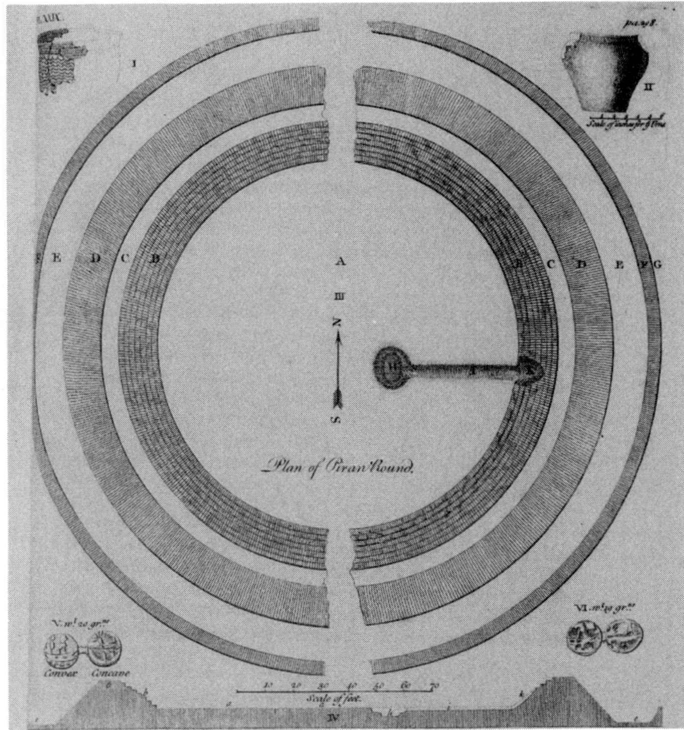

47. Perran Round, Cornwall. Borlase, *The Natural History of Cornwall* (1758). By permission of the British Library.

the people, to quiet and delight them," according to Borlase. He further notes that "these are call'd with us in Cornwall (where we have great numbers of them) *Plan an guare*; viz. the level place, or Plain of sport and pastime." Finally, he says, "The benches round were generally of Turf."[51]

Treve Holman, however, has suggested that these rounds may have been forts rather than theaters, and returns to the statement in Richard Carew's *Survey of Cornwall* in which he identifies the earthen amphitheaters of this region as much smaller—forty or fifty feet in diameter.[52] Archaeological evidence also suggests, according to this writer, that Borlase was being fanciful in his description of the seating and the ditch in these rounds.[53] This sceptical view has not been entirely confuted by the excavation of the St. Just round, the only portion of which that can definitely be designated as medieval being the circular space surrounded by "a low . . . ring mound."[54]

The use of round spaces like the St. Just and Perran rounds, or smaller rounds, for theatrical presentations is nevertheless corroborated by the diagrams of the stage that appear in manuscripts containing the extant drama in the Cornish language. The *Ordinalia* (c.1375), contained in MS. Bodley 791, contains three such diagrams (figs. 48–50), one for each of the three plays included in the three-day cycle. Stages, identified as tents (*tentum*) or pulpits (*pulpitum*), are indicated in the plays according to their use. Jane A. Bakere suggests that each may have been "a rectangular structure, roofed and curtained on three sides with front curtains that could be opened or closed at will."[55] They were clearly raised, with steps to provide access for the actors. In each diagram, heaven (*celum*) is at the top, which represents the east. From the stage directions we know that this location involved a raised stage,[56] and if the dramatic records of St. Just are to be trusted with regard to the staging scheme of the *Ordinalia*, we may surmise that it was a wooden structure.[57]

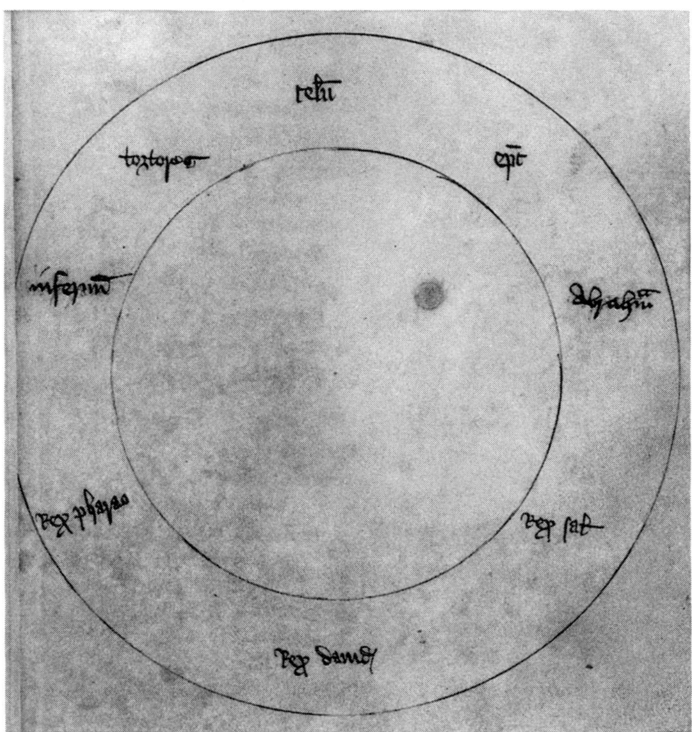

48. Stage diagram for the Cornish *Origo Mundi*. Oxford, Bodleian Library, MS. 791, fol. 27.

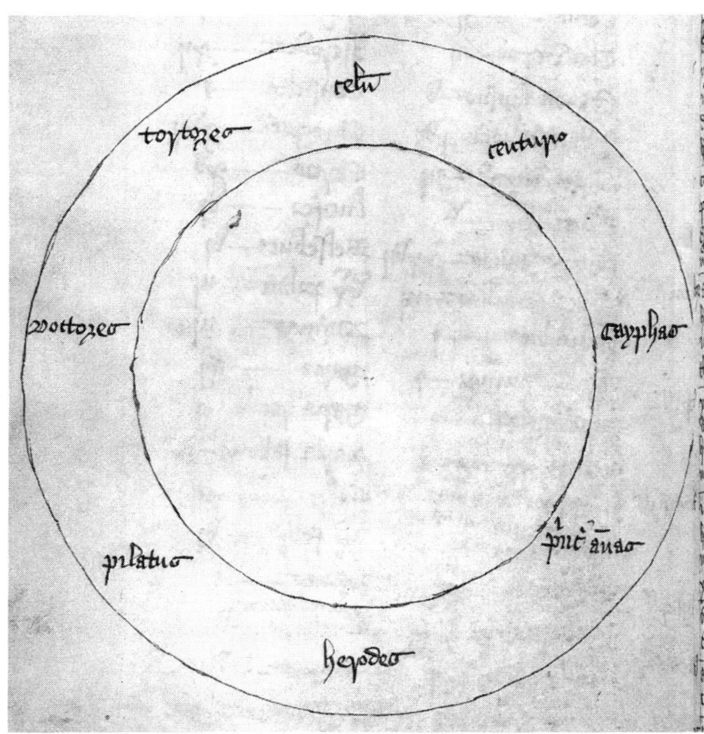

49. Stage diagram for the Cornish *Passio Domini*. Oxford, Bodleian Library, MS. 791, fol. 56v.

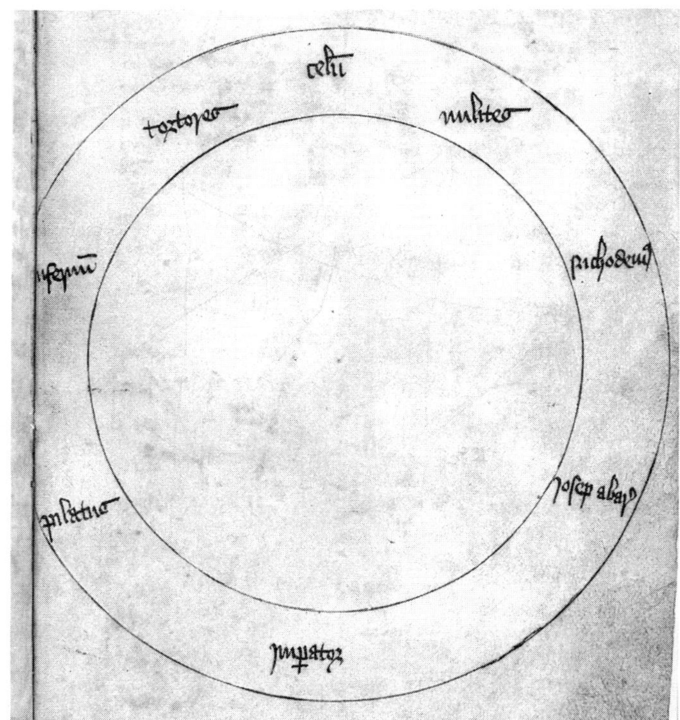

50. Stage diagram for the Cornish *Resurrexio Domini*. Oxford, Bodleian Library, MS. 791, fol. 83.

Circling to the left, the station at the northeast is consistently associated with God's enemies (*tortores*), and the next, at the north, is where hell mouth is located in the Old Testament (*Origo Mundi*) and Resurrection (*Resurrexio Domini*) plays. (In the second play, on the topic of the Passion or *Passio Domini*, where no hell mouth is specified, the north location is given to the *Doctores*.) This orientation is consistent with the conventional understanding of the symbolism of the east and of north, since prayers conventionally were spoken to the east—the direction of the Second Coming—and the Gospel was read to the north as a challenge to the powers of darkness.[58]

In the Old Testament play, the other stations are intended for Pharaoh (northwest), King David (west), Solomon (southwest), Abraham (south), and the evil bishop (southeast). The Passion substitutes Pilate for Pharaoh, and the same position is retained for Pilate in the last play of the cycle. Interestingly, the Centurion, the only good character to have a station among those named on the second *Ordinalia* diagram, is placed in the Passion at the location held in the previous play by the evil bishop, at the southeast. Caiaphas is in the south, with Annas nearby in the southwest position. Herod is located in the west. The western location is given to Tiberius in the play of the Resurrection, which has the soldiers associated with the resurrection event at the southeast, Nicodemus at the south, and Joseph of Arimathea at the southwest. The placement of the stations for these three plays seems to combine symbolism and practicality.

The stages or booths, grouped in a circle in this theater, were less the sphere of the action in

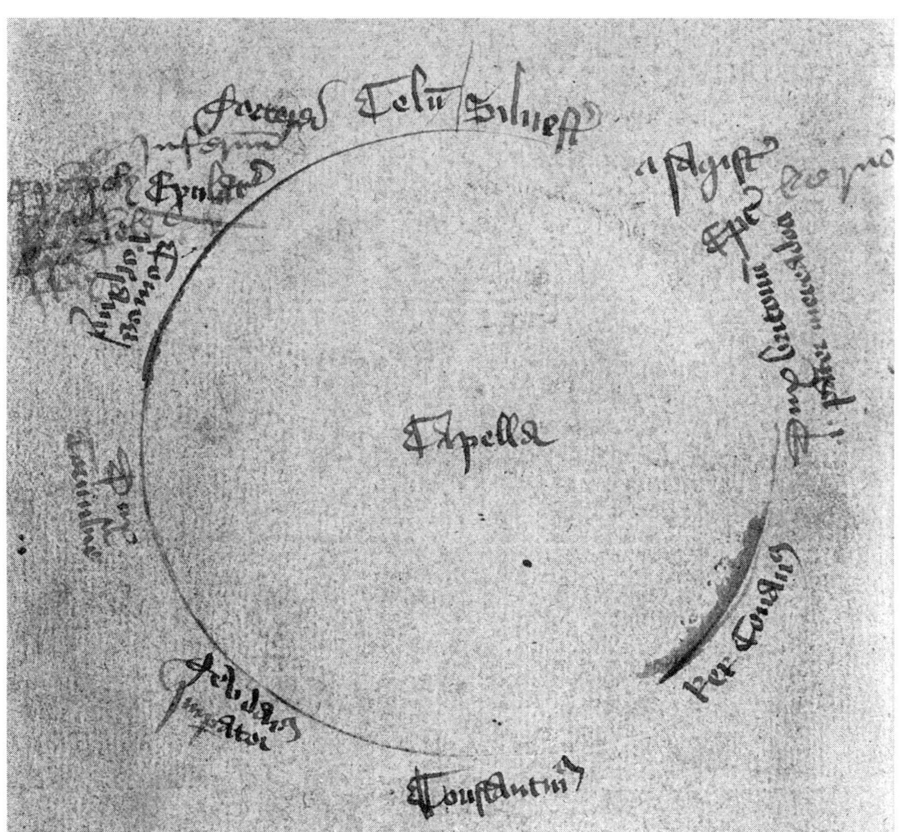

51. Stage diagram for the Cornish *Beunans Meriasek*, Part I. Aberystwyth, National Library of Wales, Peniarth MS. 105, fol. 92v.

the play than the *platea* in the center, where attention was mainly centered. Here actors could strut about or parade (*pompabit*), and from this space an actor could even mount a horse and leave the playing area.[59] It would appear that Paradise in the first part of the play was located in the central *platea*, though its location is unmarked in the diagram. In *The Creacion of the World*, which, though copied in 1611, was probably written sometime in the previous century prior to the accession of Queen Elizabeth to the throne and is not independent of the *Ordinalia*, Paradise contains two trees "and an appell upon the Tree, and som other frute one the other."[60] For the creation of Adam and Eve, the Devil's Spoon may have been used to hide them until their creation, though, as Bakere admits, such a suggestion can be only an appealing speculation.[61]

It is interesting to compare the diagrams for the *Ordinalia* with those accompanying the text of another Cornish play, *Beunans Meriasek* (c.1495–1501), which is contained in a manuscript (MS. Peniarth 105) in the National Library of Wales, Aberystwyth. The play, which has been associated with Camborne where there had been a nearby "plain-en-gwarry" at Treswithian,[62] dramatizes the life of a local saint.[63] The stage plans for this drama (figs. 51–52; see also figs.

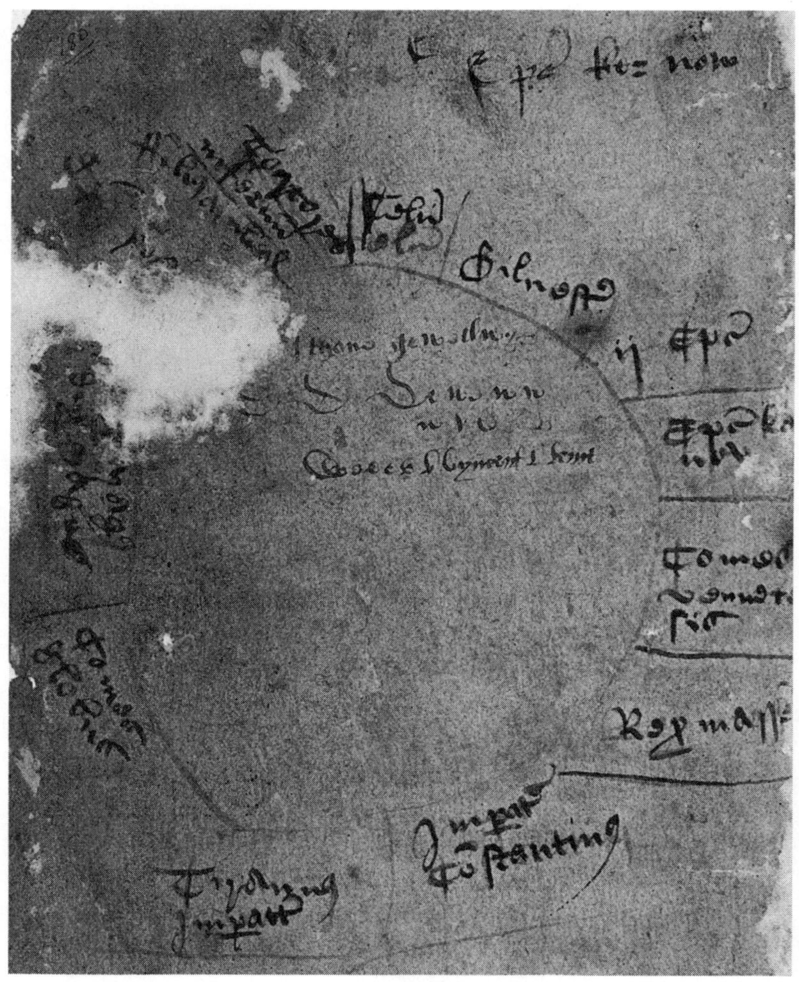

52. Stage diagram for the Cornish *Beunans Meriasek*, Part II. Aberystwyth, National Library of Wales, Peniarth MS. 105, fol. 92ᵛ.

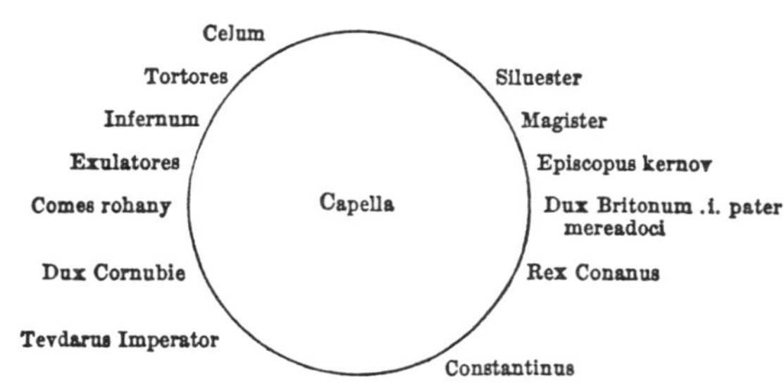

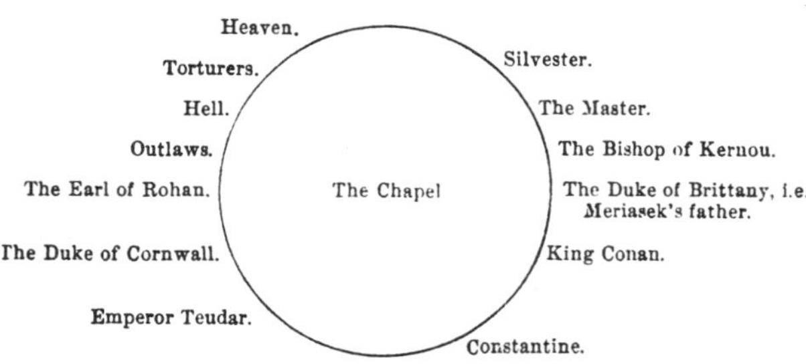

53. Stage plan for Cornish *Meriasek*, Part I, from Whitley Stokes, ed. and trans., *The Life of Saint Meriasek, Bishop and Confessor: A Cornish Drama* (1872).

53–54), included only for the first two parts of the play, again place the heaven stage at the top of the diagram—i.e., to the east—and the *Tortores* and hell stages counterclockwise from heaven. Hell is more or less aligned to the north (and there is reference in this play to the Devil as "your patron saint of the north side"[64]), but the distribution of the other scaffolds around the *platea* does not seem to conform to any identifiable principles which determine the arrangement. In the first part of *Beunans Meriasek*, there is to be a chapel in the center, while in the second part St. Samson's church at Dol is to be substituted for it. As the stage direction makes clear, the staging again allows for numerous special effects, in this drama including such effects as a dragon breathing fire, fighting, men on horseback, and a ship. Processions also played a major role in the spectacle.

Yet another stage diagram, accompanying the Middle English *Castle of Perserverance* (fig. 55), is not only well known but also controversial in large part because of the conjectures concerning the staging of the play contained in Richard Southern's *The Medieval Theatre in the Round* (1957). *The Castle of Perseverance* is to be associated with East Anglia. In date it falls between the two Cornish plays for which diagrams exist, and has been fairly reliably placed at the end of the first quarter of the fifteenth century. The scaffold of the devil, here identified as Belial, is once more in the north where we have come to expect it, and God is in the east. The other members of the unholy trinity known as the Three Enemies of Man are included, with the scaffolds of Flesh placed in the south and of World in the west. Another stage, given over to the character Covetous, is positioned in the northeast, counterclockwise from God. In the center is the fortified castle, which represents sacred space reserved for man in a state of grace. It is the Castle of Virtue, a stage property that shares its iconography with the visual arts.[65]

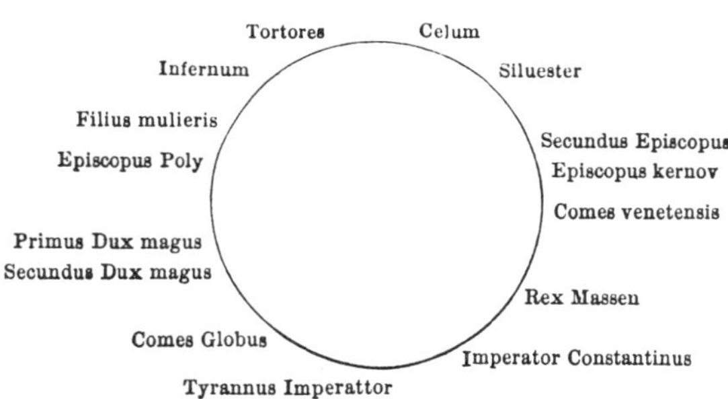

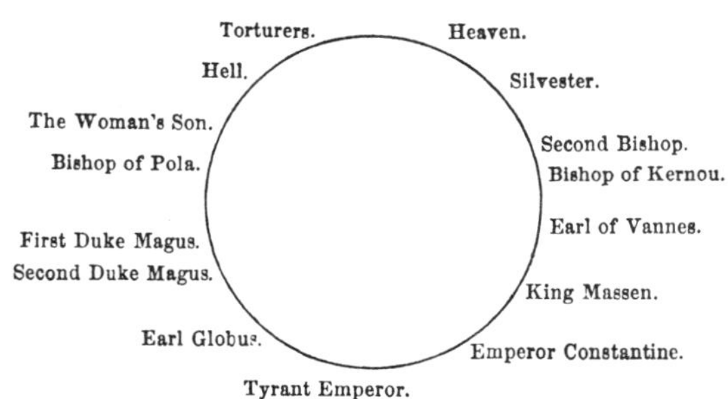

54. Stage plan for Cornish *Meriasek*, Part II, from Stokes, ed. and trans., *The Life of St. Meriasek.*

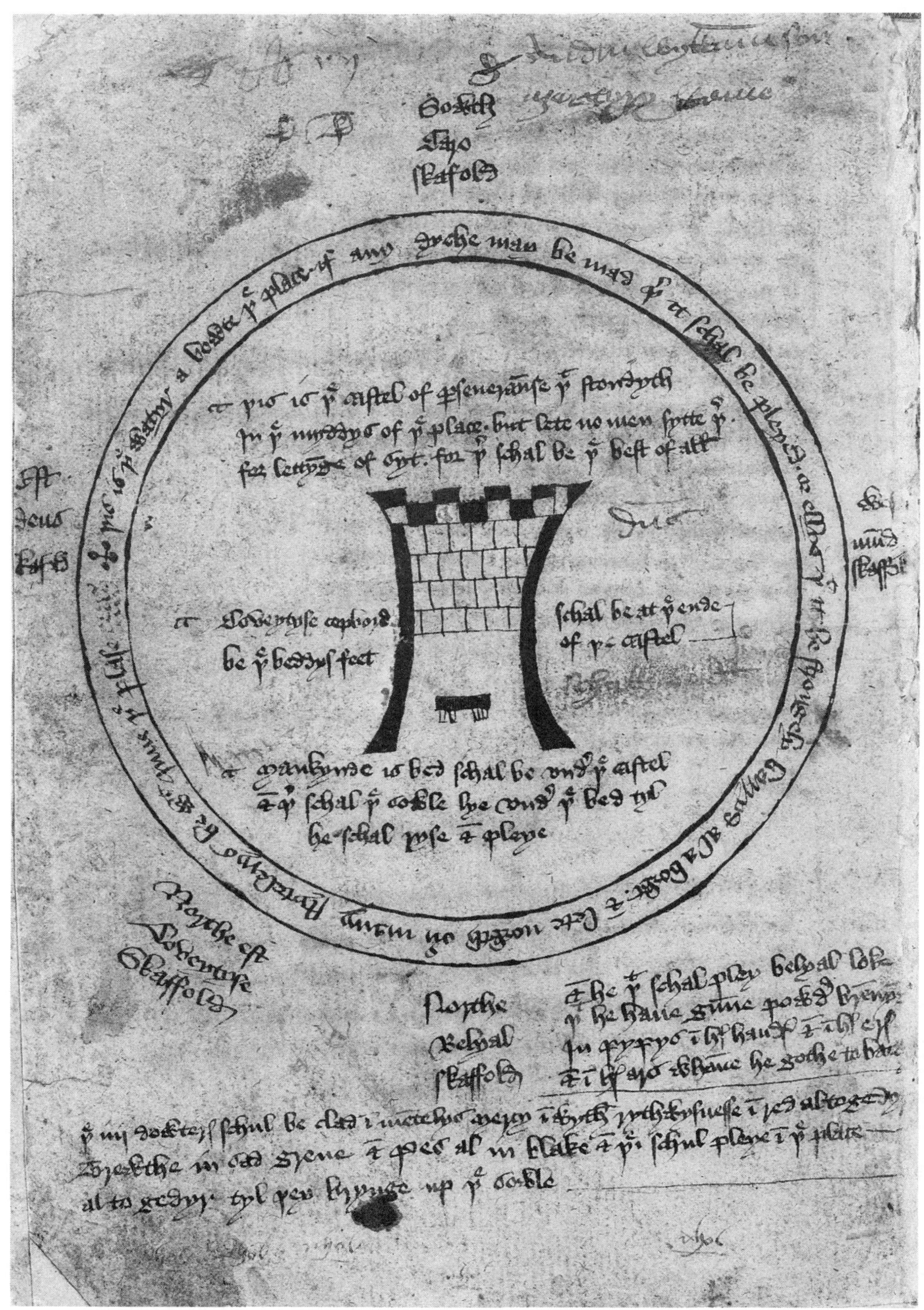

55. Stage diagram for *The Castle of Perseverance*. Macro Manuscript, Folger Shakespeare Library, MS. V.a.354, fol. 191v. By permission of the Folger Shakespeare Library.

Around it is a ditch, and within it is a bed in which Humanum Genus will die. There also, at the bed's foot, will be the cupboard with Humanum Genus' wealth—wealth which will not only be taken by another when he has departed from this life but also will stand him in little stead in the end.

The text of *The Castle of Perseverance* seems thus to have been written with a particular kind of theater in mind—a theater remarkably similar to the Cornish rounds but not limited to that region of the country. Such theaters were designed for multiple use as game places and as locations in which plays might be performed. For use as locations where plays would be seen by audiences, place-and-scaffold staging of the type exemplified by this morality reached a level of sophistication that has often not been recognized.

V

ILLUSTRATED MANUSCRIPT PLAYBOOKS

Two English manuscripts, separated by three centuries, contain play texts and illustrations showing dramatic action. The earlier is a copy of the plays of Terence (c.195–c.159 B.C.), the classical playwright who remained well known throughout the Middle Ages in spite of his reputation for writing dramas about seductions and love affairs. Although the classical dramatists named by Isidore of Seville were usually names only,[1] manuscripts of Terence were available in the Middle Ages, and at least one medieval playwright, the canoness Hrotsvita of Gandersheim (c.935-c.1002), modelled the structure of her dramas on his comedies. There is also some evidence that his plays were performed or at least were recited to audiences in this period.[2] John of Salisbury, complaining in his *Policraticus* about contemporary actors and mimes, compared them unfavorably with those who had been "intimate with our favorite Terence."[3]

Written in a single twelfth-century hand, the manuscript of the comedies of Terence now in the Bodleian Library (MS. Auct. F.2.13) contains 139 pen-and-ink drawings by perhaps as many as four contemporary English artists showing the various scenes in the plays.[4] These drawings are not merely products of the twelfth-century imagination, however, for they are immediately based on a Carolingian tradition of manuscript illustrations of Terence that may go back to the late days of the classical theater itself. It has been established that the illustrations in the English manuscript, which was once in the library of the Abbey of St. Albans though it seems not to have been copied by the resident scribes and artists,[5] were mainly modelled on those contained in Bibliothèque Nationale MS. lat. 7899.[6]

With a single exception, the illustration at the beginning of *Phormio*, the miniatures appear to have been added after the text had been written out by the scribe.[7] Jones and Morey plausibly suggest that the first artist, whom they designate as

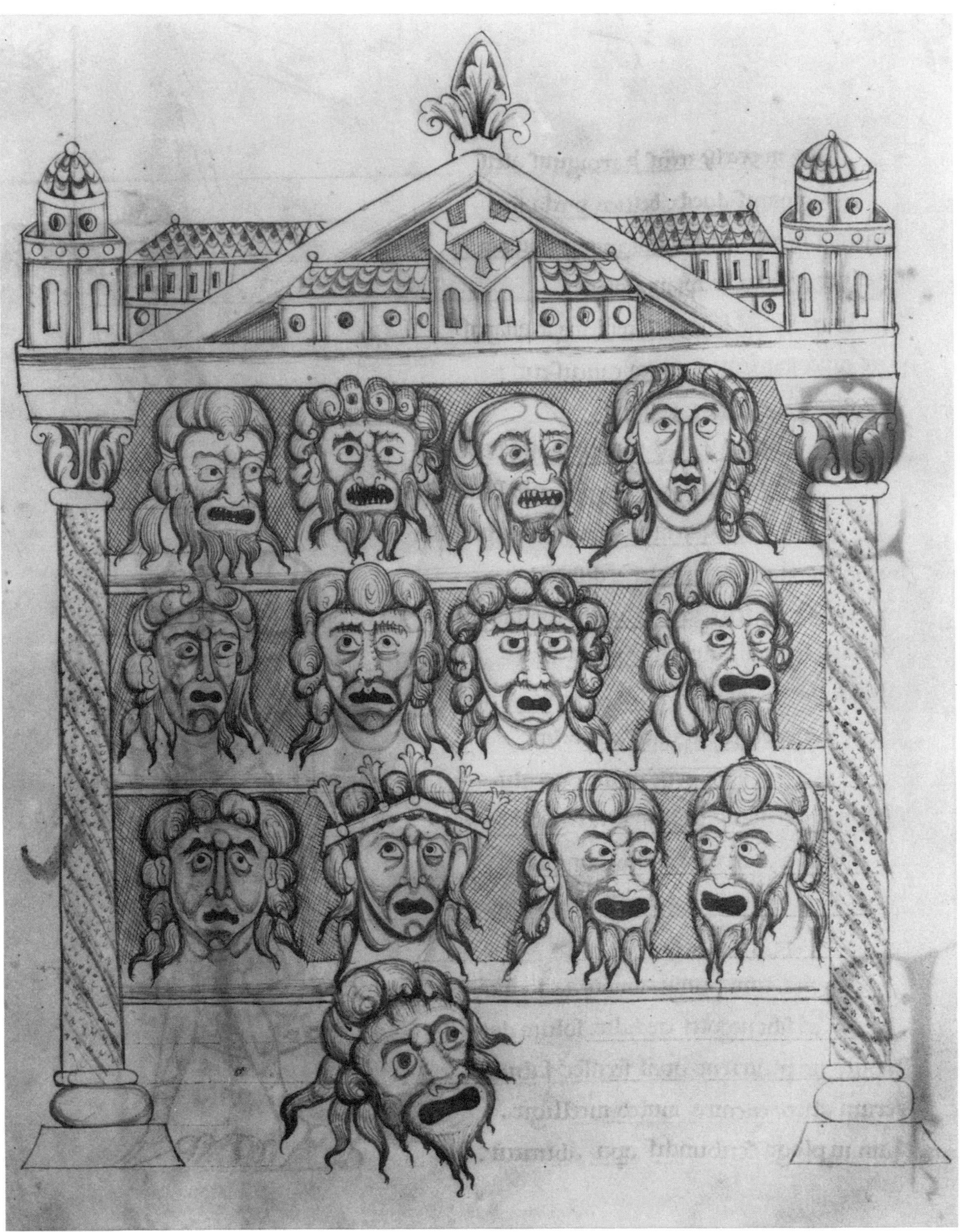

56. *Terence.* Cabinet of masks. Oxford, Bodleian Library, MS. Auct. F.2.13, fol. 3^{r}. Twelfth-century manuscript from St. Albans.

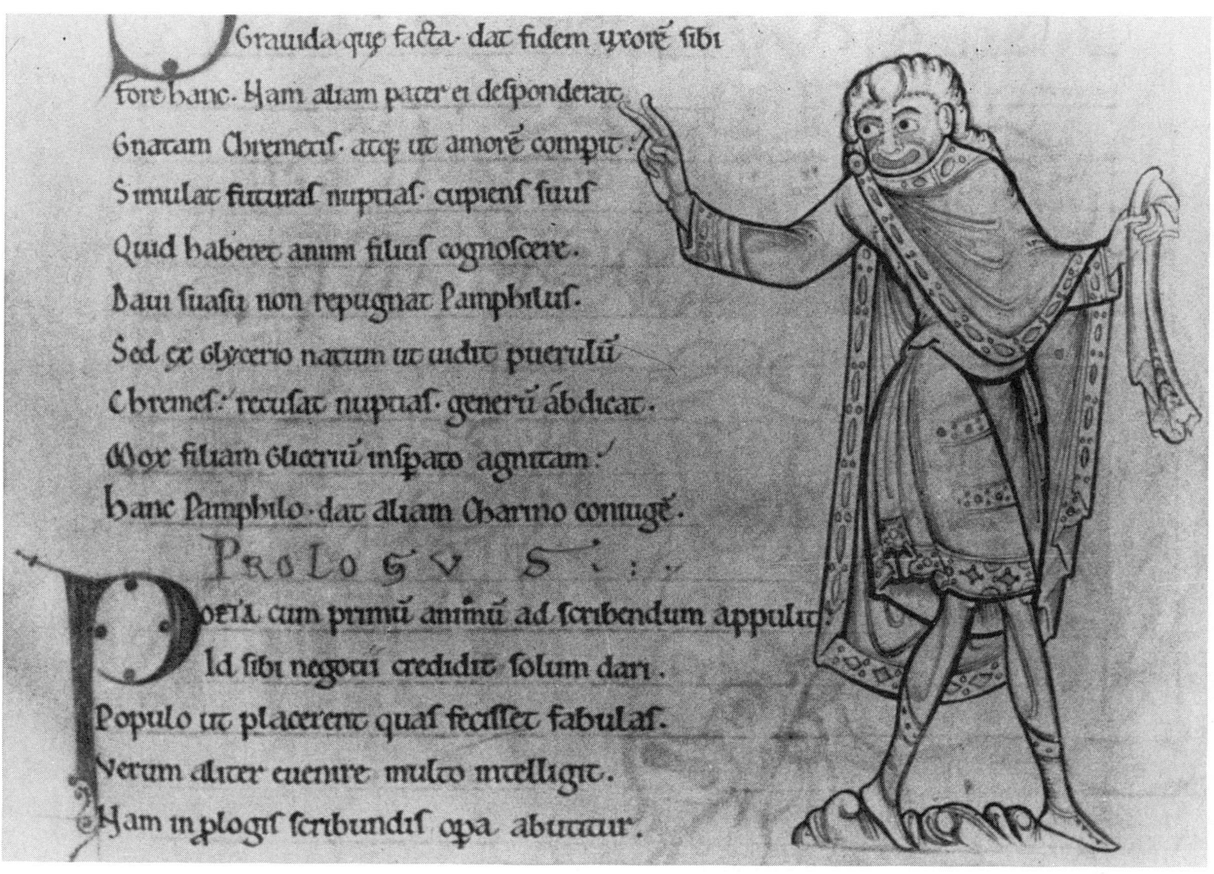

57. Terence, *Andria*: Prologue. Oxford, Bodleian Library, MS. Auct. F.2.13, fol. 3^{v}.

Artist A, may have been the head of the scriptorium in which the manuscript was produced;[8] this artist has been further identified as the "Master of the Apocrypha Drawings" in the Winchester Bible.[9] His work is marked in the Terence manuscript by round, bulging eyes and distinctive male actors' masks. The hair on the male actors' masks frequently has a "scalloped contour," while young women's hair is "hatched."[10] The male actors wear high boots with jewels on their tops. A comparison with this artist's source will demonstrate that he made significant changes from his original, and the effect is a rather striking theatrical quality and a liveliness surpassing the earlier miniatures. Margaret Rickert comments, "The poses and gestures are stagy; and the masks which cover the faces introduce a new type of head with exaggerated features and grotesque, often coarse, expressions."[11] A scholar writing in the early part of this century claimed that this artist's work and the work of the other illustrators of this collected edition of Terence show "unmistakable traces of medieval influence" and demonstrate inferior artistic ability when compared to earlier continental versions.[12] The charge of inferior draughtsmanship seems, however, to be thoroughly unfair except for some of the miniatures on fols. 114^{v}–159 for which neither Artist A nor Artist B, also recognized as a master, was responsible.

At the beginning of the manuscript is an account of Terence and his plays, and a miniature (fol. 3^{r}) depicts the masks worn by the male actors (fig. 56); these masks are placed in a cabinet (*aediculae*) that seems intended to bear some resemblance to the frame of the *scena* or stage building. Isidore had described the Roman stage as "built in the form of a house, with a platform" before it.[13] (An interesting resemblance to the English Renaissance stage will immediately be noted, since the latter had a canopy, also supported by two pillars, partly extending over the playing area or platform stage.) The design of the classical theater, including its *scena*, was reported by Isidore to involve a "stage building" and an "orchestra"; the former was described by him as "a place down in front of the theater built in the form of a house, with a platform which was called the orchestra, where comic and tragic poets recited, and actors and mime-players performed." The orchestra "was the platform of the stage building where a dancer could perform or two [persons] dispute between themselves. There comic and tragic poets mounted in competition, and while they recited, others gesticulated."[14]

On fol. 3^{v}, the Prologue to *Andria* appears—an adaptation from the illumination in the much earlier manuscript now in the Bibliothèque Nationale.[15] The figure representing the Prologue has his right hand with two fingers raised in a gesture demanding attention from the audience, and he with his other hand holds up a scarf (fig. 57). The buskins of the original drawing have become high boots, while concern with clothing fashions has led the figure to be shown wearing a shortened garment that reaches only to the knees. Costume is in fact adapted so that it is characteristic of designs used in contemporary English and continental artistic practice, probably reflecting designs learned from current model books; he wears a tunic under a cloak, and has the familiar mask and wig.

In an illustration assigned to *Andria*, Act I, Scene ii, the aged Simo and his slave Davus appear outside a "house," presumably the stage structure associated with the old man. The artist has adapted the line drawing of his original, which was only indicative of a door,[16] and has developed not only a precisely drawn romanesque doorway but also a structure with a turret and tiled roof from which an animal head protrudes. Davus points back through the door. Glycerium's house, pictured in fol. 17^{v} where she appears with Lesbia (fig. 58), also has similar features.[17]

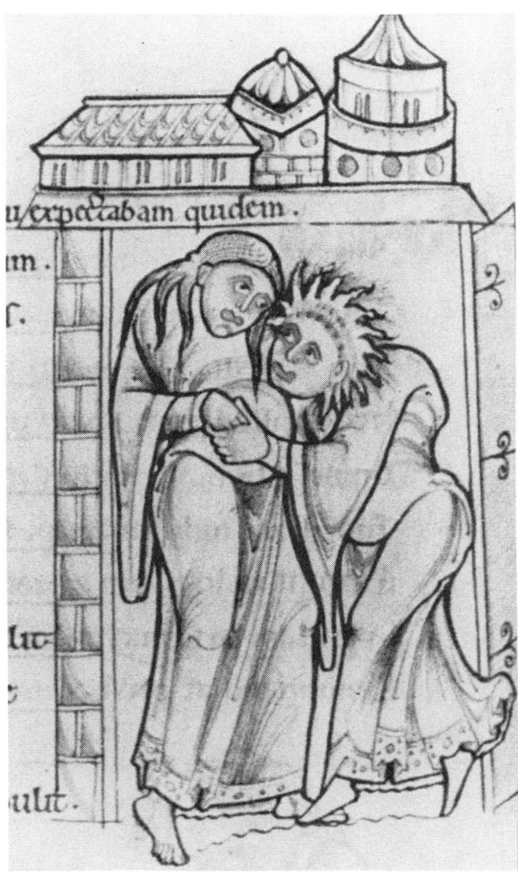

58. Terence, *Andria*: Glycerium (before her house) and Lesbia. Oxford, Bodleian Library, MS. Auct. F.2.13, fol. 17^{v}.

The prominence of hand gestures in the Terence drawings has been noted, and it has been suggested that they are based in an established system.[18] At fol. 30^{v}, the illustration (drawn, according to Jones and Morey, by Artist B) shows Pamphilus, returning to the stage with Crito whom he is indicating with two fingers and a thumb extended (the other two fingers are folded back) on his right hand (fig. 59). Crito's negative statement "Say no more" ("Mitte orare") is reflected in his gesture: his right hand is turned palm down, also with the little finger and the finger next to it turned under. Chremes' "Whom do I see? Crito of Andros?" ("Andrium ego Critonem video?") then follows with Chremes' gesture of the index finger pointed to the eye. Finally, Simo points with the index finger of his right hand at Crito, presumably

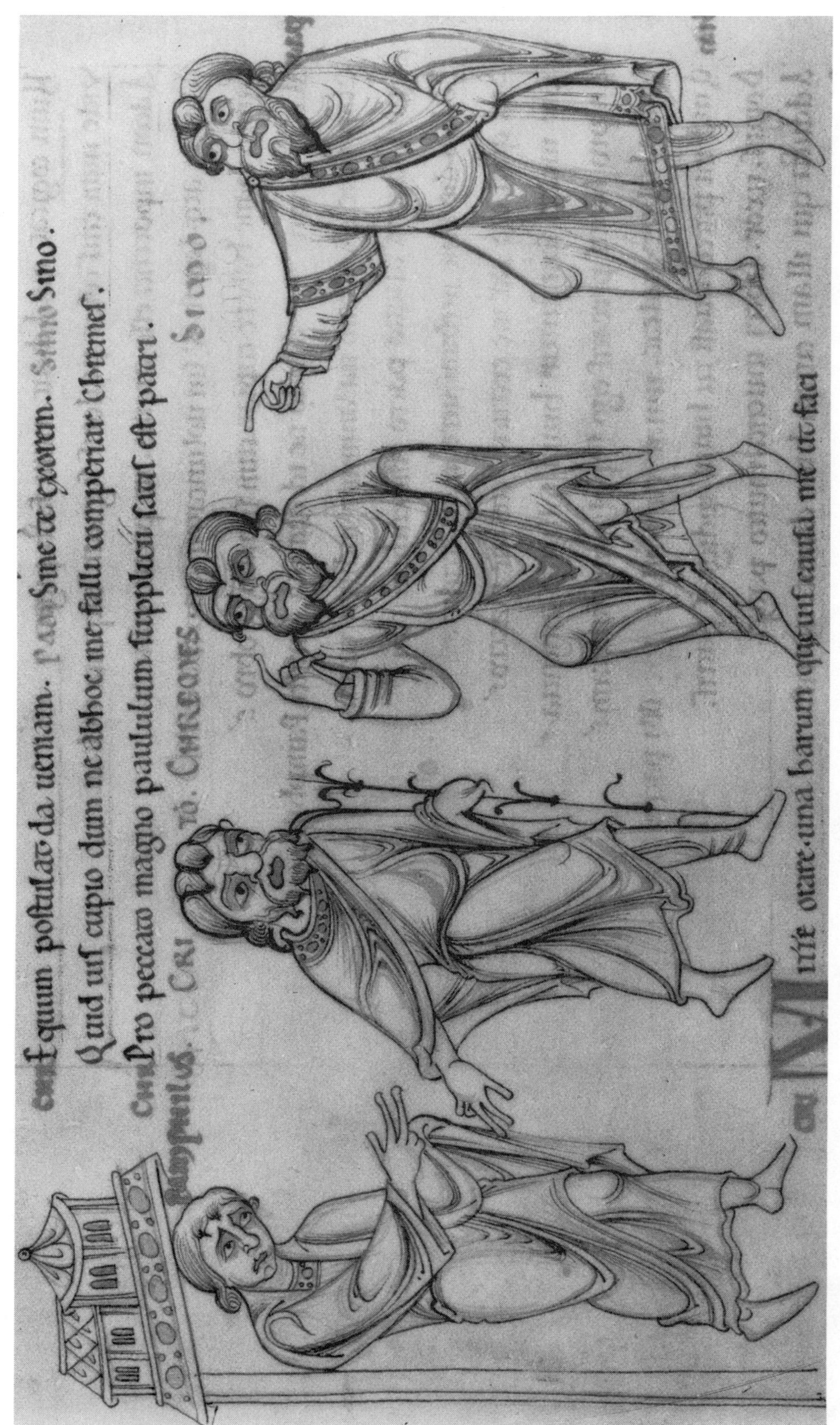

59. Terence, *Andria*: Pamphilus and Crito; Chremes gestures with index finger pointed to eye. Oxford, Bodleian Library, MS. Auct. F.2.13, fol. 30v.

reflecting his surprise as he inquires further into the news that Glycerium is an Athenian. The picture reads from left to right.

The same artist presumably drew the illustration on fol. 47^{r}, showing the point in *Eunuchus* (Act III, Scene ii) where Parmena is pictured presenting the gifts of Phaedria to Thais: a black girl slave and a eunuch (actually Chaeria in disguise) (fig. 60). Thraso and Gnato demonstrate their envy through their gestures. The house of Thais, at the right, is less elaborate than the houses pictured by Artist A, though it is more highly developed than the illustration in the source manuscript, which has only the most bare hint of the architectural features.[19] Artist B, who has been identified with the person known as the Master of the Leaping Figures, seems to have been deeply influenced in his subsequent work through his illuminations for the Terence manuscript, and it is a characteristic of his style that his work has a "stagy" liveliness.[20]

A different artist was responsible for fol. 100^{v}, which illustrates *Adelphoe*, Act II, Scene i; here Aeschinus is carrying off the music girl as her owner, Sannio the procurer, is given only blows from Parmeno for his interference (fig. 61). However, the scene may have been drawn by Artist A. Yet another artist drew the illustrations on fols. 144^{v}–159, where the figures have characteristically turned-up toes and clumsily drawn noses, and here the drawing is less reliable than in the case of the drawings in earlier parts of the book.[21]

The drawings in the St. Albans Terence deserve much more attention than they have been given since they are likely to suggest an entire repertoire of gestures inherited by the twelfth century from the Roman drama and very likely still well understood in the Middle Ages. So too the classical concept of staging, understood or misunderstood, seems to have been influential in medieval production, which in many cases utilized a kind of presentation that set off various locations or "houses" from each other, as in the case of the well-known Valenciennes stage. At the same time, the limitations of the Terence drawings as evidence for understanding the early English stage must be fully recognized, since the artists who illustrated the Bodleian manuscript were far more dependent on the traditions of the visual arts than on the theater.

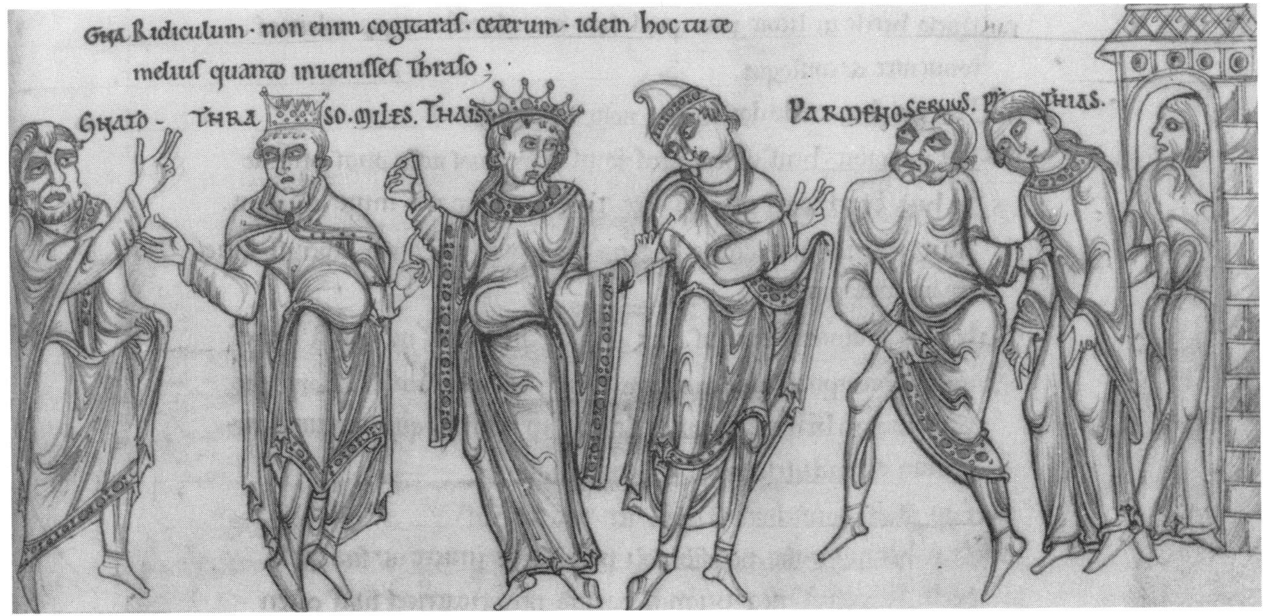

60. Terence, *Eunuchus*: Parmena presenting slave girl and "eunuch" to Thais. Oxford, Bodleian Library, MS. F.2.13, fol. 47.

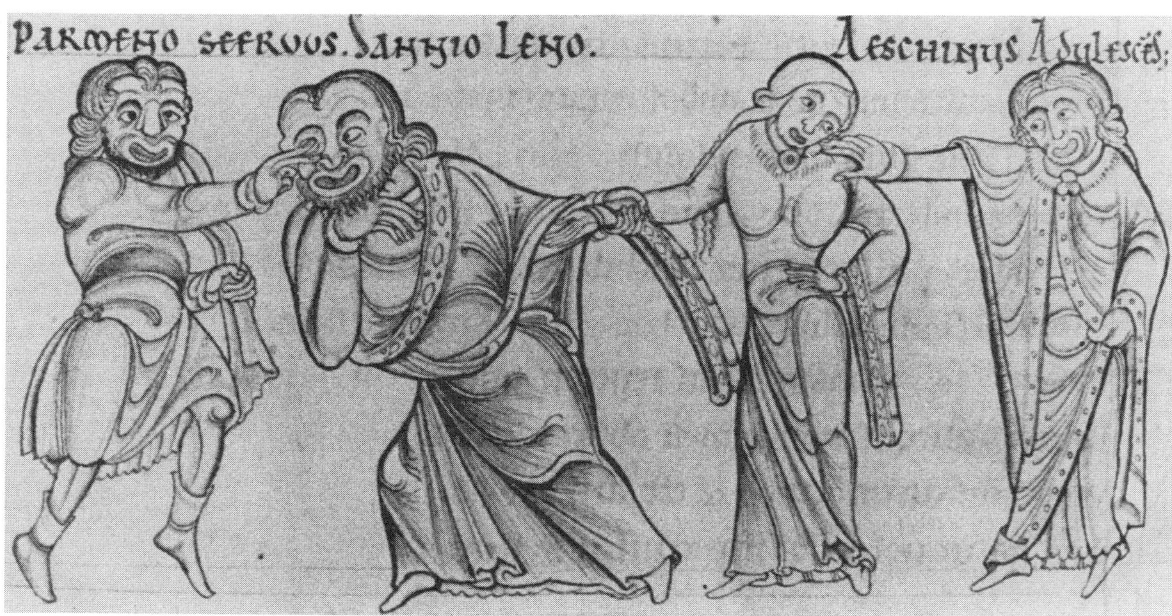

61. Terence, *Adelphoe*: Aeschinus, with music girl, Sannio, Parmeno. Oxford, Bodleian Library, MS. F.2.13, fol. 100ᵛ.

The second medieval English manuscript including illustrations of a play is Cambridge, Trinity College MS. R.14.5, which contains the text of Thomas Chaundler's *Liber Apologeticus*, an academic drama, along with fifteen illuminations, six of which are reproduced here. Closely related to the morality play tradition, the drama's hero is a representative of mankind, who is poised between Reason and Sensuality. Its author, who dedicated the work to Bishop Thomas Bekynton of Wells (d. 1465), was in succession Warden of Winchester College and of New College, Oxford; he was twice elected Chancellor of the University of Oxford, and thereafter also acted as Vice-Chancellor.[22] The play has been dated c.1457–61—i.e., during his first term as Chancellor. The manuscript, however, was copied with some other purpose than the stage in mind, though the work itself is very definitely a drama with act divisions and rubrics which may be designated as stage directions.[23] Theatrical activity is recorded at Oxford in this period, and under the circumstances it would actually be surprising to learn that this drama was not presented in one of the college halls, with New College being the leading candidate.

The illuminations are monochrome, and represent a style that has been designated as either non-English or foreign-influenced.[24] Doris Enright-Clark Shoukri, who has edited the *Liber Apologeticus*, comments that the initial

> impression which the drawings give is one of great elegance, —elegance of subject and of artistic idiom. One notes the exquisite sartorial fashions, the handsomely carved furniture, the absence of scenes overcrowded either with persons or with paraphernalia; there is no clutter. . . . The artist . . . has succeeded in conveying a wide gamut of emotions with discipline and restraint.[25]

While it is extremely doubtful that the artist had the stage in mind when producing the various illuminations which illustrate the various scenes of the play, the pictures are nevertheless useful in establishing one way in which a drama would have been visualized by a contemporary.

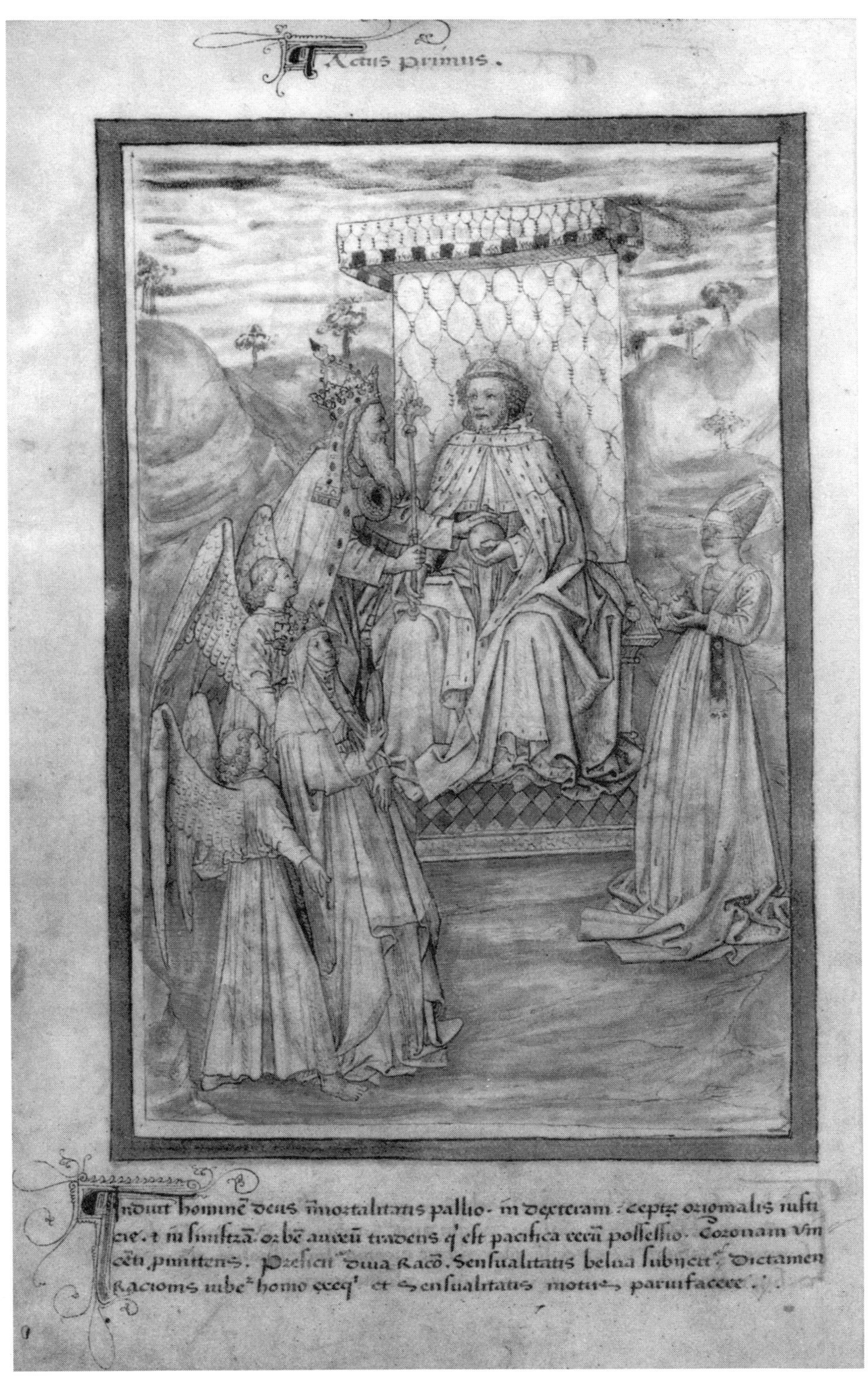

62. Chaundler, *Liber Apologeticus*: Man, enthroned by Deity, is given scepter and orb. Cambridge, Trinity College, MS. R.14.5, fol. 2v. c.1457–61. Courtesy of the Master and Fellows of Trinity College, Cambridge.

The first illustration, on fol. 2r of the manuscript, shows God the Father, crowned and seated on a throne, with the good angels at his right and the followers of Lucifer falling into hell at his left. Simultaneously with the fall of the angels, God is creating Adam, whose nude figure is being raised by him out of the slime. Unfortunately, Act I of the play does not actually dramatize the story of the fallen angels, though the events are recounted by the Father as prelude to the raising up of Adam "from *the slime of the earth* . . . stamp[ed] . . . with some visible likeness of [his] Creator."[26] The privileged position of Man (Homo) is then shown in the second illustration (fol. 2v): he is enthroned by the Deity, and the scepter of uprightness and a golden orb are placed in his hands as symbols of justice and his rulership over the created universe (fig. 62). He is wrapped in a royal cope of ermine which is in fact identified as the garment of immortality. He is not yet, however, given a crown, for that can only be promised to him at the end of his earthly journey. Reason, who retains the image of God and bears the responsibility of ruling the body, stands by at his right to guide him; however, at his left is another figure—blind Sensuality, holding an apple and here wearing a distinctive blue girdle—who is to be a servant rather than a master.[27] Thereafter, in fol. 3r, though the mirror of Reason is placed in man's breast, through an error of judgment the forbidden fruit which Sensuality offers will be accepted by the Man as a mistaken sign of his freedom. Immediately (on fol. 3v) the royal garment of immortality will be taken from him, and he will be shown nude and shivering, seated on the throne, with the canopy removed, along with Sensuality who has been raised up above Reason. According to the caption under the illustration, Man is "stripped of the gifts freely given him, injured in his natural powers, and ashamed of his nakedness, like a madman takes to flight and concealment."[28] The scepter, now broken, and the orb lie on the blue and gray tiles upon which the throne is placed.

The first miniature illustrating the second act (fol. 4v) shows Reason complaining about the wickedness of mankind, while God calls him to repentance out of his hiding place (fig. 63). In the play, however, Reason does not appear at this point as a character—a sign that the picture in this instance may be regarded as a gloss on the text, specifically mirroring Man's complaint about his nakedness. The next illustration shows Man, dressed in a hair shirt for penance, receiving a spade and a whip from the Father (fol. 5), with whom he carries on an extended conversation in the text of the play. The whip, the spade, and the "garment of skins" are substitutes for the scepter, orb, and royal garment of immortality, which he has lost. The whip, held in his right hand, is a sign of penitence, of self-flagellation as a means of restraining one's propensity to irrational acts. In his left hand he holds the spade, which God gives him "so that you may know by it that you have lost lordship over all . . . things" under the heavens. With the use of the spade, therefore, he will work the soil, which will bring forth the "thorns and thistles" predicted in *Genesis* 3.18 as by the sweat of his brow he tills the earth until such time as he himself returns to its dust.[29] The spade, an iconographic sign for Adam and also a sign of Man's mortality, also appears in the morality play of *Mankind* in the Macro manuscript.

Act III opens a judgment scene at the throne of God with Justice and Truth accusing man of his sins, though Peace and Mercy speak in his favor (fol. 5v). The illumination at fol. 6r in the manuscript shows the Judge to be strongly affected by Peace's speech, and thus he will have pity on Man—pity which is shown through the motion of stepping down from his high throne. This movement is emblematic of his Incarnation. Furthermore, the settling of the issues involved also forces Justice and Peace to overcome their differences and to kiss, and Truth and Mercy to embrace (fig. 64).[30] Man, who still holds the spade and whip, is embraced by God, who asks Mercy to "clothe [him] in the clothing of Man" so that by taking on human nature he "may strengthen his weakness and cleanse him from the filth of sins." Thus he is able to hail Man as his "Brother!"[31] Unfortunately, the four daughters of God are here dressed in

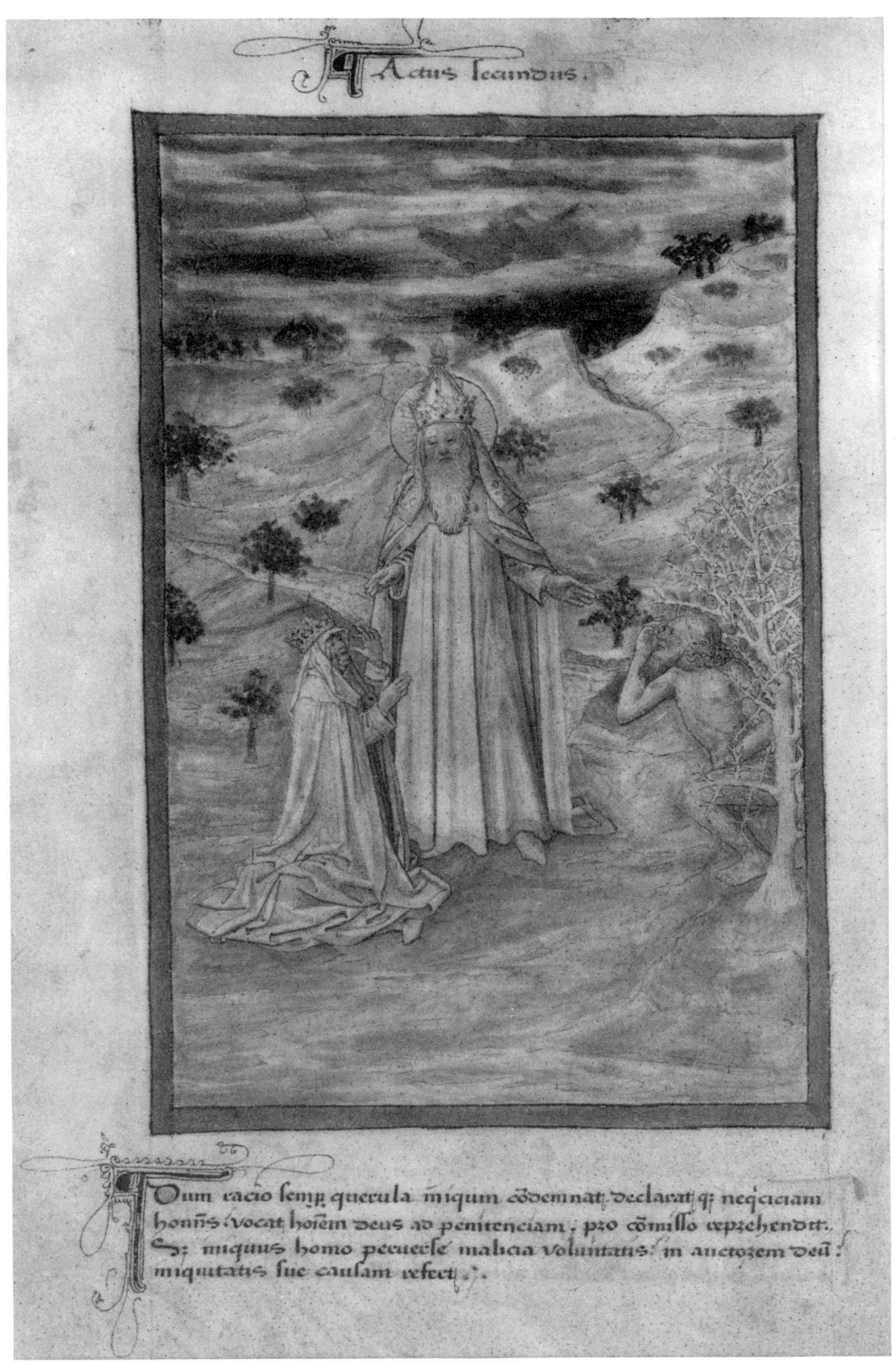

63. Chaundler, *Liber Apologeticus*: Reason complains about Man's sinfulness to God, while Man crouches in his nakedness at right. Cambridge, Trinity College, MS. R.14.5, fol. 4v. Courtesy of the Master and Fellows of Trinity College, Cambridge.

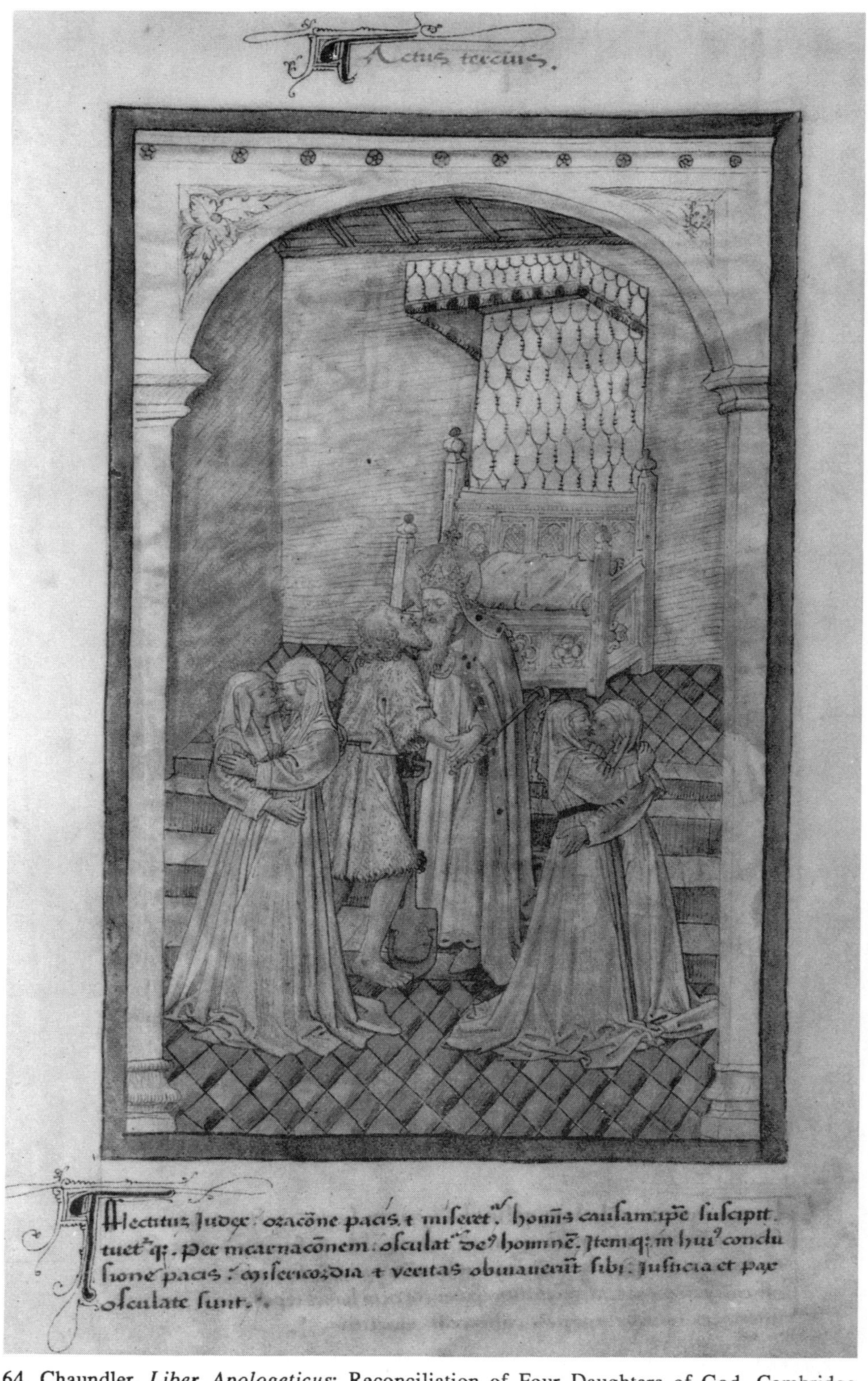

64. Chaundler, *Liber Apologeticus*: Reconciliation of Four Daughters of God. Cambridge, Trinity College, MS.R.14.5, fol. 6r. Courtesy of the Master and Fellows of Trinity College, Cambridge.

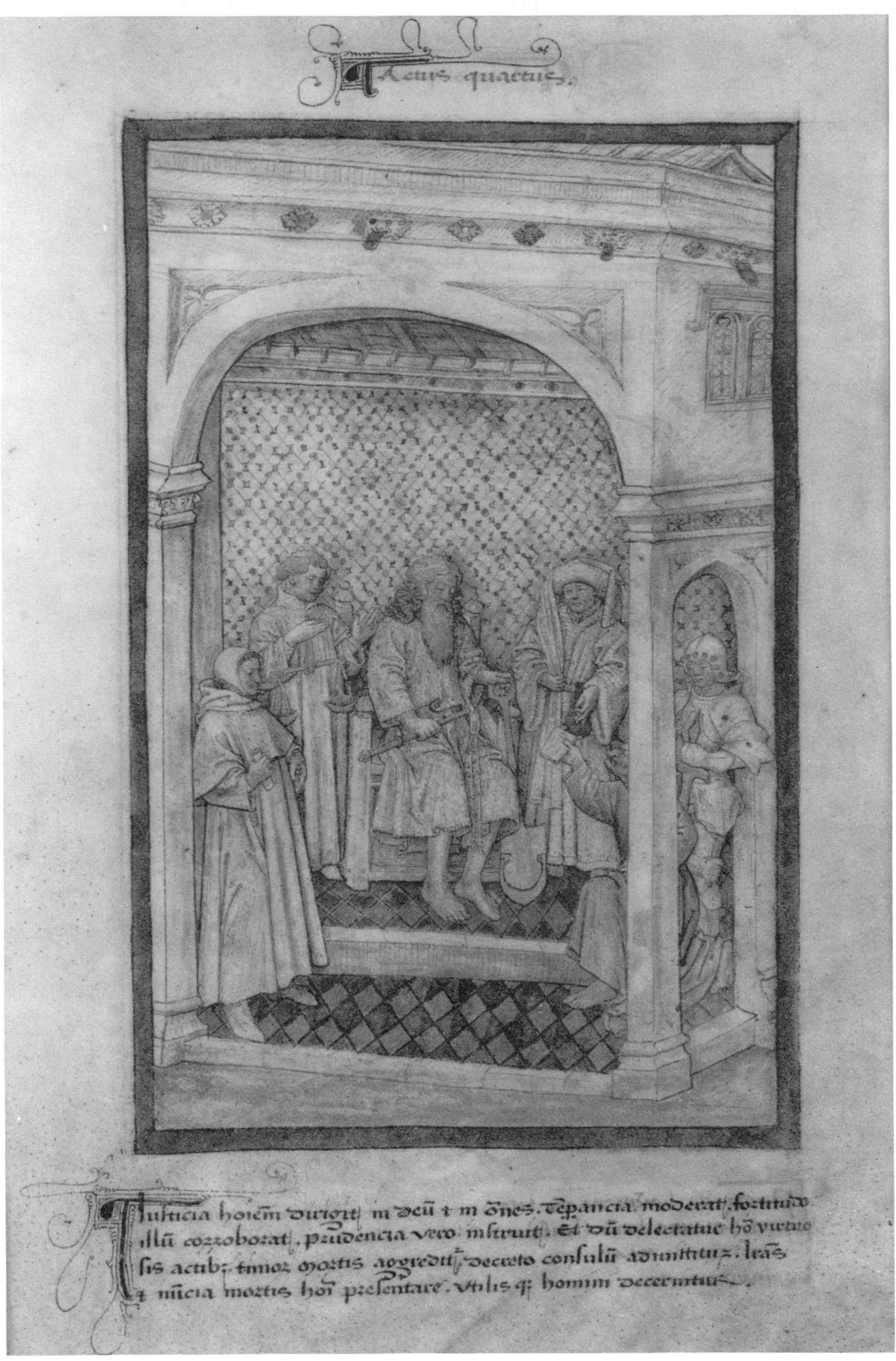

65. Chaundler, *Liber Apologeticus*: Man as penitent with virtues. Cambridge, Trinity College, MS. R.14.5, fol. 7r. Courtesy of the Master and Fellows of Trinity College, Cambridge.

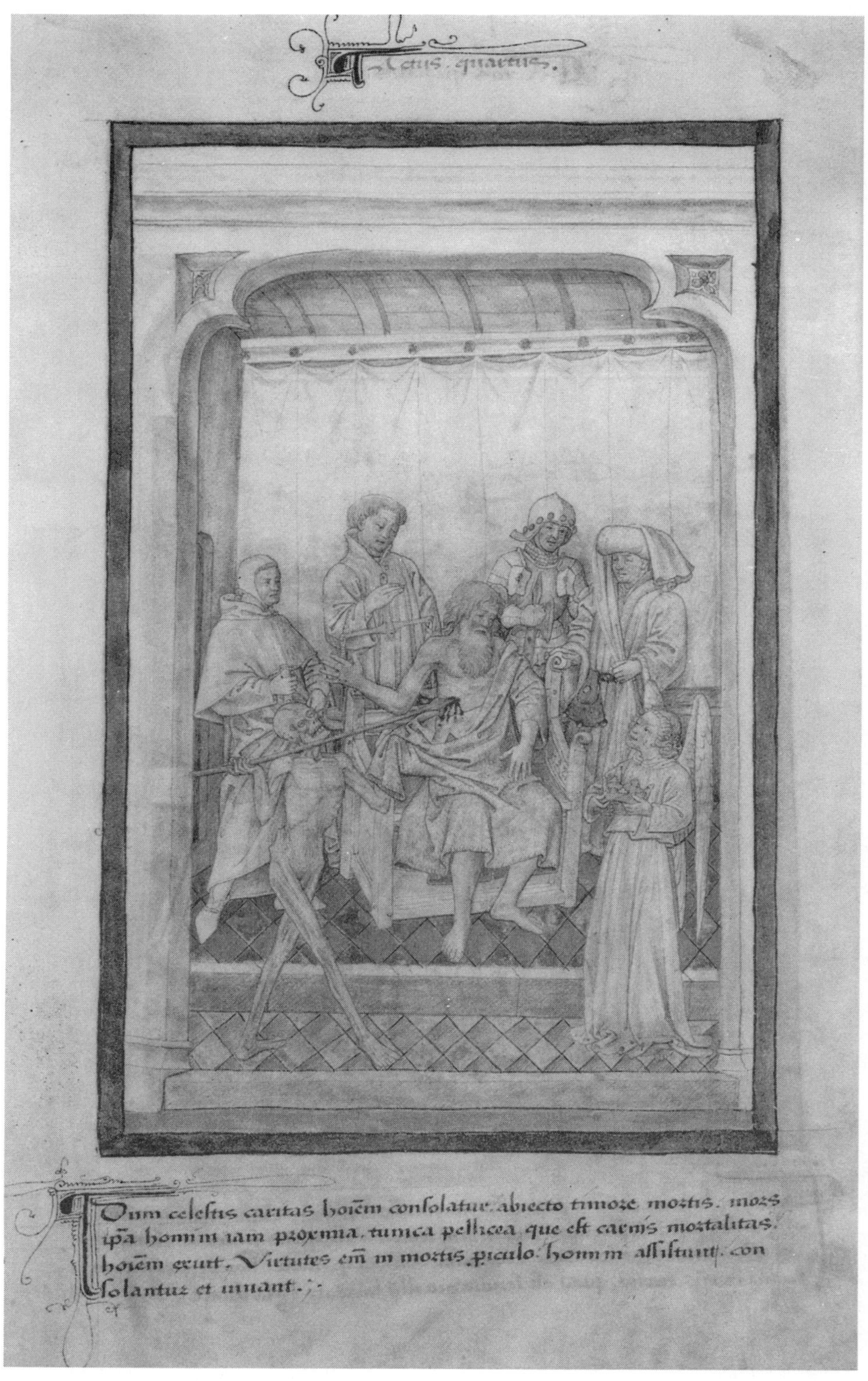

66. Chaundler, *Liber Apologeticus*: Man, with cardinal virtues, and Death with spear. Cambridge, Trinity College, MS. R.14.5, fol. 8^{r}. Courtesy of the Master and Fellows of Trinity College, Cambridge.

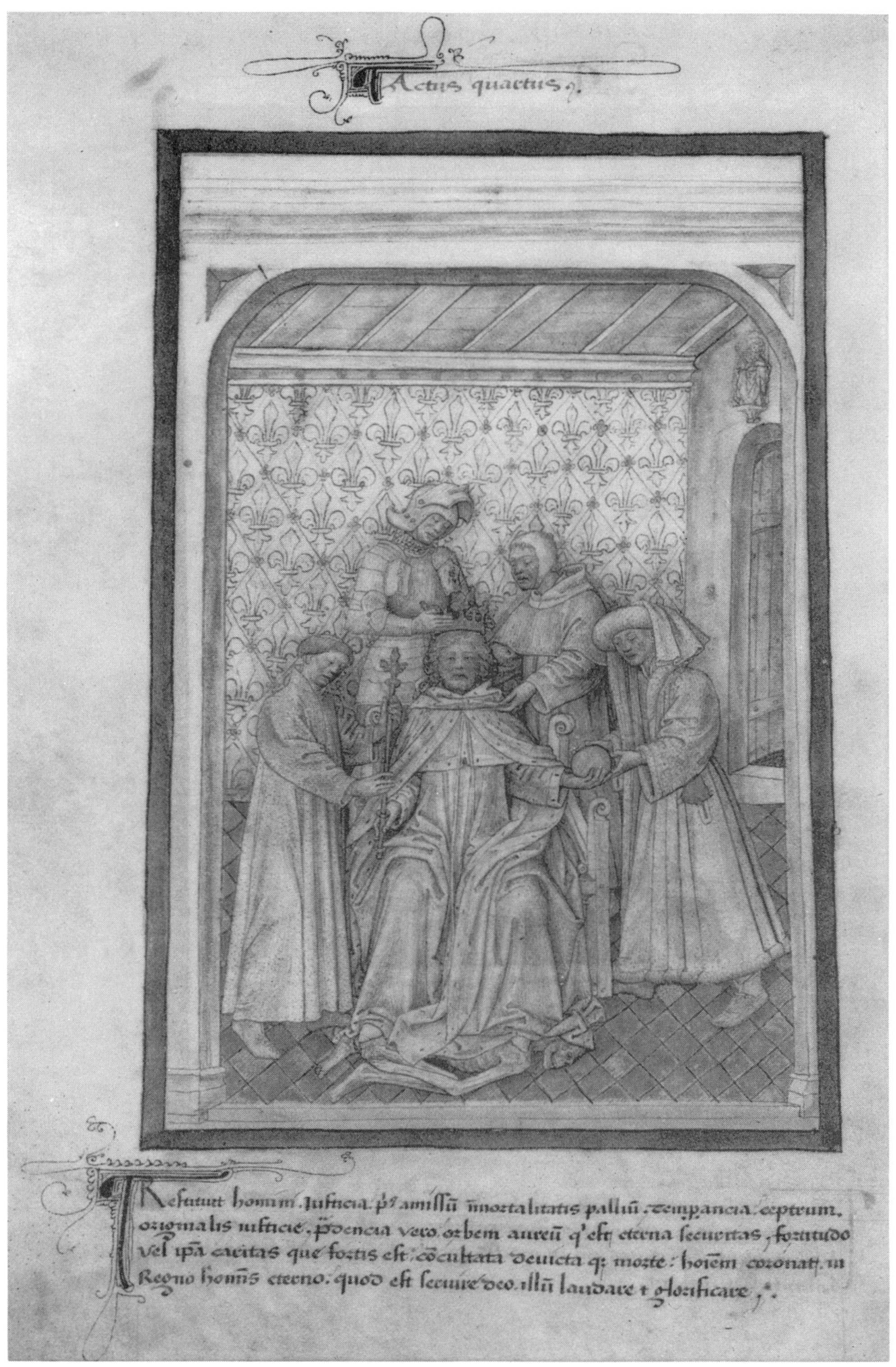

67. Chaundler, *Liber Apologeticus*: Man receiving again cloak, scepter, and orb as well as, at last, the crown. Cambridge, Trinity College, MS. R.14.5, fol. 8^{v}. Courtesy of the Master and Fellows of Trinity College, Cambridge.

costumes that are very much alike, and hence cannot reliably be distinguished from each other.

There is a shift in the iconography at the beginning of Act IV. The figure of Justice who appears in the next miniature (fol. 7^{r}) is not at all the same as the Justice who is one of the Four Daughters of God in the third act, for we have here a young man with a tonsure who holds the scales which stand for fairness at law (fig. 65). Fortitude also is easily recognizable since he wears armor and holds his sword. The figure at Man's left side is almost certainly Temperance, whose influence moderates his behavior, while Prudence, who is to instruct him and hence holds a paper or parchment roll,[32] stands at the doorway as porter. Through their efforts, Man, still holding the whip and spade and wearing his garment of humility, is again placed in the throne prepared for him. The figure approaching behind the pillar is Fear of Death, who is delivering a letter from Death himself and written inside hell where Satan is serving as his secretary. In the next miniature (fol. 7^{v}), a new letter will be delivered, in this instance from Charity, whose heavenly message counteracts that of Fear of Death and banishes the messenger with the letter from hell.

Death, however, will not fail to arrive on the scene (fol. 8^{r}). Man, still seated and surrounded by the four cardinal virtues, has his side bared so that Death's spear may pierce his side in a location reminiscent of the wound in Christ's side (fig. 66). Man's wound is sharply depicted as a bright blotch of red caused by the steel point of the spear. Death's appearance is consistent with the figure of life's termination that appears frequently in Dance of Death series following the arrival of the Black Plague in the fourteenth century. He is skeletal, emaciated, and vindictive. Justice's scales immediately behind Man are indicative of the justice of his death, but hope is offered in the figure of the angel who stands in the front at the left of Man and holds the heavenly crown with which he will eventually be graced.

Finally, in the last miniature illustrating the play (fol. 8^{v}) Man will receive again the cloak of immortality, the scepter, and the orb, making him "secure from all the perils and tribulations of the world"[33] (fig. 67). Then he at last will be crowned with the crown of gold, whereafter it is promised to him that he will be raised up "above the stars and . . . above the choirs of angels, who will advance to meet [him] with hymns and canticles to receive [him] into the holy assembly where, in the sight of God your Creator, [he] will rejoice with them eternally."[34]

VI

FOOLS AND OTHER ENTERTAINERS

Fools not only have a long stage history, but also they are well documented in the visual arts of the Middle Ages. As entertainers, the fools of ancient Greece and Rome achieved very great popularity through their deliberately inept imitations of the actions and speech of principal actors. Such a fool, or secondary mime, was also termed the *stupidus*, a figure recognized by his baldness and his role to be one who, according to St. John Chrysostom, "is slapped at the public expense."[1] One fool of the time of the persecution of Diocletian, St. Genesius (Genest), having been mockingly baptised, was converted suddenly even while performing in an anti-Christian satire and was eventually martyred. A bench-end at Combe-in-Teignhead, Devon, is said to show St. Genesius in a late medieval fool's outfit with ass's ears, fool stick, and bells (fig. 68),[2] but we can only assume that this figure was modelled on the contemporary fool-entertainer and not directly on a fool of classical antiquity.

Yet the medieval fool's appearance was not entirely an innovation of the post-classical era. The conical hat and other attributes of the fool of antiquity appear to have survived the early medieval period and to have been retained in the tenth through the twelfth centuries when this figure was also characterized by clothing made of patches of various colors. But the ass's ears and coxcomb, also derived from antiquity, were in the later Middle Ages and early Renaissance even more representative of the fool, whose foolstick or bauble may possibly be regarded as descended from the wooden sword of the ancient mime.[3] The distinctive ass's ears and, to a lesser degree, the coxcomb appear illustrated in the woodcuts in Richard Pynson's issue of the *Shyp of Folys* (1509), translated into English and adapted by Alexander Barclay from Sebastian Brant's *Narrenschiff*, written in Latin and printed on facing pages in this edition. In a woodcut (fol. 51) reflecting the fool's garrulousness, he is sticking out his tongue—a gesture

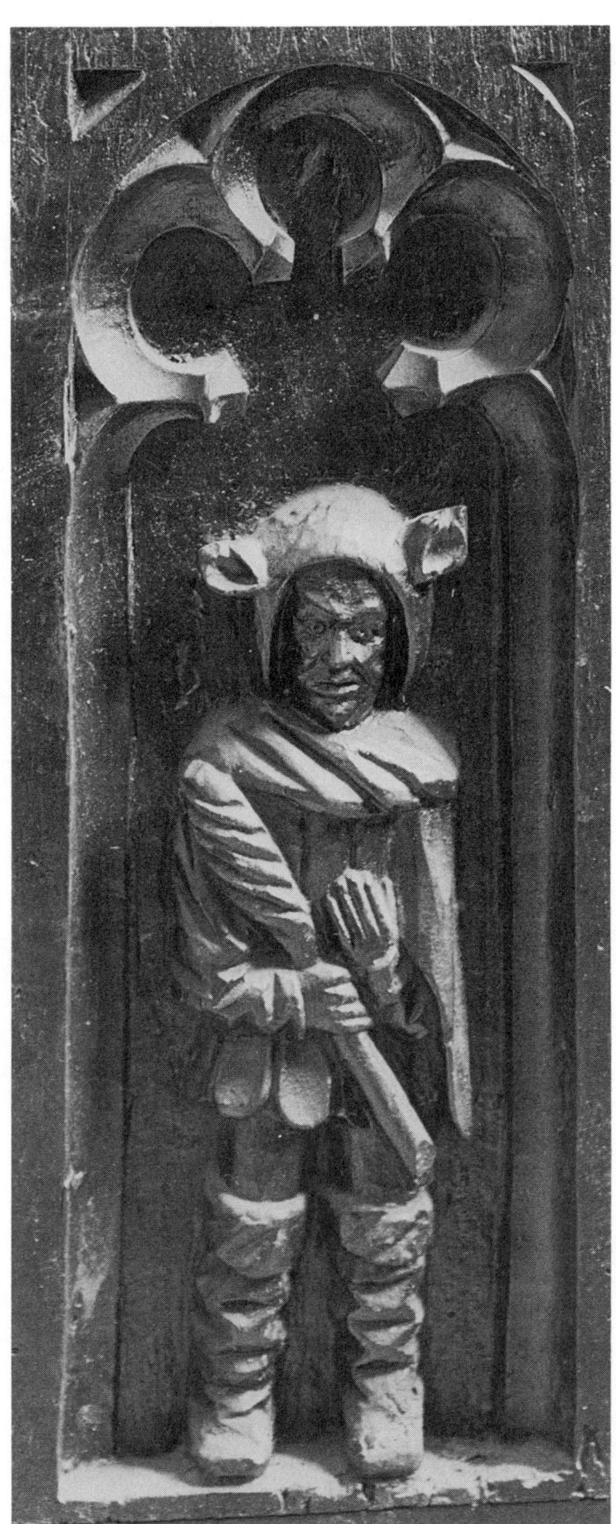

68. Fool, possibly St. Genesius. Bench-end, Combe-in-Teignhead, Devon. By permission of the Royal Commission on the Historical Monuments of England.

reflected in the miniature fool carved on his fool stick—and his loose tongue is further symbolized by the magpie on the tree in the illustration (fig. 69).

In England, there were no fool plays like the *sottie* of medieval France, and even the Feast of Fools seems not to have been of great importance, although statutes of Lincoln and Beverley indicate observance of this festival in those locations.[4] But the drama nevertheless abounds in characters which either are foolish to some extent—for example, Cain in the Towneley *Mactacio Abel*—or are in fact fully established fools. An example of such a fool is Nought in the morality *Mankind* (c.1465–70). Nought, who appears first in a dancing scene, indicates that he has "pleyde so longe the fool that I am ewyn wery" (l. 275)[5]—a weariness that is intended by the playwright to overtake the audience in its attitude to-

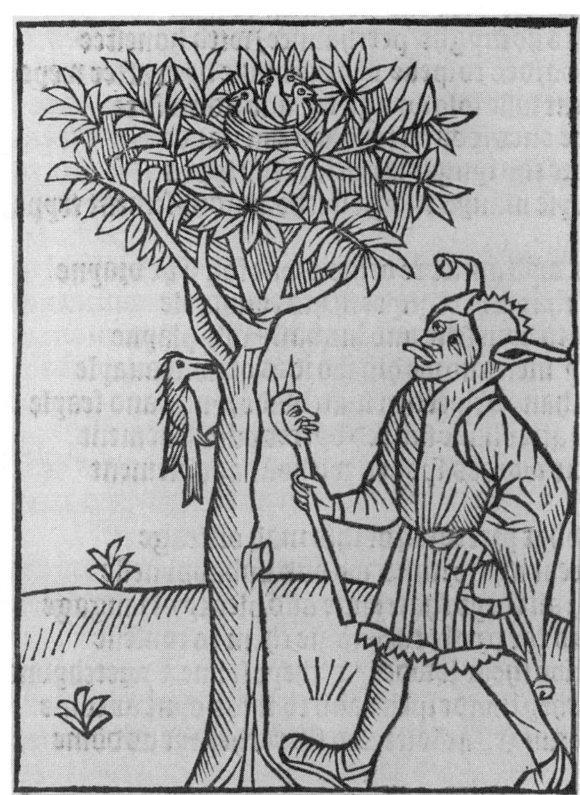

69. Fool. Alexander Barclay, *Shyp of Folys* (1509), fol. 51. By permission of the British Library.

ward this character as the play proceeds. Dancing fools are present in misericords of c.1520 at Beverley Minster,[6] where three jesters are participating in a round dance, which here involved movement in a clockwise direction (fig. 70). All have hoods with long asses' ears and scalloped tunics. The supporters also have jesters, the one on the left with pipe and tabor. As a fool, Nought is "not wyse" (l. 140), and he represents a variety of derision that both amuses and reveals an inner emptiness.[7] The latter characteristic also reflects the traditional view of the fool as one who denies reality and the God who is its creator—a view that is, as we shall see below, very important in medieval iconography.

The fool is rightfully one whose values deserve not to be established as the norm. The point is forcefully made in the Canterbury Psalter (Cambridge, Trinity College MS. R.17.1), copied in the twelfth century by the scribe Eadwine from an earlier source, the ninth-century Utrecht Psalter[8]—a source which may in turn depend on a model from late antiquity. The illustration for Psalm 53 (52) on fol. 92 shows a fool-prince, seated under a dome and presiding over a scene of violence. Two men are bringing heads to him, and below a battle rages. On the right men on horses with lances are pursuing a group of women who are imploring a man with a lance and shield at the top of the hill. The figure of Christ in heaven above indicates the psalmist and the angels who are behind him. The scene is similar to the illustration for Psalm 13 (12) on fol. 22, where once again the robed fool sits under a canopied dome and holds a sword across his knees (fig. 71). Before him there is lying a dead man, and snakes have wound themselves around two of the pairs of supporting columns—an indication of the poison associated with asps. On the left once again two men hold severed heads and swords, while on the right is a woman with four children and before her is an open coffin. On the right, the psalmist points at the fool and protests at his foolishness.[9] Here the fool, whom we can identify positively since the scene reflects the incipits of the psalms which open with the words *Dixit insipiens in corde suo: Non est Deus* ("The fool hath said in his heart: There is no God"), is seemingly placed on the stage of the actual world, where the denial of God and of Christian values will result in social chaos.

In the centuries that followed, illuminations in psalters at Psalms 13 and 53 con-

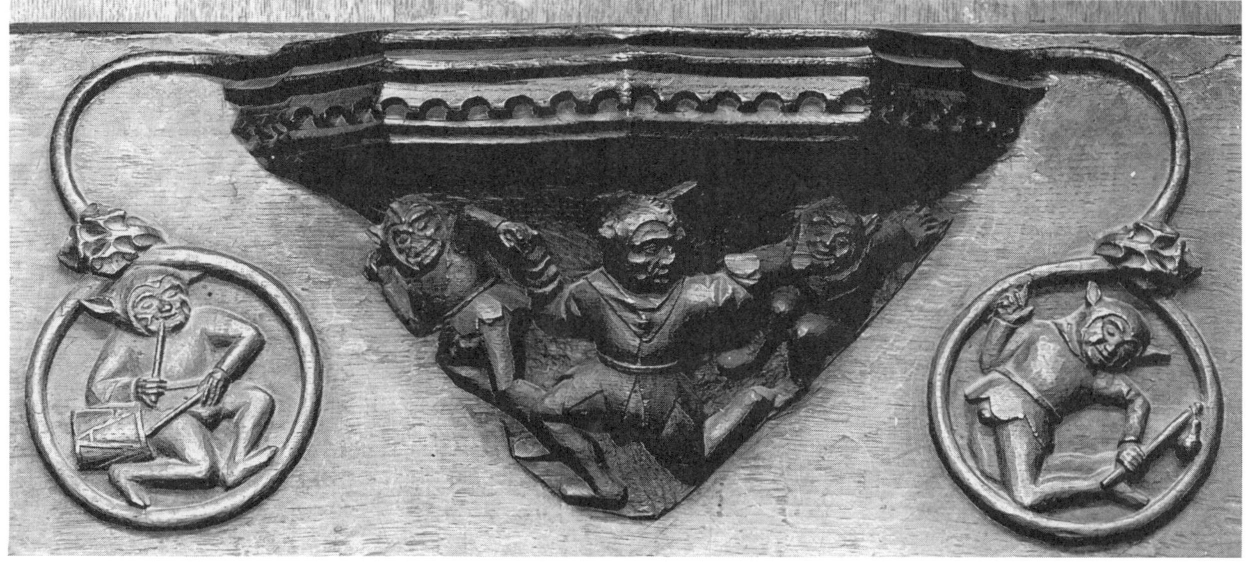

70. Fools dancing a round dance. Misericord, Beverley Minster, c.1520. By permission of the Royal Commission on the Historical Monuments of England.

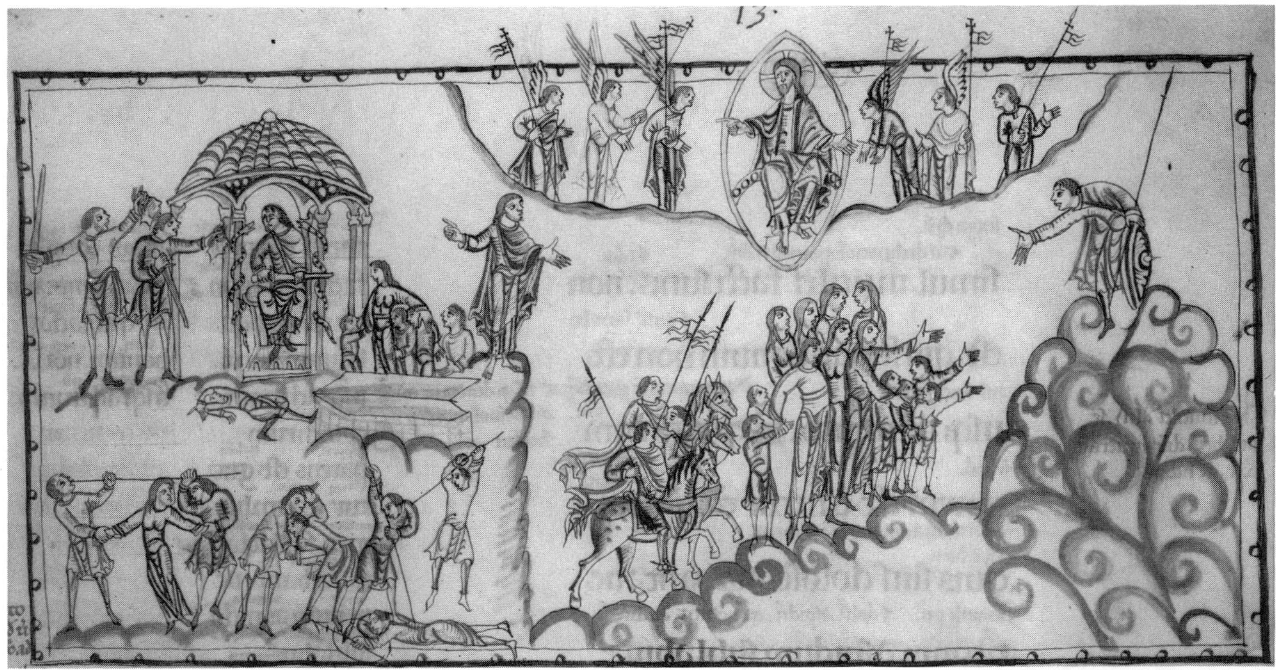

71. Fool-prince (at left), presiding over violence. Cambridge, Trinity College, MS. R.17.1, fol. 22. Twelfth-century copy of earlier manuscript. Courtesy of the Master and Fellows of Trinity College, Cambridge.

veniently continued to represent the fool, both in his natural aspect and in his professional role as entertainer. As an entertainer in real life, the fool at first merged with other figures such as minstrels, acrobats, and dancers,[10] a fact that is reflected in the Peterborough Psalter (Brussels, Bibliothèque Royale MS. 9961–2, fol. 14) where a fool, wearing a hood and holding a foolstick with a scarf draped over it, appears on stilts in the left border (fig. 72).[11] English psalters, however, tended to sort out this specific type of character, whose development can thus be traced rather exactly through the thirteenth to sixteenth centuries.[12] The earlier examples tended to stress the natural fool, who was shabbily dressed and hardly courtly in his demeanor,[13] although he not infrequently was juxtaposed with a king, perhaps Solomon because of his reputation for wisdom. Thus in a Bible illuminated by the workshop of William of Devon (Cambridge, Emmanuel College MS. 2.1.6, fol. 174)[14] a bald fool is biting on a disk that he holds with his right hand and is holding a club with his left (fig. 73). A king, holding a scepter in his left hand and gesturing disappoval with his right (his index finger is raised as if making a point), is seated at the left.[15] The Coldingham Breviary (c.1270–80) has a king and a fool at Psalm 53 (British Library, MS. Harley 4664, fol. 145ᵛ); here the fool, who holds a dish in his right hand and has his left hand raised, perhaps in a mock blessing, wears a long gown with a hood which is thrown back in the customary manner (fig. 74). Nigel Morgan comments that he is "perhaps the most truly foolish-looking fool in 13th-century illumination."[16] Another thirteenth-century example, in the psalter illustrated for Lacock Convent in Wiltshire in the middle of the century (Bodleian MS. Laud Lat. 114, fol. 71), shows the fool appearing before a seated king and holding a foolstick in his right hand and bladder on a stick in his left hand (fig. 75). He wears particolored clothing of red and blue, and has bells about his legs, hanging from his neck, and at the top of his hood. The hood, likewise of red and blue, also has asses' ears attached.[17] The Mostyn Psalter, now in a private collection, shows a "half-naked fool

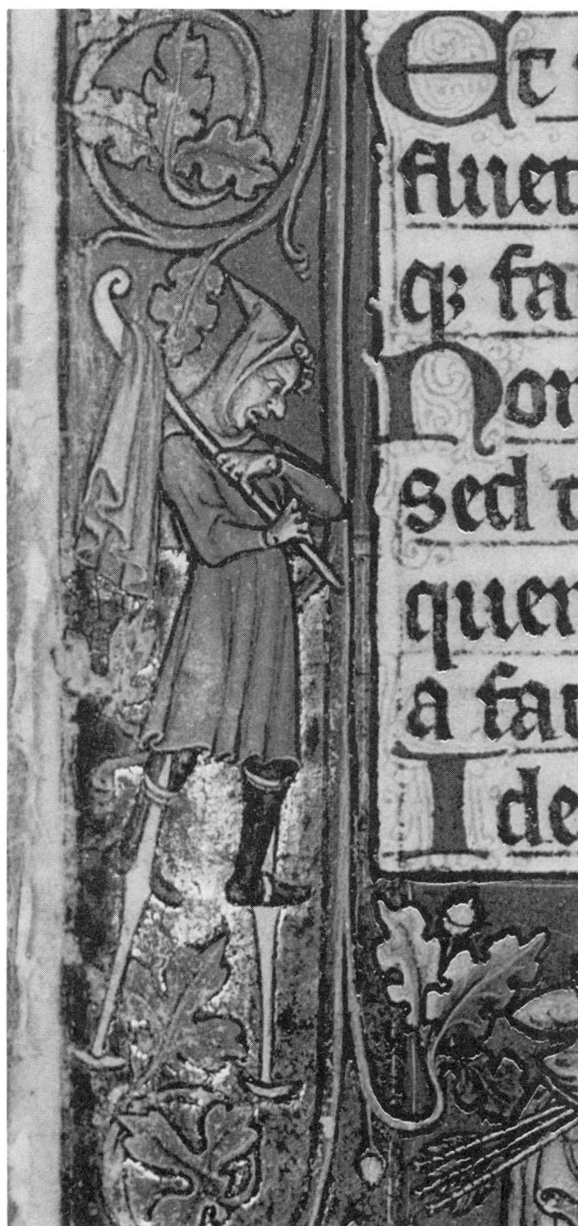

72. Fool on stilts. Peterborough Psalter. Brussels, Bibliothèque Royale, MS. 9961-2, fol. 14. Fourteenth century. Copyright Bibliothèque Royale Ier.

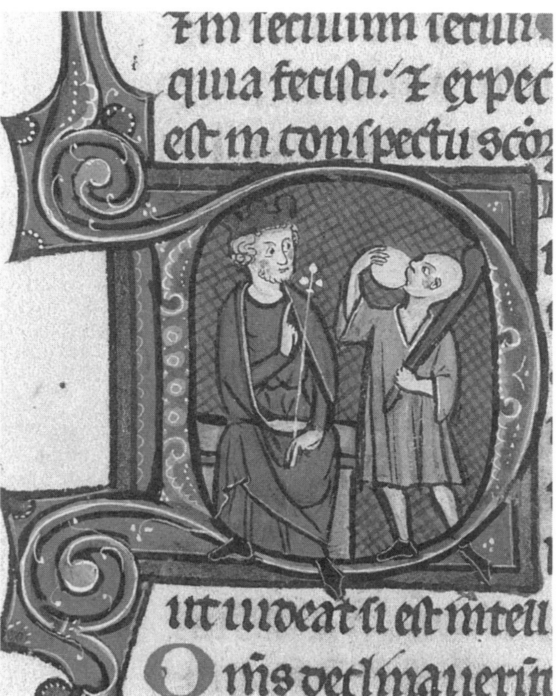

73. Fool, biting on disk. Psalter. Cambridge, Emmanuel College, MS. 2.1.6, fol. 174. c.1260–70. Reproduced with the permission of the Master and Fellows of Emmanuel College.

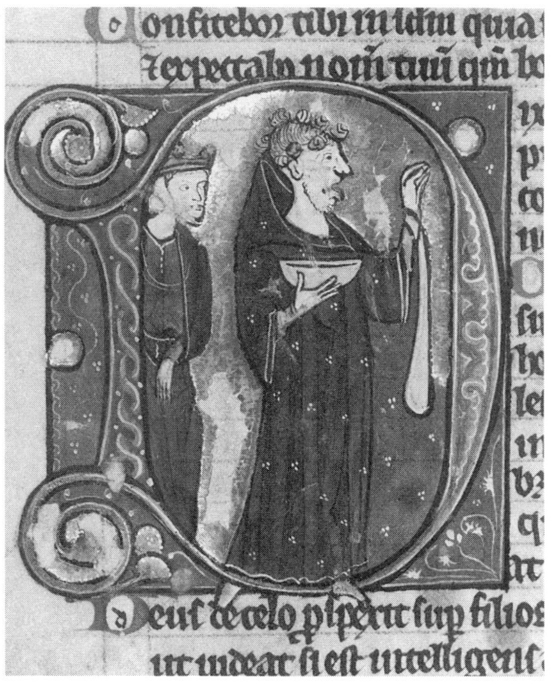

74. Fool and king. Coldingham Breviary. British Library, MS. Harley 4664, fol. 145v. c.1270–80. By permission of the British Library.

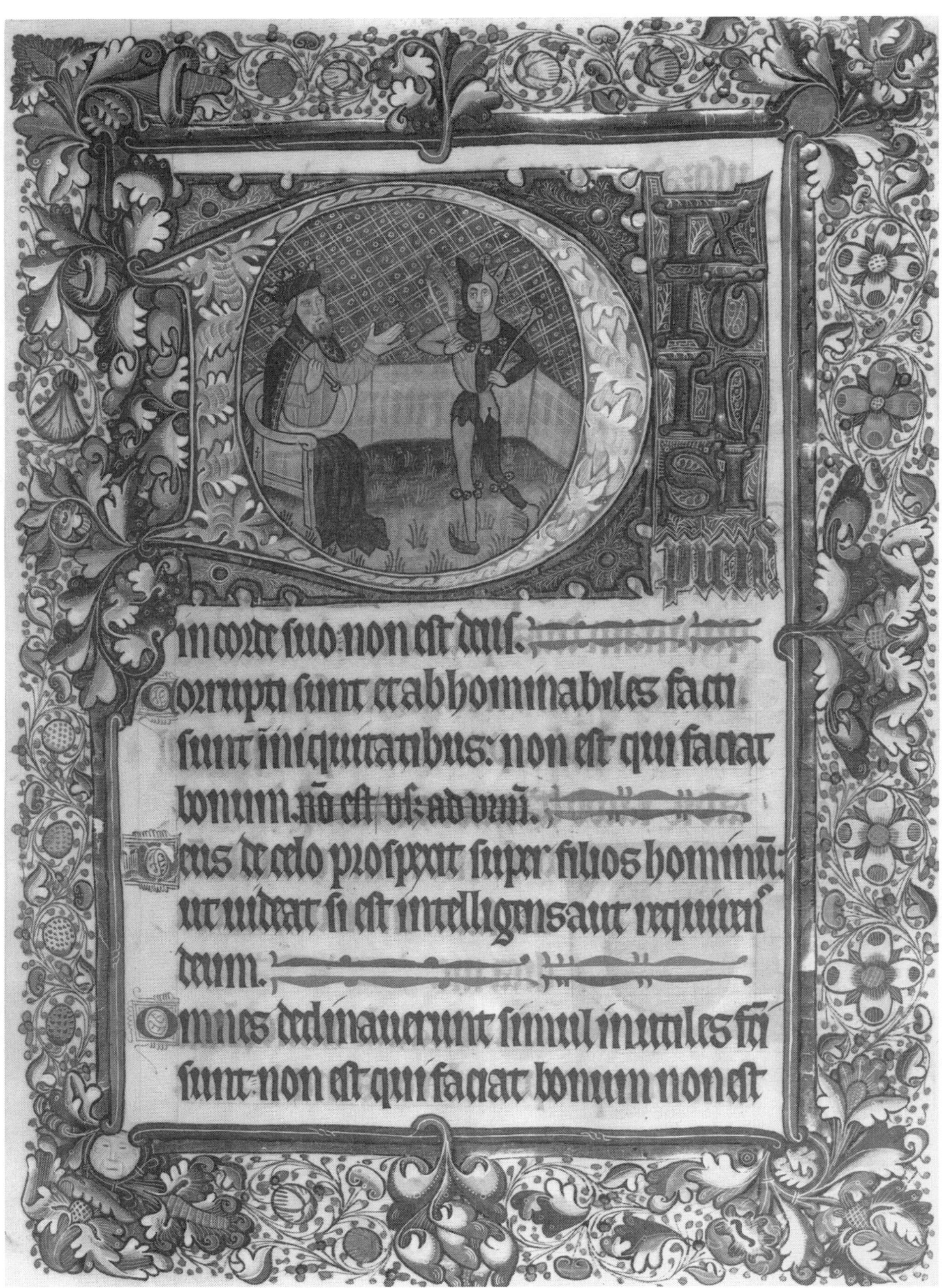

75. Fool. Lacock Psalter. Oxford, Bodleian Library, MS. Laud Lat. 114, fol. 71. Mid-thirteenth century.

holding a ball and a club" (fol. 52[v]).[18]

In an initial in the fourteenth-century Bromholm Psalter (Bodleian MS. Ashmole 1523, fol. 66) from Bromholm Priory in Norfolk, the barefoot fool in a tunic at the left, wearing cap and bells and holding foolstick and bladder in his right

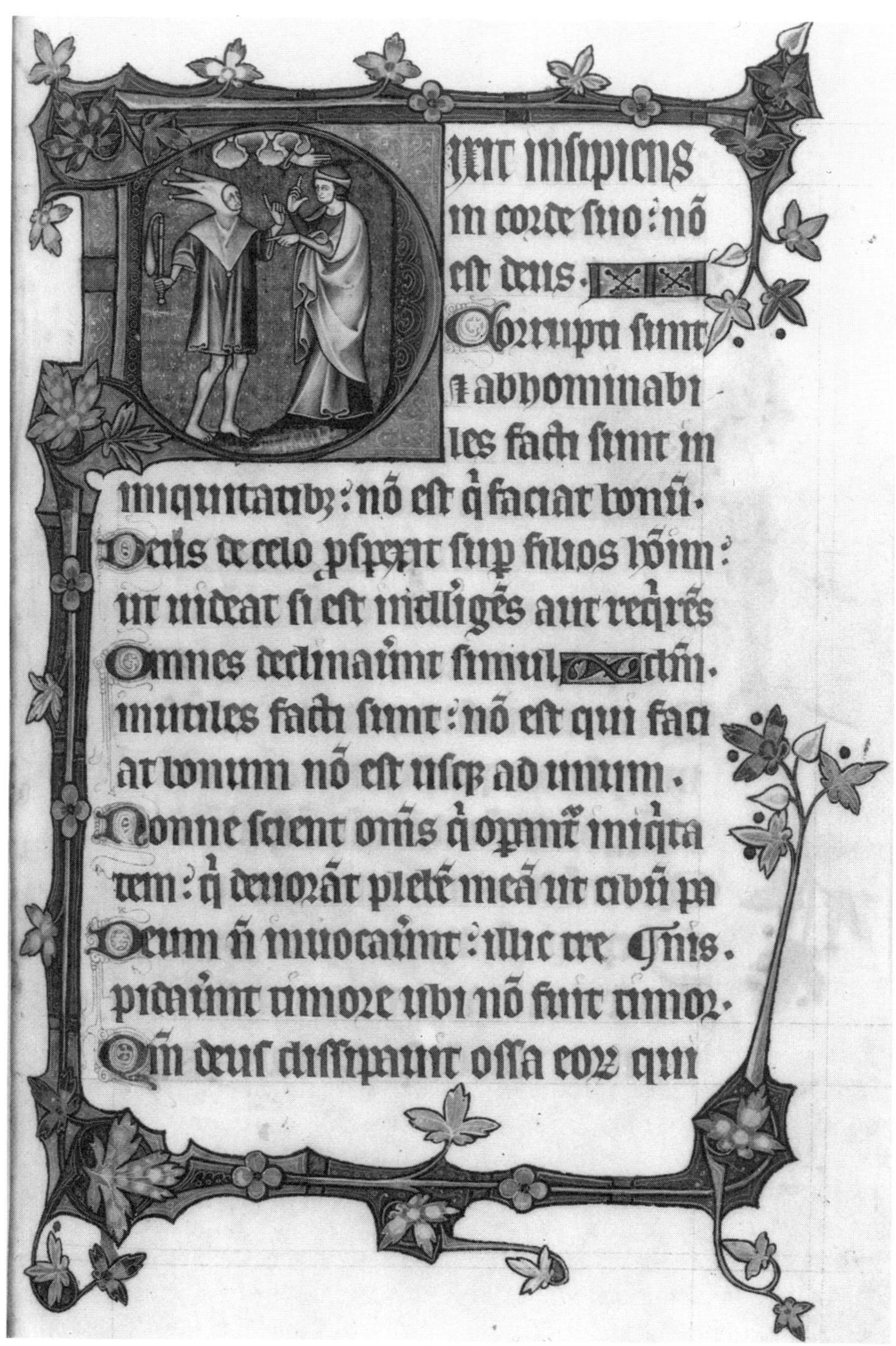

76. Fool arguing with righteous man. Bromholm Psalter. Oxford, Bodleian Library, MS. Ashmole 1523, fol. 66. Fourteenth century.

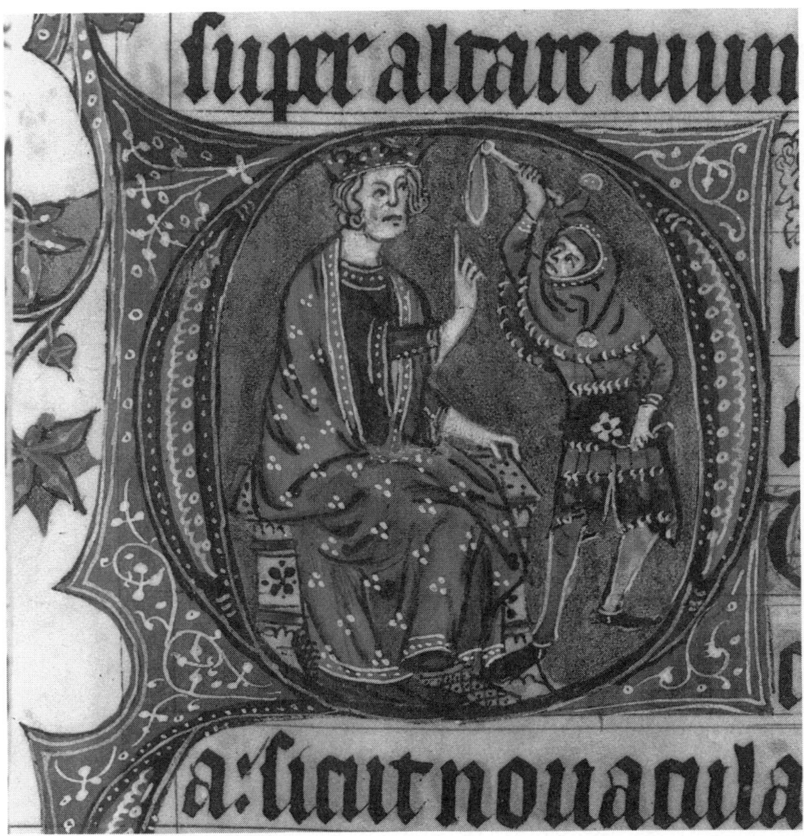

77. King and Fool. Psalter from Christ Church, Canterbury. Oxford, Bodleian Library, MS. Auct. D.2.2, fol. 60. Second quarter of fourteenth century.

hand, argues with another figure at the right above whom God's hand reaches out of a cloud in blessing (fig. 76).[19] A similar juxtaposition is evident in Bodleian MS. Auct. D.2.2, fol. 60, a psalter created in the second quarter of the fourteenth century for Christ Church, Canterbury. Here a king, seated, points upward with his index finger, while at the right the fool, wearing a red hood, a tunic made up of bands of cloth, and hose of different colors, raises a bladder (attached to his foolstick) with his right hand and holds a flower in his left (fig. 77). In the Psalter of Humphrey de Bohun of c.1360–73 (Oxford, Exeter College, MS. 47, fol. 34), kings and fools appear in canopied compartments (fig. 78).[20] At this time, woodcarvings of fools also begin to appear, as in the case of the intriguing misericord (c.1390) at St. Botolph, Lincolnshire, which shows two fools squeezing cats and biting their tails (fig. 79).[21] At Winchester Cathedral, a misericord dated c.1305 shows a fool sticking out his tongue and trying to draw out a sword (fig. 80).[22]

A logical development in the fifteenth and early sixteenth centuries is that the fool depicted in psalters and similar sources influenced by Psalms 13 and 53 will tend to be visualized as a court jester though a king may not always be present. An interesting transformation is present in an initial in Bodleian Library MS. Liturg. 198, fol. 47, a psalter copied for an Augustinian house in the northeastern part of England: the king, seated in regal posture at the left but obviously not a symbol of wisdom in this case, commits suicide by stabbing himself while the fool looks on (fig. 81).[23] The garment worn by the latter seems very like the leather body stocking worn in plays to simulate

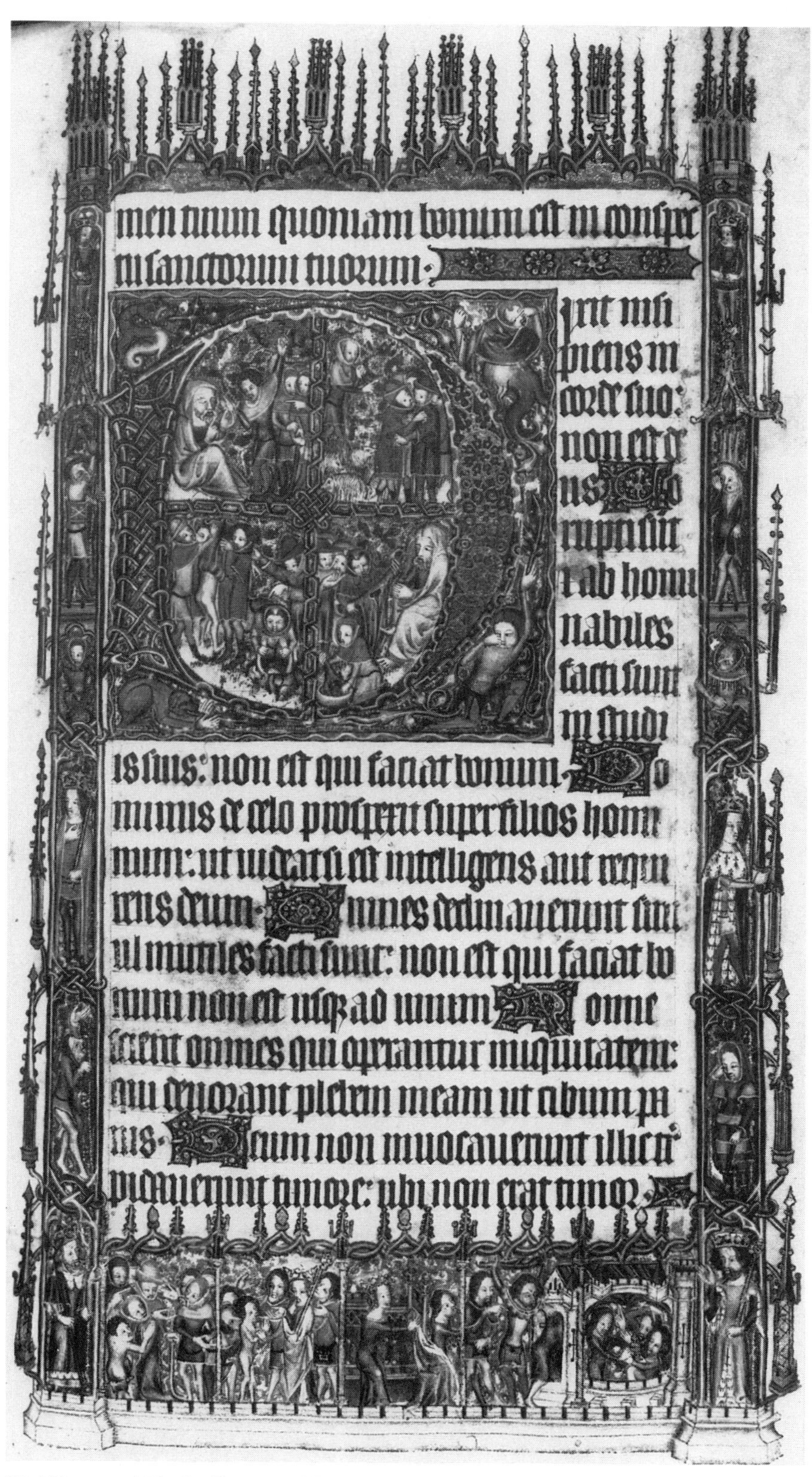

78. Kings and Fools. Psalter of Humphrey de Bohun. Oxford, Exeter College, MS. 47, fol. 34. c.1360–73.

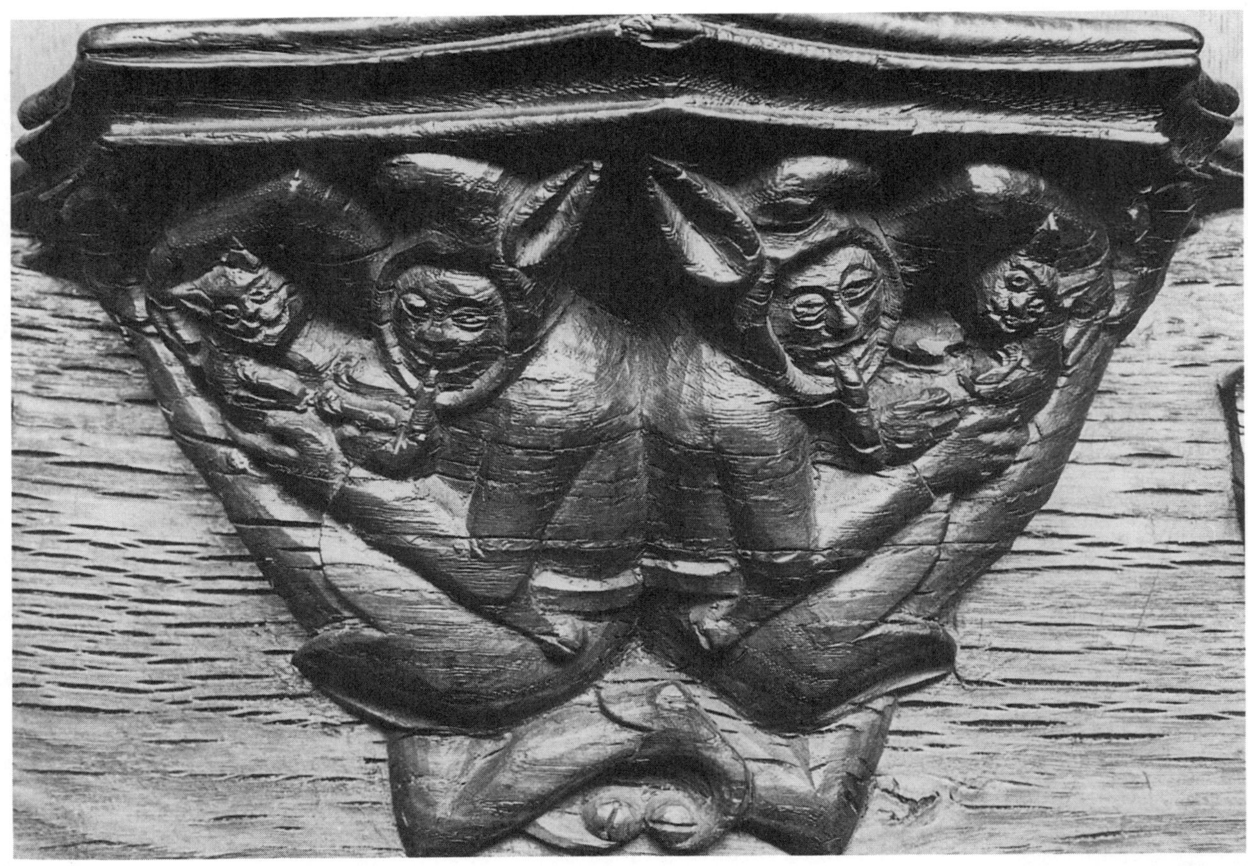

79. Two fools squeezing cats and biting their tales. Misericord, St. Botolph, Lincolnshire. c.1390. Photograph: Jennifer Alexander.

nudity. The fool may also appear as a musician, playing bagpipes on a misericord in the parish church at Faversham, Kent[24] (fig. 82), and on a misericord of c.1477–84 on the south side of the choir at St. George's Chapel, Windsor (fig. 83).[25] Among the figures on the misericords dated 1430–40 at the church of the Holy Trinity in Stratford-upon-Avon, one of the fool grotesques is playing a pipe (fig. 84).[26] Barclay's *Shyp of Folys* (1509) includes a woodcut of a fool playing bagpipes in preference to the lute or harp (fig. 85). Barclay castigates the one who "in his Bagpipe hath more game and sport/ Than in a Harp or Lute more swete of melody" (fol. 107). The early sixteenth-century glass formerly at Betley, famous for its illustration of morris dancers, also includes a fool (fig. 86).[27] The fool here holds a yellow bauble with asses' ears, and wears a blue hood "edged with yellow at its scalloped bottom" with a coxcomb and bell in addition to the expected asses' ears. Other bells are attached to his ankles, arms (at the wrists and elbows), hood, and the tail of his tunic, which is of two shades of red and edged with yellow. His girdle and his left stocking are yellow, and his right stocking is blue. His shoes are of red leather.[28] Billington points out that in the fifteenth-century Wingfield Psalter (New York Public Library, Spencer Collection, fol. 38^r) there is a figure of the court fool in the central panel and a natural fool, wearing less elaborate costume, in the border (fig. 87). Billington comments:

> The central figure in the illustration of Psalm 13 is a large and beautiful painting of a fool in full

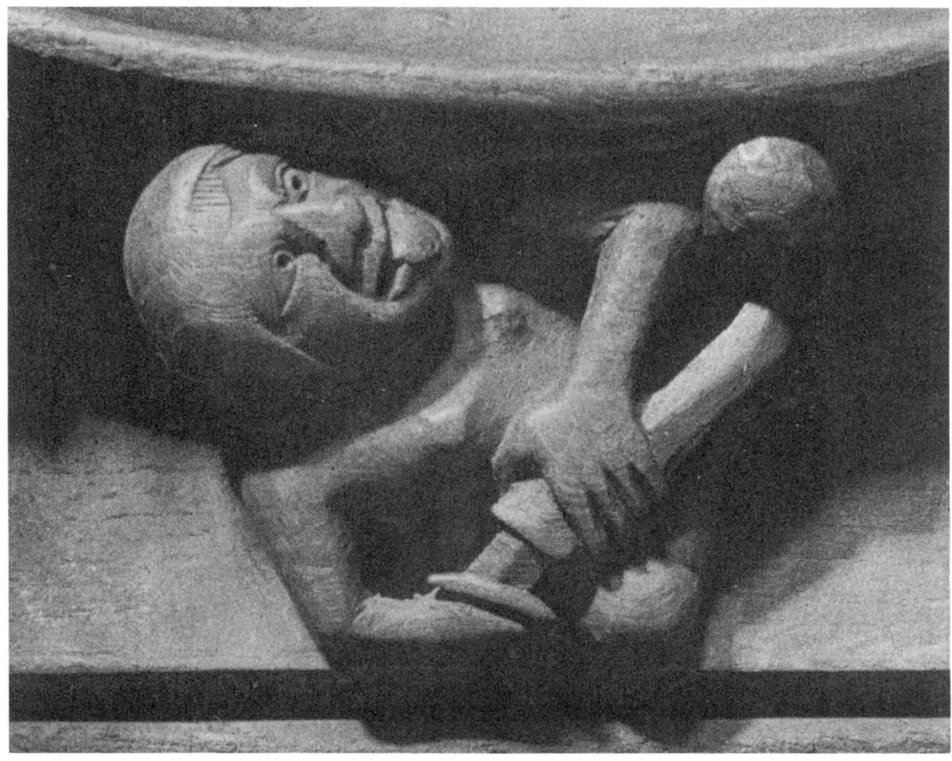

80. Fool sticking out tongue. Misericord, Winchester Cathedral. c.1305. By permission of the Royal Commission on the Historical Monuments of England.

> regalia. He wears parti-colouring of pink, red, yellow, purple and blue, and the colours are part of a carefully tailored coat and hose. There are also bells on his eared hood, round his wrists, waist, legs, and on one toe. He carries two baubles and plays the pipe, to which he is dancing. Finally, he is watched in admiration by two small dogs, one of which is also belled. The elaborate costume must have been paid for by a man of means, and it seems likely that the fool was jester to a wealthy family.[29]

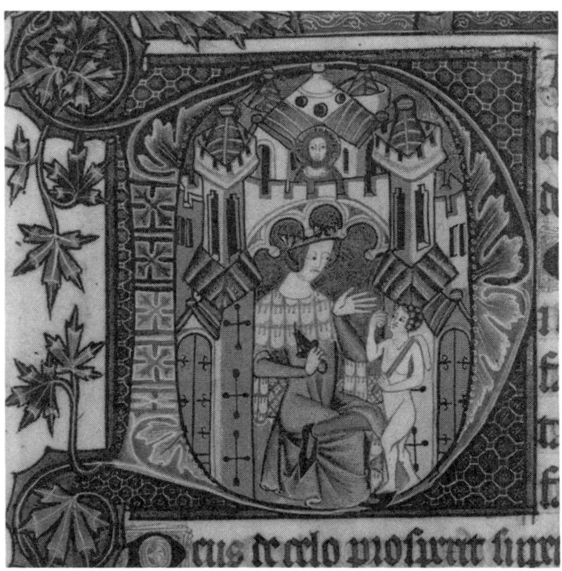

81. King, committing suicide, and fool. Psalter. Oxford, Bodleian Library, MS. Liturg. 198, fol. 47. Fifteenth century.

In a footnote Billington suggests that the wealthy family in this case might have been the Stafford family since the psalter belonged to them.[30] The

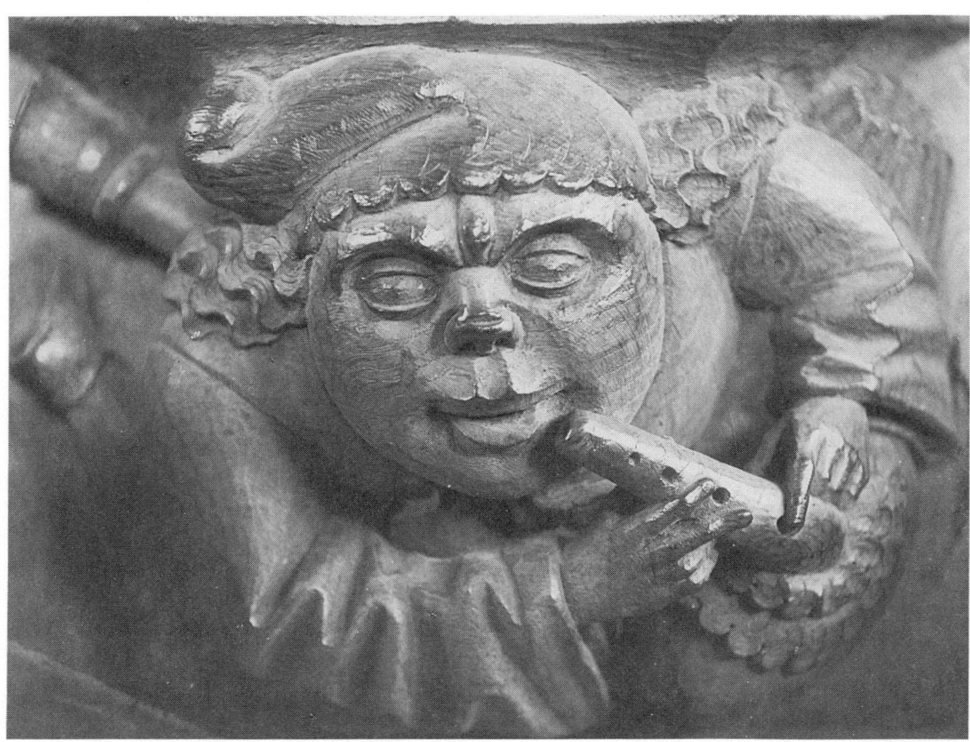

82. Fool playing bagpipes. Misericord, Faversham, Kent. Fifteenth century. By permission of the Royal Commission on the Historical Monuments of England.

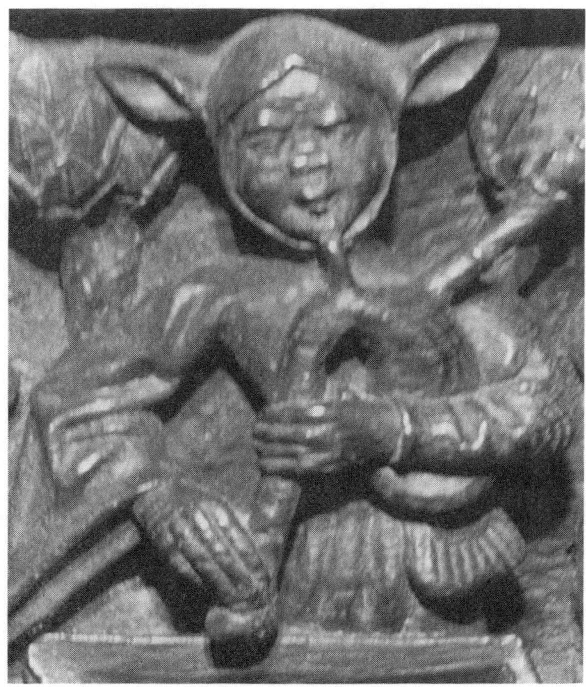

83. Fool playing bagpipes. Misericord, St. George's Chapel, Windsor. c.1477–83. Courtesy of the Dean and Canons of St. George's Chapel.

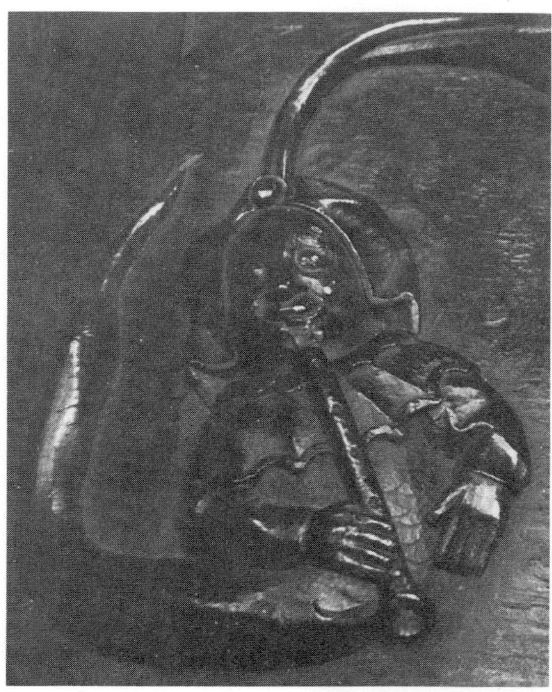

84. Fool-grotesque playing a pipe. Misericord, Holy Trinity Church, Stratford-upon-Avon. c.1430–40. Photograph: Jennifer Alexander.

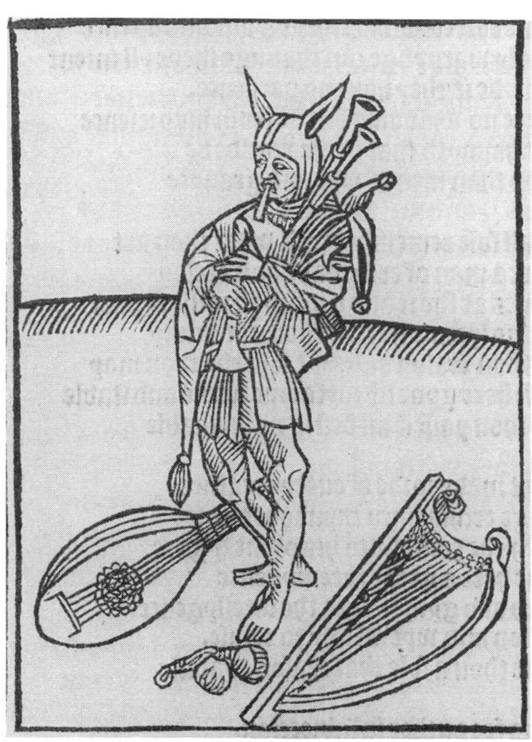

85. The Fool rejects the lute and harp for the less pleasing bagpipes. Barclay, *Shyp of Folys* (1509), fol. 107. By permission of the British Library.

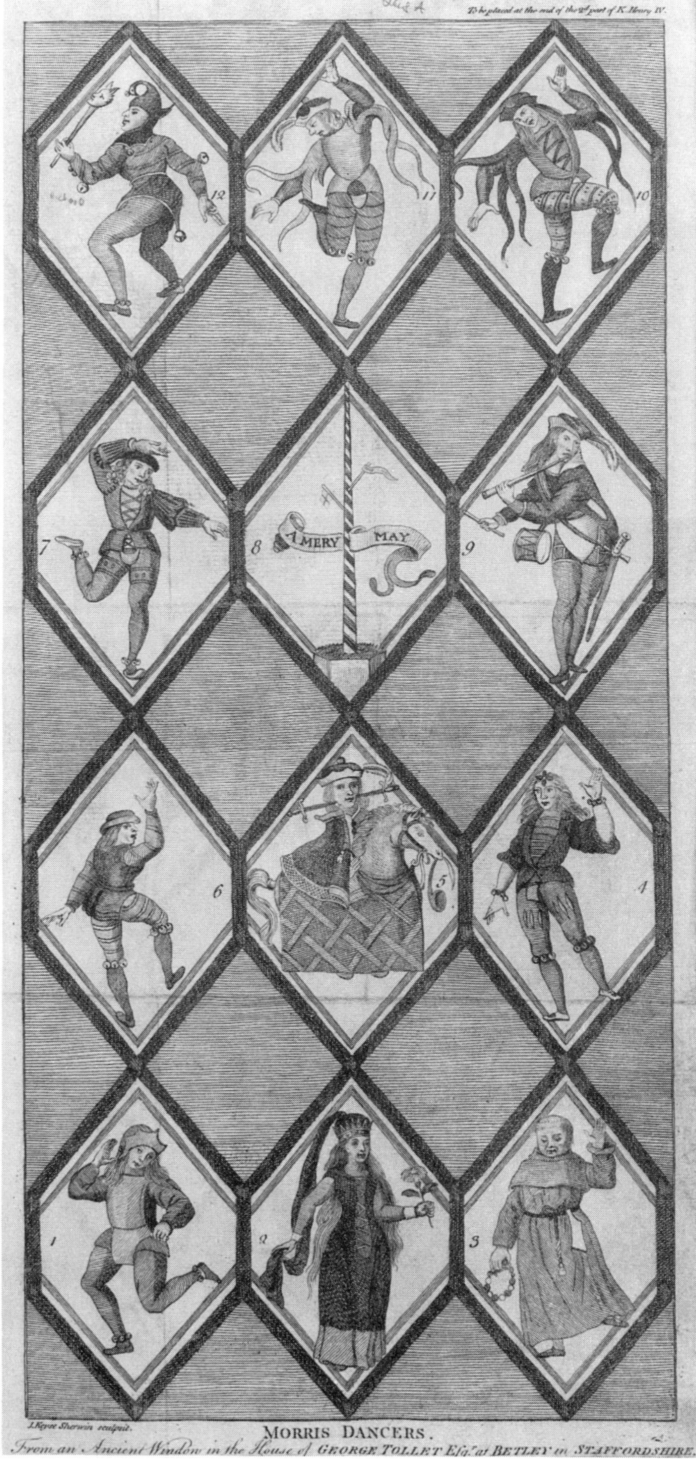

86. (At right) Morris dancers and other figures. Painted glass formerly at Betley (removed to Leigh Manor). Engraving from Samuel Johnson and George Steevens, eds., *The Plays of William Shakespeare* (1778), V, Pl. facing p. 248. c.1500-20. By permission of the British Library.

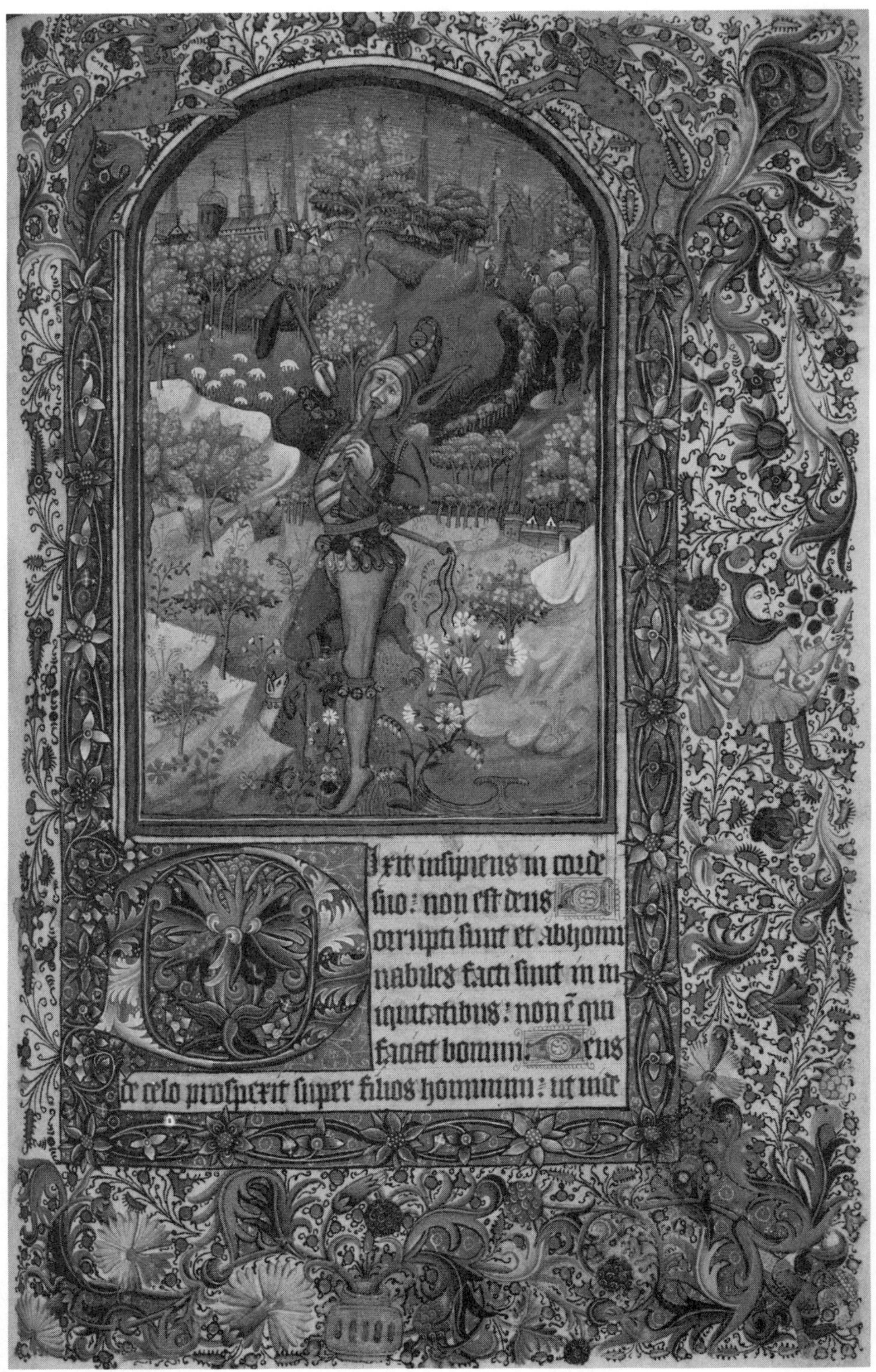

87. Court fool (in central panel) and natural fool (right hand marginal illustration). Wingfield Psalter. New York Public Library, Astor, Lenox, and Tilden Foundations, Spencer Collection, fol. 38r. Fifteenth century.

fool in the margin, however, wears only a hood and a single bell as well as a simple yellow and pink tunic and stockings with a stripe along the side.

The existence of court fools as entertainers is of course well documented. They had appeared in court records as early as William the Conqueror, and the "artificial" fool Rahere during the reign of Henry II had founded the Priory and Hospital of St. Bartholomew as well as Bartholomew Fair after his conversion.[31] The elaborateness of the wardrobe of a fool in the service of a king is indicated in the records extant for Henry V's reign in April 1416.[32] Henry VIII's jester, Will Summers, remained legendary into the seventeenth century when there was published *A Pleasant History of the Life and Death of Will Summers* (London, 1637). This publication contains eight woodcuts by the same artist who illustrated a play, Heywood's *A Maidenhead Well Lost.*[33] One woodcut (sig. C5^{v}) shows Summers welcoming another fool, Patch, who had been in the retinue of Cardinal Wolsey; the latter fool has an elaborate coxcomb hat and a garment with scalloped edges (fig. 88). Summers, on the other hand, has a distinctive headdress and a unique garment of motley, both of which seem to be made up of different colors. Like Patch, he has bells at his elbows, but he may also have had bells attached elsewhere on his clothing. It appears that his doublet was made of worsted or fustian, with a cotton and canvas lining. His cap and coat were green with a red crepe or white fringe, while his hood similarly was green with a white fringe.[34] Summers' bauble and bells had been retained in the collection of Walter Cope where they were seen in 1599 by Thomas Platter on his visit to England.[35] However, there is also a contemporary illustration of Summers in the Psalter of Henry VIII (British Library MS. Royal 2.A.XVI, fol. 63^{v}) which shows him standing at

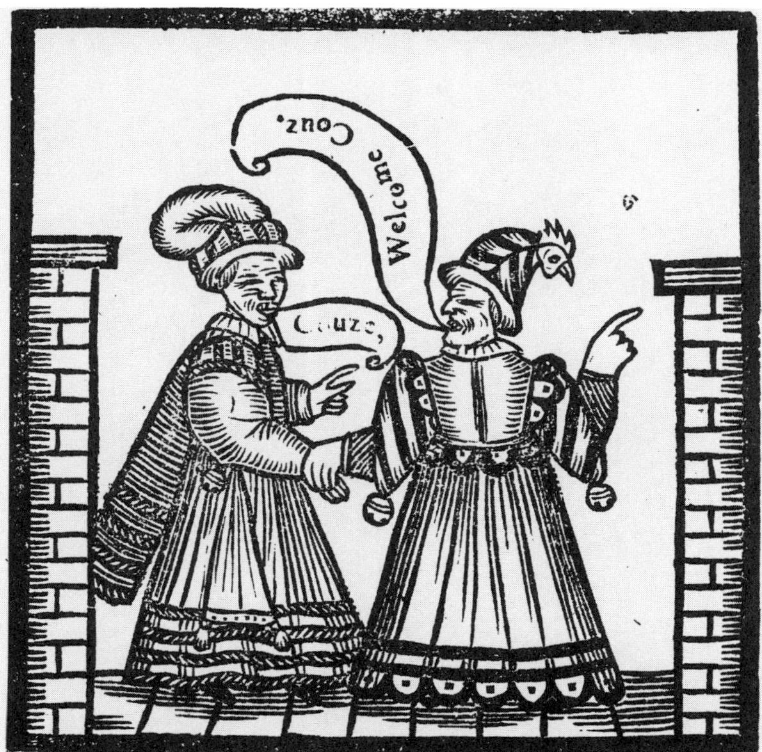

88. Will Summers (left) welcoming Patch. *A Pleasant History of the Life and Death of Will Summers* (1637). By permission of the Folger Shakespeare Library.

the right while at the left Henry VIII himself sits at a table and plays a harp (fig. 89). Even a household such as Sir Thomas More's could boast a fool, in this case Henry Patenson, a former mummer.[36] Patenson's likeness was included with the More family in Holbein's Basel sketch of 1527 or 1528 (fig. 90) and the copies made by Rowland Locky in the 1590's, though he was left out of Holbein's family portrait in the National Portrait Gallery.[37]

The court jester's role is described in Thomas Fuller's account of Richard Tarlton, who appears to have enjoyed a reputation as a natural fool, was adopted as a favorite of Queen Elizabeth, and also became a popular actor on the stage in the mid-1570's to his death in 1588.[38] According to Fuller,

> Our Tarlton was master of his faculty. When Queen Elizabeth was serious (I dare not say sullen), and out of good humour, he could *undumpish* her at his pleasure. Her highest favourites would, in some cases, go to Tarlton before they would go to the

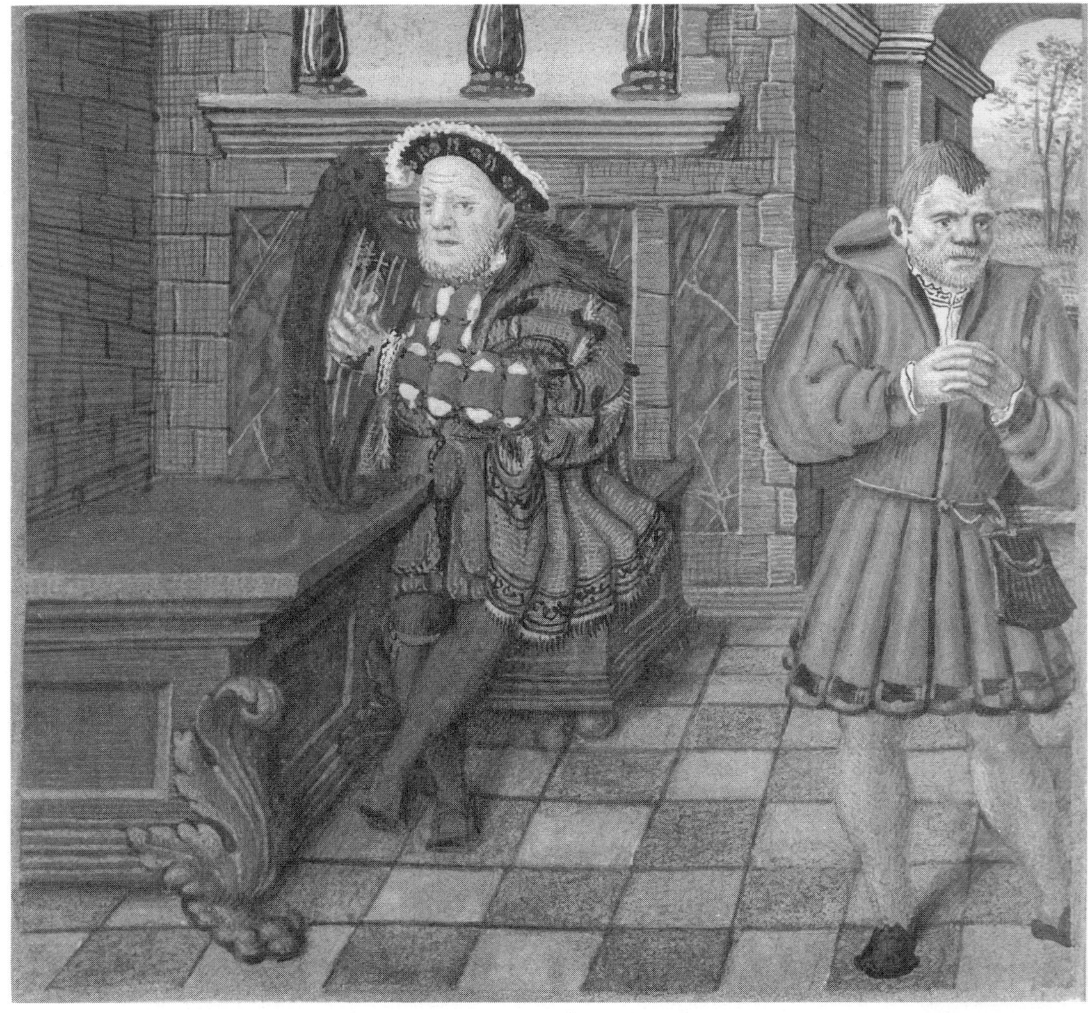

89. King Henry VIII playing harp (left), and his fool Will Summers (right). Psalter of Henry VIII. British Library, MS. Royal 2.A.XVI, fol. 63^{v}. By permission of the British Library.

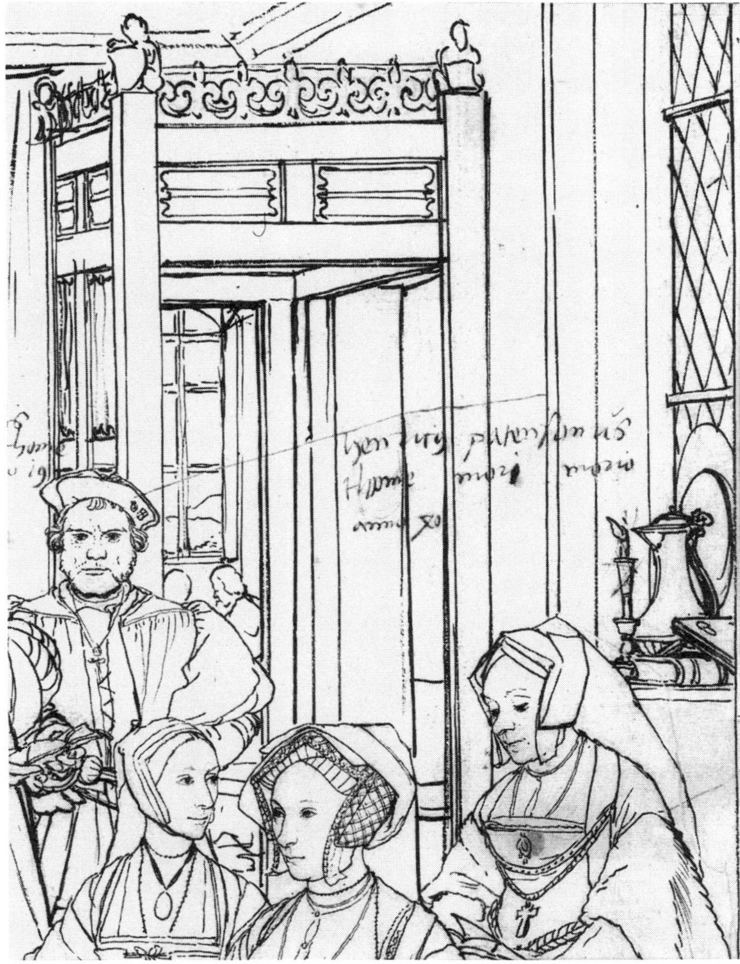

90. Henry Patenson (above, left), fool in household of Sir Thomas More. Detail from Basel Sketch by Holbein. Öffentliche Kunstsammlung, Kupferstichkabinnett Basel.

> Queen, and he was their usher to prepare their advantageous access unto her. In a word, he told the Queen more of her faults than most of her chaplains, and cured her melancholy better than all her physicians. Much of his merriment lay in his very looks and actions. . . .
>
> Indeed, the selfsame words, spoken by another, would hardly move a merry man to smile; which, uttered by him, would force a sad soul to laughter.[39]

Such too would be the stage fools who were to appear in Shakespeare's plays, and it is not surprising to encounter the opinion that Tarlton might have been the model for the deceased jester named Yorick whose skull is turned up by the gravediggers in Act V, Scene i, in *The Tragedy of Hamlet, Prince of Denmark.*

Tarlton's appearance was described two years subsequent to his death in a publication which claimed that its author had seen his ghost following his return from purgatory; prior to recognizing the ghost as Tarlton, he describes him as "attired in russet with a buttond cap on his head, a great bagge by his side, and a strong bat in his hand, so artificially attired for a Clowne, as [the dreamer] began to call *Tarltons* woonted shape to remembrance."[40] We also know of him that he had a flat nose and a squint. His portrait, drawn by John How of Norwich, appears in British Library MS. Harl. 3885, fol. 19, where he appears, playing

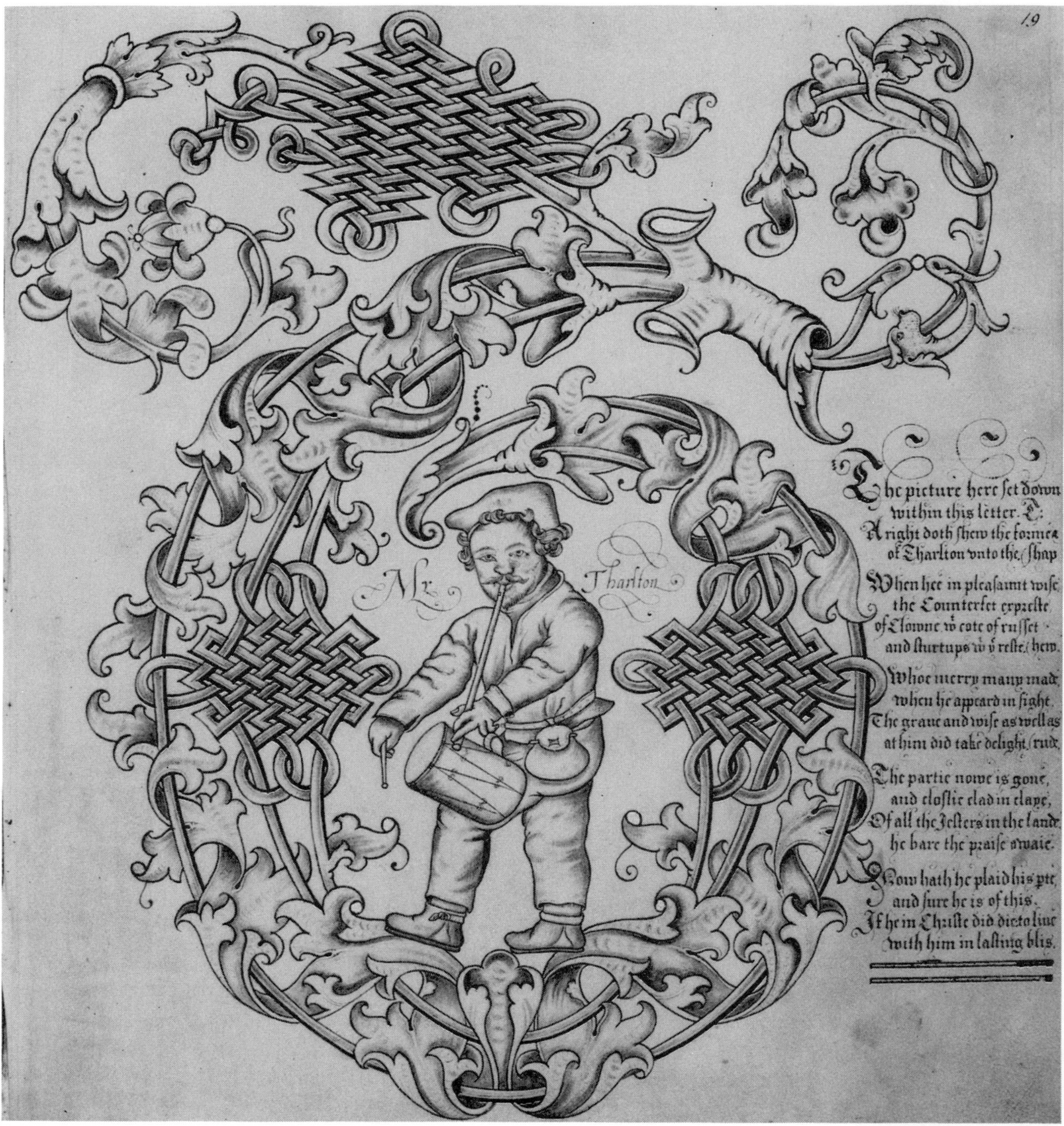

91. Richard Tarlton. Sketch by John How of Norwich. British Library, MS. Harl. 3885, fol. 19. By permission of the British Library.

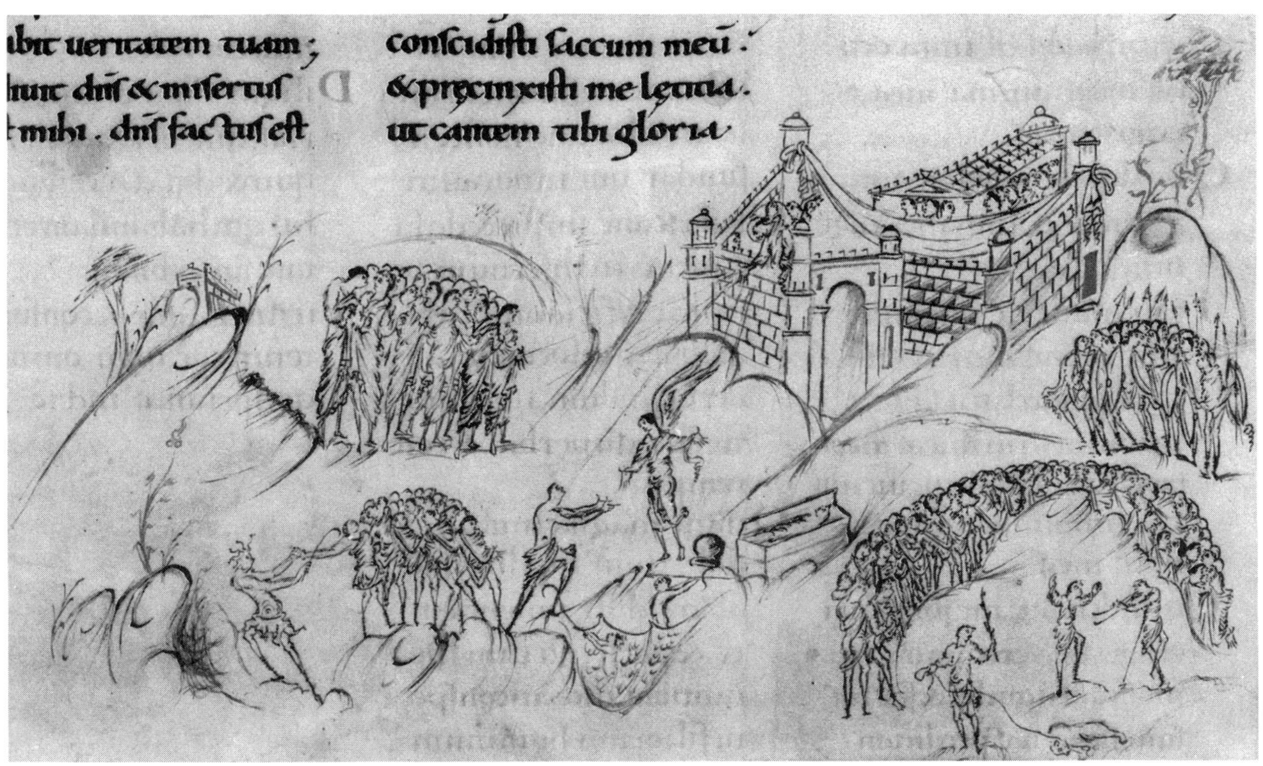

92. Crowd watching entertainers (at right). Harley Psalter. British Library, MS. Harl. 603, fol. 17ᵛ. Twelfth century. By permission of the British Library.

fife and drum, in "cote of russet" (fig. 91).[41]

As noted above, the distinction between fools and other kinds of entertainers was much less rigid than we might expect. A fool existed either as an independent entertainer or as a member of a troupe of entertainers or actors. So too many others of these professions performed as individuals, as in the instance of sword swallowers and bear wards,[42] while others were organized into itinerant groups. It is instructive to note the way in which John of Salisbury in his *Policraticus* links together "mimics, jumping or leaping priests, buffoons, Aemilian and other gladiators, wrestlers, sorcerers, jugglers, magicians, and a whole army of jesters."[43] Like fools, many of these followed practices that had not very greatly changed from classical antiquity, and representations in the visual arts provide clues to their continuous presence in European society over the centuries. In the twelfth-century Harley Psalter (British Library MS. Harl. 603, fol. 17ᵛ), a crowd watches a group of entertainers, which include a bearward, a minstrel, and a dancer (fig. 92).

The interconnectedness of such entertainers is neatly suggested in the Beatus page in the Glazier Psalter (Pierpont Morgan Library, MS. Glazier 25, fol. 5ᵛ), a manuscript believed to have been illuminated in London in c.1220–30; here in addition to minstrels, one of whom is David playing for King Saul, there are also tumblers leaning backward into somersaults and a sword swallower (fig. 93).[44] The latter entertainer performed a trick that was related to another act, fire eating, a feat that was recorded in 1500 at the court of Henry VII; the king's privy purse accounts list payment of 6s 8d "To a felow for eting of coles."[45] The same accounts indicate that on one occasion in 1505 a minstrel, Watt the luter, "pleyed the fole."[46]

The fuzzy distinction made between vari-

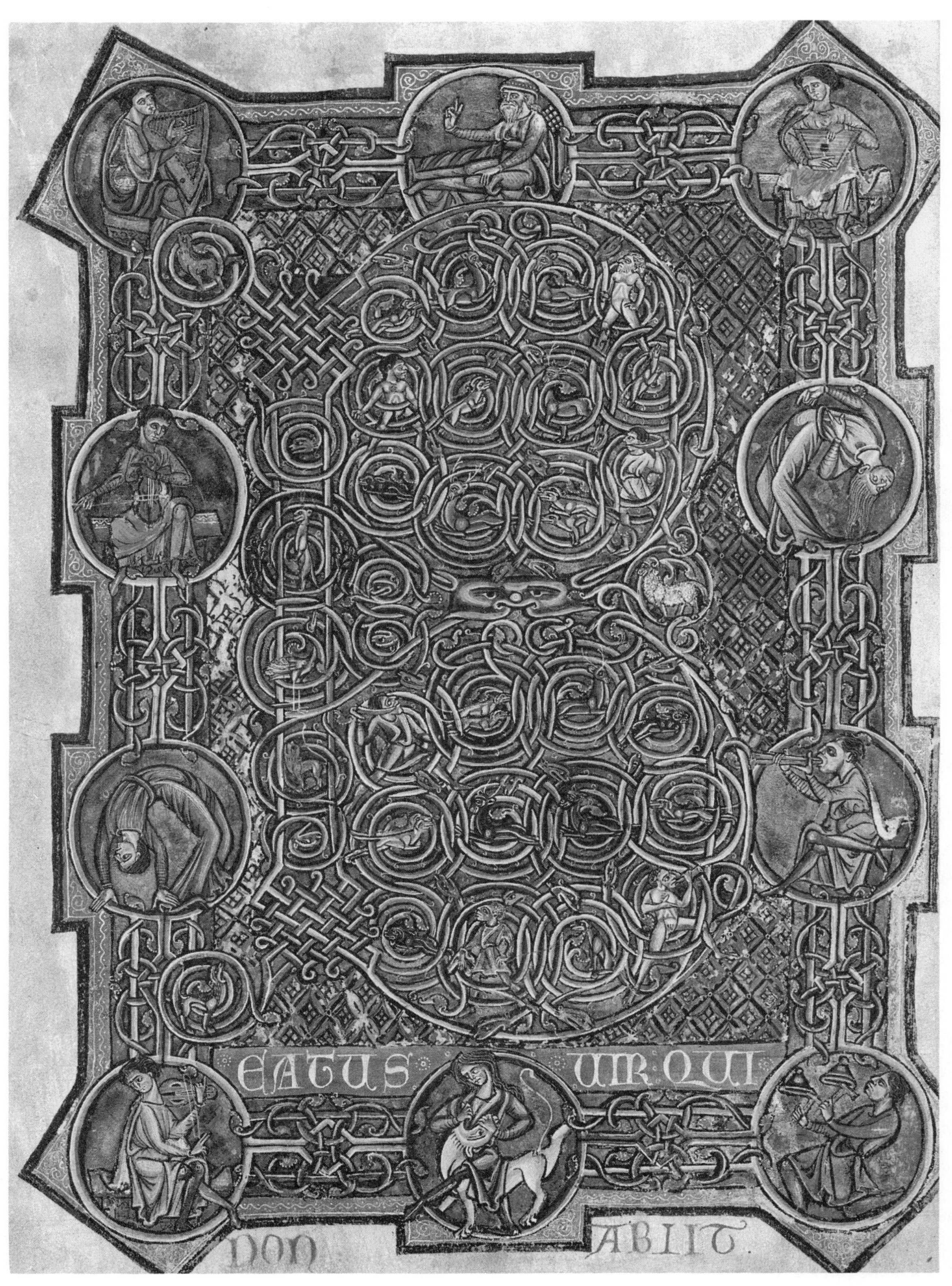

93. Beatus page. Glazier Psalter. Pierpont Morgan Library, MS. Glazier 25, fol. 5v.c.1220–30.

ous entertainers is usefully illustrated in the merging of acrobatics and dancing, especially as shown in numerous illustrations of Herodias' daughter dancing before Herod at the feast immediately prior to the beheading of John the Baptist. According to the biblical text, "on Herod's birthday, the daughter of Herodias danced [*saltavit*] before them: and pleased Herod" (*Matthew* 14.6). In picturing the scene, the daughter, known traditionally as Salome, is from the twelfth century invariably shown as a female jongleur tumbling or doing somersaults as part of her acrobatic dance before the members of Herod's court who are seated at table.[47] Owst calls attention to a passage in a Middle English sermon in which "Herodias doughter . . . was a tumbestere, and tumblede byfore him and other grete lordes of that contre,"[48] but, as Strutt points out, the substitution of *tumbling* for ordinary *dancing* took place as early as the Anglo-Saxon translations of the Gospels.[49] As an amateur entertainer, she was legendary. In a manuscript of c.1220 (British Library MS. Arundel 157, fol. 7) perhaps from Oxford, she is dressed in a long gown and is leaning over backward as she goes into her erotic tumbling act (fig. 94).[50] Other narrative elements are conflated with this action—i.e., the beheading at the left, and the bringing of the head to the table.[51] No other entertain-

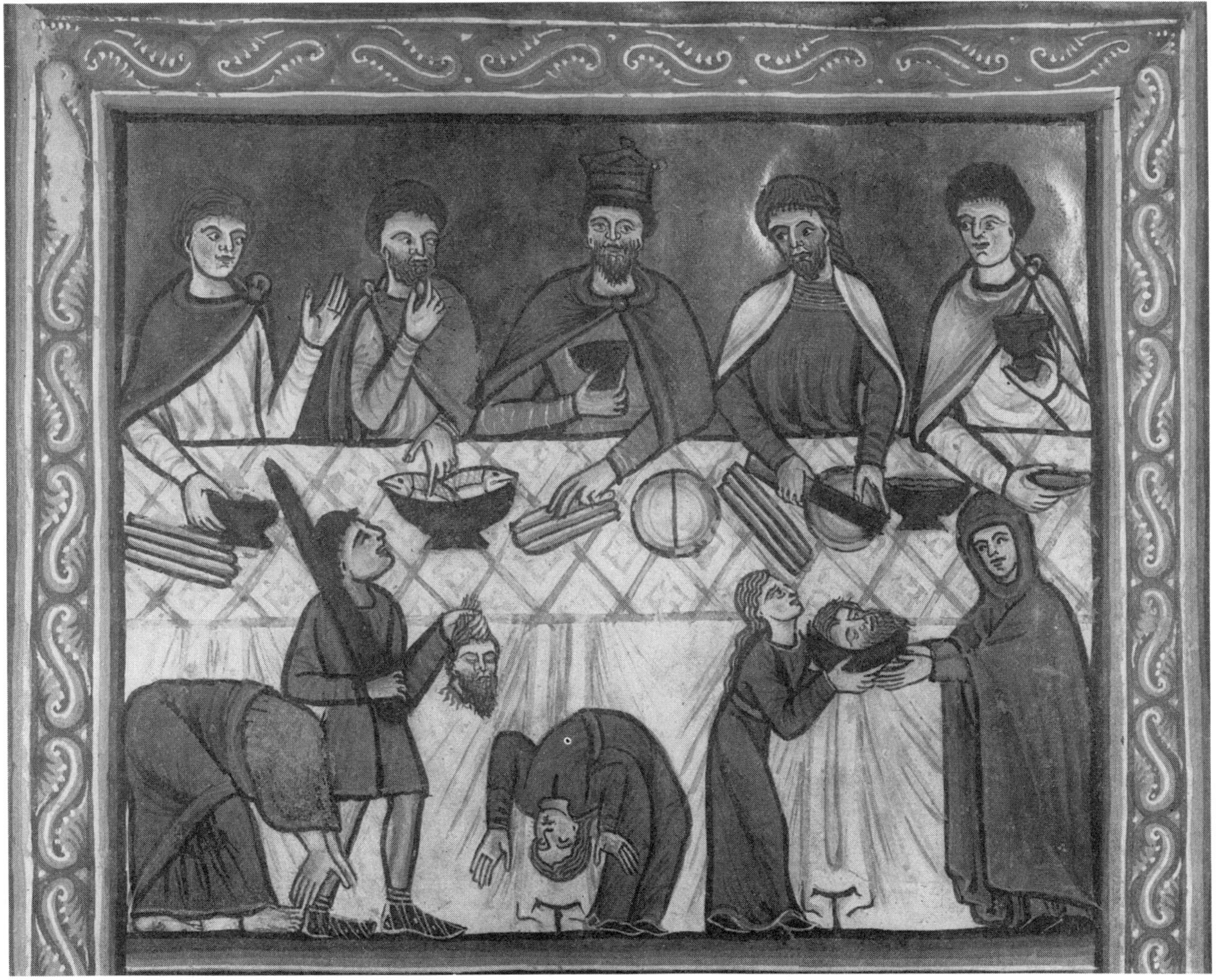

94. Salome dancing before Herod. British Library, MS. Arundel 157, fol. 7. c.1220. By permission of the British Library.

ers are present here, but the ambience of the feast often dictates musicians,[52] as in a misericord dated 1339–41 at Ely Cathedral where the dancer-acrobat is tumbling to the music of a harp, which is played by a harpist placed beside her in front of Herod's table (fig. 95).[53] Sometimes her skirt is parted in front to show her legs, a feature which is included to display her genitals to the spectators at the feast and thus to explain why Herod was so "pleased" at her act.[54] Eroticism seems definitely a factor in the illumination in the fourteenth-century *Holkham Bible Picture Book* (British Library MS. Add. 47,682, fol. 21ᵛ); here her hand rests on Herod's foot, and he gazes and points at her parted legs (fig. 96). A useful comparison may be made with a thirteenth-century drawing, though it is probably not English, in British Library MS. Add. 18,719, which also illustrates the king looking intently at the place where her gown shows cleavage between her legs, while at the same time his right hand touches the hand of another woman, who is not his wife (fig. 97).[55] In painted glass probably

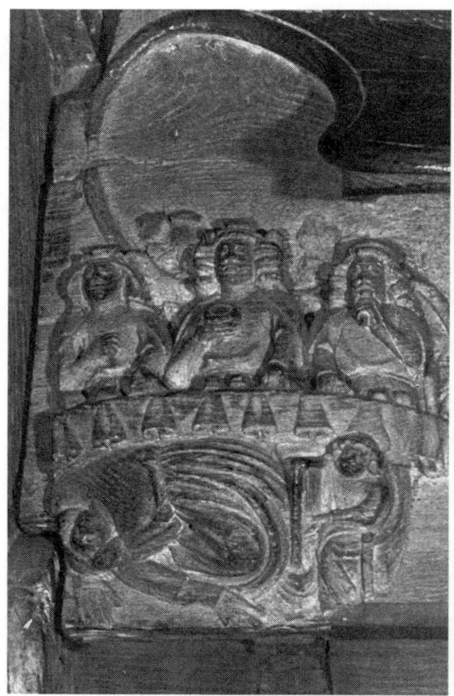

95. Salome dancing before Herod. Misericord, Ely Cathedral. c.1339–41. By permission of the Royal Commission on the Historical Monuments of England.

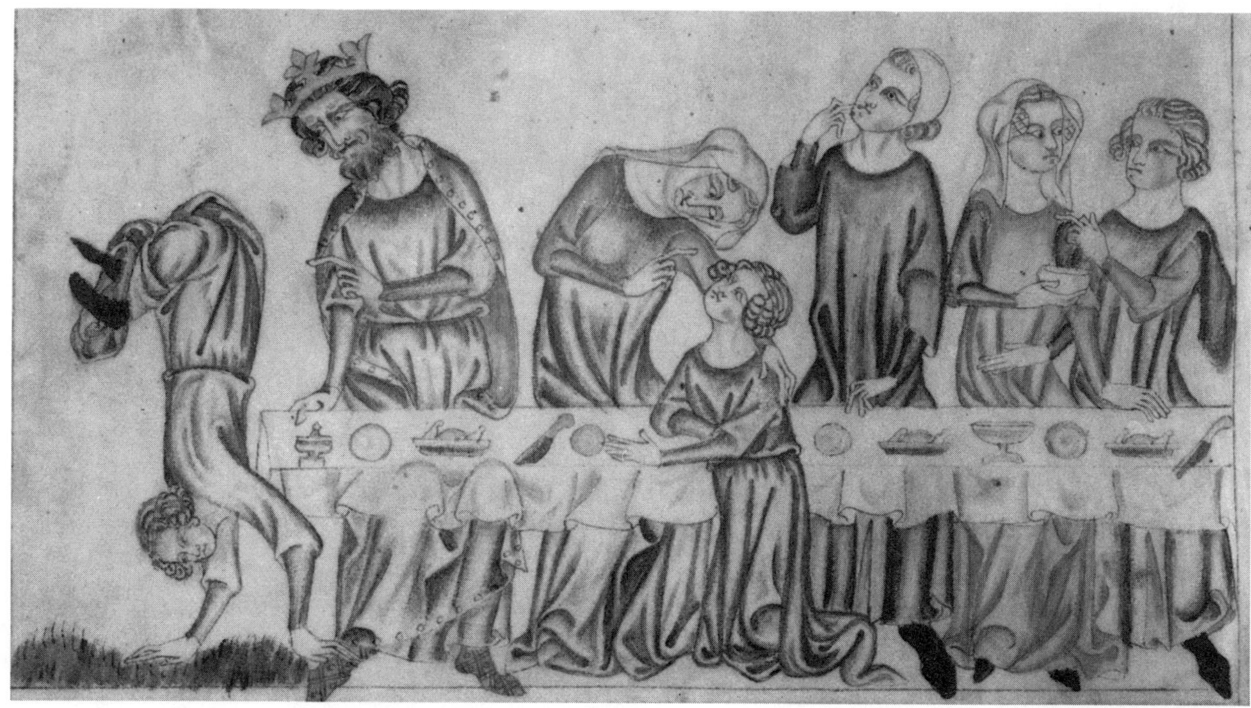

96. Salome dancing before Herod. *Holkham Bible Picture Book.* British Library, MS. Add. 47,682, fol. 21ᵛ. Fourteenth century. By permission of the British Library.

of the third decade of the fifteenth century at York Minster, Herod's feast is attended by a fidel player in one of the martyrdom scenes—i.e., when the head of the saint is brought in on a platter after the conclusion of the dance (fig. 98). Salome is shown in her most usual posture, leaning over backwards, in other glass at York in the Chapter House (c.1285) and in St. Denys' Church.[56] The fragmentary panel in the window at St. Denys' shows the dancer-tumbler wearing kerchief and wimple of fourteenth-century style.[57] In a wall painting at Idsworth, Hampshire, her somersault includes more complex acrobatics, since she holds a sword in each of her hands and is juggling a dagger, which is in the air above her head (fig. 99).[58] This iconography dates from at least as

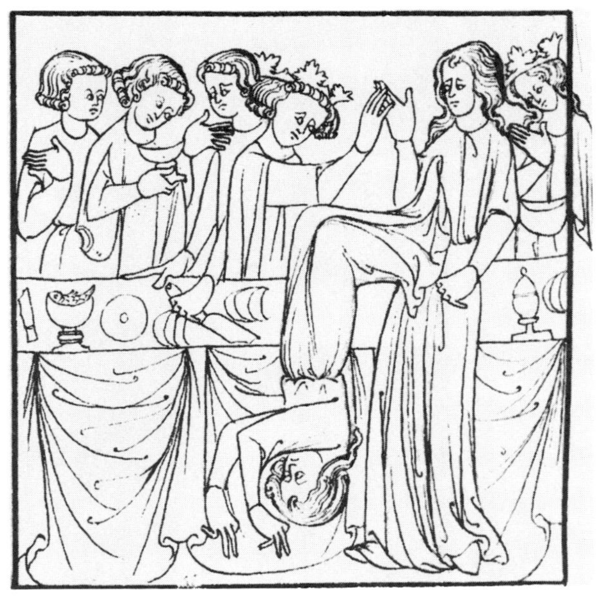

97. (Above) Salome dancing before Herod. Illustrated Bible. British Library, MS. Add. 18,719, fol. 253v.

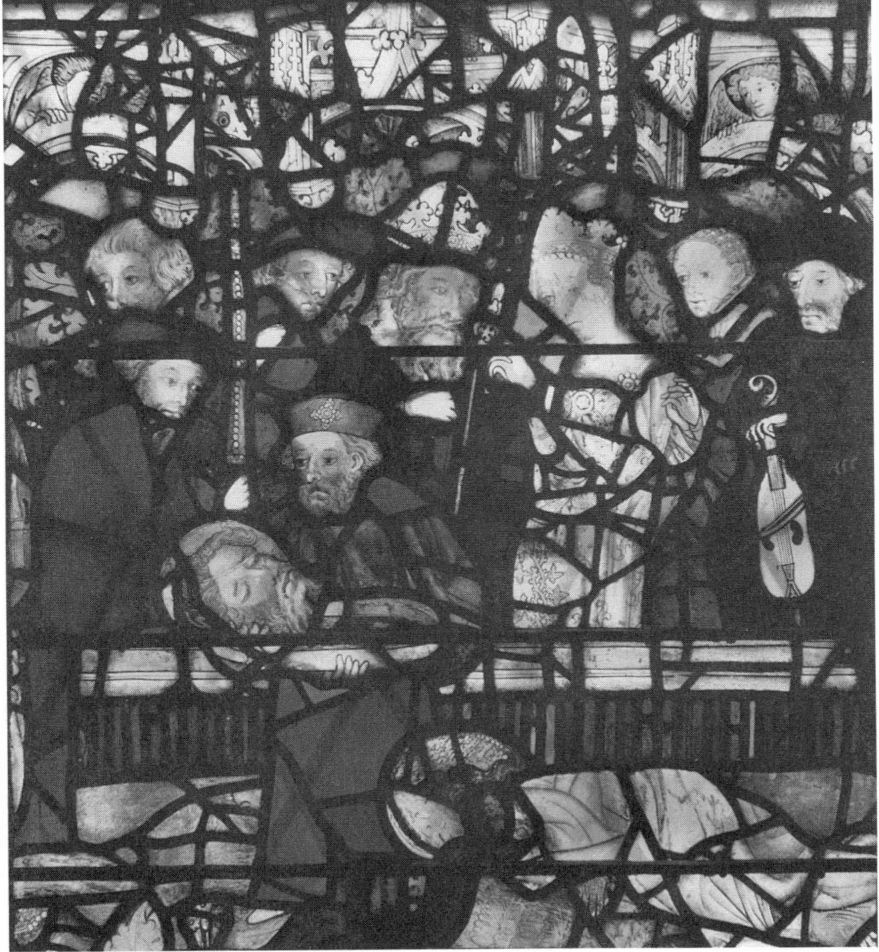

98. (Below) Conclusion of Salome's dance and head of John the Baptist being brought in to feast. Painted glass, York Minster. c.1420–30. By permission of the Royal Commission on the Historical Monuments of England.

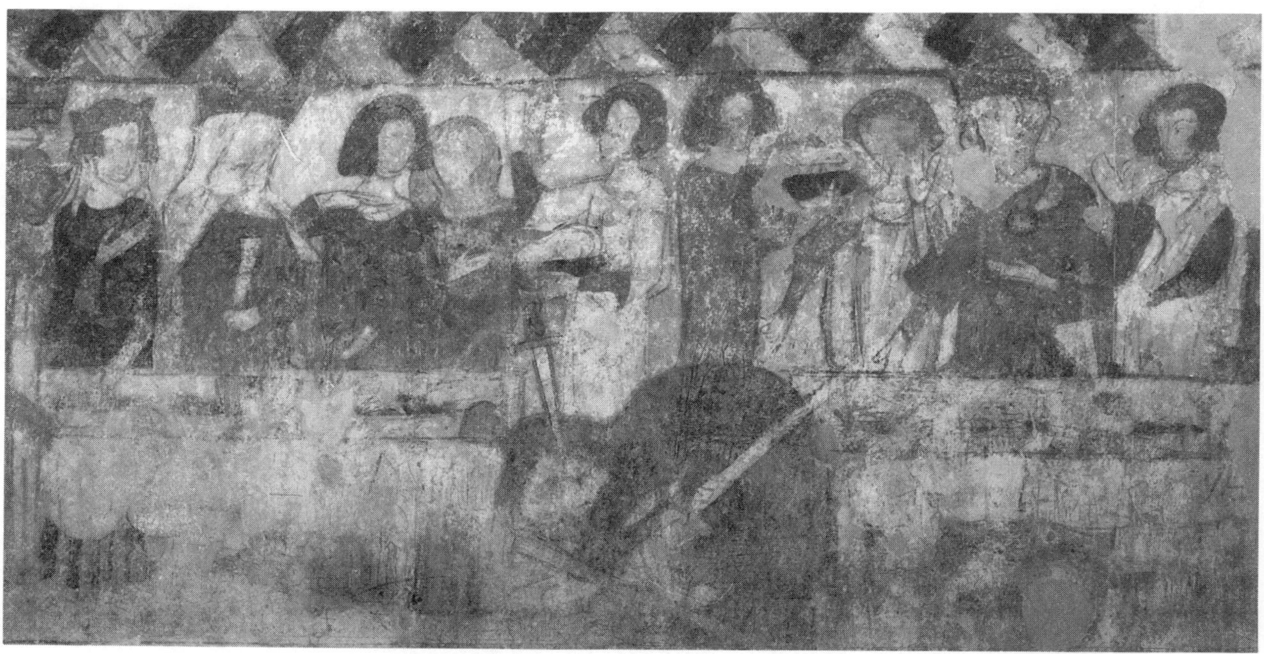

99. Salome dancing a sword dance. Wall painting. Idsworth, Hampshire. Fourteenth century. By permission of the Royal Commission on the Historical Monuments of England.

early as the twelfth century since it appears in a line drawing in an illustrated Gospel book from Bury St. Edmunds (Cambridge, Pembroke College MS. 120, fol. 5v); in this illustration, which was meant to be colored but was left unfinished, Salome holds a sword by the hilt in each hand as she turns a somersault in front of the table where Herod's feast is taking place, though the focus is upon the arrival of John the Baptist's head on a platter before the king (fig. 100). Female tumblers are recorded in medieval England—e.g., Matilda Makejoy, "acrobat," whose appearances at court functions date from 1296 to 1311.[59]

Early acrobats and tumblers in English art include those on a crypt capital at Canterbury Cathedral, where a bearded man holding a bowl and fish in his hands is seated on the head of another man, who reaches up and grasps his arms for balance (fig. 101), and the man who is performing in a roundel of c.1135 on the east jamb of the prior's door (fig. 102) at Ely Cathedral.[60] The Ely sculpture illustrates a posture reminiscent of the acrobatics in the Feast of Herod scenes cited above. The figure is very worn, but seems to be

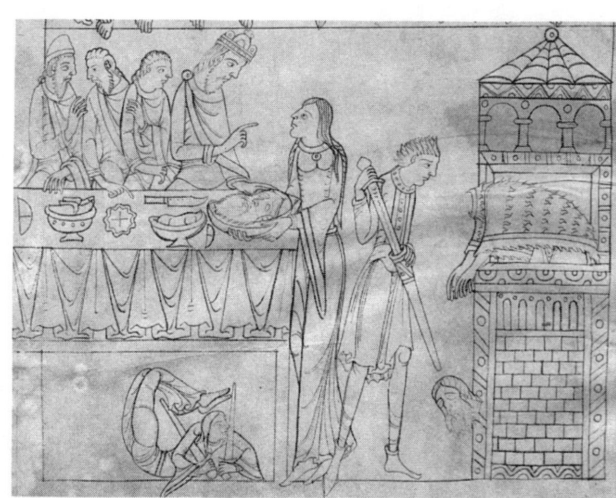

100. Salome dancing a sword dance. Illustrated Gospel book. Cambridge, Pembroke College, MS. 120, fol. 5v. Twelfth century. Reproduced by kind permission of the Master and Fellows of Pembroke College, Cambridge.

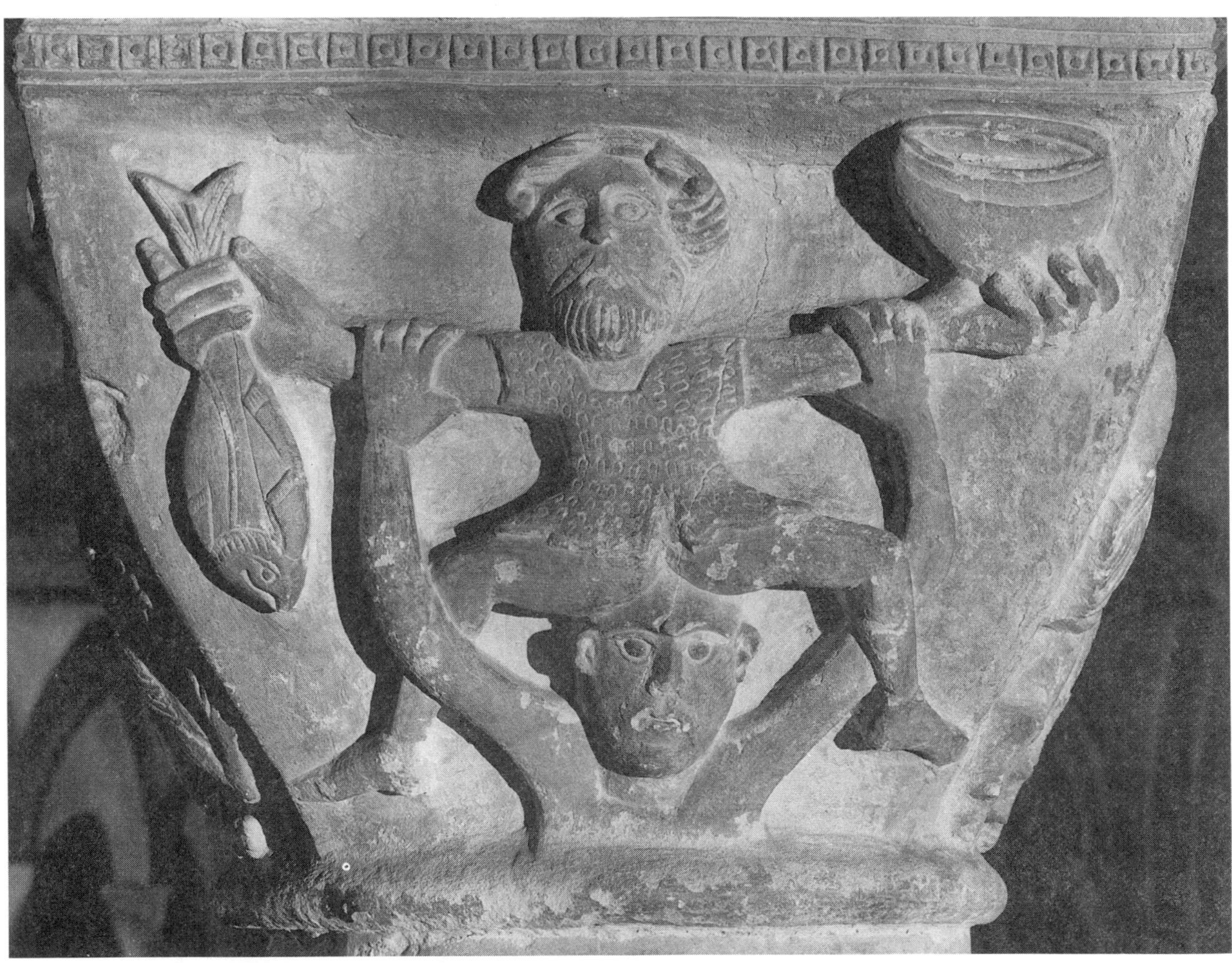

101. Acrobats. Crypt capital, Canterbury Cathedral. By permission of the Royal Commission on the Historical Monuments of England.

wearing a tunic. A misericord dated c.1290 at St. Mary's Hospital, Chichester, Sussex, shows a tumbler standing on his head.[61] The Huth Psalter (British Library MS. Add. 38,116, fol. 89) of c.1280 shows a very skillful acrobat performing a somersault in front of the figures of King David, playing bells at left, and a fidel player, wearing orange hose, at the right (fig. 103).[62] Acrobatics and similar subjects are also shown on misericords with frequency. At Winchester Cathedral, a misericord dated c.1305—i.e., roughly contemporary with Matilda Makejoy—illustrates a female tumbler on the left supporter holding one foot, while on the right supporter there is a male tumbler (fig. 104).[63] A remarkable acrobatic feat in which a woman tumbler balances upon the points of two swords, which in turn are balanced upon two small white balls, appears in the Smithfield Decretals (British Library, MS. Royal 10.E.4, fol. 58 (fig. 105). Two musicians flank her, one playing a pipe and drum, and the other plays two pipes simultaneously in the manner of pan-pipes. A contortionist and an acrobat appear at Christchurch Priory, Dorset (formerly Hampshire), in a misericord dated 1515 (fig. 106). The acrobat sticks out his tongue irreverently and holds the liripiping of his hood with his right hand and a foot with the left.[64]

Recognizable dancing, however, appears illustrated as early as Anglo-Saxon times; in an illuminated manuscript containing Prudentius' *Psy-*

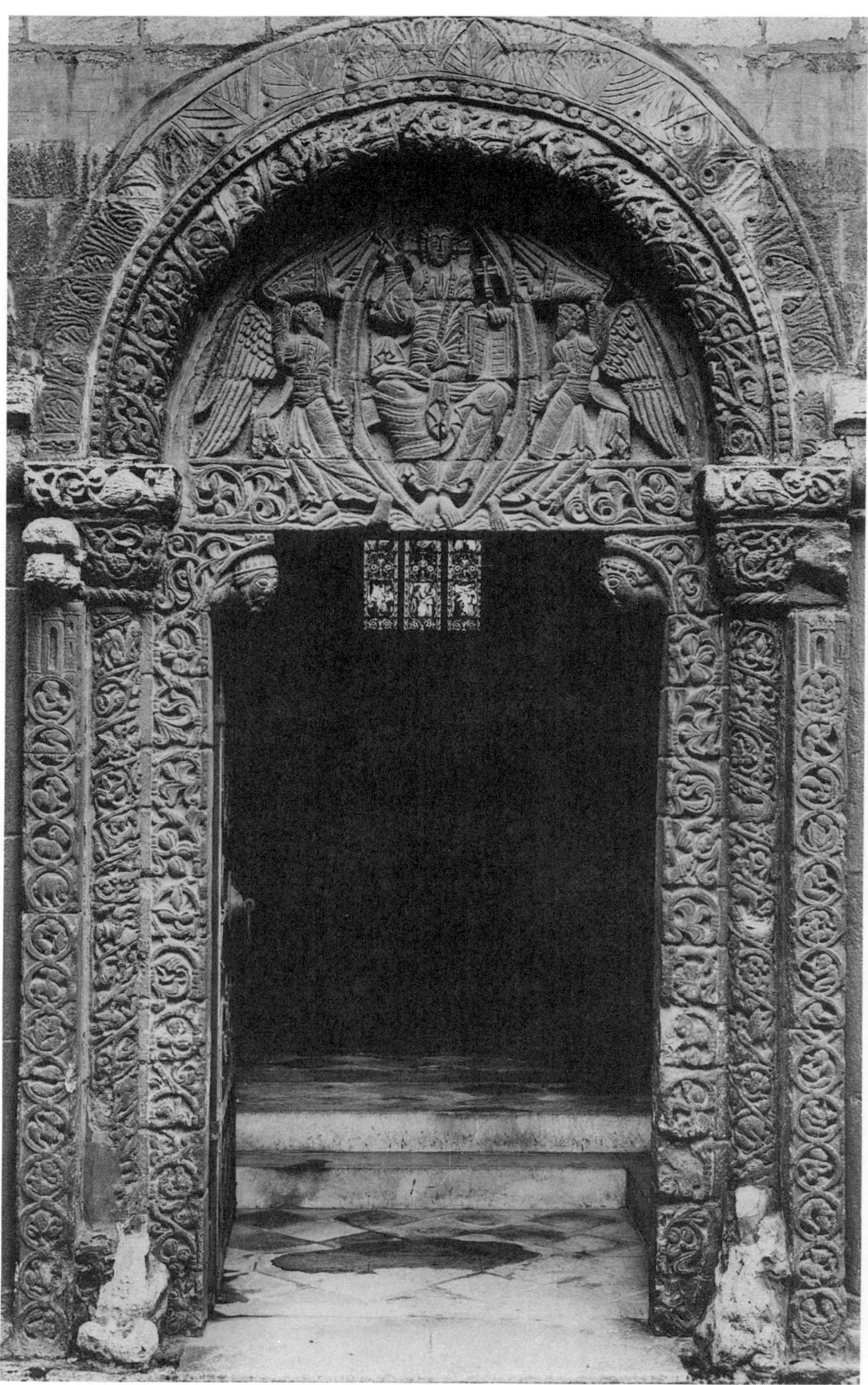

102. Prior's door, Ely Cathedral. c.1135. The Conway Library, Courtauld Institute of Art.

chomachia (British Library MS. Cotton Cleopatra C.viii, fol. 19ᵛ), a dance by a gleeman—he is dancing to music played by two other gleemen on lyre and double pipe—is shown along with an appreciative audience looking on (fig. 107). Another *Psychomachia* (British Library, MS. Add. 24,199, fol. 18) includes a tenth-century drawing showing a similar scene, with the dancer in this case distinctively feminine and identifiable as Luxuria (fig. 108).[65] In a book of hours (British Library MS.

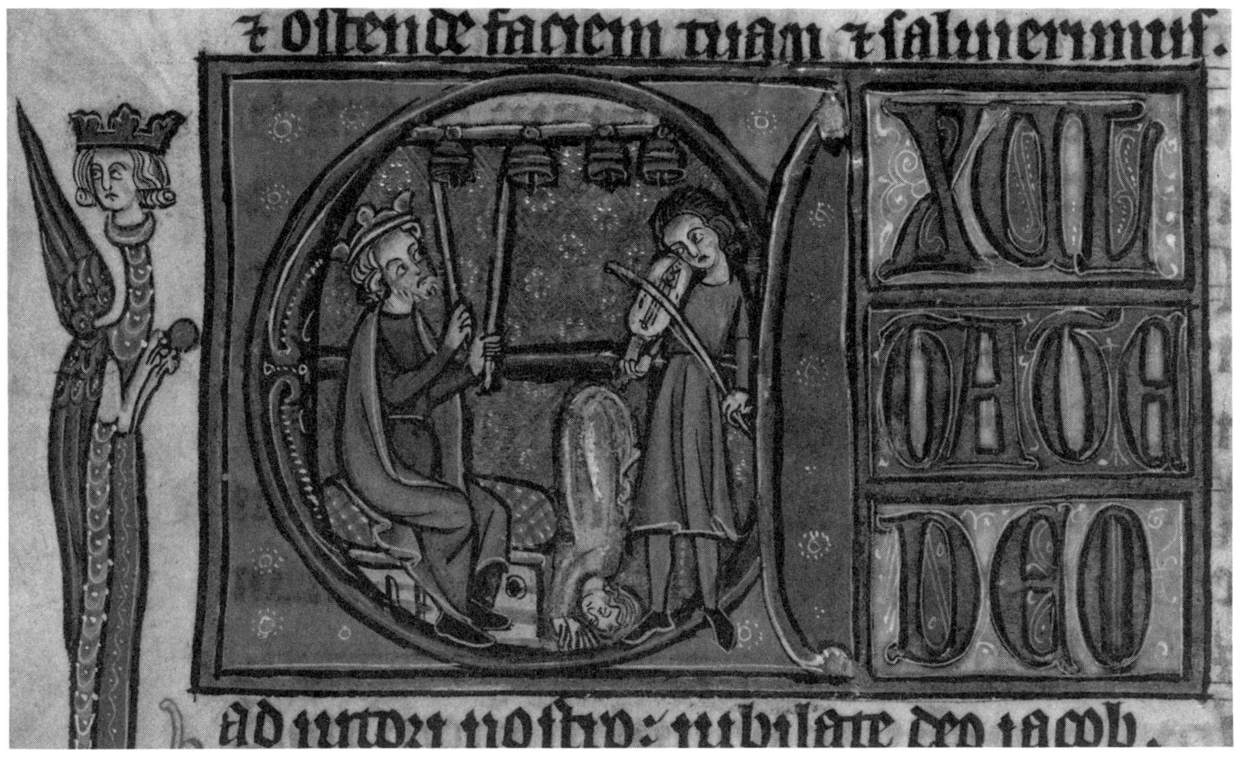

103. Acrobat performing for King David. Huth Psalter. British Library, MS. Add. 38,116, fol. 89. c.1280. By permission of the British Library.

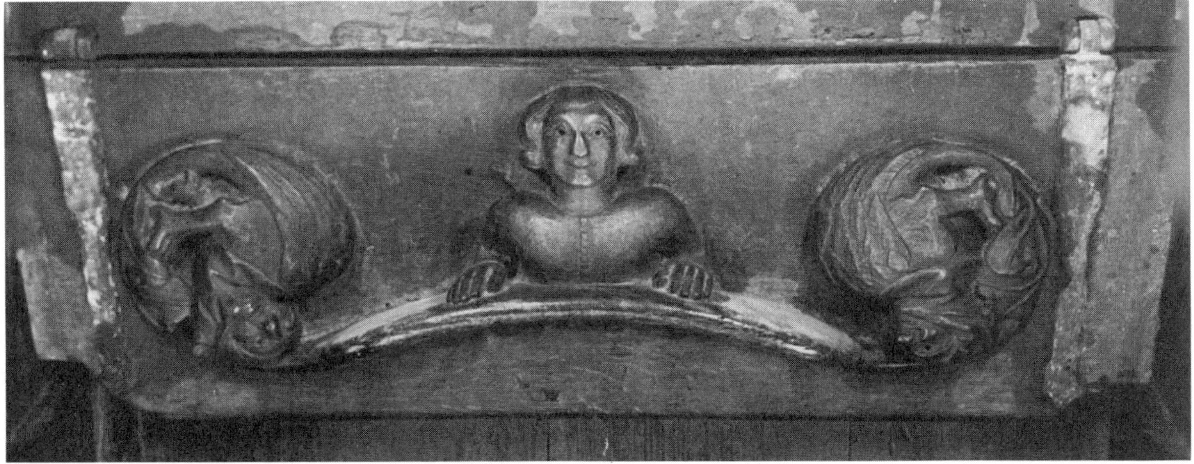

104. Male and female tumblers on supporters. Misericord, Winchester Cathedral. c.1305. By permission of the Royal Commission on the Historical Monuments of England.

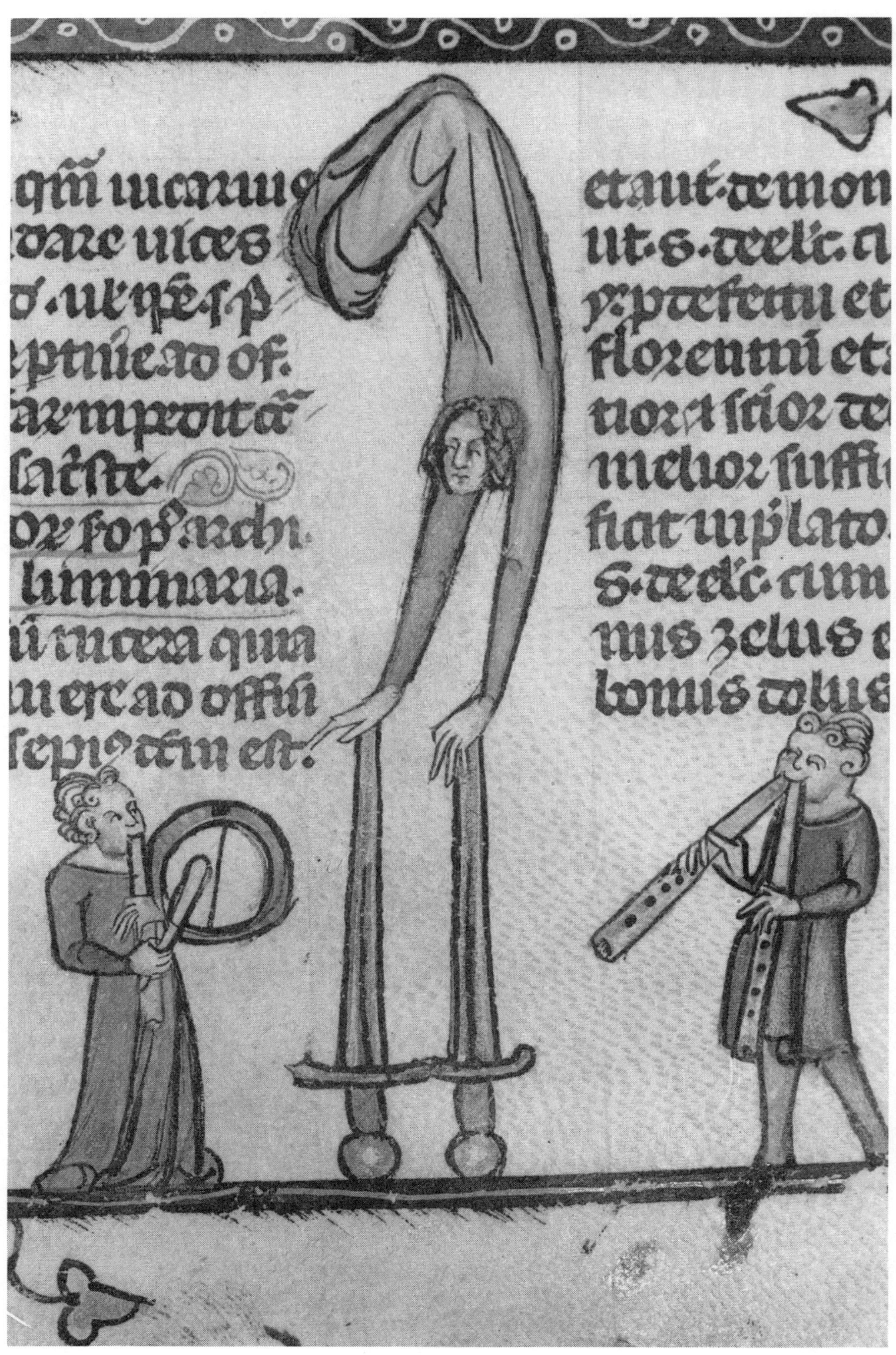

105. A woman acrobat balances on the points of two swords while musicians play. British Library, MS. Royal 10.E.IV, fol. 58. c.1340. By permission of the British Library.

Egerton 1151, fol. 47), possibly from Oxford (c.1260–80), a man and two women are dancing to the music of fidel and gittern (fig. 109).[66] The De la Twyere Psalter (New York Public Library, MS. Spencer 2), which has been identified as from the York diocese and as illuminated in the early fourteenth century, includes an illuminated border at fol. 161^{v} that illustrates dancers as well as musi-

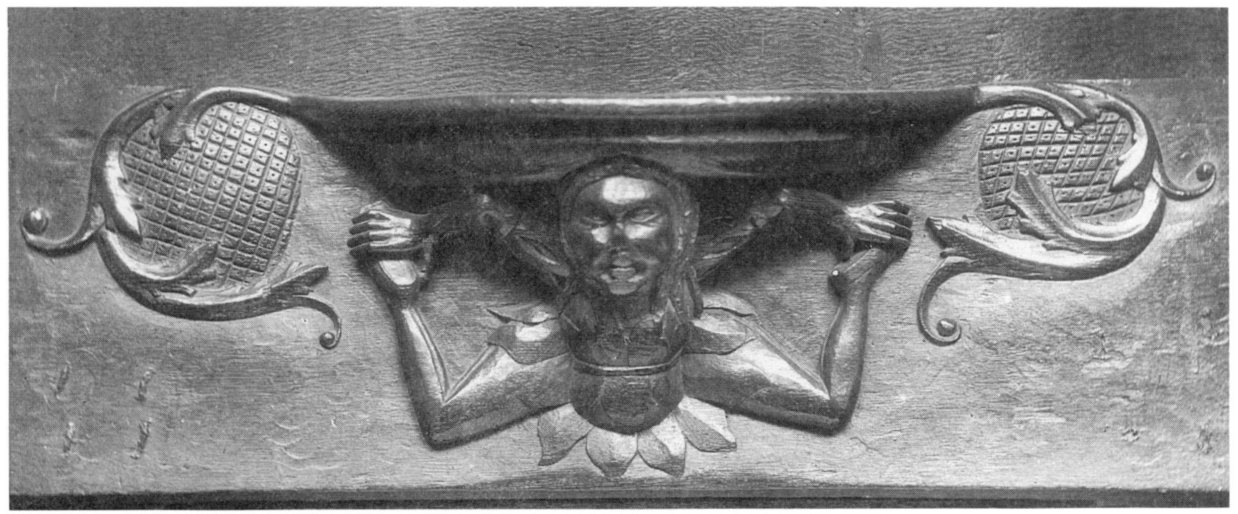

106. Contortionist. Misericord, Christ Church Priory, Dorset (formerly Hampshire). 1515. By permission of the Royal Commission on the Historical Monuments of England.

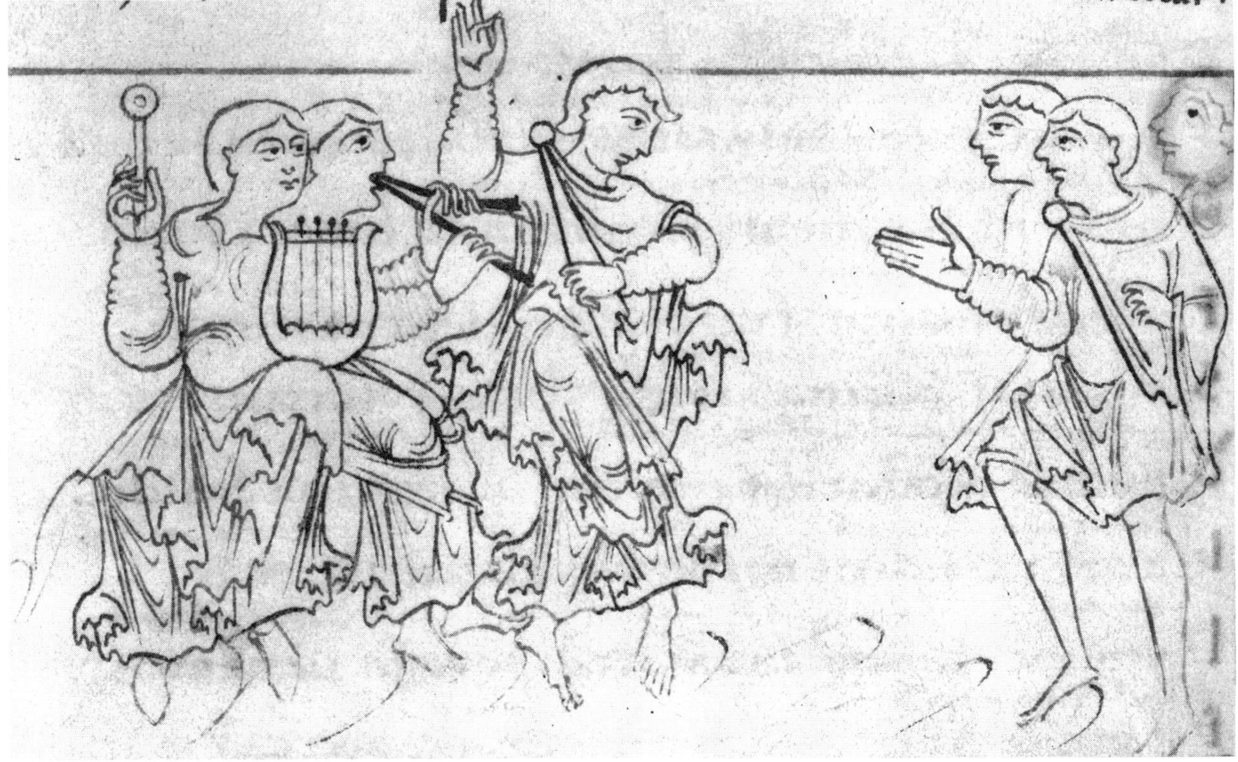

107. Dancing before an audience: Prudentius, *Psychomachia*. British Library, MS. Cotton Cleopatra C.viii, fol. 19^{v}. Anglo-Saxon. By permission of the British Library.

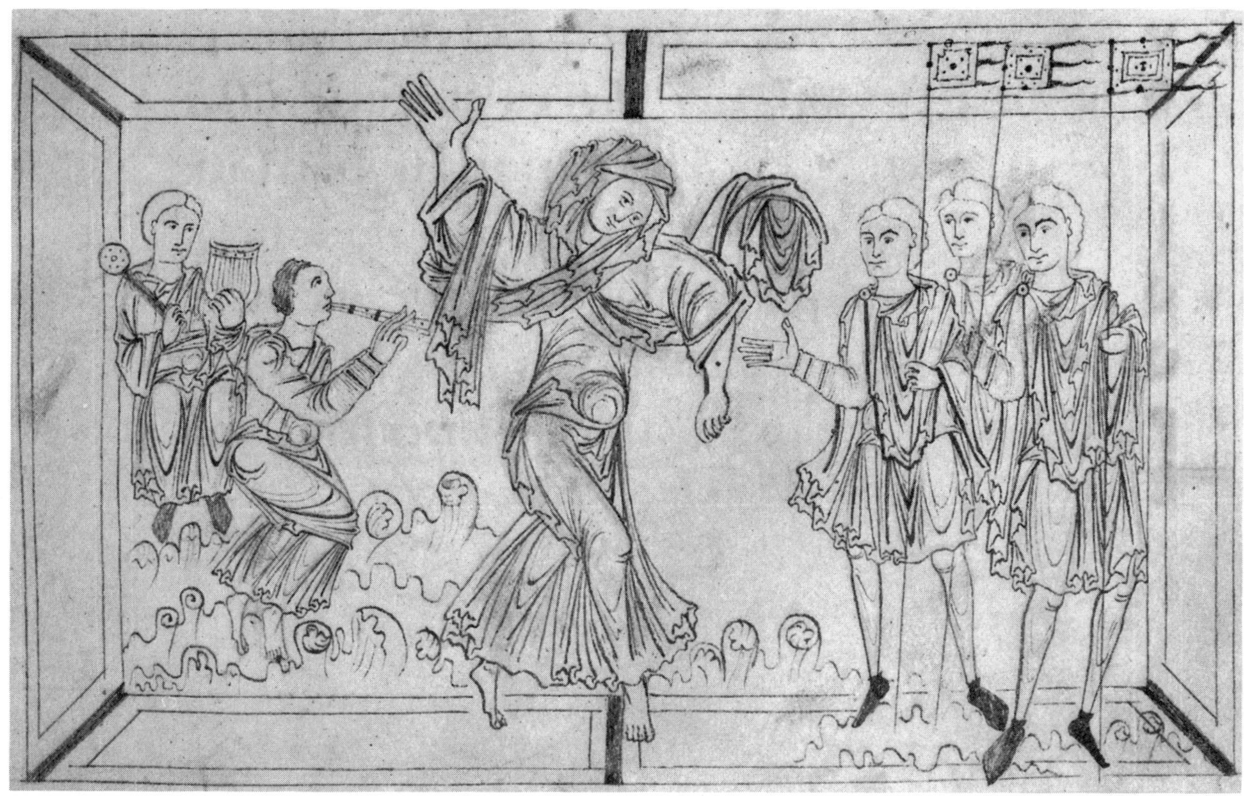

108. Luxuria dancing before an audience. Prudentius, *Psychomachia*. British Library, MS. Add. 24,199, fol. 18. Tenth century. By permission of the British Museum.

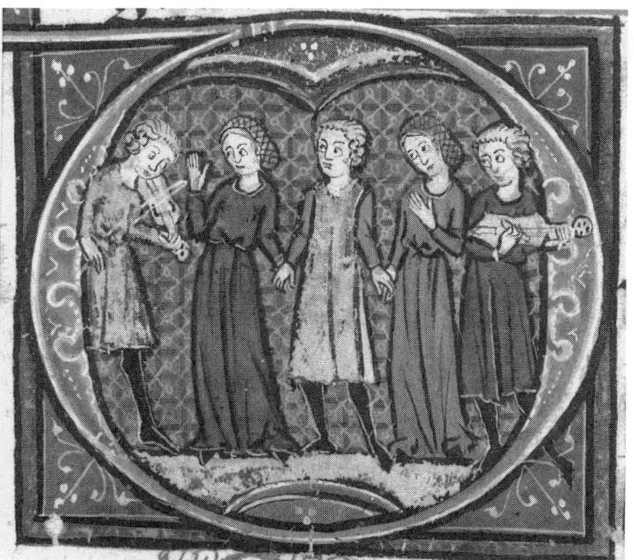

109. A man and two women are dancing, flanked by musicians playing fidel and gittern. Book of Hours. British Library, MS. Egerton 1151, fol. 47. c.1260–80. By permission of the British Library.

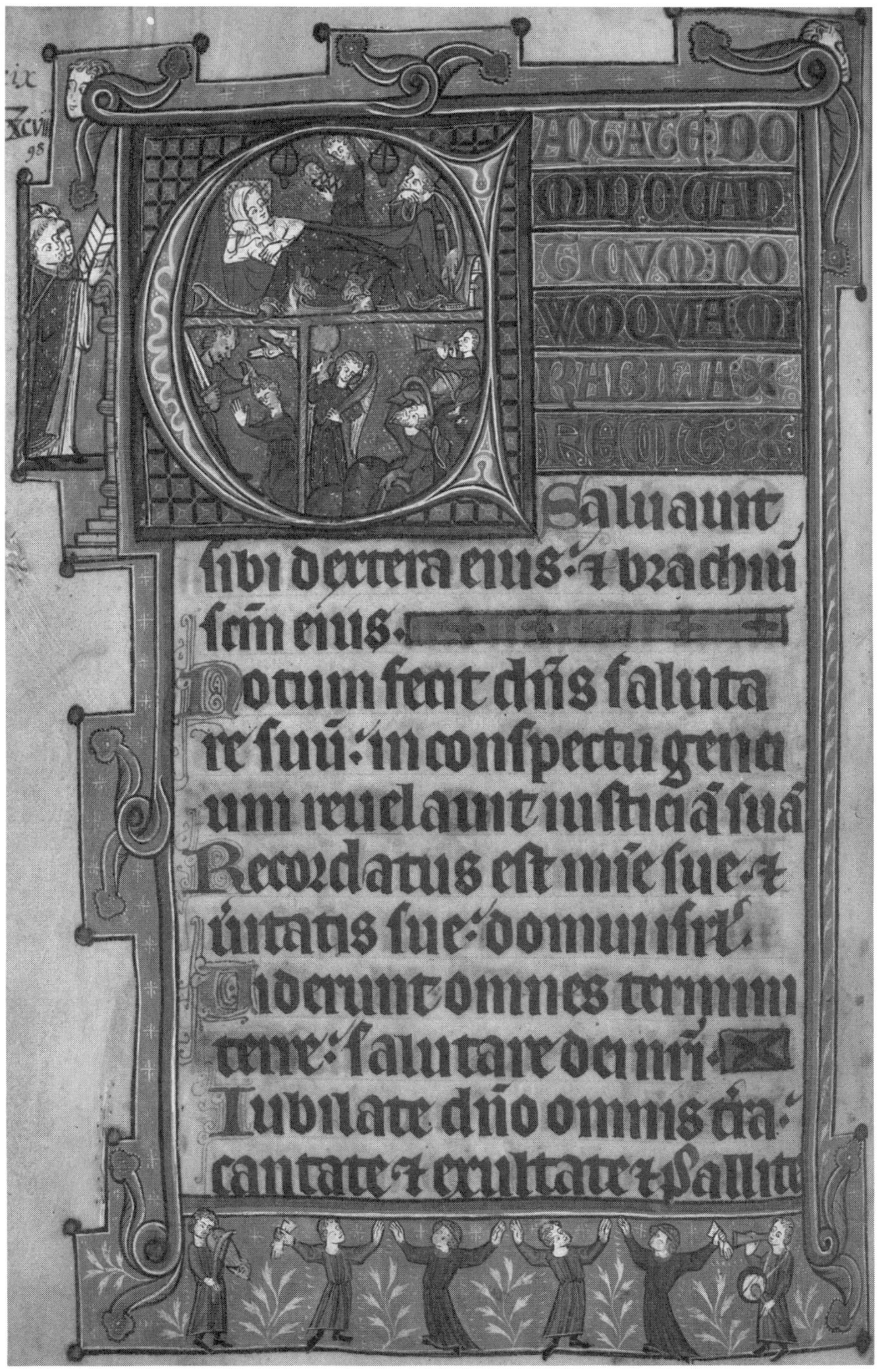

ANTATE DO
MINO CANT
ICVM NO
VVM QVIA MI
RABILIA
FECIT.
Saluauit
sibi dextera eius: ⁊ brachiū
scm̄ eius.
Notum fecit dn̄s saluta
re suū: in conspectu genti
um reuelauit iusticiā suā
Recordatus est mīe sue: ⁊
ueritatis sue: domui isrl.
Uiderunt omnes termini
terre: salutare dei nr̄i.
Iubilate dn̄o omnis tra:
cantate ⁊ exultate ⁊ psallite

110. Borders contain dancers, musicians, and chanting clerics. De la Twyere Psalter. New York Public Library, Astor, Lenox, and Tilden Foundations, MS. Spencer 2, fol. 161v. Early fourteenth century.

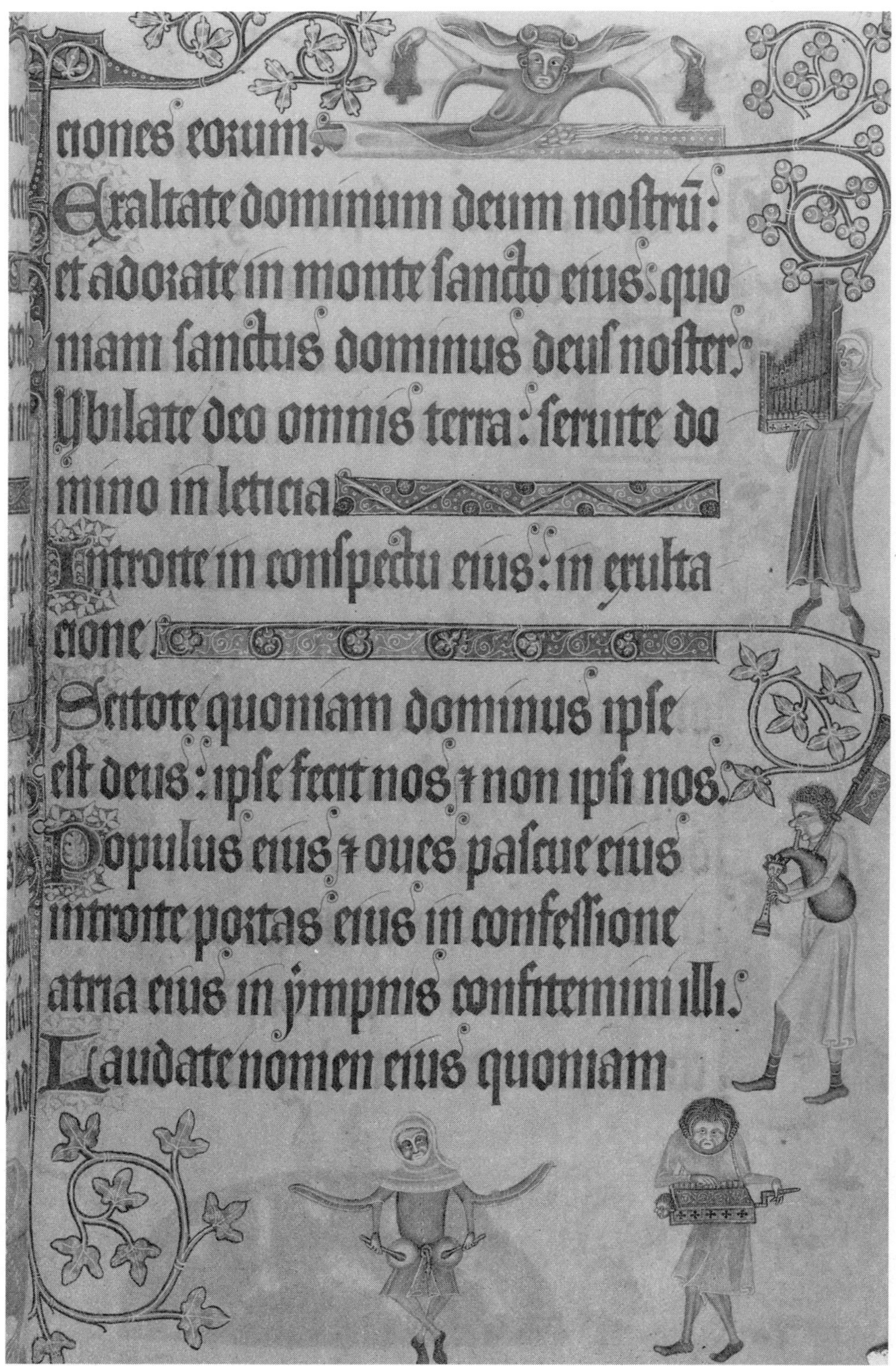

111. Margins have illustrations showing dancing nakers player and other instrumentalists playing symphony, bagpipes, and portative organ. Luttrell Psalter. British Library, MS. Add. 42,130, fol. 176. c.1325–30. By permission of the British Library.

cians playing a fidel and a pipe and tabor and chanting clerics (fig. 110).[67] In the famous Luttrell Psalter, illuminated in approximately 1325–35, a dancing nakers player is illustrated (fig. 111).[68] Minstrels and dancing also appear in the apocalyptic scene showing people rejoicing at the death of the witnesses in J. Paul Getty Museum, MS. Ludwig III.I (83.MC.72), fol. 171^{v}, better known as the Dyson Perrins Apocalypse (fig. 112).[69]

George Tollet, commenting in the eighteenth century with regard to the morris dancers illustrated in the Betley Hall painted glass (more recently removed to Leigh Manor, near Minsterley, Shropshire) in connection with the Johnson and Steevens text of Shakespeare's *Henry IV*, Part I, suggests that tumbling may have been part of the act of these entertainers, though such acrobatic displays would not have been their mainstay.[70] The glass (fig. 86) pictures not only the traditional morris dancers with their bells and distinctive clothing, but also includes Maid Marian and Friar Tuck—characters out of the Robin Hood story—as well as the Hobby Horse.[71] The friar, a Franciscan, has red stockings and a red girdle "ornamented wth a golden twist, and with a golden tassel."[72] Their musician is Tom the Piper, who plays the pipe and tabor. The true Morisco is at the top of the window in the center, while a Spanish morris dancer appears at his right. Both not only wear the distinctive bells, but also have characteristic streamers attached to their arms. Otherwise, if the Betley glass is correct, it appears that in English practice the dancers might incorporate a number of ranks in society from the lowly fool to a nobleman. Morris troupes, it is often assumed, were all male, and if this were the case the appearance of women characters such as Maid Marian would mean that these roles too would ha[illegible]en taken by men. However, women were inc[illegible]d at

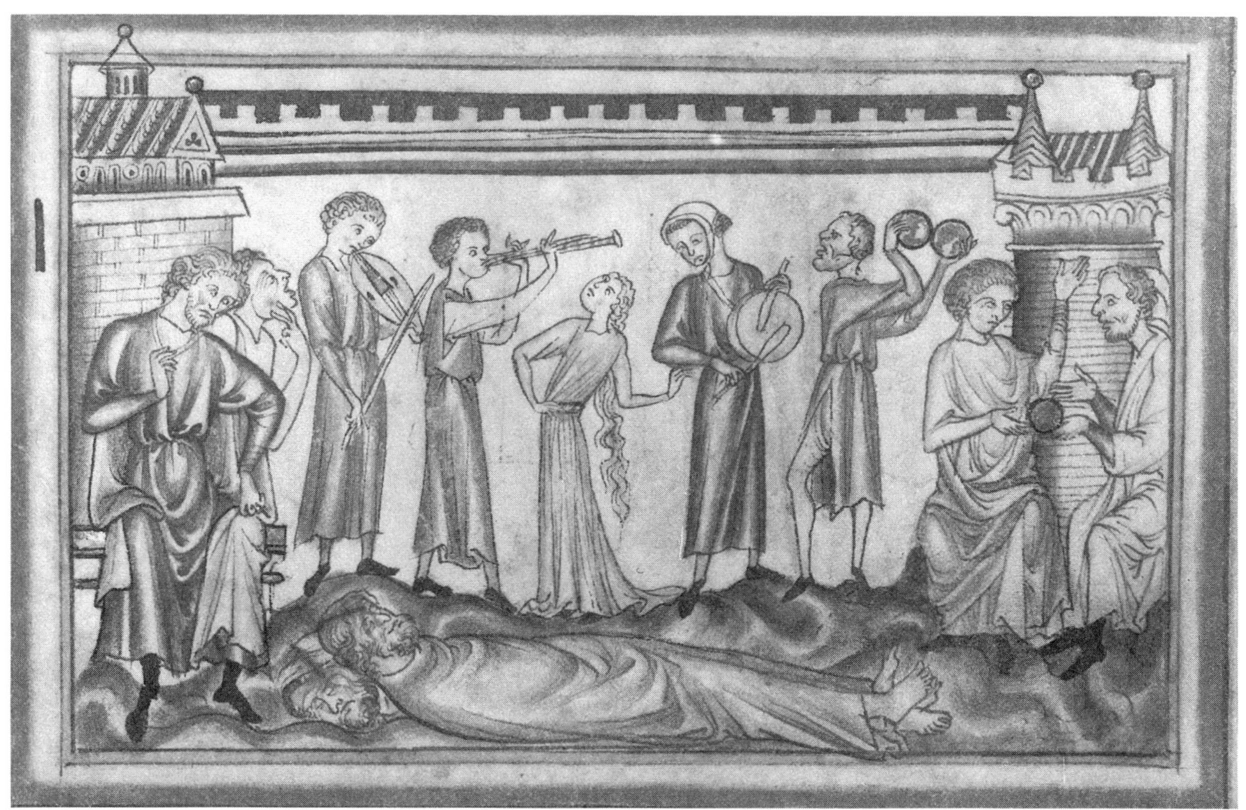

112. Death of the Witnesses. Dyson Perrins Apocalypse. J. Paul Getty Museum, MS. Ludwig III.I (83.MC.72), fol. 171^{v}.

least some of the time, as David Klausner has pointed out.[73]

In a carved panel formerly at Lancaster Castle, a row of morris dancers is assembled to the right of a Maid Marian in a short skirt who is holding out a ladle to receive money from an imagined audience.[74] The piper, playing a long pipe and beating a tabor, is next, and beside him is a nude dancer, presumably covered with a body stocking resembling flesh as in the mystery plays. Three other dancers in short tunics, only one of whom has bells attached at his knees, and finally, at the right, a fool with distinctive cap, bells, and foolstick fill out the panel. Another example of a morris dancer with a pipe and tabor appears in sixteenth-century painted glass now among the quarries collected in the Zouche Chapel in York Minster (fig. 113).[75]

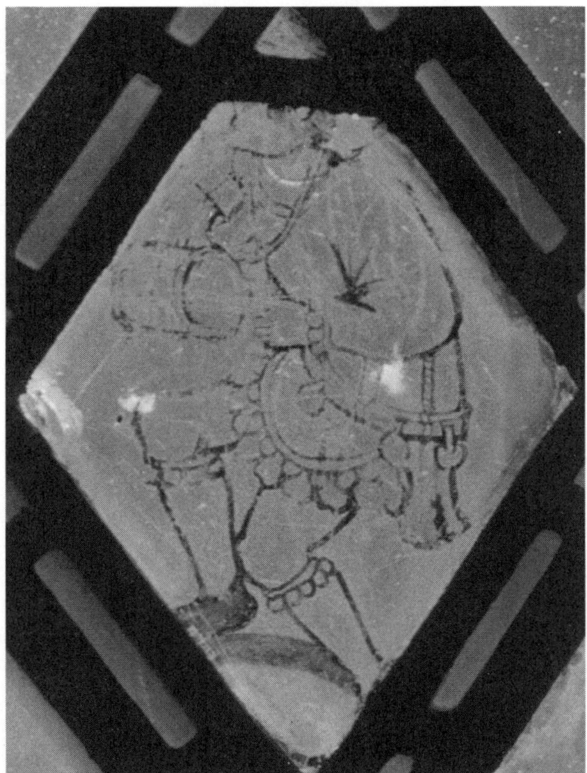

113. Morris dancer with pipe and tabor, now in Zouche Chapel, York Minster. Photograph: David O'Connor; reproduced by kind permission of the Dean and Chapter of York.

A unique, though hostile description of morris dancers appears in Phillip Stubbes' *Anatomie of Abuses* (1583):

> thei tye about either legge twentie, or fourtie belles, with riche hande kercheefes in their handes, and somtymes laied a crosse ouer their shoulders and neckes. . . . Thus all thynges sette in order, then haue thei their Hobbie horses, Dragons and other Antiques, together with their baudie Pipers, and thunderyng Drommers, to strike vp the Deuilles Daunce withall, then marche these Heathen companie towardes the Churche and Church yarde, their Pipers pipyng, their Drommers thonderyng, their stumppes Dauncyng, their belles iynglyng, their handerchefes swyngyng about their heades like madmen, their Hobbie horses, and other monsters skirmishyng amongest the throng.[76]

Stubbes complains that they would enter the church with their boisterous procession during the service, even disturbing the sermon, whereupon they would go into the churchyard where they would dance through the day and also the following night.[77]

Jugglers had appeared along with acrobats from the time of the ancient mimes;[78] both acrobatics and juggling acts are illustrated in the Rutland Psalter (British Library MS. Add. 62,925, fols. 51^{v}, 73, 90^{v}), dated c.1260 (fig. 114).[79] There is a juggler also in the Du Bois Hours (Pierpont Morgan Library MS. M.700, fol. 31^{v}) of c.1325–30 (fig. 115). This species of entertainer was also expected to do other kinds of tricks, including sleight of hand tricks like those performed by modern "magicians."[80] The sword swallowing trick illustrated on the Beatus page of the Glazier

Psalter (fig. 93) would have been identified as an act normally associated with a juggler. A more usual act would have been to juggle knives, as in the eleventh-century Tiberius Psalter (British Library MS. Cotton Tiberius C.vi, fol. 30^{v}), where a man, identified as Ethan (one of David's singers and cymbal players, named in *1 Paralipomenon* [*1 Chronicles*] 15.19), in the upper left hand corner is juggling three knives and three balls as musicians and King David play instruments (fig. 116). In another eleventh-century manuscript, St. Augustine's *Commentary on the Psalms* (Cambridge, Trinity College MS. B.5.26, fol. 1), a juggler is juggling three knives while a minstrel plays a rebec and King David (above) plays his harp (fig. 117).

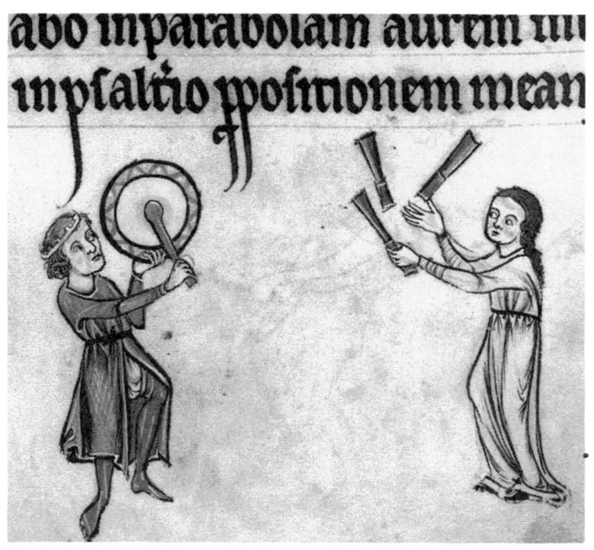

114. Juggler and tabor player. Rutland Psalter. British Library, MS. Add. 62,925, fol. 51^{v}. By permission of the British Library.

A final type of entertainer is the wild man or wodehouse, which seems strictly a medieval innovation, perhaps based on earlier regional folklore. The wild man, originally merely a woodman but sometimes identified with the idea of madness,[81] appears very frequently in dramatic records, and it has been said that he was present in pageantry in order to make way in the street for the processional display that was to follow.[82] Evidence has also been cited for the association of the wild man with fireworks.[83] These aspects are corroborated at Chester by a late description of the St. George procession in that city. Two wild men are described as follows:

> Item ij men in greene Evies set
> with worke vpon their other habet
> with blacke heare & black

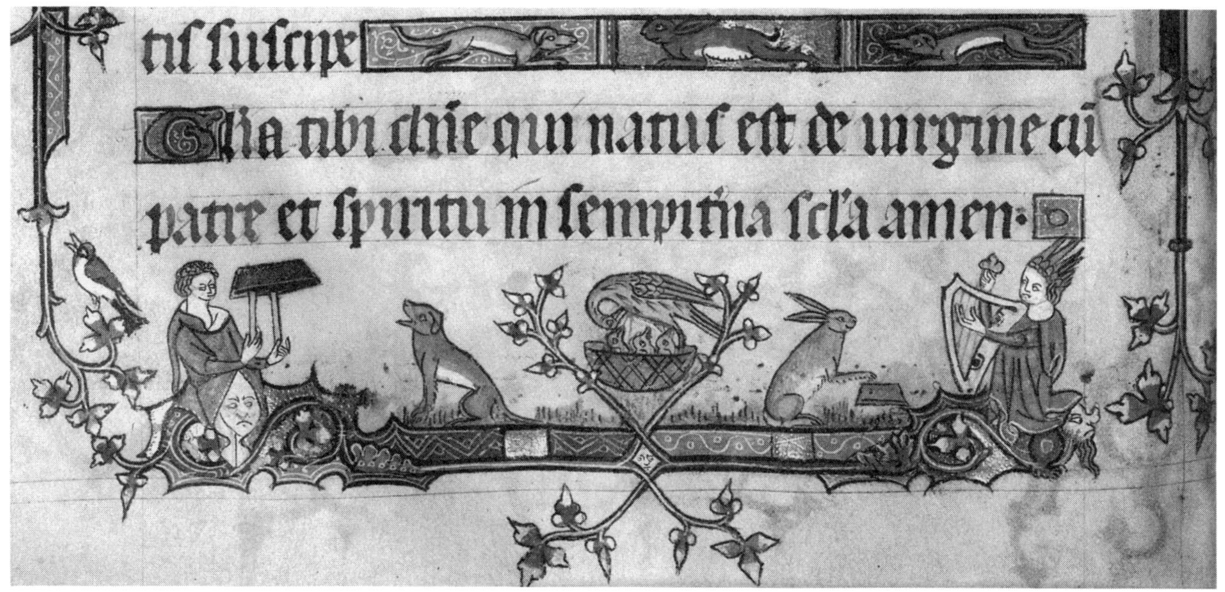

115. Juggler. Du Bois Hours. Pierpont Morgan Library, MS. M.700, fol. 31^{v}.1325–30.

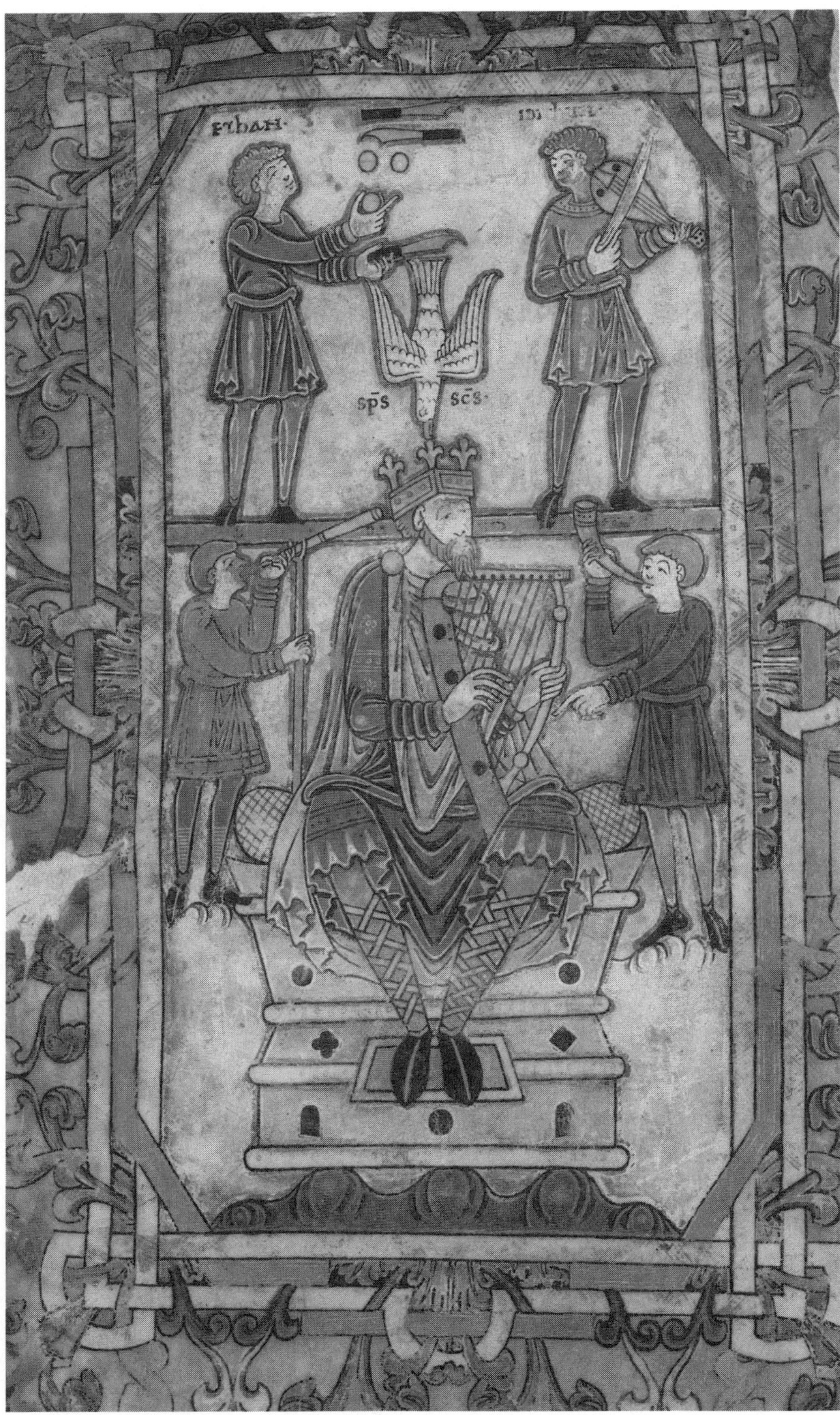

116. A juggler juggles knife and three balls while musicians play; King David plays harp. Tiberius Psalter. British Library, MS. Cotton Tiberius C.vi, fol. 30v. By permission of the British Library.

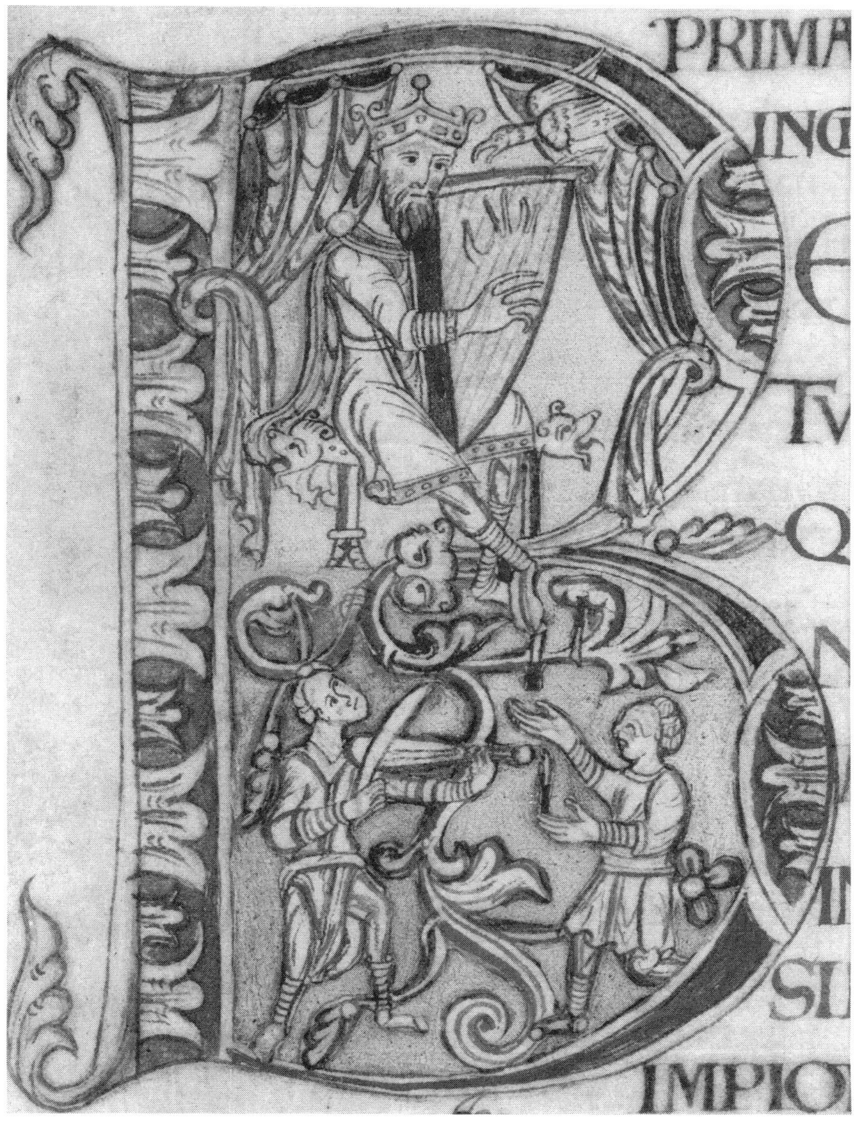

117. A juggler juggling three knives. Augustine, *Commentary on the Psalms*. Cambridge, Trinity College, MS. B.5.26, fol. 1. Courtesy of the Master and Fellows of Trinity College, Cambridge.

> beardes, very owgly to behould and garland vpon their heades with great Clubs in their handes with fier workes to scatter abroad to maintaine way for the rest of the shewe.[84]

Apparently, as the late Chester records cited here suggest, the wild man was usually arrayed in green, but at Wymondham, Norfolk, in 1537/38 his costume also included moss.[85] His rough character was seen to be prone to fighting—a scaffold for the entry of Henry VI of England into Paris in 1431 included a forest with a wild man and a wild woman engaged in a battle while the king was there to observe[86]—and additionally was given to lecherous behavior, illustrated in terms of the abduction of a lady in marginal illus-

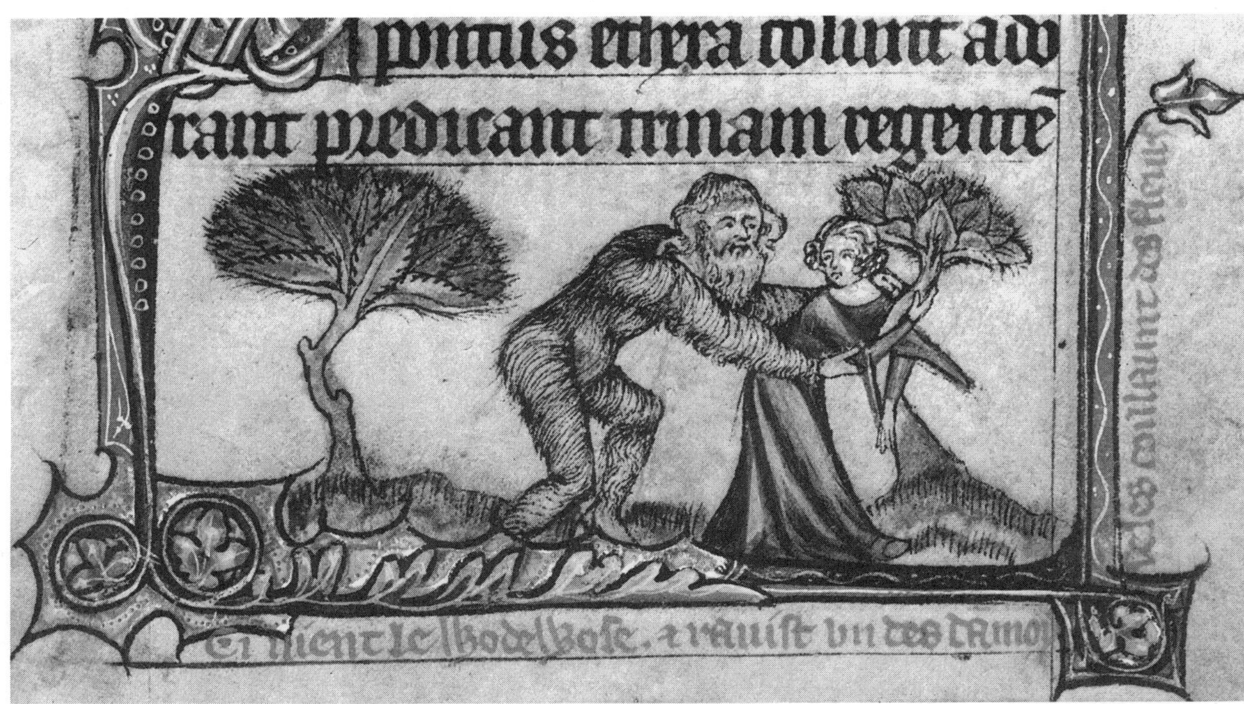

118. Wild man abducting a lady. Taymouth Hours. British Library, MS. Yates Thompson 13, fol. 62. By permission of the British Library.

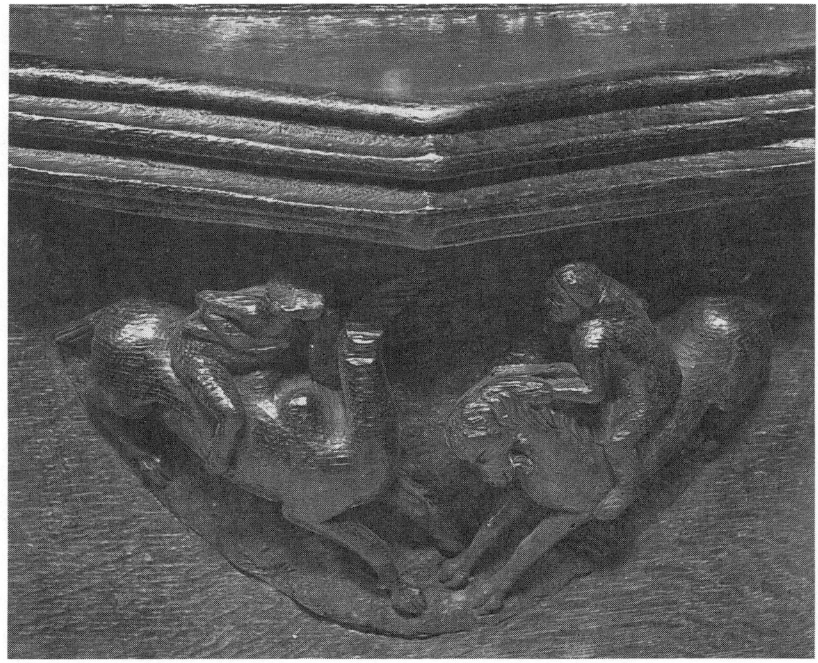

119. Mounted wild men attack each other. Misericord, Manchester Cathedral. Early sixteenth century. Courtesy of the Conway Library, Courtauld Institute of Art, and Fred H. Crossley and M. H. Ridgway.

trations in the Taymouth Hours (British Library MS. Yates Thompson 13, fols. 60^{v}–62^{v}). This wild man is big and hairy, as we might expect (fig. 118). Fortunately, the lady in this instance is rescued from rape by a knight, who fatally wounds the wild man (fol. 63). However, the knight's love (apparently improperly) is not requited by the lady.[87] The propensity to violence is shown on misericords, as in Henry VII's Chapel in Westminster Abbey, where two wild men fight with clubs,[88] or at Manchester Cathedral, where two wild men, mounted on a unicorn and a camel, are attacking each other (fig. 119).[89]

An illumination in Walter de Milemete's *De Nobilitatibus, Sapientiis, et Prudentiis Regum* (Oxford, Christ Church College MS. 92, fol. 64^{v}) shows a wild man and a wild woman, both of whom have long hair (fig. 120). M. R. James surmised that these figures may be intended to represent entertainers, either amateur or professional, impersonating male and female wodehouses.[90] If James' speculation has merit, this illustration would seem to be a most valuable one for our understanding of this theatrical type; nevertheless, we again need to be on our guard with regard to questions of verisimilitude in medieval art, which did not value drawing from life and more often than not chose the model book as its source over the depiction of actual events, whether theatrical or real-life.

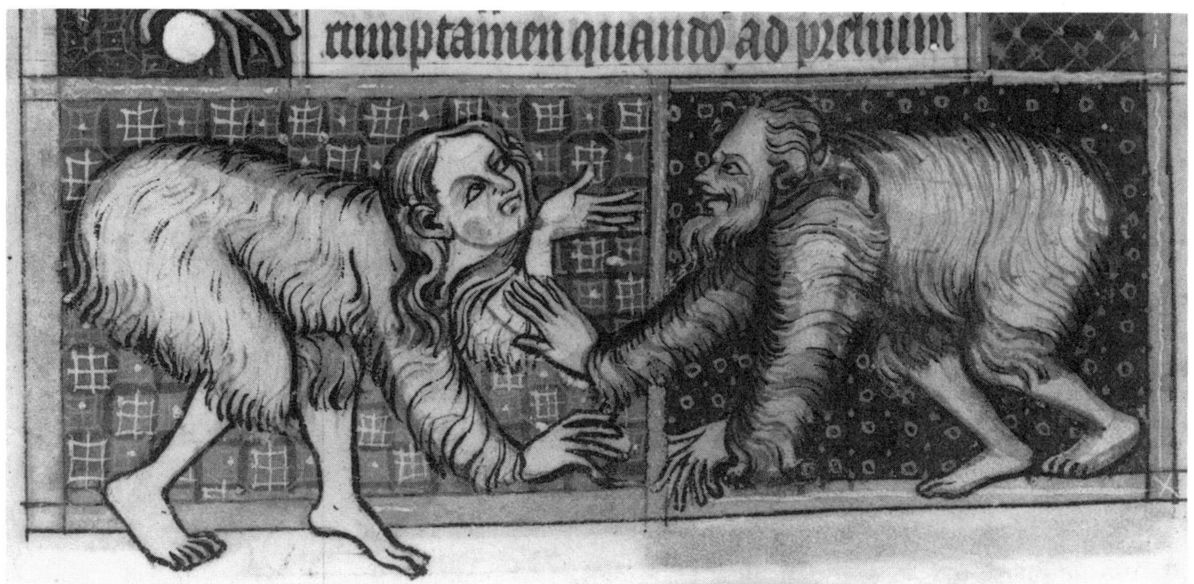

120. Wild man and wild woman. Milemete, *De Nobilitatibus, Sapientiis, et Prudentiis Regum*. Oxford, Christ Church College, MS. 92, fol. 64^{v}. Courtesy of the Governing Body of Christ Church, Oxford.

VII

MINSTRELS

Thomas de Cobham, writing in the thirteenth century, distinguished three kinds of entertainers or actors (*Tria sunt histrionem genera*).[1] The first kind engages in evil dances or acrobatics, exhibitions of nudity, or the use of horror-inspiring masks. Such actors or entertainers are utterly damned unless they give up their vocation. A second kind are given to idleness, and are lawless, prone to be vagabonds, and likely to be found around courts and individuals of power and authority. Their function is to wheedle themselves into favor and to tell slanderous stories. These too are to be condemned. A third kind of entertainer, however, is of a different variety:

> they have musical instruments to delight men with. And this kind can itself be subdivided. For some of them frequent public drinking places and licentious gatherings: there they sing various sorts of songs to incite people to licentious pleasures. And these entertainers, like the first two kinds, are in peril of damnation. But there are others, called jongleurs [*joculatores*], who sing the deeds of princes and the lives of the saints and give people comfort [*solatia*] both in sickness and in distress; these jongleurs do not perform the extremely disgusting acts that dancers do, male and female, and also those others who disport themselves in unseemly shapes and make themselves appear virtual apparitions by means of enchantments or in some other way.[2]

This kind of musician-entertainer is not to be condemned since his music refreshes the soul and he does not engage in evil or lascivious acts.

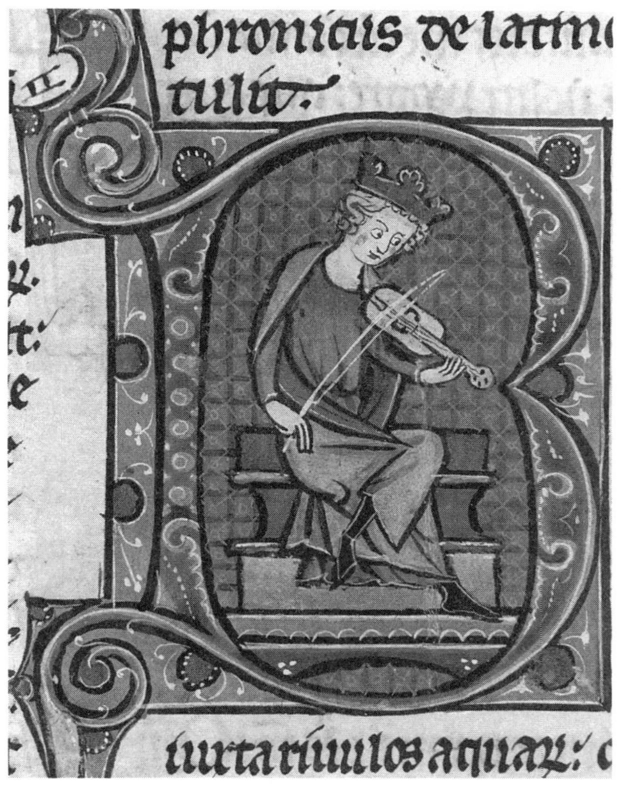

David, whose music soothed the troubled soul of King Saul, is the archetypal musician of this type, and not surprisingly the psalms came to be richly illustrated with acceptable minstrels[3] in psalters illuminated in England. Thus in a Bible illuminated by William of Devon (Cambridge, Emmanuel College MS. 2.1.6) King David plays a harp in one historiated initial on fol. 159^{r}, and in a nearby initial on the same page he is playing a four-string fidel with a long bow (fig. 121). An illumination in the Bedford Hours (British Library MS. Add. 42,131, fol. 166^{v}) presents the crowned

121. (At left) David plays a fidel. Initial at Psalm 1. Cambridge, Emmanuel College, MS. 2.1.6, fol. 161. c.1260–70. Reproduced with the permission of the Master and Fellows of Emmanuel College, Cambridge.

122. (Below) David plays a portative organ before the ark of the covenant. Bedford Hours. British Library, MS. Add. 42,131, fol. 166^{v}. Fifteenth century. By permission of the British Library.

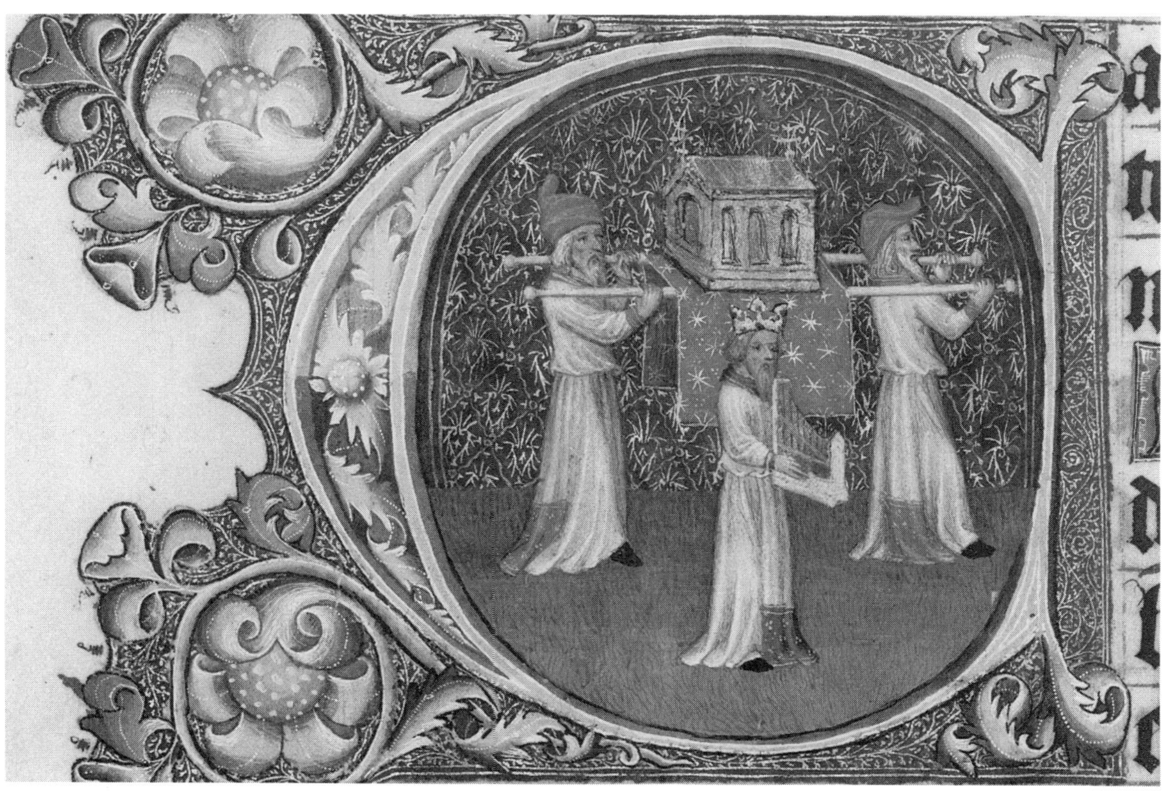

king playing a portative organ in procession in front of the ark of the covenant (fig. 122)—surely a sign of approval in this instance. In the Glazier Psalter in the Pierpont Morgan Library David as a young minstrel (at the left, top of the page) is playing a triangular harp before a king, Saul, who is reclining (center); at the right, seated behind him, is a psaltery player (fig. 93). Solace as a function of the minstrel's music is explicitly represented in a miniature in an early fourteenth-centu-

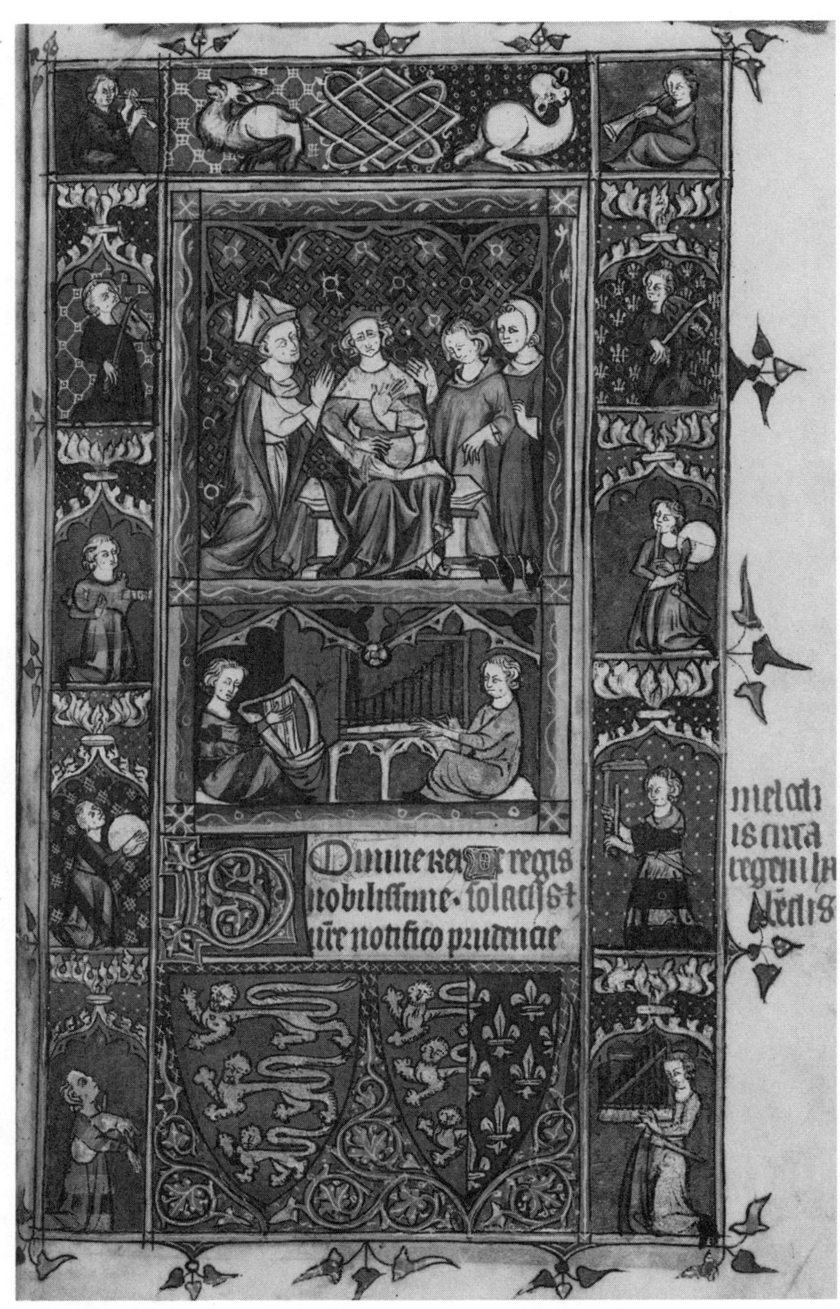

123. Instrumentalists. Walter de Milemete, *De Nobilitatibus, Sapientiis, et Prudentiis Regum*. Oxford, Christ Church College, MS. 92, fol. 43. Courtesy of the Governing Body of Christ Church, Oxford.

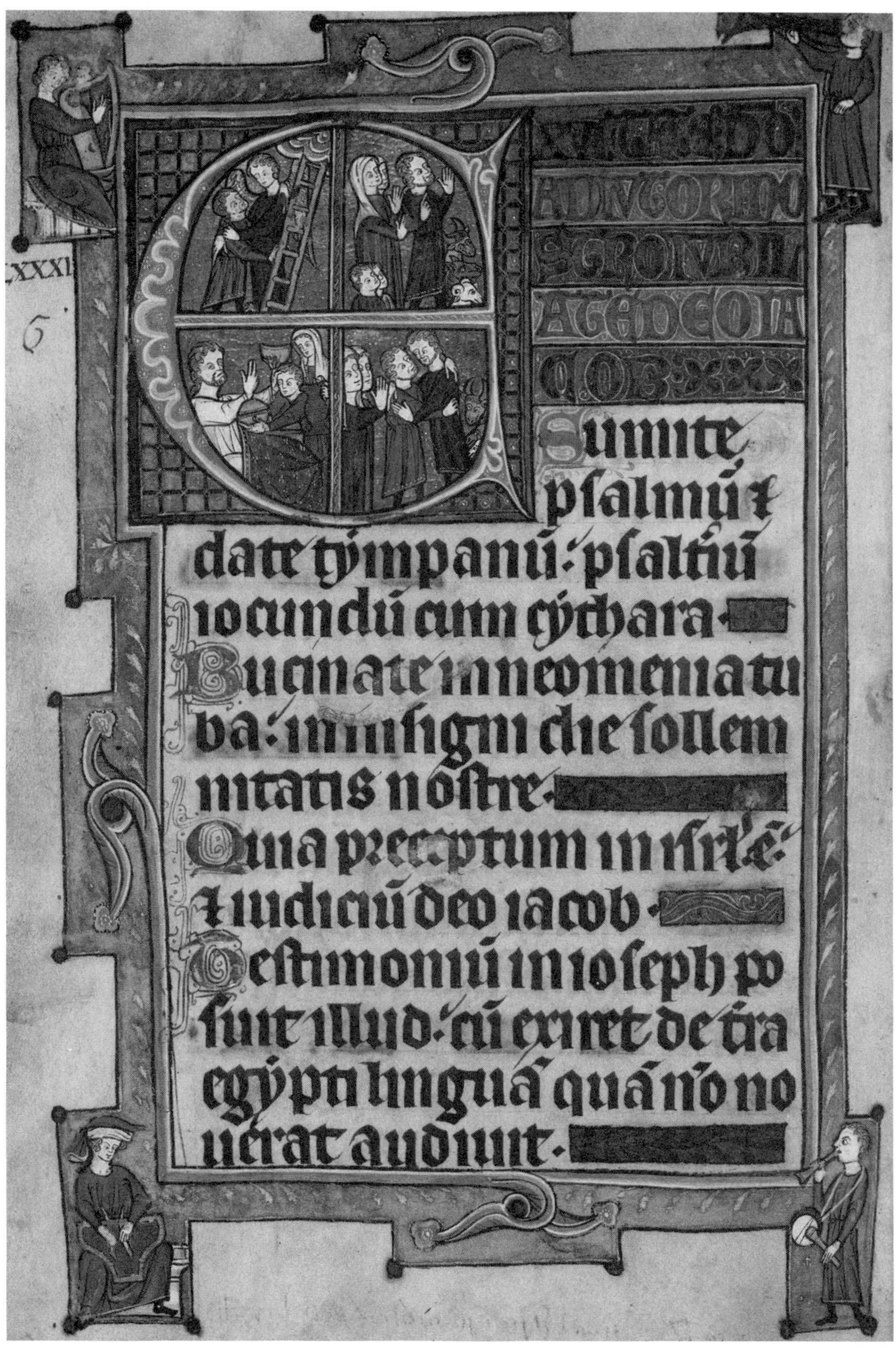

124. Minstrels. De la Twyere Psalter. New York Public Library, Astor, Lenox, and Tilden Foundation, MS. Spencer 2, fol. 137v. c.1304–10.

ry manuscript containing Walter de Milemete's *De Nobilitatibus, Sapientiis, et Prudentiis Regum* (Oxford, Christ Church College MS. 92, fol. 43); here instrumentalists are playing a harp and organ, while in the borders of the page are minstrels playing a pipe, a fidel, a gittern, a tabor, and bagpipes on the left, and a shawm, a crwth, a pipe and tabor, an unidentifiable percussion instrument, and a portative organ on the right (fig. 123).[4] The page is intended to illustrate the kind of recreation appropriate to a king.[5] But even a recreative function such as dancing could be accepted. The De la Twyere Psalter includes musicians—and perhaps also dancing minstrels in the historiated initial, at the lower right hand side—for its illustration of Psalm 81 (fig. 124), while for Psalm 96 musicians and dancers in addition to singing clerics appear in the border adjacent to the initial in the manuscript. Psalm 81 urges praise with timbrel and harp and trumpet—a crucial passage for defending the use of instruments even within the services of the Western Church. At the same time, illuminations such as these should not suggest a breaking down of the divisions which had been erected between the secular musician and the one who sang and performed in the Mass and other services. Further, the prejudice against any music other than vocal in such services still survived in many quarters up to the sixteenth century. There was also the recognition that the minstrel's music was *potentially* demonic and that it could lead astray in certain circumstances. For example, a misericord of c.1330 at Chichester Cathedral has a minstrel playing a fidel and kissing a female dancer.[6] Robert Mannyng of Brunne in *Handlyng Synne* was not alone in saying about minstrels that "Here doyng ys ful perylous."[7]

In Anglo-Saxon tradition, the *scop* was an honored poet, a reciter of verse of a distinguished kind, and, according to some scholars, an accomplished musician whose performance in the mead hall was admired by all; hence he was customarily richly rewarded by the nobles or the king for his service. The word *scop* could also be regarded as interchangeable with *comicus* (for example, with reference to Terence) and *tragicus*.[8] If the *scop*

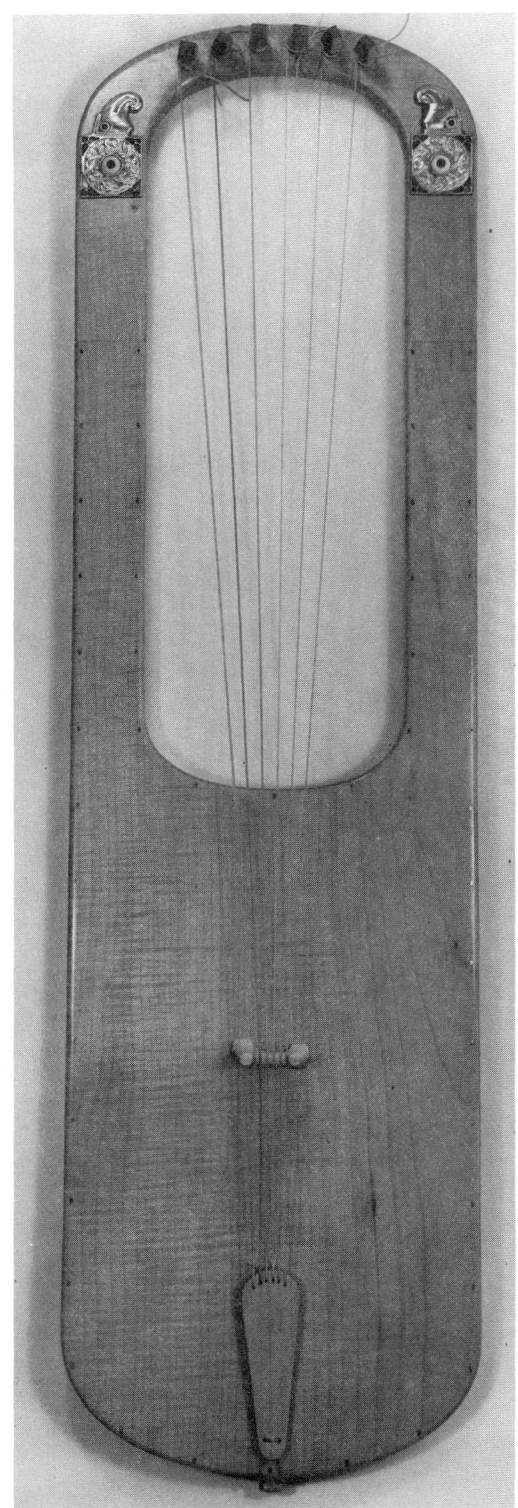

125. Reconstruction of the sixth-century lyre from the Sutton Hoo ship burial. By permission of the British Museum.

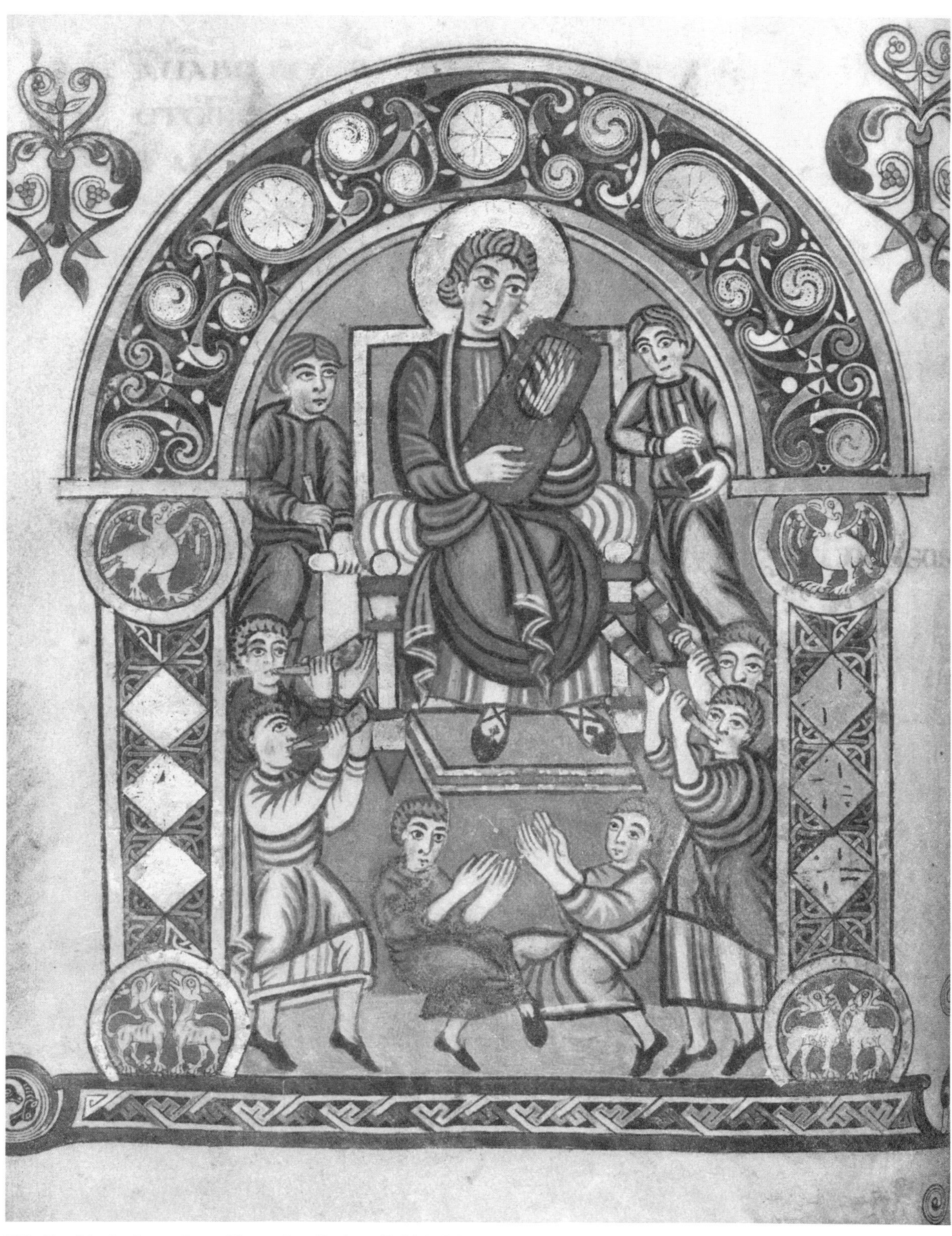

126. David playing a lyre. Vespasian Psalter. British Library, MS. Cotton Vespasian A.1, fol. 30^{v}. Eighth century. By permission of the British Library.

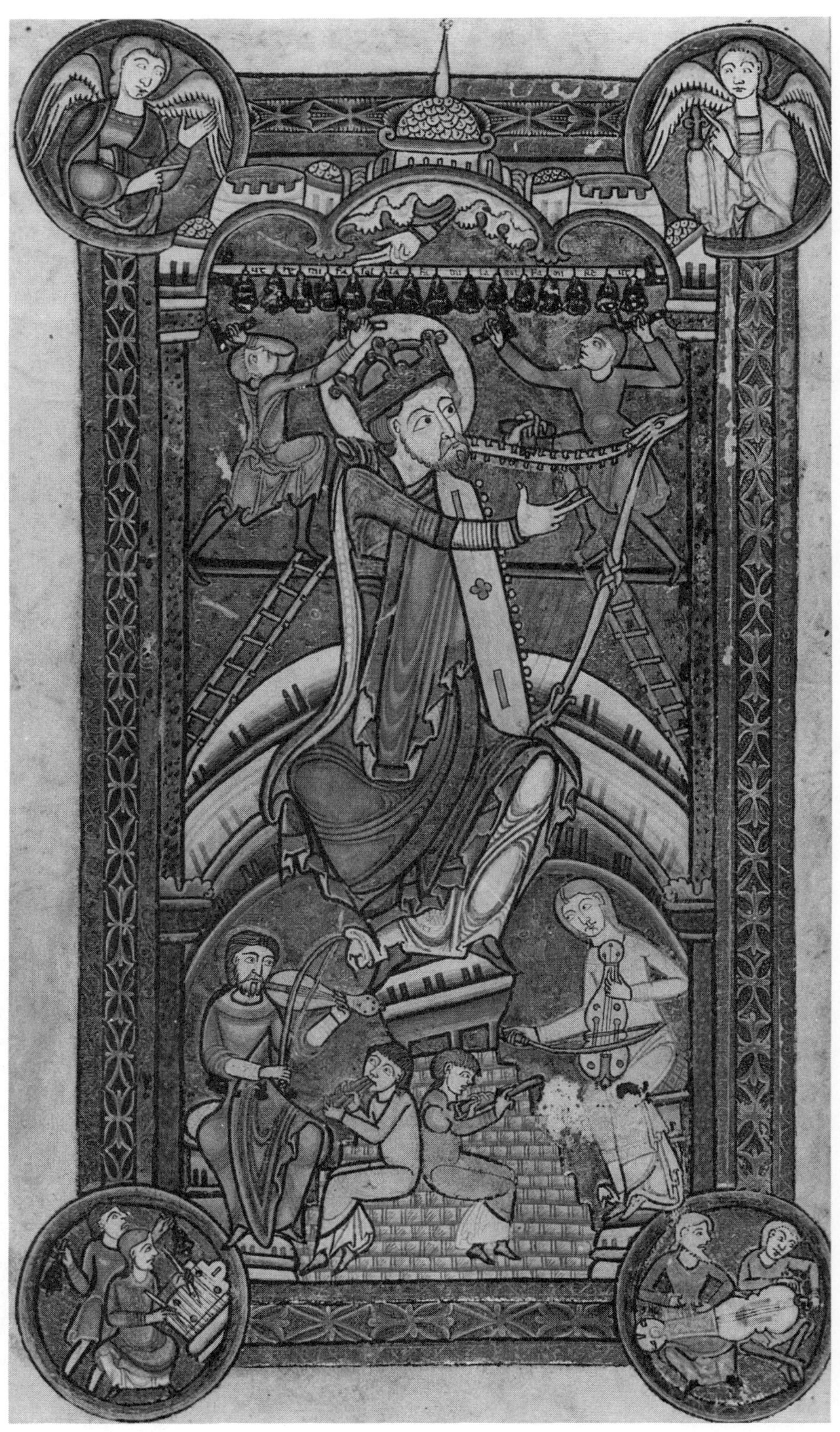

127. David and minstrels. Hunterian Psalter. Glasgow University Library, MS. Hunter 229, fol. 21^{v}. c.1170.

played a musical instrument, it was a "harp," which we may assume to have been the Germanic round harp or lyre.[9] To this instrument we shall return below. Whatever the *scop* was, however, it is important to note that he was commonly connected with theatrical activity of a serious kind.[10] And he was contrasted with the gleeman (*gleoman*) or itinerent musician-entertainer, whose role was likely "to incite people to licentious pleasures." A dancing gleeman in British Library MS. Cleopatra C.viii, fol. 19v, has already been noted above (fig. 107). As Jeff Opland notes, "gleomen were entertainers associated with those offshoots of the Roman theatres (pantomimus, mimus, scurra, jocista) who wandered about (parasitus, circulator) and were considered morally undesirable."[11] But the evidence remains ambiguous, and it seems, for example, that Widsith as a poet-performer combined the qualities of both the respected *scop* and the wandering gleeman. "Thus," says Widsith, "the minstrels [gleomen] of men go wandering, as fate directs, through many lands; they utter their need, speak the word of thanks; north or south, they always meet one wise in measures, liberal in gifts, who wishes to exalt his glory before the warriors."[12]

The presence of a Germanic lyre in the sixth-century Sutton Hoo ship burial (fig. 125) seems to militate further against Opland's thesis concerning the lack of instrumental accompaniment in the *scop*'s performance technique, for the instrument was apparently a highly valued treasure, not merely a thing to be played by low forms of entertainers who might show up at the king's hall. It was an instrument that might have been played by the king himself,[13] and the reconstruction presents us with a lyre[14] that is very much like the instrument played by none other than King David in a psalter (British Library MS. Cotton Vespasian A.1, fol. 30v) illuminated in Canterbury in the eighth century (fig. 126). In the illumination, King David is sitting on his throne and holding the lyre, which he is playing with his left hand. Four horn players and two other musicians (percussionists playing friction drums apparently related to the *rummelpot*, a Frisian instrument of the sixteenth century) stand beside him, while below two dancers are dancing. David, as a respected poet and musician, would have been identified with the *scop* rather than with the itinerant gleeman. The royal musician more commonly plays a harp rather than a lyre. He will sometimes take up other instruments, but essentially he remains an important role model who would influence the movement toward the rehabilitation of the concept of performance so that it would be rescued from derision. Chambers calls to our attention a passage in Robert Mannyng of Brunne's *Handlyng Synne* which tells us how the ascetic Robert Grosseteste later in the high Middle Ages "louede moche to here the harpe," played by his own harper, and defended his liking for this instrument by referring to the harpist King David and to its typological meaning which linked it with the cross.[15]

That harping had not been entirely free from the charge of frivolousness or dishonesty is implied in the reaction to the harping of St. Dunstan, who was accused of evil on account of his knowledge of popular traditions of song and therefore was banished from the court of King Athelstan in 935. According to an early account, "Dunstan was accustomed to play on musical instruments, in the knowledge of which he was distinguished in no ordinary way, and to lull not only his own, but the minds of many from the turbulent affairs of the world and toward the meditation of celestial harmony as much through the sweetness of his words (which he alternated, sometimes in his mother tongue, sometimes in another, [modo materna modo alia lingua]) as through the harmonious melody he expressed on those instruments."[16]As Opland argues, the continued survival in the tenth century of vernacular song and entertainment from pagan times is verified by Dunstan's accusers—a survival also indicated by the canons of Aelfric which forbid heathen songs.[17]

While the study of musical iconography has done much to define the instruments to be seen in the various visual arts of the pre-modern period—study which has led to the successful replication of many of these instruments—further scholarship will be required to understand the context of their use. In the Vespasian Psalter, for example, is the playing of lyre, trumpets, and friction drums indicative of an Anglo-Saxon orchestra at a court of a king, and further can such playing be regarded as appropriate for dancing? Or was the artist exhibiting a certain amount of creativity in drawing the musicians and dancers? More reliable, perhaps, are the costumes of the participants and their placement in two rows like the singers in the choir of a monastic church. It is thus a reasonable speculation that musicians playing and singing in groups in an Anglo-Saxon court might on occasion have lined up in such parallel rows, which would have given the place of honor to the monarch whose seat, on a raised platform, would have been placed in the same location in relation to the musicians as the high altar—the place where the Eucharist was consecrated—in a church. Other entertainments, such as dancing or miming, logically would have occurred immediately before the throne with the king as the primary spectator.

In the Tiberius Psalter (British Library MS. Cotton Tiberius C.vi, fol. 30^{v}) of c.1050, however, the arrangement of musicians around King David is different, with the king's throne placed frontally, a trumpet player and a gemshorn or hunting horn player—instrumentalists probably intended to represent the trumpets played before the ark in *1 Paralipomenon* 15.24—on his right and left behind him. And, above the wind instrument players, appear a player on a rebec—the first appearance of such an instrument in English iconography[18]—and the juggler, Ethan, noted above in the previous chapter (fig. 116). Still, the dove of the Holy Spirit descending upon David indicates that the meaning suggested above for his harping may also apply here, especially since the shape of the harp is indicative of David's role as a type of Christ at his crucifixion when his sinews would be stretched out like the strings on the musical instrument.[19] In the historiated initial from St. Augustine's *Commentary on the Psalms* (Cambridge, Trinity College MS. B.5.26, fol. 1) copied at Canterbury in c.1070–1100, David sits at the top, again playing a triangular harp, while above the harp is a dove representing the inspiration of the Holy Spirit; below are a rebec player and a juggler, who is juggling three knives (fig. 117). The Hunterian Psalter (Glasgow University Library MS. Hunter 229, fol. 21^{v}) of c.1170 has a group

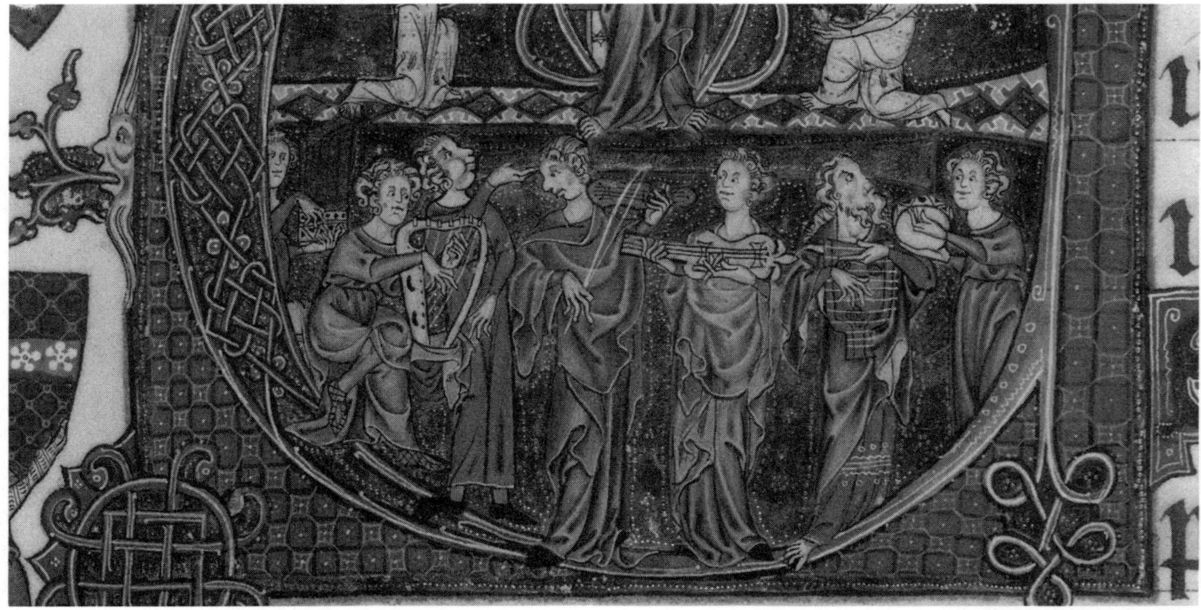

128. David and minstrels. Gorleston Psalter. British Library, MS. Add. 49,622, fol. 107^{v}. Early thirteenth century. By permission of the British Library.

of instrumentalists playing a rebec, medieval viol, pan pipes, and possibly a pipe or recorder[20] below a large figure of David with a triangular harp, while at the top of ladders above are two minstrels with hammers playing chimebells (fig. 127). In the two lower roundels are handbells and psaltery (left) and organistrum (right). Since David is tuning his harp, it has been suggested that the illustration shows a rehearsal of a type which might have taken place at a song school rather than an actual performance, though such an explanation seems rather to involve overinterpretation.[21]

A manuscript from the early thirteenth century that illustrates minstrels in some profusion is the Gorleston Psalter (British Library MS. Add. 49,622). At Psalm 80 (fol. 107^{v}), an orchestra of harp (David), rebec, gittern, psaltery, and tambourine is shown in an initial (fig. 128).[22] But one of the more interesting manuscripts for its depiction of minstrels is the Luttrell Psalter (British Library MS. Add. 42,130), which was illuminated in East Anglia in c.1325–35.[23] Among the examples of medieval minstrels in this manuscript is the figure of an organ player and his bellows blower in the bottom margin of fol. 55 (fig. 129). Elsewhere there are the dancing nakers player, which has been noted above, and other musicians playing instruments—portative organ, symphony, bagpipes—in the borders of fol. 176 (fig. 111), while on fol. 164^{v} a dancing pipe and tabor player and a shawm player lead a procession out of the city gates of Constantinople (the players of two long trumpets are yet to emerge at the rear of the dance).[24]

The variety of musical instruments in use in medieval England is also reflected in such documents as financial accounts. The minstrels attending a fourteenth-century English king, Edward III, are identified in his household accounts for the years 1344–47: five trumpet players, two clarion players, five pipers, a tabor player, a citole player, a "fideler" or player of the fidel, a nakers player, and three waits, who may have played shawms and other instruments.[25] In 1358 at the feast of the Garter at Windsor, twenty-four King's Minstrels are noted[26]—a band of considerable size,

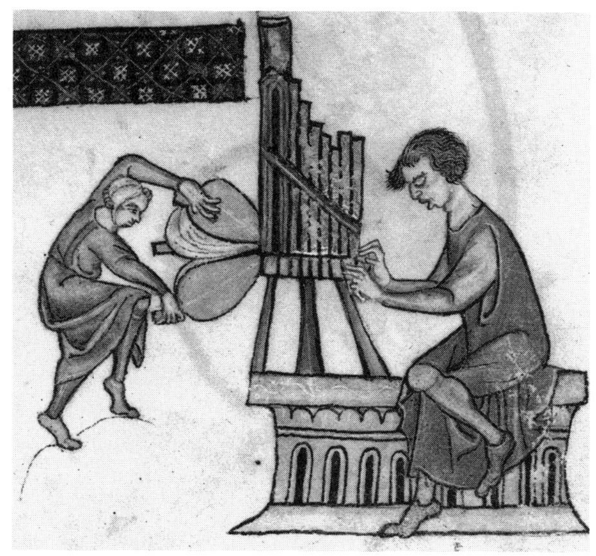

129. Marginal illustration showing organ player and bellows blower. Luttrell Psalter. British Library, MS. Add. 42,310, fol. 55. c.1325-35. By permission of the British Library.

if indeed they played together as a single ensemble.[27] Richard Rastall has provided an inventory of minstrels named in royal household records from 1296 through the first year of the reign of Henry VIII, and this listing identifies the following musical instruments in addition to those noted above: harp, viols, lute, crwth, organ, psaltery, gittern, cornemuse, bagpipes, sackbutt, recorder, rebec, and cornett.[28] The minstrels were organized under a minstrel king who had authority over the musicians and other designated persons since in the records the term 'minstrel' included some who were not actually musicians but instead were waferers, fools, dancers, bearwards, or even zoo keepers.[29] From the standpoint of the present survey it is also perhaps necessary to note that the connection between the music of town minstrels and civic dramatic activity was direct, with the local musicians along with singing men from church or cathedral providing the music needed in staging plays.[30]

A fine illumination in the French style illustrating the use of musical instruments in processions may be found in a copy of the *Romance of Alexander* (fig. 130) said, probably incorrectly, to have been produced in England (Paris, Bibliothèque Nationale MS. fr 22547, fol. 245^v) and dating from c.1380. Harp, trumpet, shawms, and lutes are played by fashionably dressed men walking in an outdoor procession and accompanying horse-drawn pageant wagons. Whether all of these instruments would in fact have been used in an outdoor situation is debatable, and by the fifteenth century there was a clear distinction between *haut* and *bas* instruments, with the loud ones being normally regarded as more appropriate for outdoor use.[31] Obviously the trumpet and shawm—loud instruments—would have been better adapted than the harp or lute for use in a procession such as the one shown in the illustration. As would have been customary for a religious festival, the street in this miniature is strewn with branches.

Processions of a lesser sort might also be indoor, and these too might be led by musicians. In the Queen Mary Psalter (British Library MS. Royal 2.B.vii, fols. 184^v–185^r) of the first quarter of the fourteenth century, a procession of servers led by a fidel player proceeds in the top margin of the page toward the table with a seated king and two others on the next page (fig. 131); before the table another server is kneeling as he places a serving dish before the monarch. The normal presence of minstrels as entertainers at feasts[32] is in-

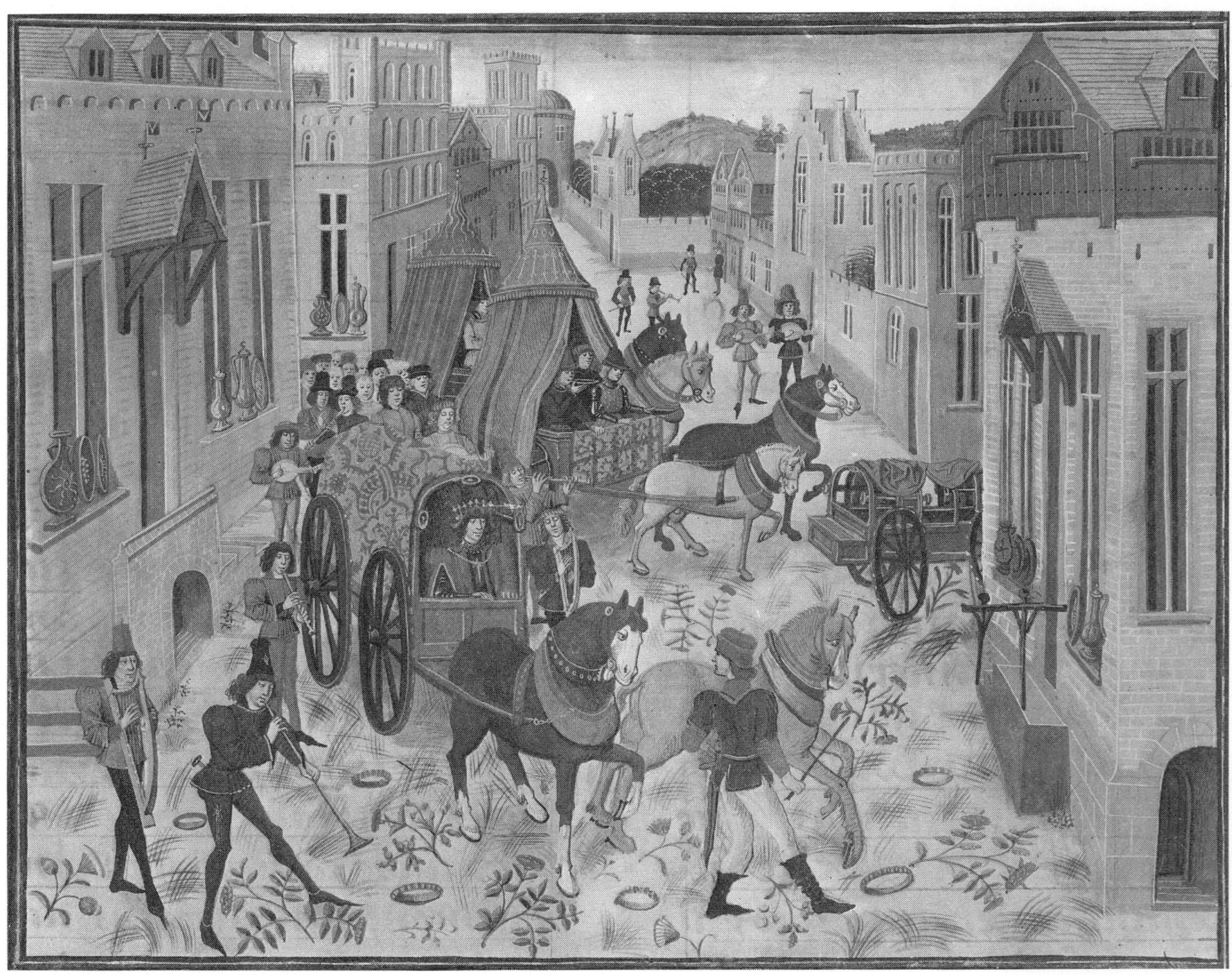

130. Minstrels in a procession. *Romance of Alexander*. Paris, Bibliothèque Nationale, MS. fr 22547, fol. 245^v. c.1380. Photograph: Bibl. Nat. Paris.

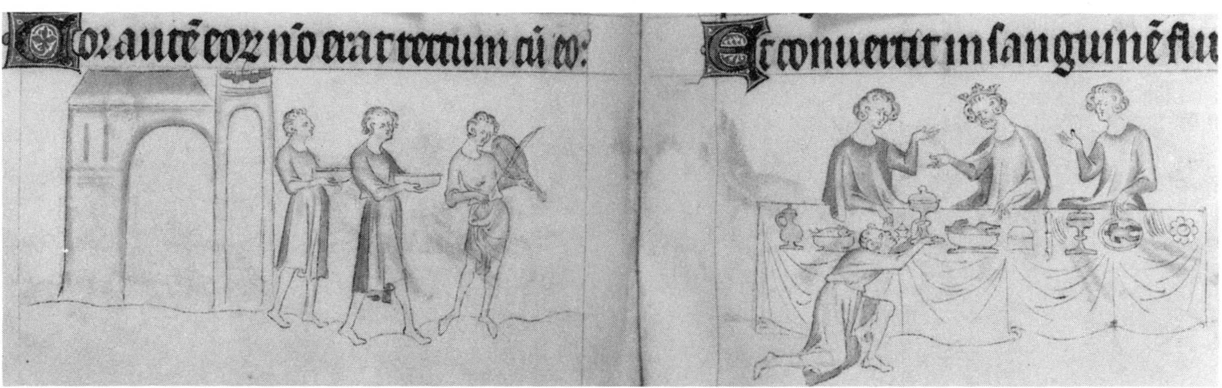

131. Procession led by minstrel. Queen Mary Psalter. British Library, MS. Royal 2.B.vii, fols.184v–185r. c.1309–26. By permission of the British Library.

dicated by the N-town cycle when Herod orders his minstrel to "blowe up . . . with all your myght" since "the servyse comyth in sone";[33] that the practice was not a late innovation is demonstrated in a single leaf from a twelfth-century Bible illuminated at Bury St. Edmunds (Pierpont Morgan Library MS. M.521) which illustrates the return of the prodigal son (fig. 132). At the right the father welcomes his son back to his home, and at the left is shown the killing of the fatted calf. Between these two scenes is the actual scene of the feast, with a minstrel on the left playing a rebec and at the right another minstrel holding a symphony.[34] A set of louder instruments is present in an illustration in a copy of the *Speculum humanae salvationis* (c.1400) now in the same library (Pierpont Morgan Library MS. M.766, fol. 64); here minstrels are playing shawms, one of which has a flared bell, and nakers at the feast of Ahasuerus (fig. 133).[35] In this instance the minstrels are standing in front of the table, which separates the entertainers from those who are feast-

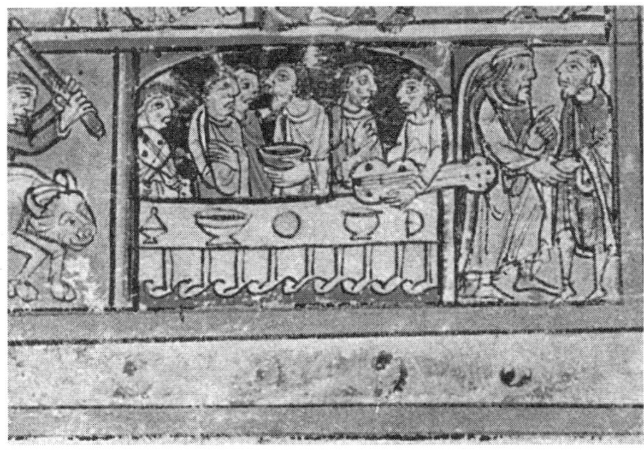

132. Return of the Prodigal Son. Bible. Pierpont Morgan Library MS. M.521. Twelfth century.

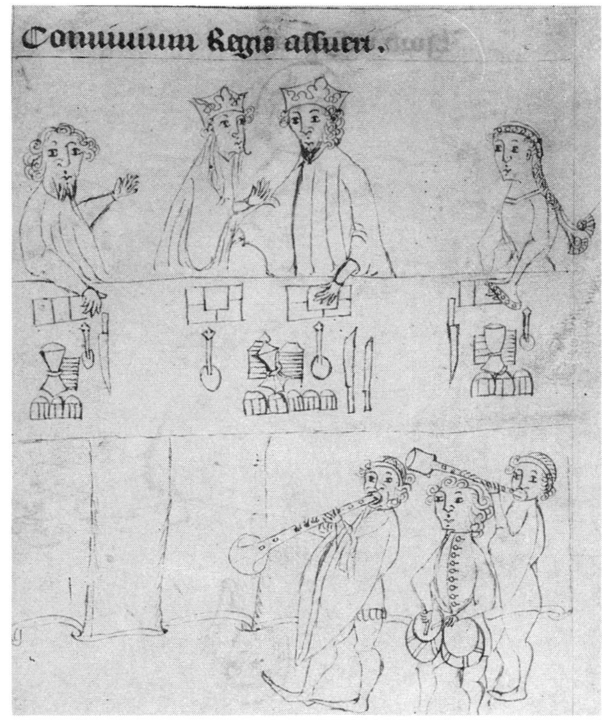

133. Minstrels at feast of Ahasuerus. *Speculum humanae salvationis*. Pierpont Morgan Library MS. M.766, fol. 64. c.1400.

ing—a conventional arrangement in aristocratic households when a minstrels' gallery is not used. A similar separation, with the musicians at one side, is present in a fifteenth-century copy of the *Speculum humanae salvationis* (British Library MS. Harley 2838, fol. 45); here instrumentalists play a straight trumpet, a tabor, and possibly a shawm (fig. 134). Another illumination on the same page shows a rebec player and a pipe player standing at one side in front of the table—soft instruments, which were often favored for such occasions.

Manuscript illuminations such as those cited above represent aristocratic traditions on the whole. But there is ample evidence from other media, which reflect various social strata from the designers of sculpture for small village churches —e.g., the fidel player-minstrel on a capital at

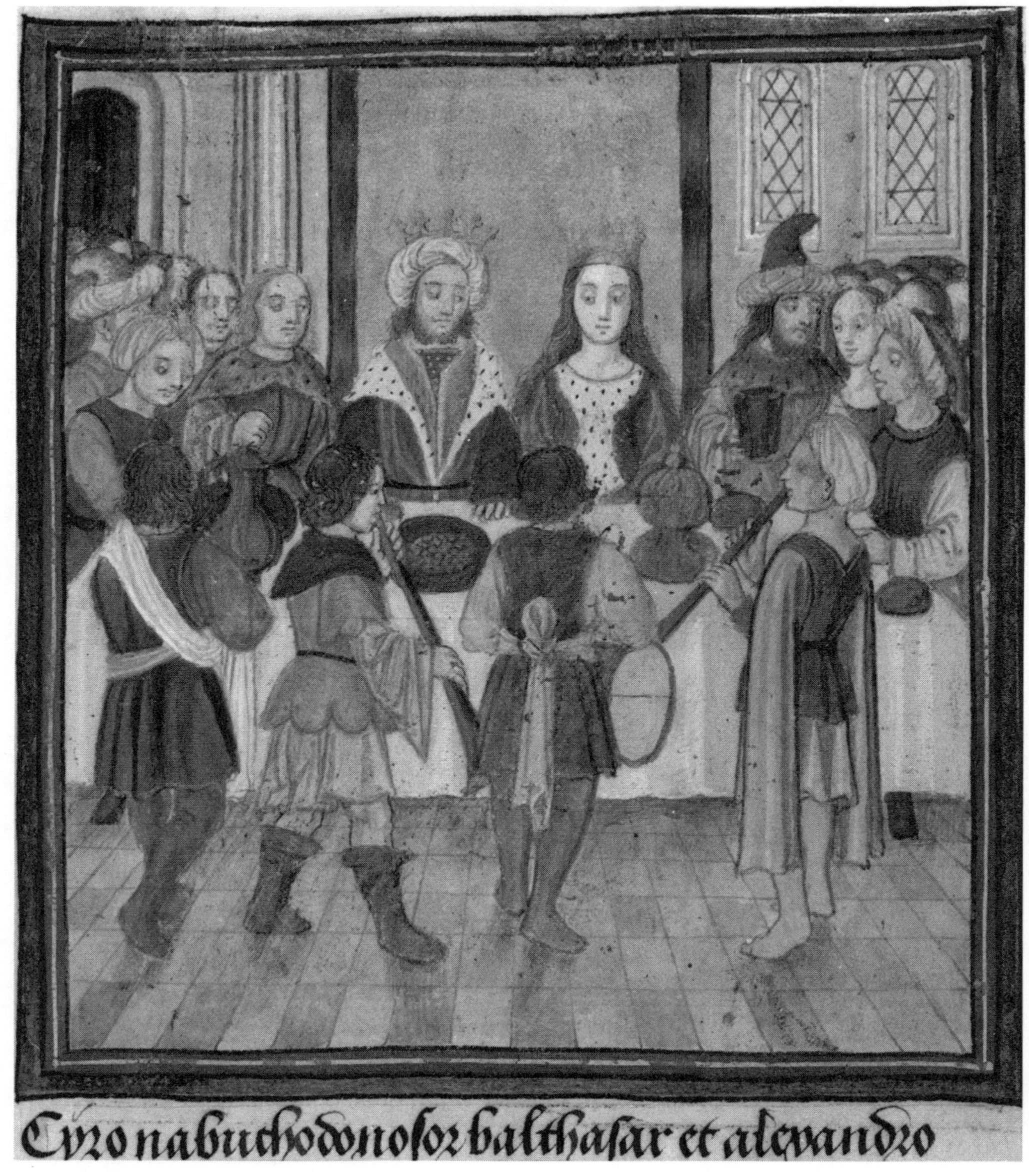

134. Minstrels at a feast. *Speculum humanae salvationis*. British Library MS. Harley 2838, fol. 45. Fifteenth century.

Hanwell, Oxfordshire (fig. 135)—to very rich ecclesiastical establishments such as Norwich Cathedral, where gittern and fidel players, riding on grotesque beasts with human heads, adorn one of the fourteenth-century bosses in the cloister (fig. 136). Another cloister boss illustrates a piper and tabor player (fig. 137). Some earlier examples are the minstrels playing pipe, harp, and fidel on roundels on the Prior's door at Ely Cathedral (figs. 138–39; cf. fig. 102); these are dated c.1135, and, though worn, are illustrative of secular music since there are also dancers, people drinking, and a couple kissing in addition to the acrobat noted above (p. 88).[36] A minstrel, who is kneeling on his right knee, is playing a pipe and tabor on a misericord of c.1260 at Exeter Cathedral (fig. 140).[37] In painted glass of the fourteenth century in St. Mary's Church, Merevale, Warwickshire, a nonecclesiastical organist is playing an organ (fig. 141), while on a bench-end at North Cadbury, Somerset, a fashionably dressed minstrel is performing on a transverse flute (fig. 142). An important example is the bench-end, carved after 1523, at the church of St. Nonna, Altarnun, Cornwall, where a minstrel is playing a fidel (fig. 143) which, according to Mary Remnant, shares some similarities with the two fragmentary instruments recovered from Henry VIII's warship, the Mary Rose, that sank on 19 July 1545.[38] This woodcarving is reputed to be by Robart Daye, who also carved a minstrel playing a bagpipe (fig. 144). In fifteenth-century painted glass there is a representation of a rebec player at All Saints, North Street[39]—he is a musician from an aristocratic household, as his garments indicate (fig. 145) —and at All Saints, Besthorpe, minstrels play a lute and a rebec (fig. 146).[40]

The minstrels' pillar, from 1524, in St. Mary's, Beverley, provides a useful example of musician-entertainers; standing around the pillar are players who played pipe and tabor, rebec, lute, and shawm (fig. 147). The central player has completely lost his instrument, and the pipe and rebec are also broken away. Other representations of minstrels roughly contemporary with the minstrels' pillar in this church appear on corbels: a bagpipe player (fig. 148) and a musician singing and playing a lute with a bow as if it were a rebec. The latter, which incorporates the artist's fantasy, illustrates a common peril in interpreting medieval illustrations of minstrels and entertainers.

But one of the richest sources of sculp-

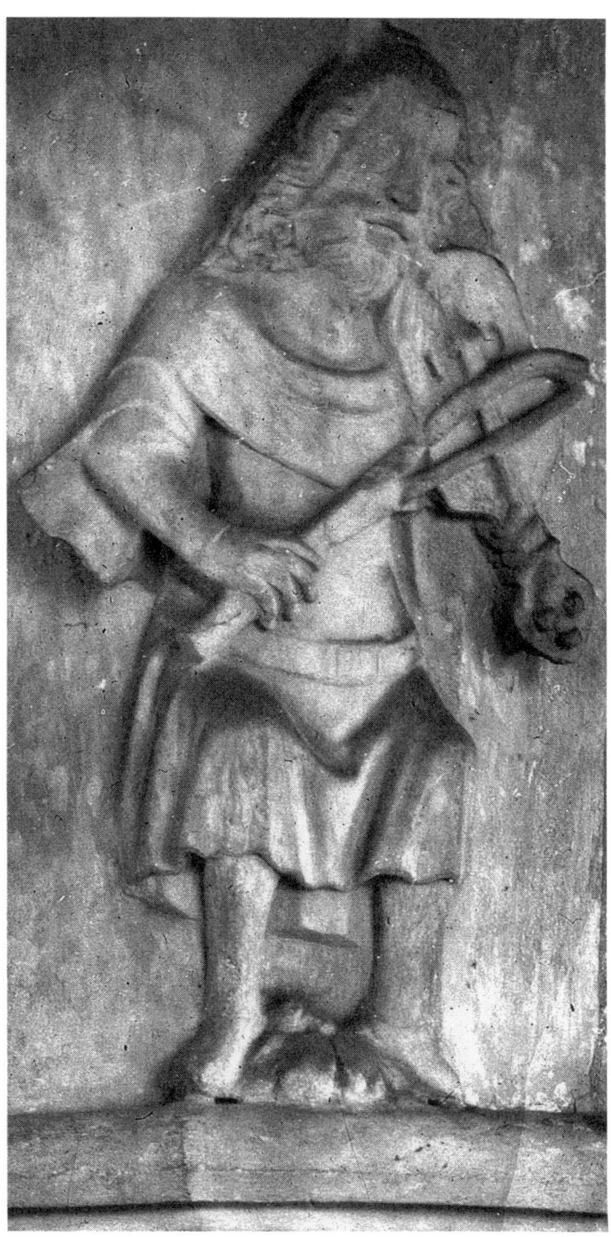

135. Minstrel playing fidel. Capital, Hanwell, Oxfordshire. By permission of the Royal Commission on the Historical Monuments of England.

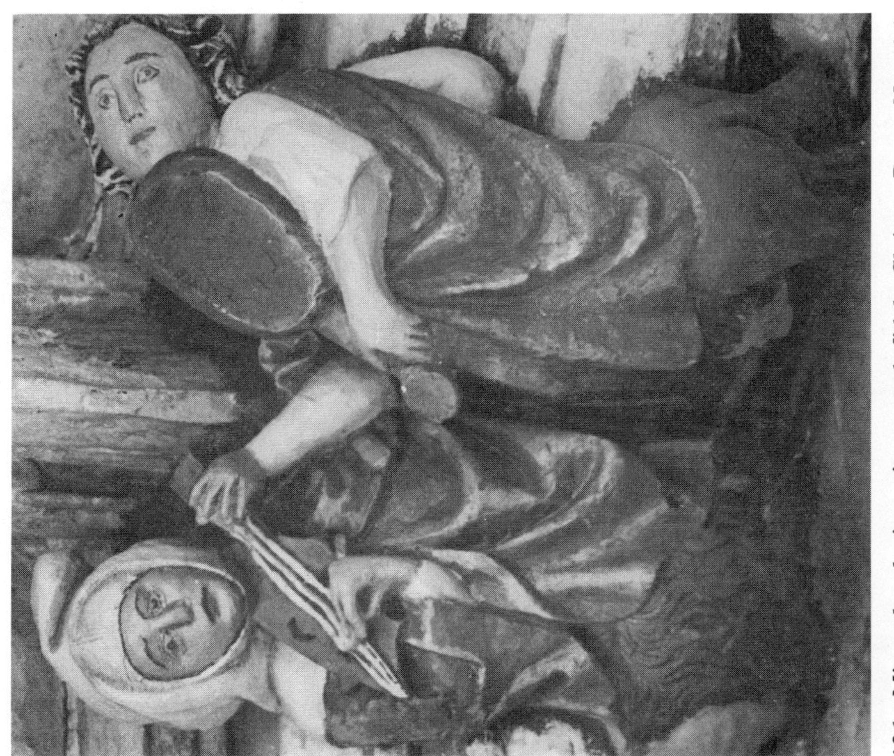

136. Minstrels playing gittern and fidel. Cloister Boss, Norwich Cathedral. Fourteenth century. By permission of the Royal Commission on the Historical Monuments of England.

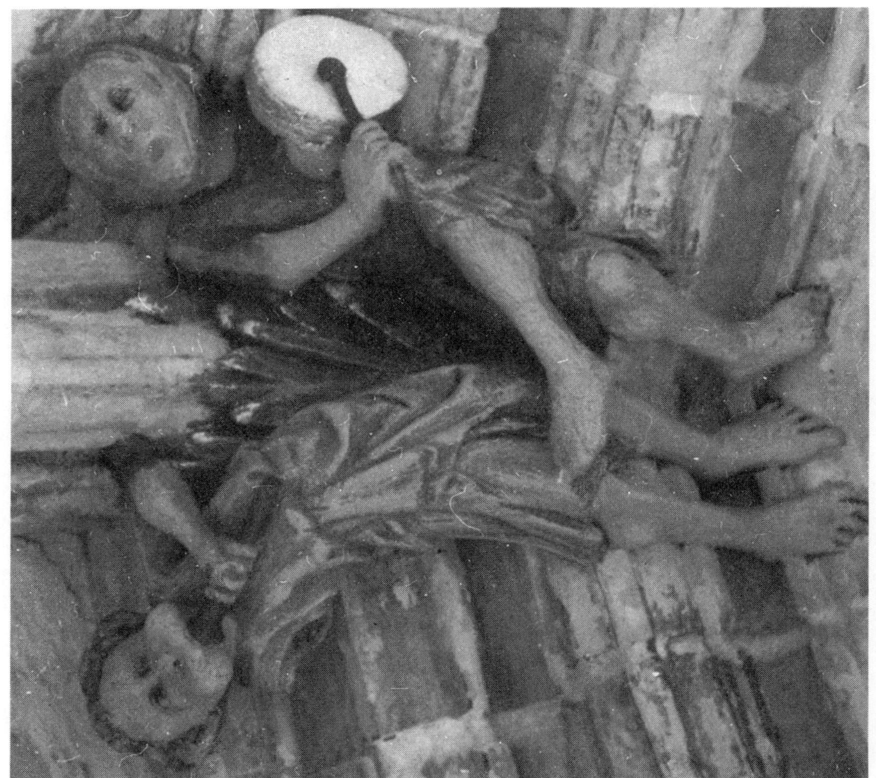

137. Pipe and tabor. Cloister boss, Norwich Cathedral. Fourteenth century. By permission of the Royal Commission on the Historical Monuments of England.

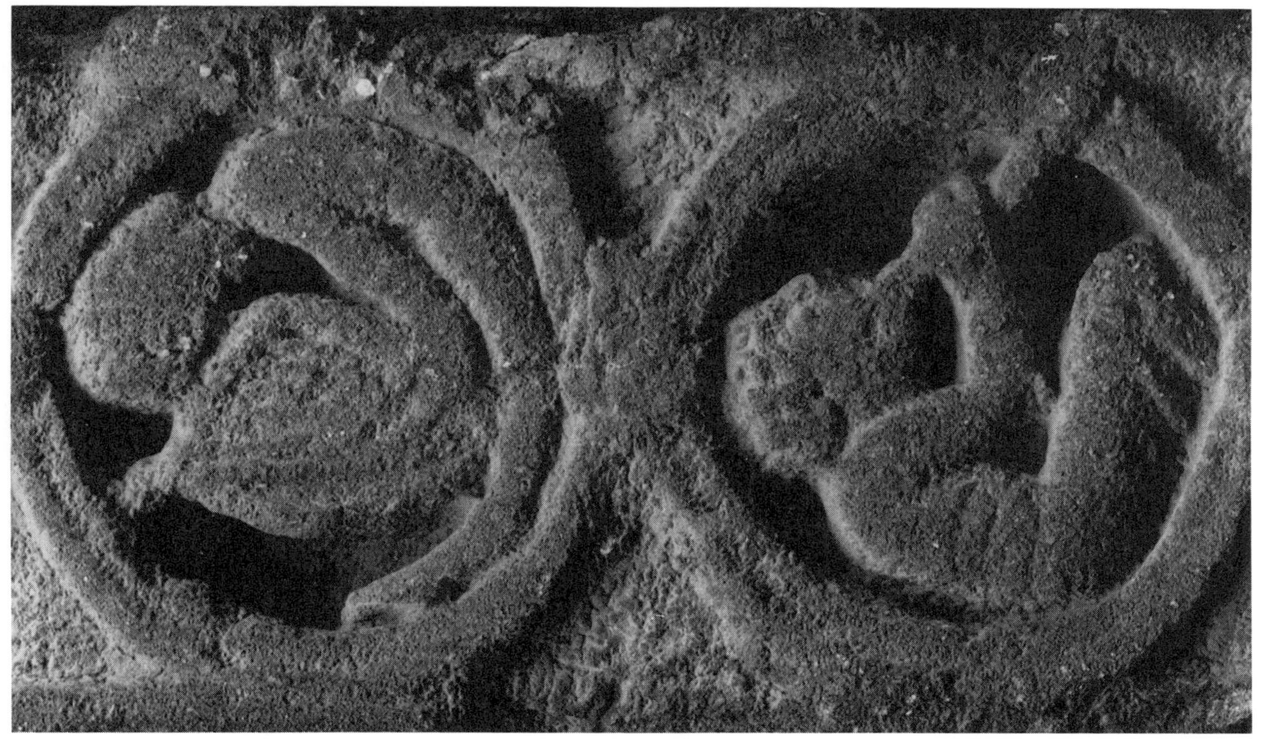

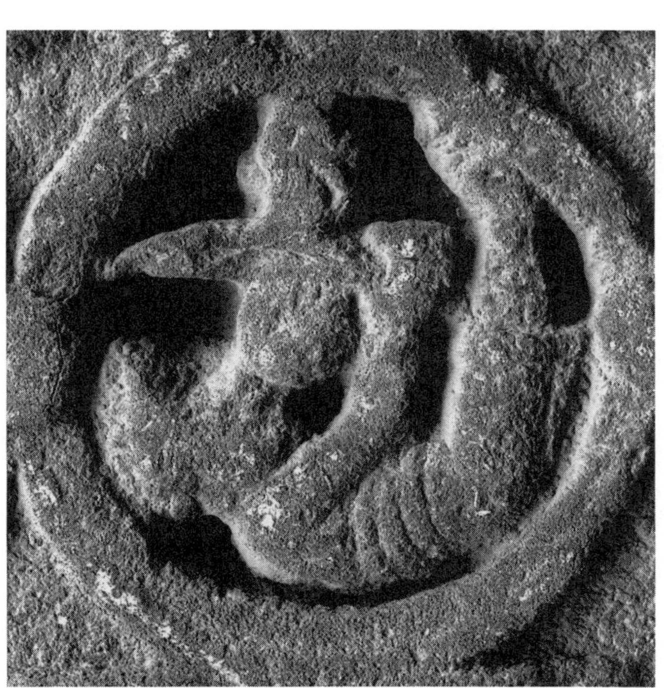

138. (Above) Minstrel playing fidel. Prior's door, Ely Cathedral, c.1135. Courtesy of the Conway Library, Courtauld Institute of Art.

139. (At right) Minstrels playing harp (above) and pipe (below). Prior's door, Ely Cathedral. c.1135. Courtesy of the Conway Library, Courtauld Institute of Art.

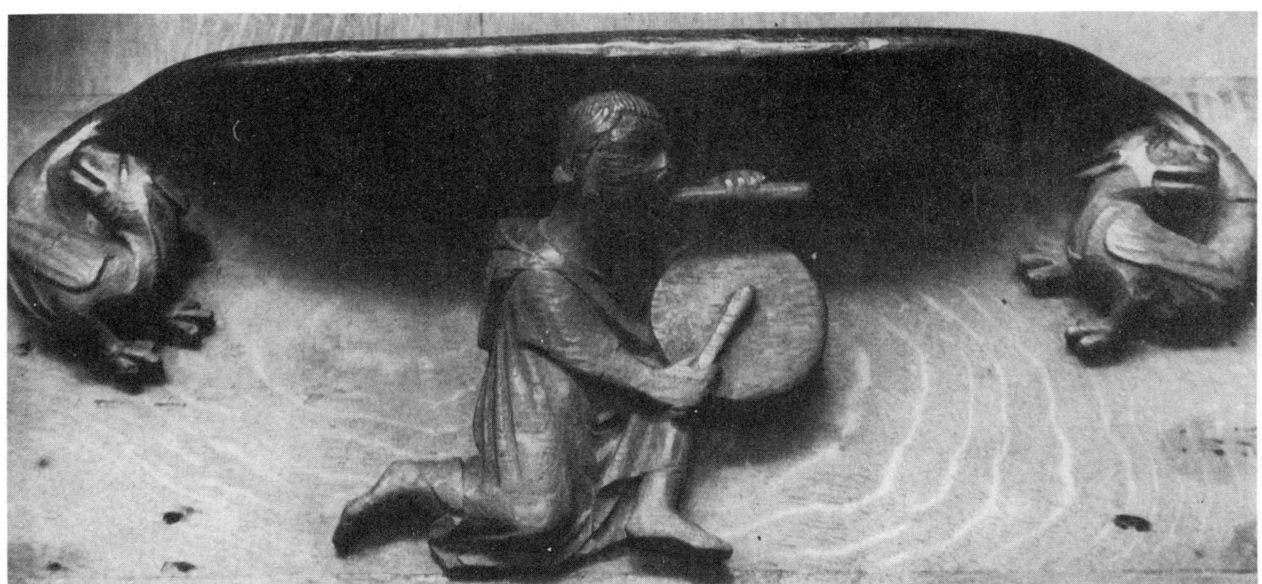

140. Minstrel playing pipe and tabor. Misericord, Exeter Cathedral. c.1260. By permission of the Royal Commission on the Historical Monuments of England.

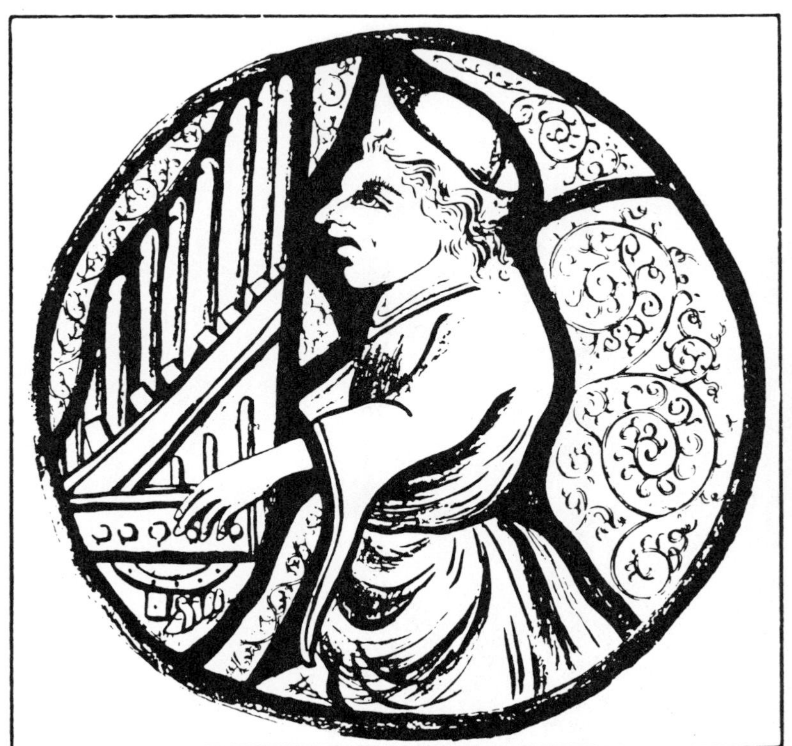

141. Organ player. Painted glass, Merevale, Warwickshire. Reproduced from J. Charles Cox, *English Church Fittings and Accessories* (London: B. T. Batsford, Ltd., 1923).

tures showing minstrels in all of England is to be found in Beverley Minster, where an entire orchestra was carved in stone, mostly in the nave and north aisle, around 1330. Unfortunately, many of the figures of minstrels were "restored," mainly by John Percy Baker in modern times, and hence their iconography needs to be approached with care. Such an attractive figure as the bagpiper (fig. 149) in the north aisle, for example, holds an instrument

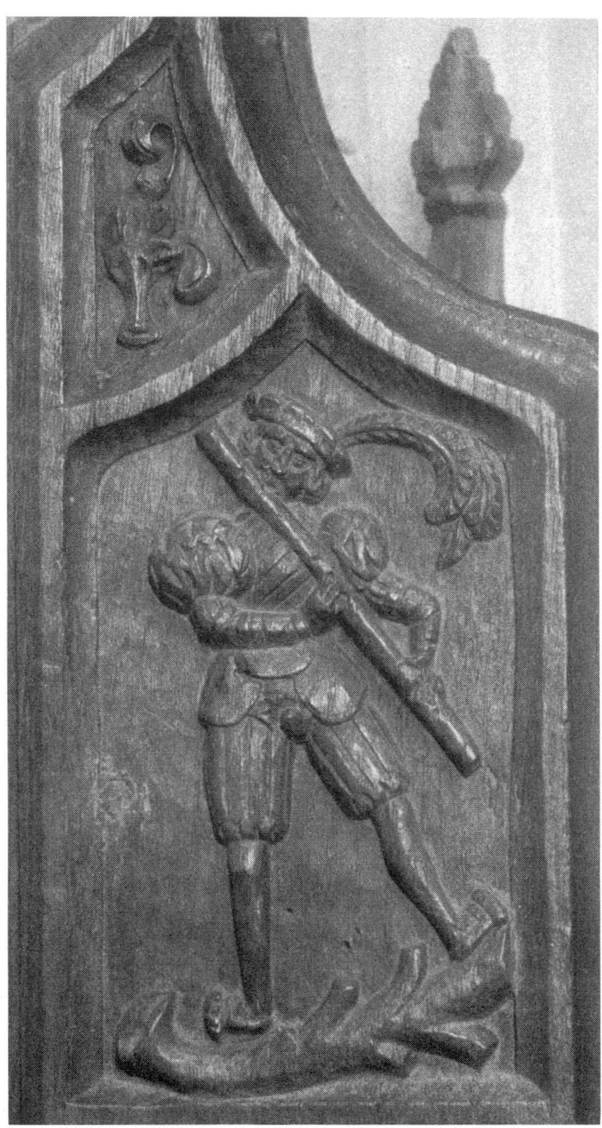

142. Minstrel playing flute. Bench-end, North Cadbury, Somerset. By permission of the Royal Commission on the Historical Monuments of England.

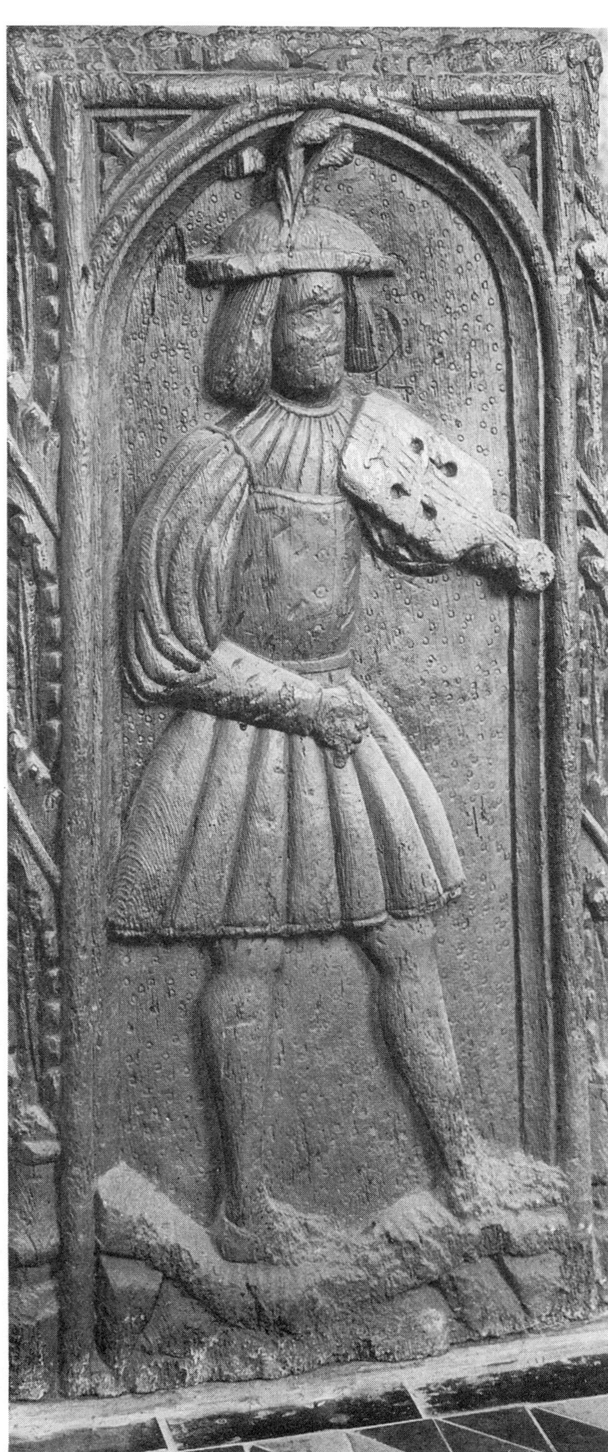

143. Minstrel playing fidel. Bench-end, Altarnun, Cornwall. After 1523. By permission of the Royal Commission on the Historical Monuments of England.

that is only in part original: while the bag is original, the chanter, along with the hands of the player, may be judged to be modern, and the blowpipe has also been questioned.[41] In the case of a gittern player (fig. 150), also in the nave aisle, a modern head illustrating a man singing suggests the practice of singing to one's own accompaniment on this instrument; however, the head is a

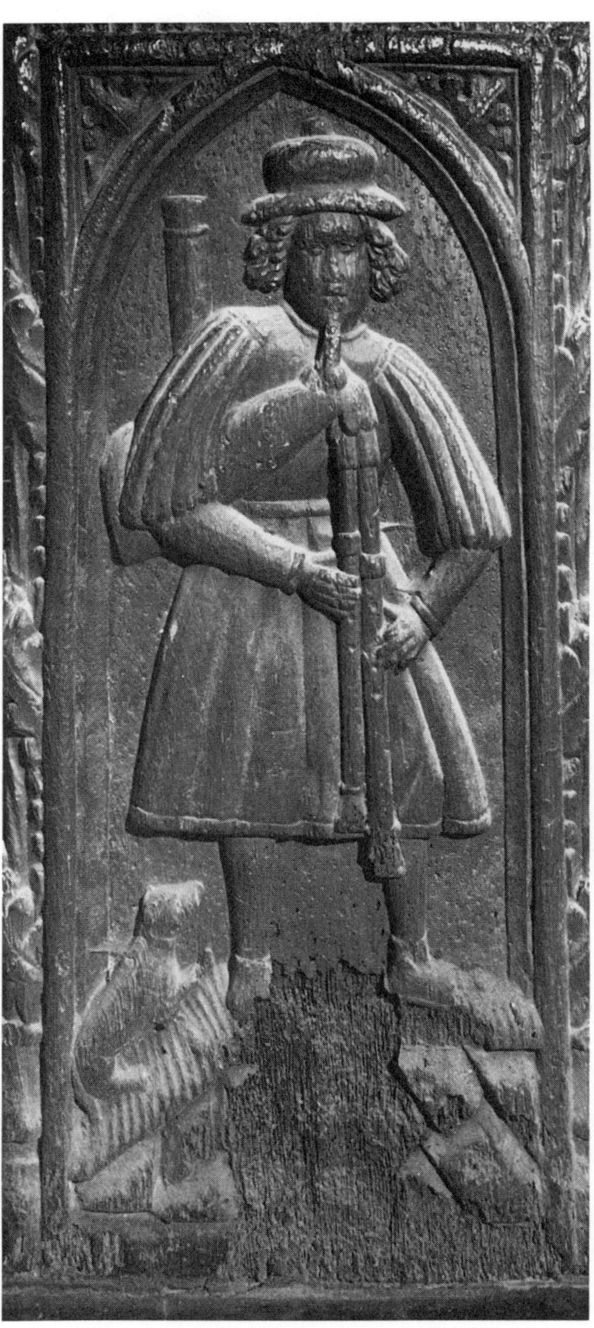

144. Minstrel playing bagpipes. Bench-end, Altarnun, Cornwall. By permission of the Royal Commission on the Historical Monuments of England.

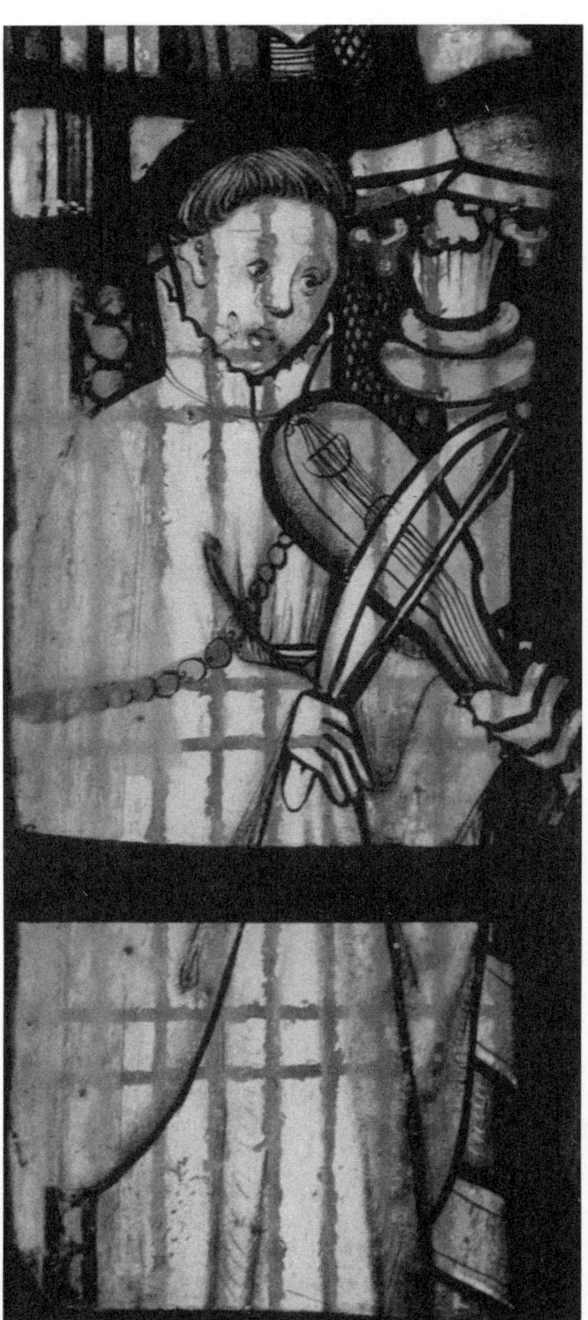

145. Rebec player. Painted glass, All Saints, North Street, York. Fifteenth century. Photograph: David O'Connor.

modern insertion—a lesson, actually, in the potential of "restored" examples of the visual arts to mislead. The original sculpture might have included the feature of the singing musician, but on the other hand there is no reason to believe that this was the case. However, in this instance the instrument is in very good condition except for the peg box, which has been copied from elsewhere in the minster.[42]

More reliable among this set of minstrels

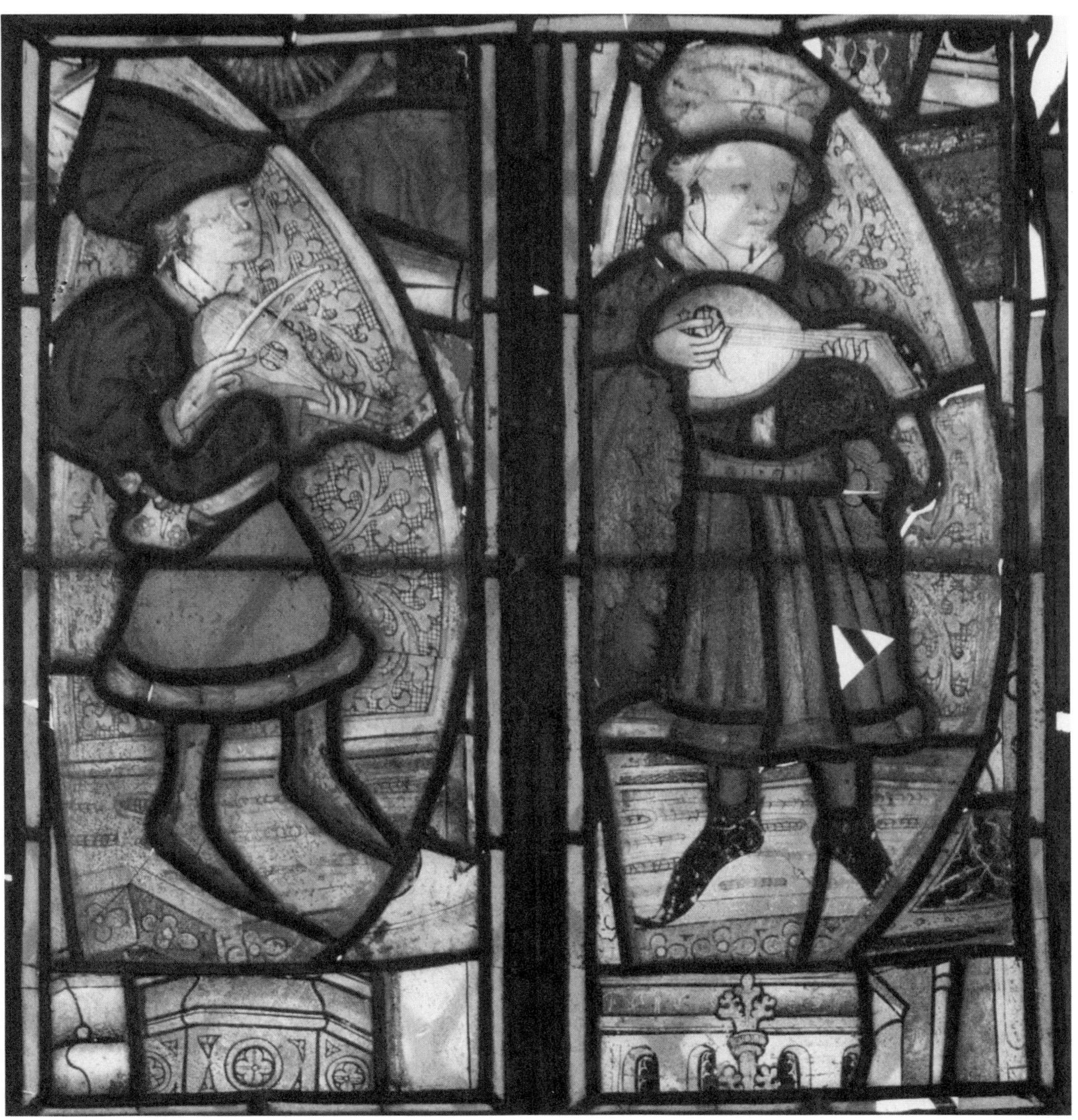

146. Minstrels playing rebec and lute. Painted glass, All Saints, Besthorpe. Fifteenth century. By permission of the Royal Commission on the Historical Monuments of England.

is the psaltery in the north aisle (fig. 151). This psaltery is a very careful rendition of a fourteenth-century instrument, and is played by a man in a costume appropriate for a minstrel of this date. A different costume is suggested by the fidel player, also in the north aisle, who does in fact look as though he is singing to the accompaniment of his instrument (fig. 152).

Attached to companies of actors, the singer-entertainer would still perform an important function up to the closing of the theaters in 1642, as the texts of the plays for the stage of the age of

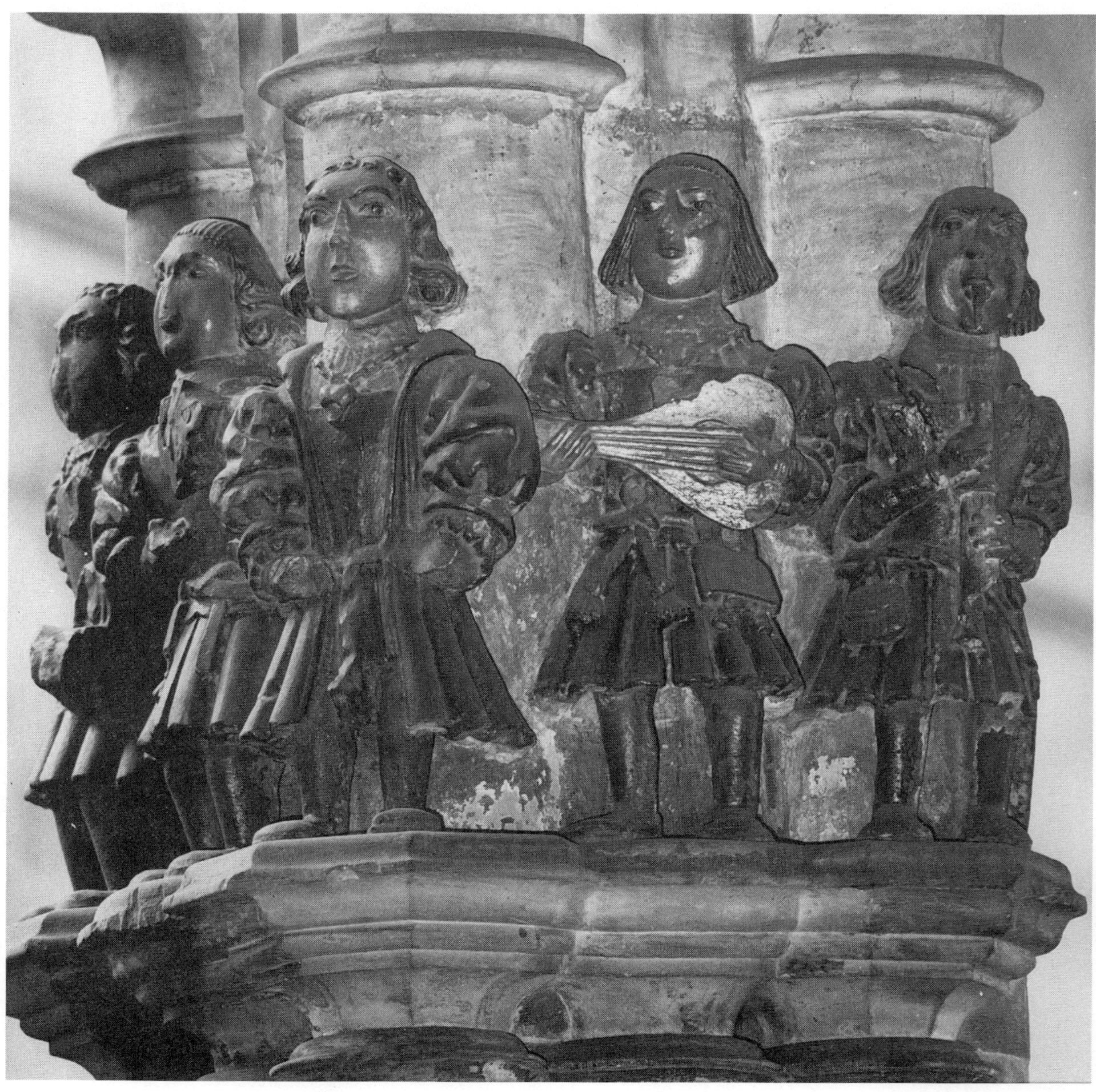

147. Minstrels' pillar. St. Mary's, Beverley. 1524. By permission of the Royal Commission on the Historical Monuments of England.

148. Bagpiper. Corbel, St. Mary's, Beverley. c.1520. Courtesy of the Conway Library, Courtauld Institute of Art, and of Fred H. Crossley and M. H. Ridgway.

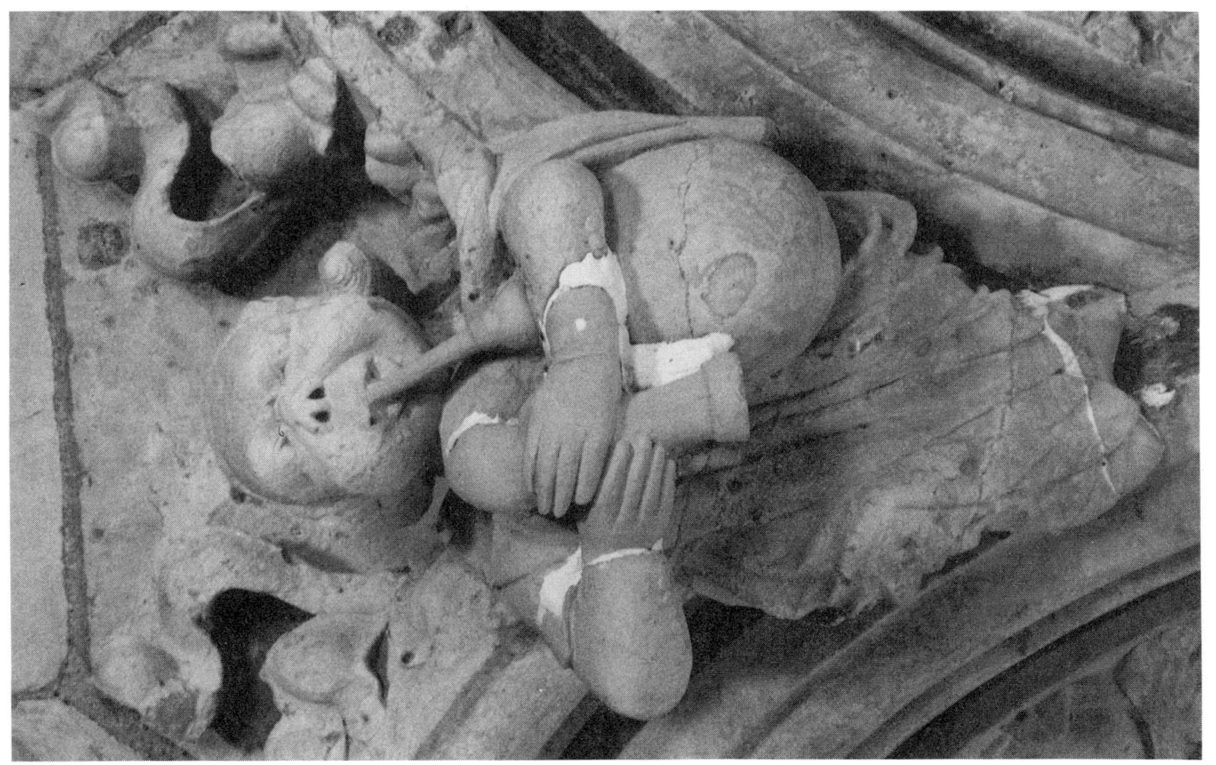

149. Bagpiper. Label stop, Beverley Minster. c.1320–35. Photograph: Jeremy Montagu.

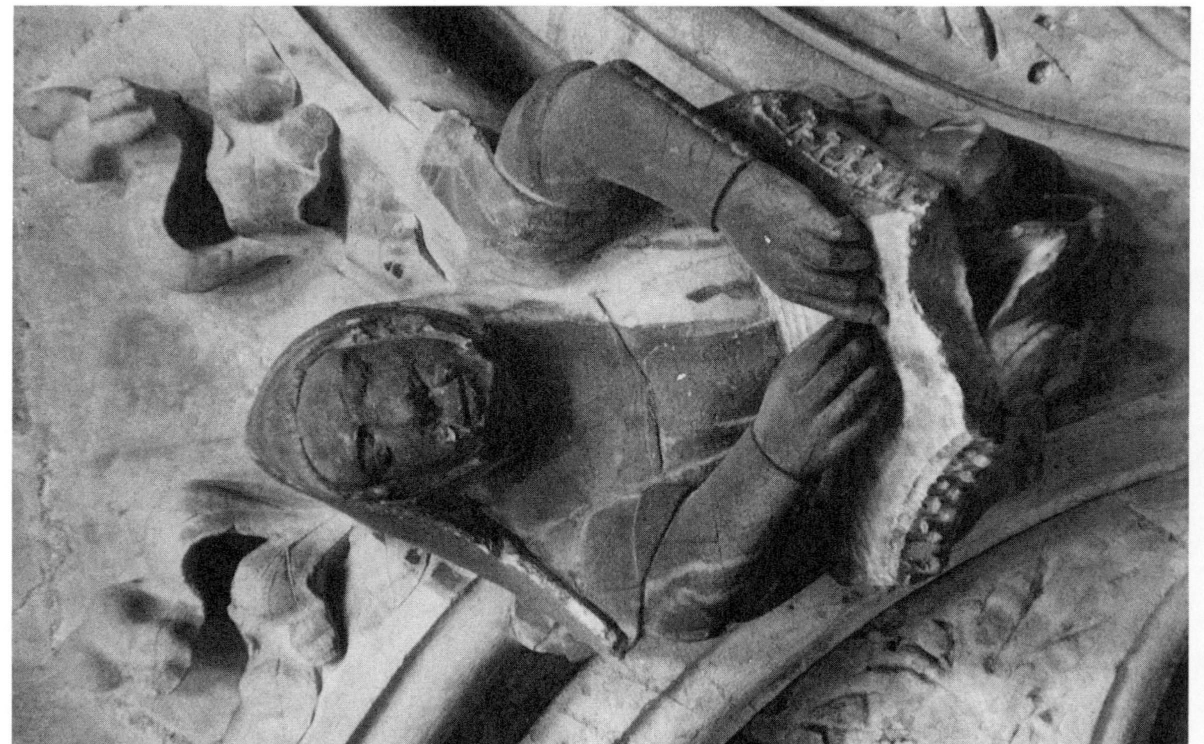

151. Psaltery player. Label stop, Beverley Minster. c.1320–35. Photograph: Jeremy Montagu.

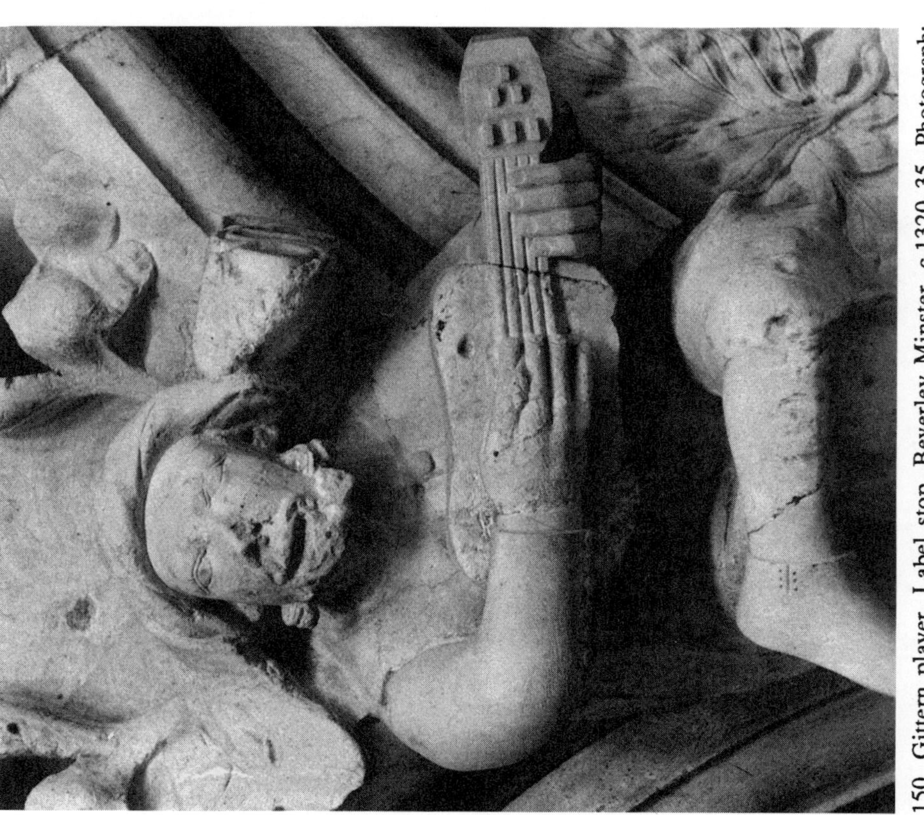

150. Gittern player. Label stop, Beverley Minster. c.1320–35. Photograph: Jeremy Montagu.

Elizabeth I, James I, and Charles I will demonstrate. The songs embedded in these dramas are very numerous, and the men and boys who sang them must be seen as the inheritors of the medieval minstrels who cast their spell upon listeners from very ancient times.

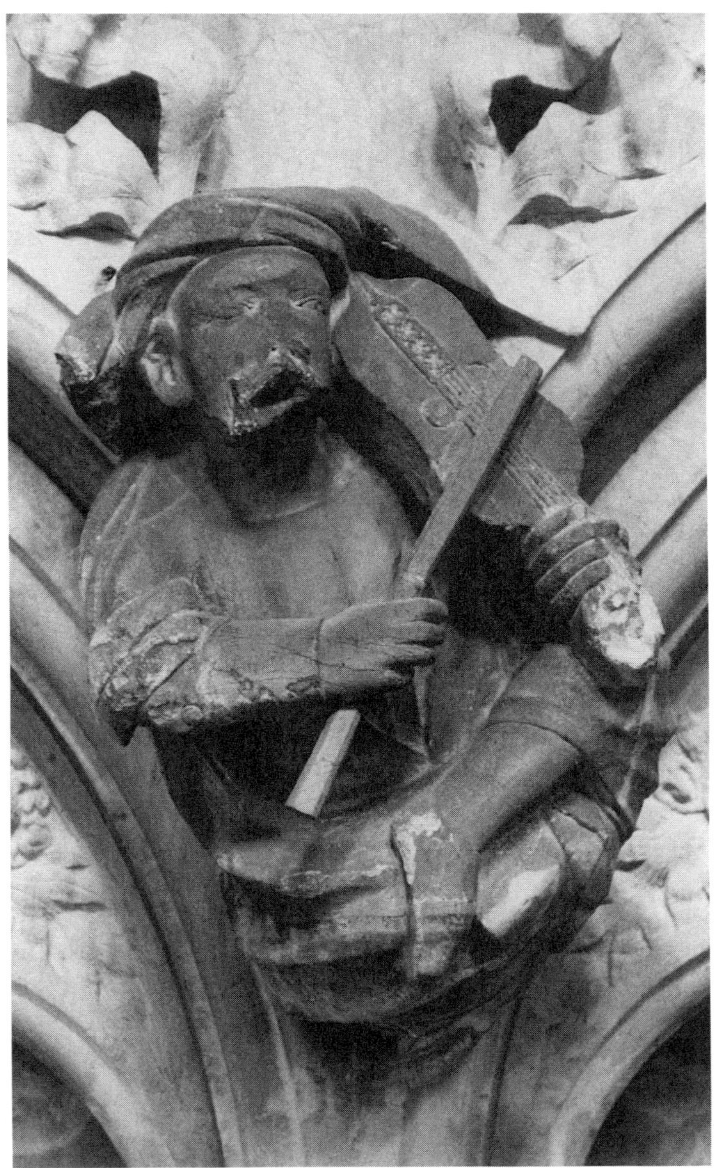

152. Fidel player, who is singing. Label stop, Beverley Minster. c.1320–35. Photograph: Jeremy Montagu.

VIII

ILLUSTRATIONS IN PRINTED PLAYBOOKS

The earliest illustration in a printed playbook from England is the woodcut on the title page of Henry Medwall's *Fulgens and Lucrece*, printed by John Rastall, the brother-in-law of Sir Thomas More, sometime between 1512 and 1516 (fig. 153).[1] In the play, the young lady Lucrece is wooed by two young men, one of whom represents wealth (Cornelius) while the other demonstrates traits more desirable in a potential husband (Gayus). But the illustration, even though it seems to show a wooing scene, does not show an actual production of the play, nor is it even an artist's visualization of the probable staging of a contemporary drama, for the woodcut is in fact copied (in reverse) from an impression made by a woodblock used on the colophon page of *L'Art et instruction de bien dancer* printed by Michel Toulouze in Paris prior to 1496[2] but also used on the recto and verso of the initial leaf of a romance, *Paris et Vienne* (Paris: Denis Mellier, n.d.).[3]

Yet, the illustration may accurately show an aristocratic young woman wearing an ornate floor-length gown (buttoned in the front and belted) and an elaborate headdress. She has her left hand raised as if in response to something that the man, on the right, is saying, presumably in favor of his suit to her. The man, wearing a gold chain upon his fashionably elaborate gown (lined with ermine?), worn over a tunic, and a feathered hat on his head, reaches out to the lady with his right hand as if making a point in his own favor—a gesture which is re-inforced by the index finger of his left hand. Rastall was known to have been attracted to theatrical production,[4] and hence we may assume the illustration to have been at least vaguely consistent with what might have been shown by actors in a contemporary production.

Another possibility is that Rastall might have recognized the woodcut as representing a basse dance, which had been the subject of the dancing treatise in which it had previously appeared. Music and dancing, including a basse dance, were part of the spectacle in *Fulgens and Lucrece.* "Wyll ye see a bace daunce after the gyse/ Of Spayne whyle ye have no thynge to do?" Cornelius asks Lucrece (ll. 380–81). The instrumentalists include a piper, whose lip is too sore to allow him to play, and a tambourine player, but there must have been more. However, the woodcut does not really give any information about the dance steps involved, and there is not even any proof that it is intended to represent dancing.[5] It

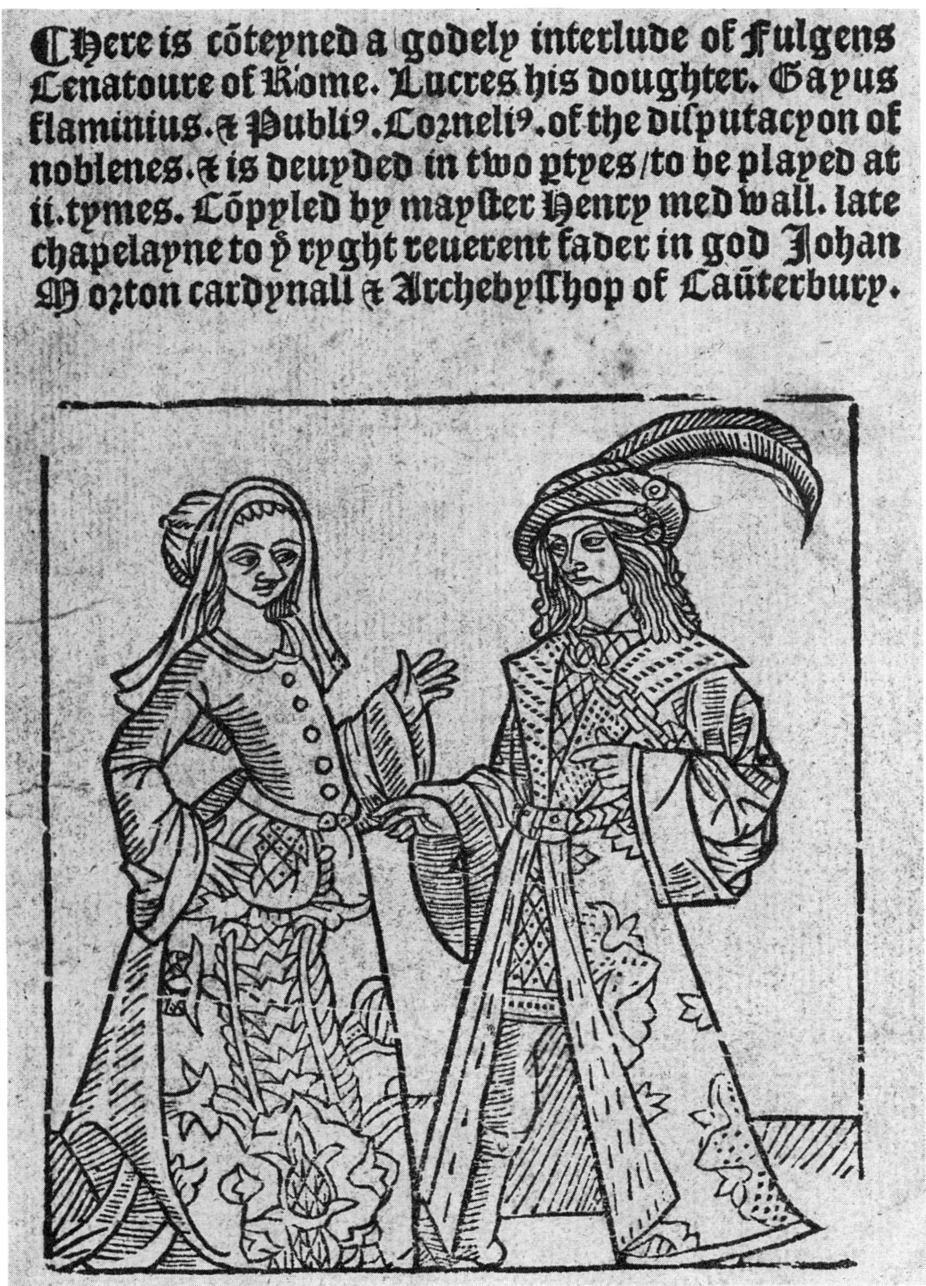
¶ Here is cōteyned a godely interlude of Fulgens
Cenatoure of Rome. Lucres his doughter. Gayus
flaminius. & Publiꝰ. Corneliꝰ. of the disputacyon of
noblenes. & is deuyded in two ꝑtyes/to be played at
ii. tymes. Cōpyled by mayster Henry medwall. late
chapelayne to yͤ ryght reuerent fader in god Johan
Morton cardynall & Archebysshop of Cāuterbury.

153. Man and woman either in conversation or dancing. Title page of *Fulgens and Lucrece* (c.1512–16). By permission of the Huntington Library, San Marino, California.

seems likely after all that we cannot assume the man and woman in the woodcut to be dancing at all.

The next playbook to have an illustrated title page is the anonymous morality *Hick Scorner*, printed in 1515 or 1516 by Wynkyn de Worde (fig. 154).[6] At the top of the page is the title of the play, and under it is a woodcut showing workmen with a spade, a hammer, and a hoe, while in the background on the right a mason is at work.[7] This woodcut has absolutely nothing whatever to do with the play, but is merely intended to be decorative. It first was used as an illustration in de Worde's *Robert the Deuyll* of c.1502 (fol. 8^{v}) and was repeated on the title page of his *How the plowman learned his pater noster*. Richard Pynson had also used the woodcut in his edition of Lydgate's translation of Guido delle Colonne's *Hystory of Troye* (1513), sig. $E6^{v}$. The king in the lower right-hand corner[8] would be re-used several times

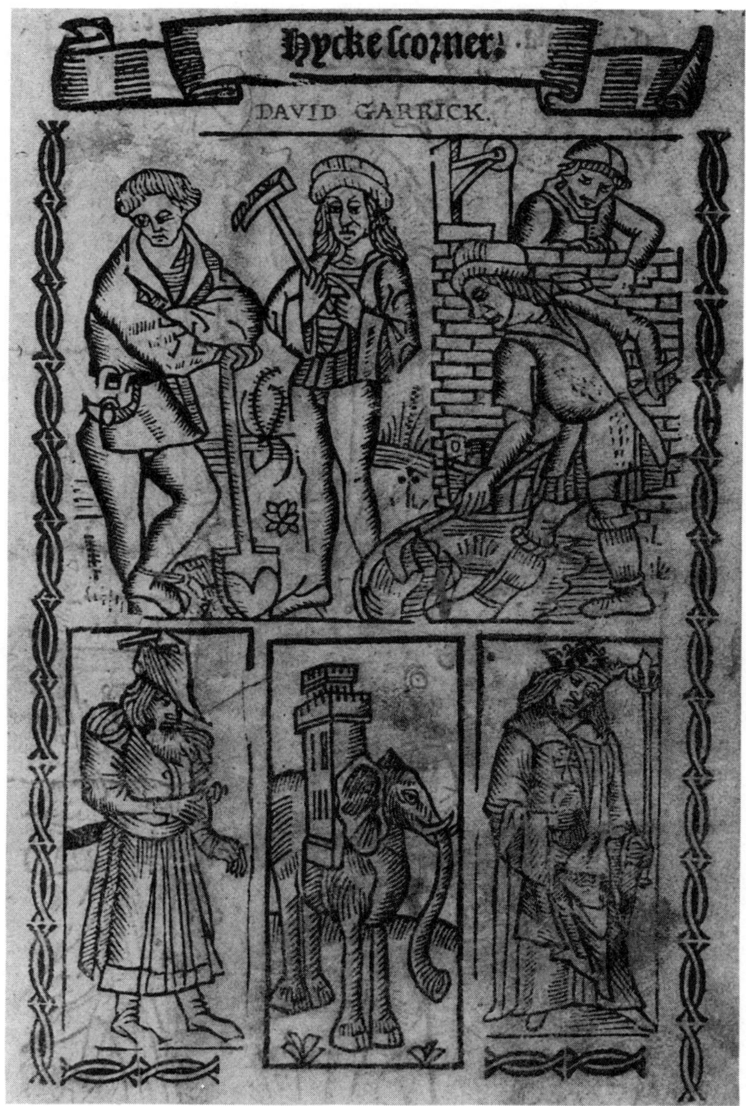

154. Title page of *Hick Scorner* (c.1515–16). British Library, shelfmark C.21.c.4. By permission of the British Library.

after its appearance in *Hick Scorner*, including use in Jacobus de Voragine's *Legenda aurea* (Wynkyn de Worde, 1527), sig. E8^{v}, while the old man at the lower right likewise would also be re-used in the same edition of the *Legenda aurea*, fol. 4^{v}. The other woodcut on the title page—the elephant in the center of the bottom row—appears also to involve a *factotum* block of the type used by English printers to fill in illustrations in early books. These blocks frequently were not English but French in origin. Such French woodblocks were used by English printers after about 1506 when a

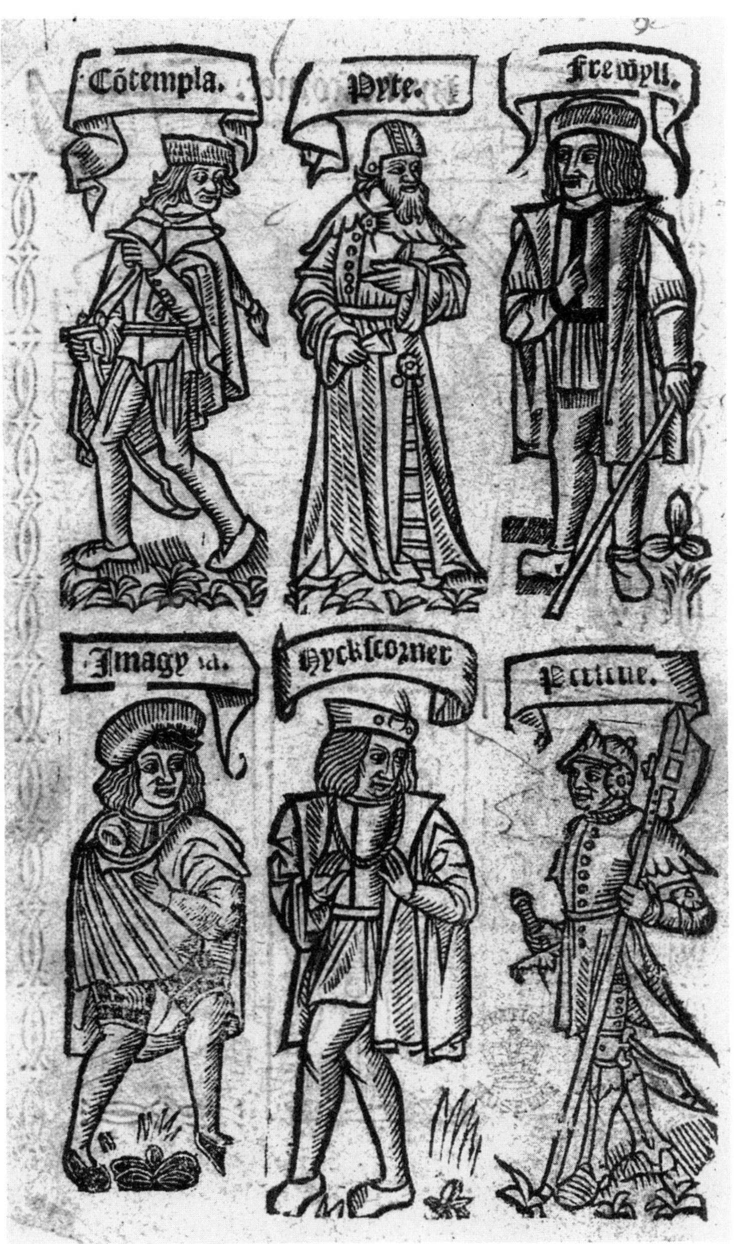

155. Woodcuts purporting to illustrate characters in *Hick Scorner* (c.1515–16). British Library, shelf-mark C.21.c.4. By permission of the British Library.

set was acquired by Pynson for his edition of the *Kalender of Shepardys* in that year. The woodblocks were copied, and copies of copies were also cut for use in numerous books printed through the sixteenth century in England. Hodnett explains, "so many of these cuts exist and differ so minutely from one another that they cannot be identified by verbal description, and since nothing short of the reproduction of every one would be useful, they have not been included in [his] Catalogue."[9]

The *verso* of the title page of *Hick Scorner*, though often regarded as showing "the portraits of the dramatis personae, with their labels over their heads,"[10] are far less significant than they at first seem (fig. 155). While the names of the characters have been inserted into the labels at the top of each woodcut, the illustrations are all prints from *factotum* blocks, some of which originated with the French printer Antoine Vérard who had used them for his edition of Terence (*Therence en francois* [Paris, c.1500]). Thus, as A. W. Pollard indicated long ago, the figures initially used for Davus and Pamphile in Vérard's *Therence* are transformed into Contemplation and Hick Scorner, in the latter case involving rather crude re-cutting;[11] these woodcut figures thus can hardly be considered reliable as depictions relating to the stage.

Nor is the edition of *Hick Scorner* printed by William Copland for John Walley around 1550[12] any more useful for the purpose of studying actual illustrations of the stage or acting. Copland re-used the woodcut initially used by Vérard for Davus without any identification in the ribbon above and added two other ill-matching woodcuts, one with two men who seem on the page to be following him (center) and the other with a single figure facing the other direction (right). Both the single figures had already appeared in John Skot's second edition of *Everyman* (c.1530) where they were identified as "Felawshyp" and "Strengthe," while the figure at the right on the title page of *Hick Scorner* also had been used in Wynkyn de Worde's *A lyttell treatyse called the Lucydarye* (c.1528), sig. A3^{v}. Nor should any more value be placed on the larger woodcut at the top of the title page in the Copland-Walley edition of *Hick Scorner*; the two men, meeting in the center of a room with a tiled floor and windows in each of the three visible walls, seem to be disputing but without any necessary connection to the action of the play.

The most famous sixteenth-century playbook with an illustrated title page is Skot's *Everyman*, issued in two undated editions, the later of which is c.1530.[13] Each edition has an illustration on the title page printed from two woodblocks showing, at the right, a rectangular scene with Death standing in a churchyard and, to the left, a smaller figure intended to depict Everyman but so labeled only in the second edition (fig. 156). The two illustrations also have significantly different borders; instead of the non-matching left and lower borders in the first edition,[14] the second chooses two segments of a vine and column left border and also substitutes pieces of border motifs instead of the flower and leaf designs below Everyman's feet.

The figure of Everyman is actually printed from one of the *factotum* woodblocks originating with Vérard, and represents a better block than the copy which had been used for the figure of Hick Scorner in de Worde's edition[15] and for an illustration in the *Lucydarye* of c.1528 (sig. A2). On the other hand, Death is closely copied from a woodcut[16] in de Worde's edition of the *Kalender of Shepeherdes*, first published in 1508. The woodcut in the *Kalender of Shepeherdes* was, of course, also a copy, taken from the *Kalendrier et compost des bergiers* printed at Paris in 1493.[17] As in the woodcuts from which it is derived, the figure of Death on the *Everyman* title page holds a coffin lid with his left arm (the shape of the coffin lid is surprisingly imprecise when compared with the original French woodcut), and he points with his index finger—an accusatory gesture which is surely appropriate to the play of *Everyman*. Comparison with the French woodcut will show that the design was originally intended to show a cadaver stepping forth out of the tomb, though in Skot's illustration the tomb is replaced by an arched gateway into the cemetery, which is identified through the bones which lie under the feet of Death.

Death's grave clothes hang loosely over him, but he does not display an open abdomen as in the French woodcut. On the whole, the quality of the woodcut is rather crude, especially when compared to the original illustration in the *Kalendrier et compost des bergiers*.

As A. C. Cawley comments, the two woodcuts of the finely dressed man and Death on the title page of *Everyman* "were brought together presumably in order to make a suitable *memento mori*. . . . The figures thus used by Skot are not, however, particularly appropriate to the play they

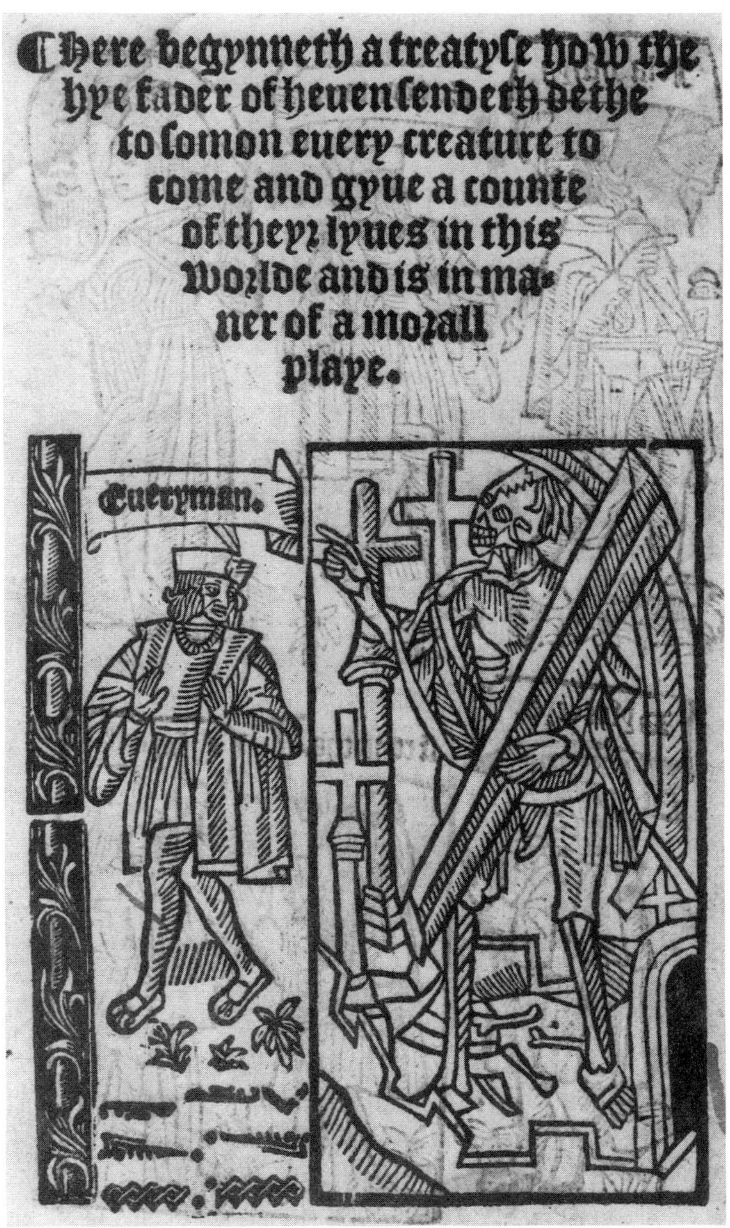
¶ Here begynneth a treatyse how the hye fader of heuen sendeth dethe to somon euery creature to come and gyue a counte of theyr lyues in this worlde and is in maner of a morall playe.

156. Death and Everyman. Title page of *Everyman* published by John Skot (2nd ed., c.1530). British Library, Huth 32. By permission of the British Library.

are meant to illustrate."[18] It may be objected here, as in the case of the illustrations accompanying *Hick Scorner*, that the choice of woodcuts was arbitrary, especially in light of the fact that Death in the woodcut does not match very well with the character in the play. Death in *Everyman* is a figure who serves as the messenger of God. Like Death as he appears in the illustration of Chaundler's *Liber Apologeticus*, he is here apparently armed with a traditional attribute, a "darte" (l. 76), which is commonly associated with him in the fifteenth and sixteenth centuries and in fact is held

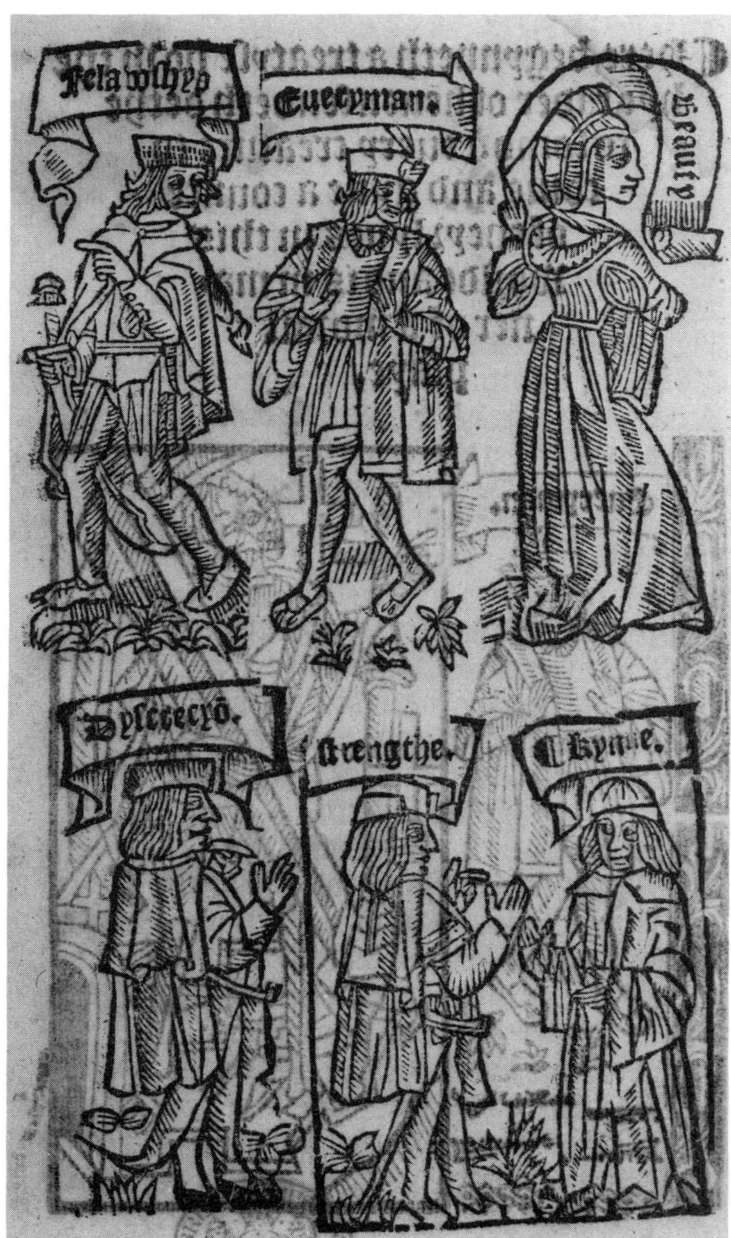

157. Woodcuts purporting to illustrate characters in *Everyman*, published by John Skot (2nd ed., c.1530). British Library, Huth 32. By permission of the British Library.

by him in Pynson's *Kalender of Shepardys* (sig. H5).[19] Reference is made to such a "darte" when Death threatens: "Nor no man wyll I respyte,/ But to the herte sodeynly I shall smyte/ Without ony aduysement" (ll. 177–79). In no sense, therefore, can the made-up woodcut on the title page of the play be regarded as an illustration showing an actual production of *Everyman*. Nevertheless, the woodcuts used in Skot's editions of *Everyman* will show how, when attempting to visualize a scene in drama, the printer drew directly on traditional tableaux in the visual arts as these were represented by blocks available to his print shop.

The figure of Everyman is also repeated on the verso of the title page of Skot's edition of c.1530 where he further appears with similar woodcut illustrations of "Felawshyp," "Beauty," "Dyscrecyon," "Strengthe," and "Kynne" (fig. 157).[20] As noted above, the blocks used for Discretion and Fellowship will be repeated in the Copland-Walley edition of *Hick Scorner*, while Strength and Kin also have appeared in the *Lucydarye* where they are labelled "the discyple" and "the mayster" respectively (sig. A3v).

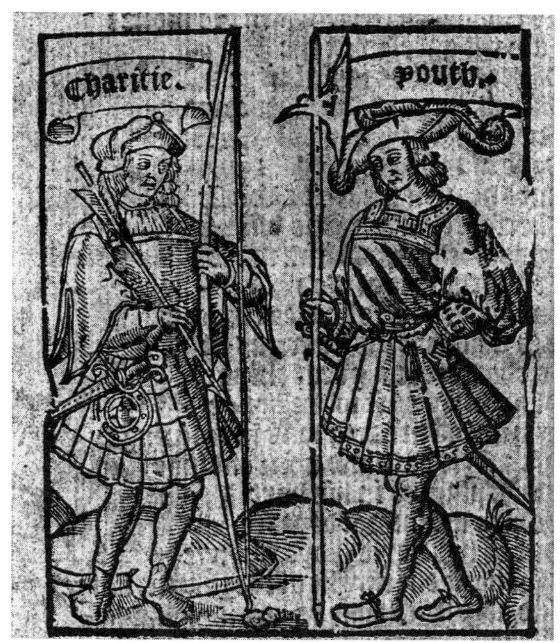

158. Woodcuts purporting to illustrate *Youth*. Edition published by John Walley (c.1557). British Library, shelf-mark C.34.b.24. By permission of the British Library.

Nor do the *factotum* woodcuts used as illustrations of drama end with the playbooks already cited. *Thenterlude of Youth* printed by de Worde in c.1530 contains three such figures, one of which had already been used in his edition of *Hick Scorner* where he was identified as "Pyte."[21] In this edition of *Youth* the three figures have no identifying inscriptions in the labels above them. And, while the edition of c.1557 produced for John Walley has a woodcut representing "Charitie" and "Youth" that in spite of its decorative quality might reflect stage possibilities (fig. 158),[22] Copland's edition, printed in the mid-1560's, returns to the well known *factotum* woodblocks.[23] "Charite," at the left, repeats the figure of an old man previously seen in *Lucydarye* (labeled "the mayster," sig. B5 and repeated) approximately thirty-five years before. Even more striking is the reappearance of the woodcut which had illustrated Everyman in Skot's edition and is now designated as Youth. Another matching woodcut showing an older (but not old) man, unidentified, holding a staff (cut off at the edge of the woodblock), appears on the right. These woodblocks were clearly selected because the side figures seem to point accusingly toward the figure of the young man and because they represent persons from the appropriate stages of life—youth in the middle, with old age at the left, and one whom we should identify as middle-aged on the right. This right-hand figure had previously appeared, with the staff already cut off, in *The Playe called the foure PP* by John Heywood, printed by William Middleton in c.1544.[24] Middleton's title page was in turn re-using a woodcut which had been recut rather crudely—the young man, unidentified, at the left—that had appeared in c.1530 in de Worde's *Youth* and previously in Pynson's *Kalender of Shepardys* (sig. D2). None of these figures has anything to do with the occupations of the characters of Heywood's play—the palmer, the pardoner, the apothocary, or the pedler.[25]

Repeated figures, including the "Everyman" woodcut, make up the stereotyped three figure title page of *An new enterlude of Impacient Pouerte* printed by Copland in c.1561.[26] The same arrangement of three figures, including the "Everyman" woodcut which is now intended to represent the galant Boungrace (center), appears in Copland's edition of *A New Enterlued for Chyldren to playe named Jacke Juggler*, printed sometime between 1559 and 1565.[27] Here the person identified as "Jak iugler" (left) is a figure in a long gown—not a likely representation at all. In a close reprint of *Jack Juggler* by Copland,[28] the "Everyman" woodcut is once more repeated, along with a more satisfactory Jack Juggler, though the block chosen is of much smaller size. There is also a new Dame Coye, though again clearly chosen from among the available woodblocks in the printer's repertoire.

Two woodcut figures, printed from *factotum* blocks, appear on the title page of a book entitled *A mery geste of Robyn Hoode and of hys lyfe, wyth a newe playe for to be played in Maye games very plesaunte and full of pastyme*, issued by Copland in the early years of Queen Elizabeth's reign (fig. 159).[29] The larger figure intended to represent Robin Hood at the left shows a man in a feathered hat who is holding a bow and arrows. His garments are reminiscent of the earlier part of the century, as was common in woodblocks which had been frequently re-used. On the right is a figure labeled "Lytel Iohn," a man in armor (his visor is up) who is holding the hilt of a broadsword with his right hand and a poleaxe with his left; this figure, which originated with Vérard, is repeated from de Worde's edition of *Hick Scorner* where he is curiously identified as Perseverance in the bottom row of illustrations purporting to show the characters in the play. (As Richard Southern has noted, however, the character of Perseverance in *Hick Scorner* wears instead the garment of a priest or doctor![30]) A second edition of *Robin Hood*, published by Edward White who along with his son of the same name was a printer in London from 1577 to 1612, uses re-cut blocks of Robin Hood and Little John.[31] The latter figure is significantly altered.

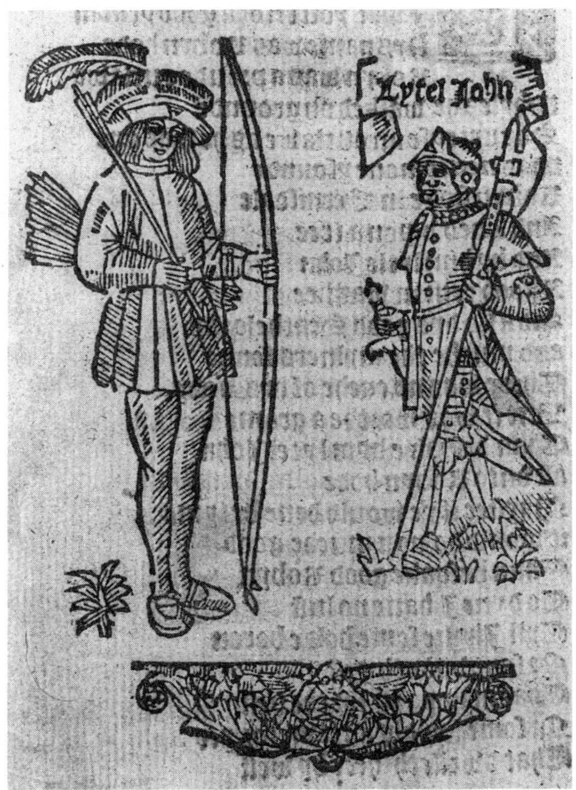

159. Woodcuts purporting to illustrate Robin Hood and Little John. From title page of *A mery geste of Robyn Hoode and of hys lyfe* (c.1560). British Library, shelfmark C.21.c.63. By permission of the British Library.

Such title pages stand in contrast to the more appropriate illustration of a play on the title page of the *Interlude of the Worlde and the Chylde, otherwyse called Mundus and Infans*, printed by Wynkyn de Worde in 1522 (fig. 160).[32] Here a regal figure is seated on a throne with a canopy overhead. He is crowned, and wears an ermine robe. With his left hand he holds an orb and with the right a scepter. The king in the illustration is Mundus, who is shown at the beginning of the drama bragging to the audience that he is "ruler of realmes . . ./ And ouer all fodys [?folys] I am kynge" (sig. [A1^{v}]). His alliance with Wanton and his role with regard to Infans will quickly define his kingship as regal in appearance and demonic in function.

The first unified decorative border on a title page in an English playbook appears in John Bale's *A Comedy concernynge thre lawes, of na-*

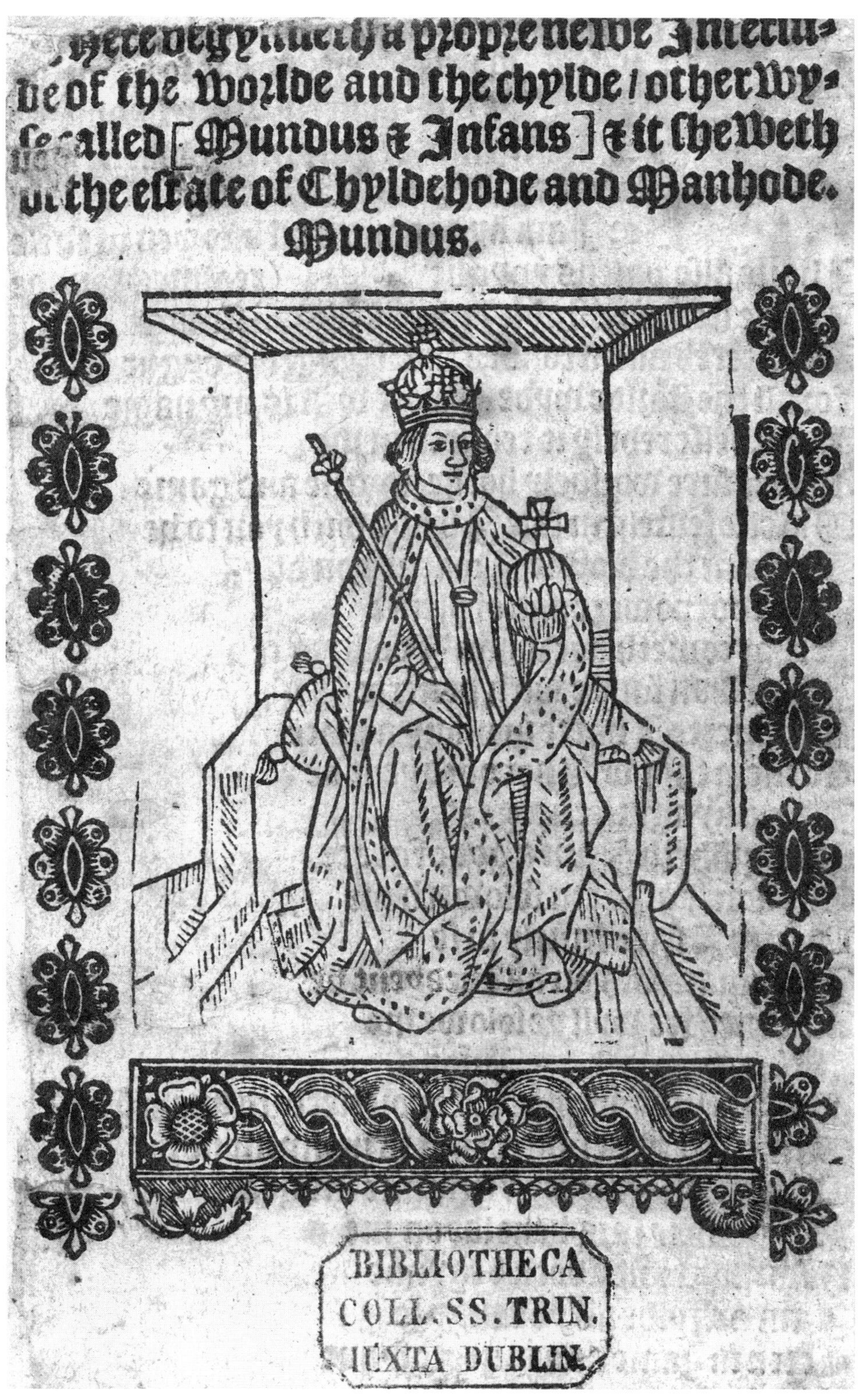

160. Infans, in royal garments, seated. Title page of *The Worlde and the Chylde* (1522). Dublin, Trinity College Library. Courtesy of the Board of Trinity College Dublin.

ture, Moses, and Christ, corrupted by the Sodomytes, Pharysees and Papystes (1538).[33] It is a narrative design, beginning at the left with the creation of Eve, then proceeding clockwise through the Fall, Expulsion, and labor of Adam and Eve, who appear with several children. Eve, pictured as nude even following the Expulsion, holds up a child, presumably a sign of her function of bringing forth offspring in pain in the post-lapsarian world. Unfortunately, the woodcut not only fails to depict anything of the action of the play,[34] but also is of foreign manufacture, used by the continental printer[35] who produced this edition of Bale's play.

Two other English playbooks prior to 1580 have illustrations on their title pages. *The Enterlude of Johan the Euangelist*, issued by John Walley,[36] contains a woodcut of St. John the Evangelist within made-up borders (fig. 161). The play may have been an old one,[37] and there is some reason to suspect that the woodblock used by the printer may also have derived from a supply of pre-Reformation blocks in his possession. The figure of the beardless apostle, his head surrounded by a halo of light and his right hand raised in blessing, represents conventional iconography. In his left hand he holds a chalice with a dragon emerging from it—a reference to the cup of poi-

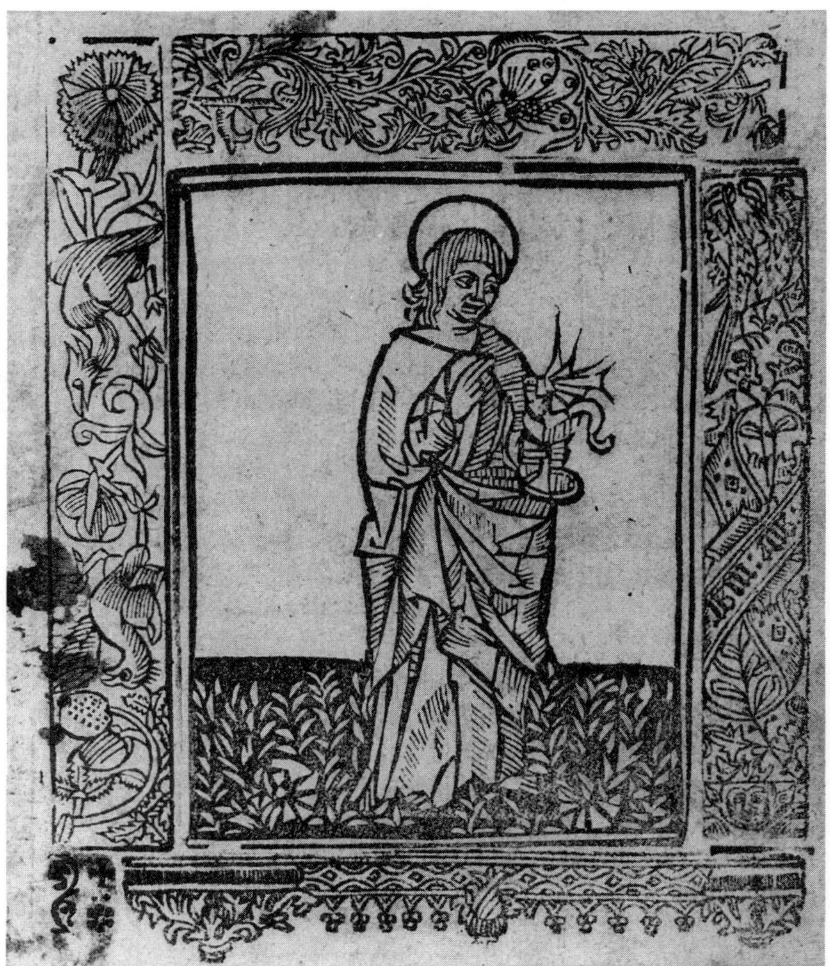

161. St. John. From title page of *The Enterlude of Johan the Euangelist*, published by John Walley. British Library, shelf-mark C.34.i.20. By permission of the British Library.

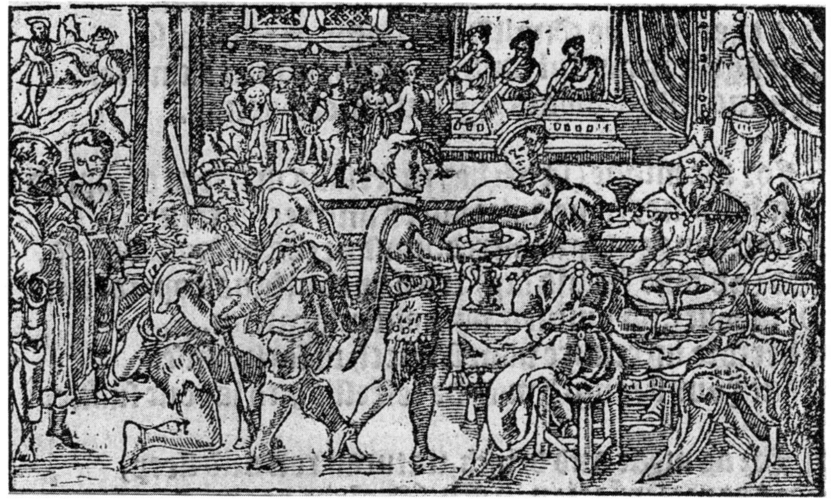

162. Feast of the Prodigal Son. From title page of *Jack Juggler*, published by John Allde (n.d.). By permission of the Folger Shakespeare Library.

soned wine given to him by the Emperor Domitian and from which the poison left the drink in the form of a snake or small dragon.[38] This legend of St. John is not part of the drama, which instead focuses on characters that are given an interpretation in terms of the parable of the Pharisee and the Publican by the saint when he makes an appearance at the end of the play.

Another wood engraving, in this instance of considerable interest, appears on the title page of an undated edition of *Jack Juggler* published by John Allde.[39] Later than the other editions of this play which have been cited above, the playbook would need to have been issued prior to 1582, when Allde seems to have discontinued his vocation.[40] The scene is the feast of the prodigal son, who is kneeling as he is welcomed by his father upon his return at the left and then is feasted at a table at the right (fig. 162). A servant is bringing more food on a platter to the table, while in the background three musicians are playing trumpets to announce the entrance of yet another course of food. Near the musicians are apparently dancers, though they are so indistinctly carved that little can be determined about the kind of dance that is represented.

Woodcuts also appear as illustrations within a playbook in the case of Arthur Golding's translation of Theodore Beza's *A Tragedie of Abrahams Sacrifice* (1577).[41] Four scenes are pictured. In the first, at sig. B1^r, Abraham stands (center, holding a long staff) in the enclosed yard (there are two chickens, a cock and a hen, in it) beside his house, which has a thatched roof, while Sara is at the right (fig. 163). The caption above the woodcut says: "*Abraham commeth out of his house and sayth.*" The text which follows is his lament to God over his childless condition. The next woodcut, at sig. C2^v, shows Abraham preparing to take his son on a journey, while the child Isaac is asking his mother not to weep since he "shall returne ageine/ (I hope) in better plyght." Abraham's house is again shown at the right, and donkey and servants wait for Abraham and his son in the background at the left. At sig. C7^r, a third woodcut presents the child Isaac walking with a staff, Abraham at the right, also walking but holding the hilt of his sword with his left hand, and the donkey, riderless, at the left. Two trees separate the main scene (at the right) from the donkey and a group of travelers, presumably servants, in the background above the animal (at the left). Following behind Abraham is the Devil with claw feet, horns, and a flesh hook in hand. Below at the right are a burning lamp and the bundle of sticks that will be used for the sacrifice. Isaac has said, "Sir

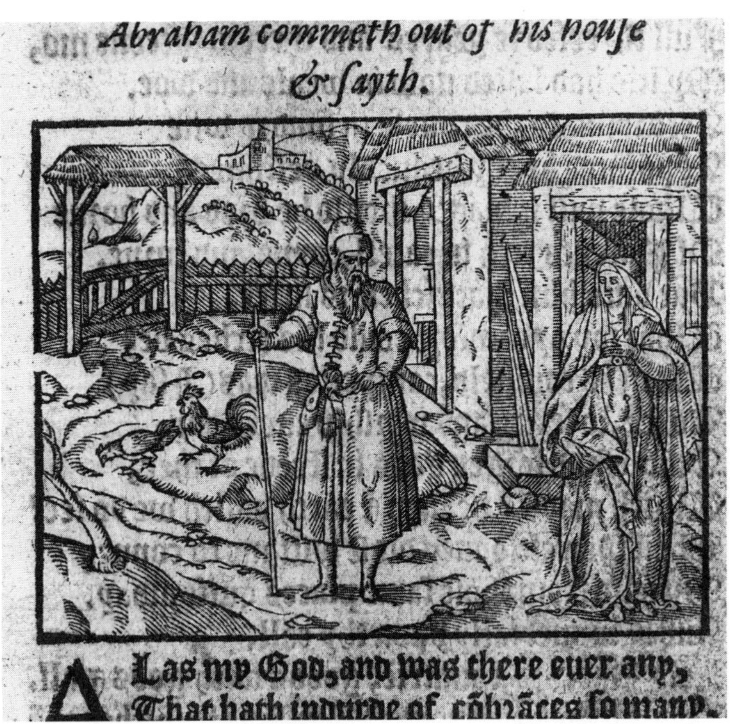

163. Abraham and Sara. Woodcut in Beza, *A Tragedie of Abrahams Sacrifice* (1577), sig. B1^{r}. Courtesy of the Bodleian Library, Oxford.

here is woode, with fire, and knyfe redy:/ But as for sheepe or lambe I see none here./ For you to offer." Abraham insists that "God will prouide," but cannot hide his great grief from his son.

The final woodcut from Beza's *Abraham* (sig. D6^{r}) shows the famous scene in which Abraham prepares to strike his son with his sword (fig. 164). Isaac, whose garment has been stripped off leaving only a loincloth, is blindfolded and holds his hands joined in prayer—a gesture for praying that had been adopted in the thirteenth century—as he kneels upon the wood. The angel in the cloud above, however, has reached down toward the sword with his right hand. In the text of the play, Isaac has begged Abraham to put away his fear, for he is anxious to be with God. Abraham then ("*Heere he intendeth to stryke him*") asks his son's forgiveness and exclaims that "It kills me that thou may not liue." In the text immediately below the woodcut the angel calls Abraham's name. Though the other travelers and the riderless donkey remain at the left on the other side of two trees, another actor in this drama, the sheep which shall be substituted for the son Isaac, is not present.

Neither Beza's play nor its woodcuts are typical, but they do demonstrate that the interest in making visible biblical scenes had not yet died out completely. In 1577 the biblical drama which had been instituted prior to the Reformation in various cities and towns was under increasing pressure and indeed was nearly suppressed everywhere.[42] Beza's play, however, avoided some of the charges leveled at the biblical drama since it was verifiably Protestant and avoided scenes from the New Testament. While the woodcuts hardly illustrated a stage production, they do help us to see how scenes in the play might have been visualized at that time.

A final woodcut illustrating a play is a scene in which a fool with ass's ears seems about to attack one of two young men standing in a Renaissance street on the last page of *The enterlude of the .iiii. cardynal vertues* (c.1541), a work of which only a fragment survives.[43] Unfortunately, this woodcut too will prove disappointing when we learn that it is from the series included in Wynkyn de Worde's edition of Barclay's *Shyppe of Fooles* (1509)[44] and that it is not only a re-used woodcut but also a re-working of a German original.

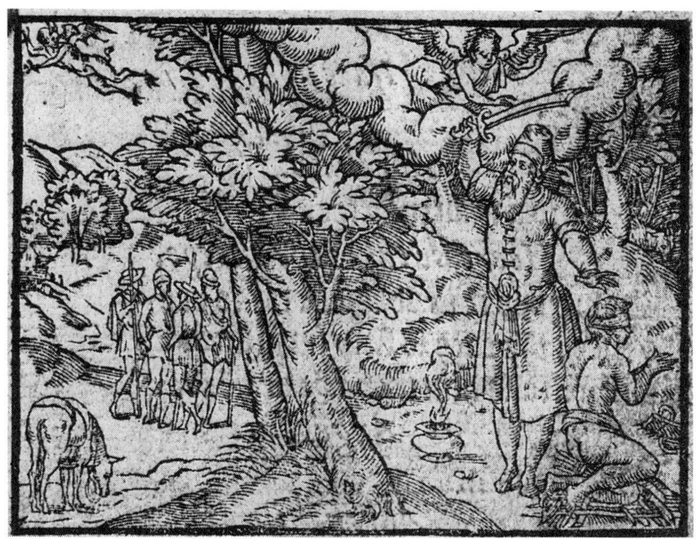

164. Sacrifice of Isaac. Beza, *A Tragedie of Abrahams Sacrifice* (1577), sig. D6r. Courtesy of the Bodleian Library, Oxford.

APPENDIX

EARLY ELIZABETHAN THEATERS AND THE ROSE

No plan or drawing of an Elizabethan theater erected before 1580 is extant except a drawing of c.1597–98 by Abram Booth which *may* include The Theater and the Curtain. This drawing, entitled *The View of the Cittye of London from the North toward the Sowth* (Utrecht University Library, MS. 1198 Hist. 147), is reproduced by R. A. Foakes (*Illustrations of the Stage, 1580–1642*, pp. 8–9), who notes that "it is not, unfortunately, very informative." The Theater, built by James Burbage in 1576, is frequently claimed to have been the first theater building in England since Roman times.[1] This claim, however, is not entirely correct, and theatrical records even demonstrate that a regular theater structure was constructed as early as 1567 when the Red Lion was established, taking its name from its location at the Red Lion Farm at Stepney. Fortunately, the contracts for providing the stage and a turret in this theater have survived on account of litigation which occurred when the financier, John Brayne, found himself dissatisfied with the workmanship of the carpenters.[2]

The stage at the Red Lion appears in the records as having "one Skaffolde or stage for enterludes or playes of good newe and well seasoned Tymber & boords" five feet in height. Assuming that the carpenters had reproduced the measurements in the specifications in the contract, its "lenghte" was forty feet, and "in bredthe" it was thirty feet.[3] Also a turret, which Herbert Berry has suggested might be a tower like the castle structure in *The Castle of Perseverance*, extended twenty-five feet above the stage with a room at the top.[4] It would thus appear that the design for the stage with its turret was based on the traditional scaffolds which had been used in the late Middle Ages as fixed stages. In any case, the design may well have involved a mistaken technology resulting in an unsuitable stage, since Brayne blamed the carpenters' incompetence for the failure of this theater, which seems to have had a very short life.

On the other hand, The Theater, located in Shoreditch outside Bishopgate, was a success. The building, designated as "a theater or playinge place,"[5] was substantial and expensive, costing a considerable sum of money, and even when the lease on its location was expired the timbers would be used to build the Globe. Thus it has mainly been to the Globe—known until recently only through small illustrations of the theater and its successor, the second Globe, on maps[6]—that scholars have gone to derive some idea about the possible size and design of the earlier building. The discovery of the foundations of the Globe in Southwark in the fall of 1989 has, however, opened up a new avenue for information. But only a small portion of the Globe can presently be excavated because the foundations are to a large extent inaccessibly located under Southwark Bridge Road and a nineteenth-century building, Anchor Terrace, deemed to have historical importance. Almost all that can be ascertained is that the Globe was set on chalk footings under foundations of brick and that these foundations were round or nearly so.[7]

The only detailed drawing of an Elizabethan theater is the copy by Aernout van Buchel of the DeWitt sketch of the Swan (c.1596), which nevertheless has proved controversial for a number of reasons.[8] Johannes DeWitt was apparently less interested in perspective than in the ways in which the English theaters were used in play production; further, he seems also to have been interested in the relationship, real or imagined, of such theaters to the classical theaters of ancient Rome.[9] The large stage (identified as *proscaenium*), set upon short columns, is only partly covered by the thatched roof of the canopy, which in turn is supported by long columns of a classical design; the actors are playing as far downstage as practical, while in the gallery over the stage a number of persons, not impossibly musicians, look on. Behind the stage façade with its two doors (and lacking a discovery place or "inner stage"[10]) is the tiring house (*minorum aedes*). From a door in the hut atop the tiring house a trumpeter is announcing the beginning of a play. The three levels of seating are identified as *orchestra* (the lowest), *sedelia*, and *porticus*. Even the roofs over the galleries are given a label (*tectum*). Entrances to the galleries are indicated at each side of the pit.

But what actually, for example, was the shape of the Swan's stage? Was it in fact square, as it appears to be in the DeWitt drawing? Using the scientific methodology offered by the mathematical field of theoretical and artistic perspective restitution, Henryk Limon and Jerzy Limon have examined the DeWitt drawing with mostly negative results; on the whole they caution against accepting the proportions or dimensions that seem to be represented in the drawing for the Swan Theater.[11] Specific descriptions for other theaters and identification of their dimensions have been elusive, except for some specifications in contracts and records which pertain to the Fortune and Hope;[12] even these details have been frustratingly difficult to interpret.

Many of the mysteries surrounding the design of the Elizabethan theaters may never be solved, but the finding of the foundations of the Rose Theater (fig. 165) in December 1988 meant that considerable advance would be made in the coming months toward mapping the theater in which Marlowe's plays were presented and in which Shakespeare's earliest dramas were staged. In Henslowe's diary, the new play of "hary the vj"—a part of the *Henry VI* trilogy—is recorded on 3 March 1591/92, and "titus & ondronicus," also new, is noted on 23 January 1593/94.[13] These plays were thus written by Shakespeare for Lord Strange's Men, the company that was then playing at the Rose in 1592–93.[14]

The recent discoveries at the site of the Rose, according to John Orrell and Andrew Gurr, produced "the first really trustworthy evidence about any of the playhouses that flourished in Shakespeare's day."[15] Knowledge about the construction techniques used in the Rose had previously been based mainly on the accounts kept by Henslowe in his diary during the refurbishing of the theater in 1592; other entries in his diary appeared in 1595 when he noted "what I haue layd owt abowt my playhowsse ffor payntinge & doinge it a bowt with ealme bordes & other Repracyones."[16] Together these accounts indicated only that the building was set on brick foundations

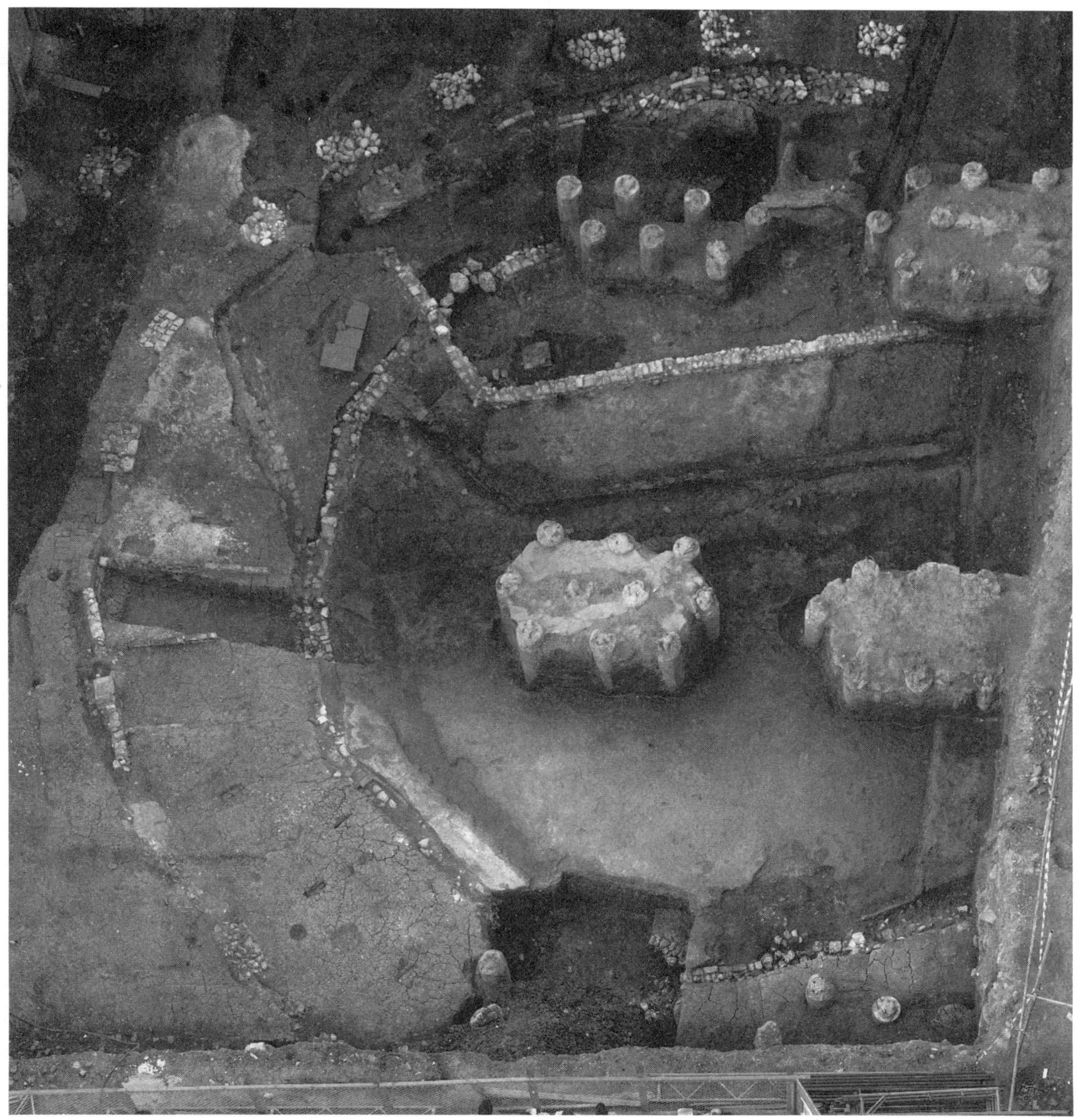

165. Site of the Rose Theater during excavations in 1989. Copyright Museum of London; photograph by A. Fulgoni.

and made of wood and plaster with at least a partially thatched roof.[17] But there was also reference to the tiring house which had a room at the top[18]—information that is reminiscent of the design of the turret at the Red Lion more than two decades earlier.

The excavation of the site of the Rose confirmed that brick had been used in the foundations. The foundations had been set on footings of chalk, placed in trenches outlining the shape of the walls of the theater. The outline of the footings in the excavation fortuitously show the shape and

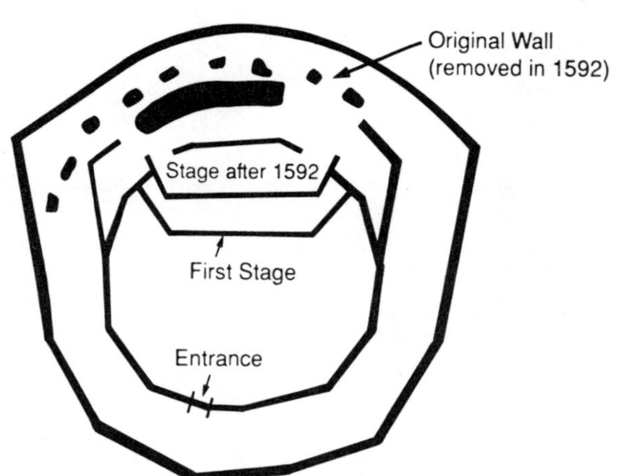

166. Plan of the Rose Theater, showing the position of the stage.

size of the building and also locate the stage and tiring house areas.[19]

Even more important, the position and size of the stage are evident for the period immediately after the initial building of the theater in 1587 and also for the relocated stage following the rebuilding of 1592 (see fig. 166). We now know the configuration and size of the Rose's stage, which was shallow, wide, and tapered toward the front. In 1587–92, the stage at the Rose was 24 feet 9 inches wide at the front and 37 feet 6 inches in the back; it was approximately 15 feet 6 inches deep.[20] At this time the stage was thrust out into the pit to a considerable extent—a design that apparently for some reason was found unsatisfactory, since in 1592 the stage was set back by 6 feet 6 inches. Columns held up the stage roof at least after 1592. As part of the reconstruction program, the tiring house was expanded, and also the northern portion of the theater was rebuilt.[21] The resulting building appears to have been irregular, though the original design seems to have been the expected polygonal shape. Orrell and Gurr estimate that the total capacity of the Rose Theater after the rebuilding of 1592 would have been 2,425, slightly larger than the previous capacity of around 2000 people.[22]

The stage of the Rose, like that of the Red Lion, is apparently a variant of a type that owes much to the fixed stages used in late medieval drama in East Anglia and elsewhere. While the acting of the professional companies who used this stage was expectedly of a superior quality when compared to the amateur theater upon which so much civic energy had been lavished in cities such as Coventry, their acting style very possibly was closer in spirit to the civic theater and other amateur theatricals than to twentieth-century practice. The conditions of repertory playing, whether an annual event such as the presentation of Corpus Christi plays or the normal rotation of plays such as those identified in Henslowe's diary, call for a method of acting grounded in traditional gestures and vocal production and inflection. At least with the discovery of the Rose Theater's remains we now are able to see the layout of an actual theater in which early drama was presented. It is thus a shame that the excavation of the Rose was prematurely brought to an end by the scandalous refusal of the government to declare it to be an ancient monument, and that the site will be now situated in an enclosure under a commercial building where future archaeological exploration will be doubtful.[23]

NOTES

I. THE ROMAN THEATER IN BRITAIN

1. Tactitus, *The Histories [and] the Annals*, trans. John Jackson, Loeb Classical Library (London: Heinemann, 1912), IV, 158–61.

2. For other examples of Gallo-Roman theaters, see Kathleen M. Kenyon, "The Roman Theatre at Verulamium, St. Albans," *Archaeologia*, 84 (1934), 245, 247–53, Pl. LXV, and Margarete Bieber, *The History of the Greek and Roman Theater* (Princeton: Princeton Univ. Press, 1961), pp. 199–201.

3. Vitruvius, *On Architecture*, ed. and trans. Frank Granger, Loeb Classical Library (London: Heinemann, 1955), p. 263 (Book V.iii.1).

4. See John Wacher, *The Towns of Roman Britain* (Berkeley and Los Angeles: Univ. of California Press, 1974), pp. 105–10.

5. Philip Crummy, "The Roman Theatre at Colchester," *Britannia*, 13 (1982), 299–302, and M. R. Hull, *Roman Colchester*, Report of the Research Committee of the Society of Antiquaries, 20 (London: Society of Antiquaries, 1958), p. 80.

6. Crummy, "The Roman Theatre at Colchester," pp. 300–01.

7. Rosalind Dunnett, "The Excavation of the Roman Theatre at Gosbecks," *Britannia*, 2 (1971), 27–47, figs. 1–5; Hull, *Roman Colchester*, pp. 267–69.

8. Sheppard Frere, "The Roman Theatre at Canterbury," *Britannia*, 1 (1970), 83–91.

9. Kenyon, "The Roman Theatre at Verulamium," pp. 213–15.

10. Ibid., pp. 215–22.

11. Ibid., pp. 222–26. See also Wacher, *Towns of Roman Britain*, pp. 210–11.

12. Kenyon, "The Roman Theatre at Verulamium," pp. 228–31.

13. Ibid., pp. 232–39.

14. R. G. Collingwood and R. P. Wright, *The Roman Inscriptions of Britain*, I (Oxford: Clarendon Press, 1965), No. 707 (p. 237).

15. P. D. C. Brown and Alan D. McWhirr, "Cirencester, 1966," *Antiquaries Journal*, 47 (1967), 194–95; Alan McWhirr, "The Roman Town Plan," in *Studies in the Archaeology and History of Cirencester*, ed. Alan McWhirr (1976), p. 11, fig. 1.

16. *Britannia*, 3 (1972), 279–80; for the presence of a small theater at this location, known in Roman times as Cataractonium, see Ian Lancashire, *Dramatic Texts and Records of Britain: A Chronological Topography to 1558* (Toronto: Univ. of Toronto Press, 1984), No. 518.

17. I. M. Stead, "A Roman Pottery Theatrical Face-mask and a Bronze Brooch-blank from Baldock, Herts.," *Antiquaries Journal*, 55 (1975), 397–98.

18. J. M. C. Toynbee, *Art in Britain under the Romans* (Oxford: Clarendon Press, 1964), p. 359. The amphitheater is described by R. E. M. Wheeler, "The Roman Amphitheatre at Caerleon, Monmouthshire," *Archaeologia*, 88 (1928), 111–218.

19. G. D. Marsh, "The 'Theatre' Masks from London," *Britannia*, 10 (1979), 263–65.

20. Ibid., p. 265.

21. Ibid., p. 265.

22. *The Historians of the Church of York and Its Archbishops*, ed. James Raine, Rerum Britannicum Medii Aevi Scriptores, 71 (1879), I, 328.

23. In the fifteenth century John Capgrave can still refer to the amphitheater as "a place all rou*n*d swech as we haue her in this lond"—i.e., in East Anglia—but more importantly he describes a theater as a half-circle used for displays of wrestling or for seeing plays (*Ye Solace of Pilgrimes: A Description of Rome, circa A.D. 1450*, ed. C. A. Mills [London: Oxford Univ. Press, 1911], pp. 17–18).

II. CEREMONIES AND LITURGICAL PLAYS

1. Karl Young, *The Drama of the Medieval Church* (Oxford: Clarendon Press, 1933), I, 249–50; Pamela Sheingorn, *The Easter Sepulchre in England*, Early Drama, Art, and Music, Reference Ser., 5 (Kalamazoo: Medieval Institute Publications, 1987), pp. 20–22.

2. Martin Biddle, "Excavations at Winchester 1966: Fifth Interim Report," *Antiquaries Journal*, 47 (1967), 269–70, and *The Old Minster: Excavations Near Winchester Cathedral, 1961-1969* (Winchester: Wykeham Press, 1970), p. 82; for a suggestion concerning the processional movement of the Marys at Winchester, see Dunbar Ogden, "The Use of Architectural Space in Medieval Music-Drama," *Comparative Drama*, 8 (1974), 67.

3. See Lawrence Butler, "The Easter Sepulchre at Cowthorpe Church, N. Yorks.," *Sciant Presentes*, 16 (1987), 8–9.

4. Sheingorn, *Easter Sepulchre*, p. 269; illustrated by Charles J. Hunt, "Old Chests," *Transactions of the Birmingham Archaeological Society*, 20 (1895), 80.

5. For a full description, see Sheingorn, *Easter Sepulchre*, p. 359.

6. For the view that this Easter sepulcher is to be seen as a unique "tomb of Christ" distinct from the Easter sepulcher in regular use for Good Friday and Easter, see Veronica Sekules, "The Tomb of Christ at Lincoln and the

Development of the Sacrament Shrine: Easter Sepulchres Reconsidered," in *Medieval Art and Architecture at Lincoln Cathedral*, ed. T. A. Heslop and V. A. Sekules, British Archaeological Assoc., Conference Transactions, 8 (1986), pp. 122–23.

7. Christopher Wordsworth, "Inventories of Plate, Vestments, &c., belonging to the Cathedral Church of the Blessed Mary, of Lincoln," *Archaeologia*, 53 (1892), 81.

8. Stanley Kahrl, ed., *Records of Plays and Players in Lincolnshire 1300–1585*, Collections, 8 (Oxford: Malone Society, 1974), p. 26.

9. See *The Pageants of Richard Beauchamp, Earl of Warwick*, introd. William, Earl of Carysfoot, Roxburghe Club, 150 (1908), and James Gairdner, "Richard Beauchamp," *DNB*, II, 30.

10. Sheingorn, *Easter Sepulchre*, pp. 43, 364.

11. Sheingorn, *Easter Sepulchre*, pp. 43, 344–46; D. U. Seth Smith and G. M. A. Cunningham, "An Inventory of Gifts to the Chapel of the Holy Sepulchre that was at Edington," *Wiltshire Archaeological and Natural History Magazine*, 55 (1953–54), 161.

12. Ed. James Raine, Surtees Soc., 15 (London, 1844).

13. Ibid., pp. 9–10.

14. Ibid., pp. 10–11.

15. E. A. Loftus and H. F. Chettle, *A History of Barking Abbey* (Barking: Wilson and Whitworth, n.d.), pp. 41–42.

16. Young, *Drama of the Medieval Church*, I, 164–66.

17. Ibid., I, 165–67.

18. Sheingorn, *Easter Sepulchre*, pp. 135–37; *The Ordinale and Customary of the Benedictine Nuns of Barking Abbey*, ed. J. B. L. Tolhurst, Henry Bradshaw Soc., 65 (London, 1927), I, 106–10; Walther Lipphardt, *Lateinische Osterfeiern und Osterspiele*, V (Berlin: Walter de Gruyter, 1976), No. 770. For facsimiles of the relevant pages in the Barking Ordinal, see Sheingorn, *Easter Sepulchre*, figs. 12–17.

19. Young, *Drama of the Medieval Church*, I, 167.

20. Nancy Cotton, "Katherine of Sutton: The First English Woman Playwright," *Educational Theatre Journal*, 30 (1978), 475–81.

21. *A History of the County of Essex*, ed. W. R. Powell, Victoria County Histories (Oxford: Oxford Univ. Press, 1966), V, 222–23; Alfred W. Clapham, "The Benedictine Abbey of Barking: A Sketch of Its Architectural History and an Account of Recent Excavations on Its Site," *Transactions of the Archaeological Society*, n.s. 12 (1913), 69–87; Eileen Power, *Medieval English Nunneries c.1275 to 1535* (Cambridge: Cambridge Univ. Press, 1922), p. 2.

22. *Somerset Wills, 1501–1530*, 2nd ser., ed. F. W. Weaver, Somerset Record Soc., 19 (1903), p. 53.

23. Sheingorn, *Easter Sepulchre*, p. 302; Nikolaus Pevsner, *South and West Somerset* (Harmondsworth: Penguin, 1958), p. 312.

24. See "Church Restoration," *The Ecclesiologist*, 3, Nos. 33–34 (August 1844), 156.

25. Reproduced in Lancashire, *Dramatic Texts and Records of Britain*, Pl. 15.

26. Young, *Drama of the Medieval Church*, I, 94–98; Hans-Jürgen Diller, "A *Palmesel* from the Cracow Region," *EDAM Newsletter*, 11 (1989), 27–30; Teresa Bela, "Palm Sunday Ceremonies in Poland: The Past and the Present," *Early Drama, Art, and Music Review*, 12 (1990), 25–31.

27. Lancashire, *Dramatic Texts and Records of Britain*, Nos. 956, 988–89, 1001, 1004, 1024.

28. Roger Martin, "The state of Melford Church and our Ladie's Chappel at the East end, as I did know it," *Gentleman's Magazine*, 146 (1830), 206.

29. See also Christopher Wordsworth, *Ceremonies and Processions of the Cathedral Church of Salisbury* (Cambridge: Cambridge Univ. Press, 1901), I, 67–68.

30. John Walton Tyrer, *Historical Survey of Holy Week: Its Services and Ceremonial*, Alcuin Club Collections, 29 (London: Oxford Univ. Press, 1932), p. 58. The boy seems, however, to be a sixteenth-century addition to the ceremony; see Nigel Davison, "So which way round did they go? The Palm Sunday Procession at Salisbury," *Music and Letters*, 61 (1980), 12.

31. David Galloway and John Wasson, eds., *Records of Plays and Players in Norfolk and Suffolk, 1330–1642*, Collections, 11 (Oxford: Malone Society, 1980–81), pp. 99–100.

32. W. S. Simpson, "On the Parish of St. Peter Cheap, in the City of London, from 1392 to 1633," *Journal of the British Archaeological Association*, 24 (1868), 263.

33. *York*, ed. Alexandra F. Johnston and Margaret Rogerson, Records of Early English Drama (Toronto: Univ. of Toronto Press, 1979), I, 1.

34. Kahrl, ed., *Records of Plays and Players in Lincolnshire*, pp. 25ff.

35. Ibid., pp. 32–33 and *passim.*

36. William Lambarde, *Dictionarium Angliae Topographicum et Historicum* (London, 1730), pp. 459–60.

37. Kahrl, ed., *Records of Plays and Players in Lincolnshire*, p. 27; for London, see Lambarde, *Dictionarium*, pp. 459–60.

38. *York*, ed. Johnston and Rogerson, I, 42–44; II, 728–30.

III. PAGEANTS AND PROCESSIONAL STAGING

1. Neil C. Brooks, "Processional Drama and Dramatic Processions in Germany in the Late Middle Ages," *Journal of English and Germanic Philology*, 32 (1933), 141–71; Alan E. Knight, "Processional Theater in Lille in the Fifteenth Century," *Fifteenth Century Studies*, 13 (1988), 347–53.

2. See especially George R. Kernodle, "The Medieval Pageant Wagons of Louvain," *Theatre Annual* (1943), pp. 58–62, and also Glynne Wickham, *Early English Stages, 1300 to 1660* (London: Routledge and Kegan Paul, 1959–81), I, figs. 25, 28.

3. *Chester*, ed. Lawrence M. Clopper, Records of Early English Drama (Toronto: Univ. of Toronto Press, 1979), p. 325.

4. Ibid.

5. Ibid., p. 239. See the discussion by Alan H. Nelson, "Six-Wheeled Carts: An Underview," *Technology and Culture*, 13 (1972), 391–416.

6. Pl. 22.

7. "On Six-Wheeled Pageant Wagons," *EDAM Newsletter*, 11 (1989), 37–39.

8. Cf. John Marshall, "'The manner of these playes': The Chester Pageant Carriages and the Places Where They Played," in *Staging the Chester Cycle*, ed. David Mills (Leeds: Univ. of Leeds School of English, 1985), pp. 23–25.

9. See the discussion by Peter Meredith and John Marshall, "The Wheeled Dragon in the *Luttrell Psalter*," *Medieval English Theatre*, 2 (1980), 70–73. There is in the case of this manuscript the need for special caution, however, since many of the illustrations are innovatively creative rather than realistic; on the other hand, its artist also had a keen eye for details in real-life scenes. See Eric George Millar, *The Luttrell Psalter* (London: British Museum, 1932), *passim.*

10. John Tatham, *Londinum* [sic]*: Londons Triumphs* (London, 1663), p. 6; cited by L. J. Morrisey, "English Pageant-Wagons," *Eighteenth-Century Studies*, 9 (1975–76), 368.

11. Cited by Morrisey, "English Pageant-Wagons," p. 368.

12. Pl. facing p. 4.

13. In the case of the pageant of Justice, the horses are fitted with unicorns' horns, and are ridden by "two beautiful young Princes" (p. 4).

14. R. Ingram, "The Coventry Pageant Waggon," *Medieval English Theatre*, 2 (1980), 7.

15. See Marjorie Nice Boyer, "Medieval Pivoted Axles," *Technology and Culture*, 1 (1960), 128–38.

16. *York*, ed. Johnston and Rogerson, I, 55–56.

17. Ibid., I, 55, 95.

18. See Peter Meredith, "The Development of the York Mercers' Pageant Waggon," *Medieval English Theatre*, 1 (1979), 5–18.

19. *York*, ed. Johnston and Rogerson, I, 11, 356–57; see Meg Twycross, "'Places to hear the play': Pageant Stations at York, 1398–1572," *REED Newsletter*, 1978 (No. 2), pp. 10–33, and Eileen White, "Places for Hearing the Corpus Christi Play in York," *Medieval English Theatre*, 9 (1987), 23–63.

20. William Dugdale, *Antiquities of Warwickshire* (London, 1656), p. 116.

21. See Ingram, "The Coventry Pageant Waggon," p. 11.

22. *Coventry*, ed. R. W. Ingram, Records of Early English Drama (Toronto: Univ. of Toronto Press, 1981), p. 549.

23. Ibid., pp. 37, 53–55, 79, 125, 233–34.

24. *Chester*, ed. Clopper, pp. lvi–lviii, 67, 239. The earlier version of Rogers' *Breviary* here is more specific about the places where the plays were played than the 1618–19 version, which merely indicates that "the places where they weare played were in euery streete of the Cittie" (*Chester*, ed. Clopper, p. 325).

25. Marshall, "The manner of these playes," pp. 38–41.

26. John Elder, *The Copie of a letter sent in to Scotlande, of the ariuall and landynge, and most noble marryage of the most Illustre Philippe, prynce of Spaine, to the most excellente Marye, quene of England* (1555), sig. B5^{v}; Robert Withington, *English Pageantry* (Cambridge: Harvard Univ. Press, 1918–20), I, 189–94; Lancashire, *Dramatic Texts and Records of Britain*, No. 1089.

27. Frank Stevens, "The Giant and Hob Nob and Their Story," in *The Festival Book of Salisbury*, ed. Frank Stevens (Salisbury: Salisbury, South Wiltshire, and Blackmore Museum, [1915]), pp. 63–64.

28. *Records of the Guild of St. George in Norwich, 1389–1547*, ed. Mary Grace, Norfolk Record Society, 9 (1937), p. 31; *The Norwich Snapdragon*, Norfolk Museums Service Information Sheet (Norwich, 1984); William C. Ewing, *Notices and Illustrations of the Costumes, Processions, Pageantry, etc. formerly displayed by the Corporation of Norwich* (Norwich: Charles Muskett, 1850), Pl. opposite p. 35 and unnumbered color plate.

29. *Norwich 1540–1642*, ed. David Galloway, Records of Early English Drama (Toronto: Univ. of Toronto Press, 1984), p. 47.

IV. PLACES TO SEE THE PLAYS

1. E. K. Chambers, *The Mediaeval Stage* (London: Oxford Univ. Press, 1903), II, 380–81; W. O. Hassell, "Plays at Clerkenwell," *Modern Language Review*, 33 (1938), 564–67. On the terrain which made this location favored for plays, see especially John Green Waller, "The 'Hole-Bourne'," *Transactions of the London and Middlesex Archaeological Society*, 4 (1875), 115–18. Waller suggests that the plays were presented north of Clerkenwell in a place where the banks of the Holbourne "bent around in a half circle, which would not only accommodate a larger number of spectators, but enable them to witness the performances at greater convenience" (pp. 117–18).

2. J. W. Robinson, "Monuments to the Medieval Theatre," *Theatre Notebook*, 33 (1979), 86.

3. See the Appendix, below.

4. See the well known continental Lucerne stage plan; for a tracing with English translation, see *The Staging of Religious Drama in Europe in the Later Middle Ages: Texts and Documents in English Translation*, ed. Peter Meredith and John E. Tailby, Early Drama, Art, and Music, Monograph Ser., 4 (Kalamazoo: Medieval Institute Publications, 1982).

5. *The Chronicle of Jocelin of Brakelond*, ed. and trans. H. E. Butler (New York: Oxford Univ. Press, 1949), pp. 94–95. For a full discussion of drama at or near Bury St. Edmunds in the later Middle Ages, see Gail McMurray Gibson, *The Theater of Devotion* (Chicago: Univ. of Chicago Press, 1989).

6. *Historians of the Church of York*, ed. Raine, I, 328–30.

7. *Chester*, ed. Clopper, pp. 23–24.

8. Further restorations were completed in 1886–87; see Nikolaus Pevsner and Edward Hubbard, *Cheshire* (Harmondsworth: Penguin, 1971), p. 148.

9. Marianne G. Briscoe, "Some Clerical Notions of Dramatic Decorum in Late Medieval England," *Comparative Drama*, 19 (1985), 1, quoting in translation from *Decretum Magistri Gratiani*, ed. Emil Friedberg (Graz: Akademische Druck, 1959), II, 452.

10. Cf. William Tydeman, *English Medieval Theatre 1400–1500* (London: Routledge and Kegan Paul, 1986), pp. 53, 75.

11. *Records of Plays and Players in Norfolk and Suffolk*, ed. Galloway and Wasson, pp. 106, 111.

12. See the line drawing illustrating a conjectural reconstruction of the staging for the play in the churchyard in Tydeman, *English Medieval Theatre*, p. 60, and the accompanying discussion, pp. 59–60. For a description of the church, see Nikolaus Pevsner, *North-West and South Norfolk* (Harmondsworth: Penguin, 1962), p. 127. For the alternate (and also quite plausible) view that Croxton in Suffolk is indicated, see David Mills, "Drama and Folk-Ritual," in *Medieval Drama*, ed. Lois Potter, Revels History of Drama in English, 1 (London and New York: Methuen, 1983), p. 147.

13. Philip Morant, *The History and Antiquities of the County of Essex* (London, 1767), II, 399; W. A. Mepham, "Mediaeval Plays in the 16th Century at Heybridge and Braintree," *Essex Review*, 55 (1946), 14–16; Clifford Davidson, "The Middle English Saint Play and Its Iconography," in *The Saint Play in Medieval Europe*, ed. Clifford Davidson, Early Drama, Art, and Music, Monograph Ser., 8 (Kalamazoo: Medieval Institute Publications, 1986), pp. 36–37.

14. Morant, *History and Antiquities of the County of Essex*, II, 399; Nikolaus Pevsner, *Essex*, 2nd ed. (Harmondsworth: Penguin, 1965), pp. 99–100.

15. *The Antiquarian Repertory*, ed. Francis Grose and Thomas Astle (1804), IV, 256, 258–59, 262; Ian Lancashire, "Orders for Twelfth Day and Night circa 1515 in the Second Northumberland Household Book," *English Literary Renaissance*, 10 (1980), 13–14, 21.

16. Lancashire, *Dramatic Texts and Records*, p. 447, citing plans and sketches in the West Sussex Record Office, Petworth House Archives 3538–47.

17. John Leland, *The Itinerary*, ed. Lucy Toulmin Smith (rpt. Carbondale: Southern Illinois Univ. Press, 1964), I, 53. For further discussion of the use of Wressle Castle for drama and entertainment, see Suzanne R. Westfall, *Patrons and Performance* (Oxford: Clarendon Press, 1990), pp. 18–23.

18. William Horman, *Vulgaria* (London, 1519), fols. 279^{v} (misnumbered as fol. 278), 281^{v} (*STC* 13811); see further citations from this source concerning playing in Lancashire, *Dramatic Texts and Records*, pp. 131–32.

19. T. H. Vail Motter, *The School Drama in England* (1929; rpt. Port Washington, N.Y.: Kennikat Press, 1968), pp. 53, 261–64.

20. Winchester MS. 33, fols. 65^r–73^v; facsimile and transcription in Norman Davis, *Non-Cycle Plays and the Winchester Fragments*, Leeds Texts and Monographs: Medieval Drama Facsimiles, 5 (Leeds: Univ. of Leeds School of English, 1979), pp. 161–78, 192–208.

21. See Lancashire, *Dramatic Texts and Records of Britain*, p. 283.

22. John Tucker Murray, *English Dramatic Companies, 1558–1642* (London: Constable, 1910), II, 404–06.

23. *Cambridge*, ed. Alan H. Nelson, Records of Early English Drama (Toronto: Univ. of Toronto Press, 1989), II, 716–17; Alan Nelson, "Contexts for Early English Drama: The Universities," in *Contexts for Early English Drama*, ed. Marianne G. Briscoe and John C. Coldewey (Bloomington: Indiana Univ. Press, 1989), p. 143.

24. *Cambridge*, ed. Nelson, I, 93–95; see also Leicester Bradner, "The First Cambridge Production of *Miles Gloriosus*," *Modern Language Notes*, 70 (1955), 400–03.

25. *Cambridge*, ed. Nelson, I, 149 and *passim.*

26. Nelson, "Contexts for Early English Drama," p. 143.

27. *Cambridge*, ed. Nelson, I, 146, 174.

28. *An Inventory of the Historical Monuments of the City of Cambridge* (London: Royal Commission on Historical Monuments, 1959), II, 172.

29. Leslie Hotson has provided a useful conjectural drawing of the Queens' College hall in use as a theater, though the scale is misleading since it makes the space seem much too large; see *Shakespeare's Wooden O* (New York: Macmillan, 1961), p. 170.

30. E. K. Chambers, *The Elizabethan Stage* (Oxford: Clarendon Press, 1923), I, 14–17.

31. The occasions were Christmas and Shrovetide; see Albert Feuillerat, *Documents Relating to the Revels at Court in the Time of King Edward VI and Queen Mary*, Materialen zur Kunde des älteren Englische Dramas, 41 (Louvain: A. Uystpruyst, 1914), p. 26.

32. Albert Feuillerat, *Documents Relating to the Office of the Revels in the Time of Queen Elizabeth*, Materialen zur Kunde des älteren Englischen Dramas, 21 (Louvain: A. Uystpruyst, 1908), pp. 213–21.

33. Ibid., pp. 213, 219. *Anthromiris* is, according to Feuillerat, probably a mistake for *Andromeda* (p. 457).

34. Ibid., p. 218.

35. Ibid., p. 219.

36. Charles Tyler Prouty, "An Early Elizabethan Playhouse," *Shakespeare Survey*, 6 (1953), 64–74.

37. Ibid., p. 70.

38. Ibid., pp. 70–71.

39. See especially Henryk Limon and Jerzy Limon, "An Interpretation of De Witt's Drawing on the Methodological Ground of Perspective Restitution," *Comparative Drama*, 17 (1983), 233–42.

40. *Acts of the Privy Council*, ed. John Roche Dasent (London: HMSO, 1893), VI, 168–69.

41. *Cambridge*, ed. Nelson, I, 199–200.

42. Fitzwilliam Museum, No. 806; see also *Cambridge*, ed. Nelson, II, 726–27.

43. *Records of the Worshipful Company of Carpenters*, ed. Bower Marsh (Oxford, 1913–16), III, 95–96, as cited by E. K. Chambers, *The Elizabethan Stage*, II, 379–80.

44. Herbert Berry, "The First Public Playhouses, Especially the Red Lion," *Shakespeare Quarterly*, 40 (1989), 133–48; see also Appendix, pp. 143-46, below.

45. Wickham, *Early English Stages*, II, Pt. 1, 186–96. Wickham's arguments are greatly overstated; see the survey of the problem by D. F. Rowan, "Inns, Inn-yards, and Other Playing Places," *The Elizabethan Theatre IX*, ed. G. R. Hibbard (Port Credit, Ontario: P. D. Meany, n.d.), pp. 1–20.

46. *Manerium de Walsham: Superuisio sive Terratorium* (1581, but copied c.1600), in Univ. of Chicago MS. Bacon 968, fols. 50^{v}–51^{r}, and *Field Book of the Manors of Walsham-le-Willows and Walsham Churchhouse*, Univ. of Chicago Bacon MS. 969, fol. 59^{v}, as quoted by Kenneth M. Dodd, "Another Elizabethan Theater in the Round," *Shakespeare Quarterly*, 21 (1970), 126.

47. William Stukeley, *Itinerarium Curiosum* (London, 1776), II, 43. Entrance and exit were cut through the banks more or less aligned with a north-south orientation. See also W. Atkinson, "On Some Earthworks Near Eamont Bridge," *Transactions of the Cumberland and Westmorland Antiquarian and Archaeological Society*, 6 (1883), 453–55, and A. C. Cawley, "The Staging of Medieval Drama," in *Medieval Drama*, ed. Potter, pp. 14–15.

48. Capgrave, *Ye Solace of Pilgrimes*, ed. Mills, pp. 17–18; quoted in Richard Beadle, "The East Anglian 'Game-place': A Possibility for Further Research," *REED Newsletter*, 1978 (No. 1), pp. 2–4; see also p. 148, n. 23, above.

49. William Borlase, *Observations on the Antiquities Historical and Monumental of the County of Cornwall* (Oxford: W. Jackson, 1754), p. 195.

50. William Borlase, *The Natural History of Cornwall* (Oxford, 1758), pp. 297–99. For speculations concerning the "Devil's Spoon," see R. Morton Nance, "The Plen an Gwary or Cornish Playing Place," *Journal of the Royal Institution of Cornwall*, 24 (1935), 203–06.

51. Borlase, *Observations*, pp. 195–96.

52. Richard Carew, *The Survey of Cornwall* (London, 1602), fol. 71^{v}.

53. Treve Holman, "Cornish Plays and Playing Places," *Theatre Notebook*, 4 (1949–50), 52–54.

54. A. Guthrie, "The Plain-an-gwarry, St. Just, Cornwall: Report on an Exploratory Excavation," *Proceedings of the West Cornwall Field Club*, 2 (1956–61), 6–7.

55. Jane A. Bakere, *The Cornish Ordinalia: A Critical Study* (Cardiff: Univ. of Wales Press, 1980), p. 156.

56. *The Ancient Cornish Drama*, ed. and trans. Edwin Norris (1859; rpt. New York: Benjamin Blom, 1968), I, 4–5. For a more recent translation, see *The Cornish Ordinalia*, trans. Markham Harris (Washington: Catholic Univ. of America Press, 1969).

57. Bakere, *The Cornish Ordinalia*, p. 160.

58. See Clifford Davidson, "Space and Time in Medieval Drama: Meditations on Orientation in the Early Theater," in *Word, Picture, and Spectacle*, ed. Clifford Davidson, Early Drama, Art, and Music, Monograph Ser., 5 (Kalamazoo: Medieval Institute Publications, 1984), pp. 43–45.

59. See, for example, *The Ancient Cornish Drama*, ed. and trans. Norris, I, 96–97, 166–67.

60. *The Creacion of the World*, ed. Paula Neuss (New York: Garland, 1983), p. 30.

61. Bakere, *The Cornish Ordinalia*, p. 165.

62. Charles Thomas, *Christian Antiquities of Camborne* (St. Austell: H. E. Warne, 1967), pp. 37–38.

63. *Beunans Meriasek: The Life of Saint Meriasek, Bishop and Confessor*, ed. and trans. Whitley Stokes (London: Trubner, 1872). For a more recent translation, see *The Life of Meriasek: A Medieval Cornish Miracle Play*, trans. Markham Harris (Washington: Catholic Univ. of America Press, 1977).

64. Quoted in translation by Richard Beadle, "The Medieval Drama of East Anglia: Studies in Dialect, Documentary Records and Stagecraft," unpubl. Ph.D. thesis (Univ. of York, 1977), p. 202; see also *Beunans Meriasek*, ed. and trans. Stokes, p. 199.

65. See Clifford Davidson, *Visualizing the Moral Life* (New York: AMS Press, 1989), pp. 63–74.

V. ILLUSTRATED MANUSCRIPT PLAYBOOKS

1. See Joseph R. Jones, "Isidore and the Theater," *Comparative Drama*, 16 (1982), 28–32.

2. See William Tydeman, *The Theatre in the Middle Ages* (Cambridge: Cambridge Univ. Press, 1978), pp. 48–49.

3. John of Salisbury, *Frivolities of Courtiers and Footprints of Philosophers*, trans. Joseph B. Pike (Minneapolis: Univ. of Minnesota Press, 1938), p. 36.

4. Otto Pächt and J. J. G. Alexander, *Illuminated Manuscripts in the Bodleian Library, Oxford*, III: *British, Irish, and Icelandic Schools* (Oxford: Clarendon Press, 1973), No. 132; Leslie Webber Jones and C. R. Morey, *The Miniatures of the Manuscripts of Terence Prior to the Thirteenth Century* (Princeton: Princeton Univ. Press, n.d.), I, 69–70; see also Larry M. Ayres, "The Role of an Angevin Style in English Romanesque Painting," *Zeitschrift für Kunstgeschichte*, 37 (1974), 220–21.

5. Rodney M. Thompson, *Manuscripts from St Albans Abbey 1066–1235* (Cambridge: D. S. Brewer, 1982), I, 35.

6. N. R. Ker, *Medieval Libraries of Britain*, 2nd ed. (London: Royal Historcial Society, 1964), p. 94; Jones and Morey, *Miniatures of the Manuscripts of Terence*, I, 78–79, 91.

7. Jones and Morey, *Miniatures of the Manuscripts of Terence*, I, 76.

8. Ibid., I, 70.

9. Pächt and Alexander, *Illuminated Manuscripts in the Bodleian Library*, No. 132.

10. Jones and Morey, *Miniatures of the Manuscripts of Terence*, I, 70.

11. Margaret Rickert, *Painting in Britain: The Middle Ages*, 2nd ed. (Harmondsworth: Penguin, 1965), p. 79.

12. John W. Basore, "The Scenic Value of the Miniatures in the Manuscripts of Terence," in *Studies in Honor of Basil L. Gildersleeve* (Baltimore: Johns Hopkins Press, 1902), p. 277.

13. *PL*, LXXXII, 658, as quoted by Jones, "Isidore and the Theater," p. 35.

14. Isidore of Seville, *Etymologiae*, ed. W. M. Lindsay (Oxford: Clarendon Press, 1910), 18.43, as quoted by Jones, "Isidore and the Theater," p. 36.

15. Jones and Morey, *Miniatures of the Manuscripts of Terence*, II, fig. 11.

16. Ibid., II, fig. 24.

17. Ibid., II, fig. 84.

18. Basore, "The Scenic Value of the Miniatures," p. 276.

19. Jones and Morey, *Miniatures of the Manuscripts of Terence*, II, fig. 203.

20. Rickert, *Painting in Britain*, pp. 79, 84.

21. Jones and Morey, *Miniatures of the Manuscripts of Terence*, I, 74–75.

22. A. B. Emden, *A Biographical Register of the University of Oxford to A.D. 1500* (Oxford: Clarendon Press, 1957), I, 398–400; A. F. Pollard, "Thomas Chaundler," *DNB*, Suppl., I, 419–20.

23. See especially M. R. James, *The Chaundler MSS.*, Roxburghe Club, 169 (London: J. B. Nichols and Sons, 1916), p. 10.

24. Eric G. Millar, *English Illuminated Manuscripts of the XIVth and XVth Centuries* (Paris and Brussels: G. van Oest, 1928), pp. 39–40; O. Elfrida Saunders, *English Illumination* (1933; rpt. New York: Hacker, 1969), I, 119–20.

25. Doris Enright-Clark Shoukri, ed., *Liber Apologeticus de Omni Statu Humanae Naturae* (New York: Renaissance Society of America, 1974), p. 25.

26. Ibid., pp. 56–57.

27. Ibid., pp. 64–67.

28. Ibid., p. 42.

29. Ibid., pp. 96–99.

30. See Psalm 84.11.

31. *Liber Apologeticus*, ed. Shoukri, pp. 130–31.

32. James, *The Chaundler MSS.*, p. 26.

33. *Liber Apologeticus*, ed. Shoukri, pp. 164–65.

34. Ibid., pp. 166–67.

VI. FOOLS AND OTHER ENTERTAINERS

1. Allardyce Nicoll, *Masks, Mimes, and Miracles: Studies in the Popular Theatre* (London: George C. Harrap, 1931), pp. 87–88.

2. J. Charles Cox, *Bench-Ends in English Churches* (London: Oxford Univ. Press, 1916), pp. 82–83. The legend of St. Genesius goes back at least to the sixth century; see David Hugh Farmer, *The Oxford Dictionary of Saints* (Oxford: Clarendon Press, 1978), p. 164, and also Chambers, *The Mediaeval Stage*, I, 10–11, 42. St. Genesius was the patron saint of minstrels and entertainers.

3. Nicoll, *Masks, Mimes, and Miracles*, pp. 160–63; Erika Tietze-Conrat, *Dwarfs and Jesters in Art* (London: Phaidon, 1957), p. 7.

4. Chambers, *Mediaeval Stage*, I, 321–23.

5. Quotations are from *The Macro Plays*, ed. Mark Eccles, EETS, 262 (London, 1969). Nought's name may be compared with the designation of a much earlier court fool who had been identified as *nebullo*—i.e., "nobody"; see Orderic Vitalis, *The Ecclesiastical History*, trans. Marjorie Chibnall (Oxford, 1969–81), IV, 186ff, as cited by Frank Barlow, *William Rufus* (Berkeley and Los Angeles: Univ. of California Press, 1983), p. 104.

6. G. L. Remnant, *A Catalogue of Misericords in Great Britain* (Oxford: Clarendon Press, 1969), p. 176; T. Tindall Wildridge, *The Misericords or Miseres of Beverley Minster* (Hull, 1877), pp. 26–28. For further discussion of dancing fools, see Sandra Billington, "'Suffer Fools Gladly': The Fool in Medieval England and the Play *Mankind*," in *The Fool and the Trickster*, ed. Paul V. A. Williams (Cambridge: D. S. Brewer, 1979), pp. 42–44. Billington, however, suggests a different interpretation of the characters in *Mankind* than I have presented here and in my book *Visualizing the Moral Life*, pp. 26–29. For further examples of dancing fools, see British Library MS. Harley 2897, fol. 42^v, and a misericord in Chichester Cathedral which illustrates a nude fool dancing with an ape-like creature; see D. J. Gifford, "Iconographical Notes toward a Definition of the Medieval Fool," in *The Fool and the Trickster*, ed. Williams, p. 20, and Remnant, *Catalogue of Misericords*, p. 154. These examples are fourteenth-century.

7. See Davidson, *Visualizing the Moral Life*, p. 26.

8. M. R. James, *The Canterbury Psalter* (London: Percy Lund, Humphries, 1935), pp. 3–4. See also the earlier Harley Psalter (British Library MS. Harley 603, fol. 7^v), likewise illuminated at Canterbury and closely related to the manuscript at Trinity College, Cambridge.

9. See also James, *Canterbury Psalter*, pp. 13, 24.

10. Enid Welsford, *The Fool: His Social and Literary History* (1935; rpt. Garden City, N.Y.: Doubleday, 1961), p. 278.

11. For an illustration in color, see Lucy Freeman Sandler, *The Peterborough Psalter in Brussels and Other Fenland Manuscripts* (London: Harvey Miller, 1974), fig. 296.

12. See especially Gifford, "Iconographical Notes," pp. 18–35.

13. Ibid, pp. 19–20.

14. M. R. James, *The Western Manuscripts in the Library of Emmanuel College* (Cambridge: Cambridge Univ. Press, 1904), No. 116.

15. Nigel Morgan, *Early Gothic Manuscripts, 1190–1250*, Survey of Manuscripts Illuminated in the British Isles (London: Harvey Miller, 1982–88), II, No. 163.

16. Ibid., II, No. 176.

17. Pächt and Alexander, *Illuminated Manuscripts in the Bodleian Library*, III, No. 436.

18. Christie, Manson, and Woods, *The Mostyn Hall Library: Printed Books and Manuscripts*, Pt. 3 (23–24 Oct. 1974); see also Lucy Freeman Sandler, *Gothic Manuscripts, 1285–1385*, Survey of Manuscripts Illuminated in the British Isles (London: Harvey Miller, 1986), II, No. 5.

19. Pächt and Alexander, *Illuminated Manuscripts in the Bodleian Library*, III, No. 537.

20. Sandler, *Gothic Manuscripts*, No. 134; J. J. G. Alexander and Elzbieta Temple, *Illuminated Manuscripts in Oxford College Libraries, the University Archives, and the Taylor Institution* (Oxford: Clarendon Press, 1985), No. 316.

21. Remnant, *Catalogue of Misericords*, p. 85; Francis Bond, *Wood Carvings in English Churches*, I: *Misericords* (London: Oxford Univ. Press, 1910), p. 226.

22. Remnant, *Catalogue of Misericords*, p. 57; Bond, *Wood Carvings*, I, 218.

23. Pächt and Alexander, *Illuminated Manuscripts in the Bodleian Library*, III, No. 651; Sandler, *Gothic Manuscripts*, No. 121. For a less surprising modification of the traditional iconography, see the Astor Hours and Psalter (Sandler, *Gothic Manuscripts*, No. 111, fig. 287), in which the fool is the one who is committing suicide.

24. For the suggestion that this misericord may have been "touched up," see Emma Phipson, *Choir Stalls and Their Carvings* (London: Batsford, 1896), p. 83; however, Phipson misinterprets the content of the misericord.

25. M. R. James, *St. George's Chapel, Windsor: The Woodwork of the Choir* (Windsor, 1933), p. 37.

26. Mary Frances White, *Fifteenth Century Misericords in the Collegiate Church of Holy Trinity, Stratford-upon-Avon* (Stratford-upon-Avon, 1974), fig. 24; Remnant, *Catalogue of Misericords*, p. 164; Clifford Davidson and Jennifer Alexander, *The Early Art of Coventry, Stratford-upon-Avon, Warwick, and Lesser Sites in Warwickshire*, Early Drama, Art, and Music, Reference Ser., 4 (Kalamazoo: Medieval Institute Publications, 1985), p. 80.

27. E. J. Nicol, "Some Notes on the History of the Betley Window," *Journal of the English Folk Dance and Song Society*, 7 (1953), 60–61; Charles G. O. Bridgeman, "Note on the Betley Morris Dance Window," *Collections for a History of Staffordshire*, William Salt Archaeological Society (London: Harrison and Sons, 1924), pp. 14–15.

28. "Mr. Tollet's Opinion concerning the Morris Dancers upon his Window," in *The Plays of William Shakespeare*, ed. Samuel Johnson and George Steevens, 2nd ed. (London, 1778), V, 432–33.

29. Billington, "Suffer Fools Gladly," p. 41.

30. See also *Illustrations from a Hundred Manuscripts in the Library of H. Yates Thompson* (London, 1914), p. 46.

31. Henry Morley, *Memoirs of Bartholomew Fair* (London: Chatto and Windus, 1880), pp. 1–12.

32. *Foedera, Conventiones, Literae*, ed. Thomas Rymer (London, 1704–17), IX, 335, as cited by John Southworth, *The English Medieval Minstrel* (Woodbridge: Boydell Press, 1989), p. 117.

33. E. W. Ives, "Tom Skelton—A Seventeenth-Century Jester," *Shakespeare Survey*, 13 (1960), 99–100.

34. John Doran, *The History of Court Fools* (1848; rpt. New York: Haskell House, 1966), p. 135.

35. See *Thomas Platter's Travels in England, 1599*, trans. Clare Williams (London: Jonathan Cape, 1937), p. 172.

36. Doran, *History of Court Fools*, pp. 146–52.

37. Stanley Morison, *The Likeness of Thomas More*, ed. Nicolas Barker (New York: Fordham Univ. Press, 1963), pp. 18–25, figs. 8–10. See also Theodore B. Leinwand, "Conservative Fools in James's Court and Shakespeare's Plays," *Shakespeare Studies*, 19 (1987), 220.

38. Charles Dalton, "Richard Tarlton," *DNB*, XIX, 369; Chambers, *Elizabethan Stage*, II, 342–45.

39. Thomas Fuller, *The Worthies of England*, ed. John Freeman (London: George Allen and Unwin, 1952), pp. 517–18.

40. *Tarlton's Newes Out of Purgatorie* (London, n.d.), p. 2.

41. See also Foakes, *Illustrations of the Stage*, pp. 44–45. The illustration from MS. Harl. 3885, fol. 19, is included by Foakes, but is reproduced here for convenience. For another illustration, based on the Harleian manuscript illumination, see Foakes, *Illustrations of the Stage*, p. 45.

42. For a bearward leading a bear (threatened by a dog) in painted glass in the Zouche Chapel at York Minster, see Clifford Davidson and David E. O'Connor, *York Art*, Early Drama, Art, and Music, Reference Ser., 1 (Kalamazoo: Medieval Institute Publications, 1978), p. 183.

43. John of Salisbury, *Frivolities of Courtiers and Footprints of Philosophers*, p. 38. A passage, identified as from a French manuscript in the Bodleian Library and included in a music textbook by Howard D. McKinney and W. R. Anderson (*Music in History* [Boston, 1940], p. 170), suggests that entertainers might perform a number of different roles from musician to acrobatics and juggling: "I can play the lute, vielle, pipe, bagpipe, panpipes, harp, fiddle, guittern, symphony, psaltery, organistrum, organ, tabor, and the rote. I can sing a song well, and make tales to please young ladies, and can play the gallant for them if necessary. I can throw knives into the air and catch them without cutting my fingers. I can jump rope most extraordinary and amusing. I can balance chairs, and make tables dance.

I can somersault, and walk doing a handstand" (quoted by Edmund A. Bowles, "Haut and Bas: The Grouping of Musical Instruments in the Middle Ages," *Musica Disciplina*, 8 [1954], 116n).

44. Morgan, *Early Gothic Manuscripts*, I, No. 50; John Plummer, *Manuscripts from the William S. Glazier Collection* (New York: Pierpont Morgan Library, 1959), p. 19, notes that the calendar and litany are for Hyde Abbey.

45. *Excerpta Historica, or, Illustrations of English History*, ed. Samuel Bentley (London: S. Bentley, 1831), p. 124. For fire eating, fire spitting, and related tricks on the Renaissance stage, see Louis B. Wright, "Juggling Tricks and Conjury on the English Stage before 1642," *Modern Philology*, 24 (1926–27), 269–84.

46. Ibid., p. 132.

47. Louis Réau, *Iconographie de l'art Chrétien* (Paris: Presses Universitaires de France, 1956), I, Pt. 2, 452–55.

48. G. R. Owst, *Literature and Pulpit in Medieval England*, 2nd ed. (New York: Barnes and Noble, 1933), p. 118, quoting British Library MS. Harl. 2398, fol. 8. The quotation is also noted by M. D. Anderson (*Drama and Imagery in Medieval English Churches* [Cambridge: Cambridge Univ. Press, 1963], p. 58), who includes a brief discussion of the daughter of Herodias as a tumbler in drama and art.

49. Joseph Strutt, *The Sports and Pastimes of England*, revised by J. Charles Cox (1903; rpt. Detroit: Singing Tree Press, 1968), pp. 174–75.

50. On this psalter, see Rickert, *Painting in Britain*, pp. 99–102.

51. For another narrative series with Salome doing an acrobatic dance or tumbling act, see the wall painting at Pickering, North Yorkshire. The painting, of the fifteenth century but restored in oils in the nineteenth century, is described by G. H. Lightfoot, "Mural Paintings in St. Peter's Church, Pickering," *Yorkshire Archaeological Journal*, 13 (1895), 359.

52. Réau, *Iconographie de l'art Chrétien*, I, Pt. 2, 454.

53. Bond, *Wood Carvings*, I, 143–44; Remnant, *Catalogue of Misericords*, p. 18; *The Victoria County History of the County of Cambridgeshire and the Isle of Ely*, ed. R. B. Pugh (London: Oxford Univ. Press, 1953), IV, 64.

54. See the comments of Barbara Palmer on the alabaster at the Chapel of St. Andrew, Ribstone Hall (*The Early Art of the West Riding of Yorkshire*, Early Drama, Art, and Music, Reference Ser., 6 [Kalamazoo: Medieval Institute Publications, 1990], pp. 95-96).

55. This manuscript, containing biblical illustrations, is probably Burgundian. See J. A. Herbert, *Illuminated Manuscripts* (London: Methuen, 1911), p. 200.

56. John A. Knowles, "Dance of Salome," *Notes and Queries*, 12th ser., 9 (1921), 197; Davidson and O'Connor, *York Art*, pp. 61–63.

57. Davidson and O'Connor, *York Art*, p. 63; Peter Gibson, "The Stained and Painted Glass of York," in *The Noble City of York*, ed. Alberic Stacpoole (York: Cerialis Press, 1972), Pl. 8A.

58. E. W. Tristram, *English Wall Paintings of the Fourteenth Century* (London: Routledge and Kegan Paul, 1955), p. 185; also noted in Anderson, *Drama and Imagery*, p. 58.

59. Constance Bullock-Davies, *Menestrellorum Multitudo: Minstrels at a Royal Feast* (Cardiff: Univ. of Wales Press, 1978), pp. 137–38. For another interesting example, a citation of a "litell Mayden the tumbler," see *Excerpta Historica*, ed. Bentley, as cited by Southworth, *English Medieval Minstrel*, p. 139.

60. George Zarnecki, *The Early Sculpture of Ely Cathedral* (London: Alec Tiranti, 1958), p. 50.

61. Remnant, *Catalogue of Misericords*, p. 157.

62. Sandler, *Gothic Manuscripts*, No. 167.

63. Remnant, *Catalogue of Misericords*, p. 57.

64. Ibid., p. 54. Cf. Chandos Herald's remarks in his biography of the Black Prince when he complains about people's preferences for "chatterers, false liars, jongleurs or jesters who will pull faces and imitate a monkey to make them laugh" (*The Life and Campaigns of the Black Prince*, trans. Richard Barber [New York: St. Martin's Press, 1986], p. 85).

65. See Francis Wormald, *English Drawings of the Tenth and Eleventh Centuries* (London: Faber and Faber, 1952), pp. 28–29, 66–67; Elzbieta Temple, *Anglo-Saxon Manuscripts 900–1066*, Survey of Manuscripts Illuminated in the British Isles, 2 (London: Harvey Miller, 1976), No. 51.

66. Sandler, *Gothic Manuscripts*, No. 161.

67. W. H. James Weale *et al.*, *A Descriptive Catalogue of the Second Series of Fifty Manuscripts in the Collection of Henry Yates Thompson* (Cambridge: Cambridge Univ. Press, 1902), No. 56; Sandler, *Gothic Manuscripts*, No. 36.

68. Sandler, *Gothic Manuscripts*, No. 107; Millar, *Luttrell Psalter*.

69. George Warner, *Descriptive Catalogue of Illuminated Manuscripts in the Library of C. W. Dyson Perrins* (Oxford, 1920), No. 10; Sandler, *Gothic Manuscripts*, No. 124.

70. *The Plays of William Shakespeare*, ed. Johnson and Steevens, V, 449.

71. The presence of the fool has already been noted; see above, p. 74.

72. Ibid., V, 427–28.

73. *Herefordshire, Worcestershire*, ed. David N. Klausner, Records of Early English Drama (Toronto: Univ. of Toronto Press, 1990), pp. 14–15.

74. Anne G. Gilchrist, "A Carved Morris-Dance Panel from Lancaster Castle," *Journal of the English Folk Dance and Song Society*, 1, No. 2 (1933), 86–88.

75. Davidson and O'Connor, *York Art*, p. 183. Mummers and dancers were also present on the mid-fifteenth-century roof bosses at the Guildhall in York; see J. B. Morrell, *Woodwork in York* (London: Batsford, 1949), pp. 94, 96. The roof of this building was destroyed by bombing in World War II.

76. Phillip Stubbes, *The Anatomie of Abuses* (London, 1583), fols. 92^{v}–93^{r}.

77. Ibid., fol. 93.

78. Nicoll, *Masks, Mimes, and Miracles*, pp. 35–37, 84–85, 109; but see also the recent comments of Alan J. Fletcher, "Jugglers Celtic and Anglo-Saxon," *Theatre Notebook*, 44 (1990), 2–10. For prosecutions of persons whose dancing occurred during the time of religious services, see *Herefordshire, Worcestershire*, ed. Klausner, *passim*.

79. Morgan, *Early Gothic Manuscripts*, No. 112.

80. See especially Strutt, *Sports and Pastimes*, pp. 167–73, and the comment by Horman, *Vulgaria*: "A iugler with his troget deceueth me*n*s syght" (fol. 280^{v}).

81. Withington, *English Pageantry*, I, 73.

82. Strutt, *Sports and Pastimes*, p. xxxv.

83. Withington, *English Pageantry*, I, 72–73; see the entry in the Coventry accounts which indicates payment "for a torch yat wodhowsse had for ye Juddasys xvj d" (*Coventry*, ed. Ingram, p. 467).

84. *Chester*, ed. Clopper, pp. 258–59, citing British Library MS. Harley 2150, fol. 186. The date of the St. George's Day show being described is 1610.

85. *Records of Plays and Players in Norfolk and Suffolk*, ed. Galloway and Wasson, p. 129.

86. Richard Bernheimer, *Wild Men in the Middle Ages* (1952; rpt. New York: Octagon Books, 1979), p. 69. For another example of a wild man doing battle with a wild woman, see James, *St. George's Chapel, Windsor: The Woodwork of the Choir*, p. 38.

87. Bernheimer, *Wild Men*, p. 123. See also the depictions of the wild man in the Smithfield Decretals (British Library MS. Royal 10.E.IV, fols. 72^{r}–74^{v}) where this figure tries to embrace a woman, to ravish her, or otherwise to force himself upon her. The final miniature shows a knight killing the wild man.

88. Remnant, *Catalogue of Misericords*, p. 97; cf. J. S. Purvis, "The Use of Continental Woodcuts and Prints by the 'Ripon School' of Woodcarvers in the Sixteenth Century," *Archaeologia*, 85 (1936), fig. 2, Pl. XXV.

89. Remnant, *Catalogue of Misericords*, p. 82; Fred H. Crossley, "On the Remains of Mediaeval Stallwork in Lancashire," *Transactions of the Historic Society of Lancashire and Cheshire*, n.s. 34 (1919), 12–13.

90. M. R. James, *The Treatise of Walter de Milemete* (Roxburghe Club, 1913), p. xxxi.

VII. MINSTRELS

1. Chambers, *Mediaeval Stage*, II, 262.

2. Thomas de Cobham, *Summa Confessorum*, ed. F. Broomfield (Louvain: Editions Nauwelaerts, 1968), pp. 291–92, as quoted in translation by John Stevens, *Words and Music in the Middle Ages* (Cambridge: Cambridge Univ. Press, 1986), p. 235. See also Chambers, *Mediaeval Stage*, II, 262–63.

3. On the term 'minstrel,' see Lawrence Gushee, "Minstrel," *The New Grove Dictionary of Music and Musicians*, ed. Stanley Sadie (London: Macmillan, 1980), XII, 347. 'Minstrel,' which properly is used only for musician-entertainers of the twelfth to the seventeenth centuries, is eventually supplanted by the word 'musician.' In the latter part of the sixteenth century, the designation of 'minstrel' was applied to only the most decadent of wandering

entertainers such as the man who was retained for the entertainment of Queen Elizabeth at Kenilworth in July 1575 though he did not in fact perform. For his appearance, see Chambers, *Mediaeval Stage*, II, 263–64.

4. Alexander and Temple, *Illuminated Manuscripts in Oxford College Libraries*, No. 283; Morgan, *Early Gothic Manuscripts*, No. 242.

5. Michael Andrew Michael, "The Artists of the Milemete Treatise," unpublished diss. (Westfield College, Univ. of London, 1986), p. 62.

6. Remnant, *Catalogue of Misericords*, p. 154, Pl. 38. Another example is the woodcut in the *Kalendar of Shepardes* (London: Julian Notary, c.1518), sig. L3^{v}, which illustrates the effects of Venus; in this illustration a fidel player and a piper perform for a man and a woman who are bathing in a tub.

7. Robert Mannyng of Brunne, *Handlyng Synne*, ed. Idelle Sullens (Binghamton: Medieval and Renaissance Texts and Studies, 1983), p. 118. For a survey of hostility to minstrels, see Chambers, *Mediaeval Stage*, I, 35–41. The idea that the folk musician serves the devil is still current folklore in Sweden where the term 'bokfot'—i.e., goat's (or devil's) foot—is applied to folk fiddlers, whose art is believed to have originally been learned from trolls.

8. Jocelyn Price, "Theatrical Vocabulary in Old English," *Medieval English Theatre*, 5 (1983), 61, 67.

9. For the view that the *scop* probably did not play a musical instrument until at least the ninth century, see Jeff Opland, *Anglo-Saxon Oral Poetry* (New Haven: Yale Univ. Press, 1980), *passim.*

10. Ibid., pp. 242–43.

11. Ibid., p. 244.

12. *Anglo-Saxon Poetry*, rev. ed., trans. R. K. Gordon (London: Dent, 1954), p. 70; *The Exeter Book*, ed. George Philip Krapp and Elliott Van Kirk Dobbie, Anglo-Saxon Poetic Records, 3 (New York: Columbia Univ. Press, 1936), p. 153.

13. According to William of Malmesbury, King Alfred is said to have deceived the Danes by disguising himself as a minstrel who played the harp; see Chambers, *Mediaeval Stage*, I, 31.

14. Angela Care Evans, *The Sutton Hoo Ship Burial* (London: British Museum Publications, 1986), pp. 69–72; see also Rupert Bruce-Mitford, *Aspects of Anglo-Saxon Archaeology* (New York: Harper and Row, 1974), pp. 188–97.

15. Robert Mannyng of Brunne, *Handlyng Synne*, p. 120; see Chambers, *Mediaeval Stage*, I, 56n.

16. *The Memorials of St. Dunstan*, ed. William Stubbs, Rerum Britannicarum Medii Aevi Scriptores, 63 (London: Eyre and Spottiswoode, 1874), p. 170, as quoted in translation by Opland, *Anglo-Saxon Oral Poetry*, p. 179; see also F. P. Pickering, *Literature and Art in the Middle Ages* (Coral Gables: Univ. of Miami Press, 1970), esp. pp. 285–307.

17. Opland, *Anglo-Saxon Oral Poetry*, p. 180.

18. Mary Remnant, *English Bowed Instruments from Anglo-Saxon to Tudor Times* (Oxford: Clarendon Press, 1986), p. 32.

19. Pickering, *Literature and Art*, pp. 285–307.

20. See T. S. R. Boase, *The York Psalter in the Hunterian Museum, Glasgow* (London: Faber and Faber, 1962), p. 28, and, especially, Frank Ll. Harrison, "Tradition and Innovation in Instrumental Usage 1100–1450," in *Aspects of Medieval and Renaissance Music: A Birthday Offering for Gustave Reese*, ed. Jan LaRue (London: Oxford Univ. Press, 1966), p. 321.

21. Jane Hetherington Brown, "The Iconography, Style and Production of the Hunterian Psalter Illuminations," in *The Hunterian Psalter*, ed. Nigel Thorp (Oxford: Oxford Microform, for Glasgow Univ. Library, 1983), p. 3; Harrison, "Tradition and Innovation," p. 321.

22. Sydney C. Cockerell, *The Gorleston Psalter* (London: Chiswick Press, 1907), p. 29; Sandler, *Peterborough Psalter*, pp. 98–99, and *Gothic Manuscripts*, No. 50.

23. Millar, *Luttrell Psalter*, p. 1; Sandler, *Gothic Manuscripts*, No. 107.

24. For discussion of some of these instruments, see Jeremy Montagu, *The World of Medieval and Renaissance Musical Instruments* (Newton Abbot: David and Charles, 1976). In the Luttrell Psalter, dancing, in this case of an acrobatic sort, is also illustrated in the margin of fol. 68; in this instance, a woman dancer stands on the shoulders of a male dancer while they perform.

25. Clair C. Olson, "The Minstrels at the Court of Edward III," *PMLA*, 56 (1941), 603; for the view that 'waits' might have been specific instruments used in the household rather than a designation of a type of musician, see Richard Rastall, "The Minstrels of the English Royal Households, 25 Edward I–1 Henry VIII: An Inventory," *Royal Musical Association Research Chronicle*, 4 (1967), 1.

26. Ibid.

27. The playing of all the minstrels together as a band is, however, very doubtful.

28. Ibid., pp. 7–41. For a fine fifteenth-century orchestra, see the carvings of angel musicians on the choir screen (c.1430–50) at York Minster who play a number of early instruments, including the tromba marine, symphony or organistrum, and clavicembalo or early harpsichord. See Davidson and O'Connor, *York Art*, pp. 188–92, fig. 41.

29. See Rastall, "Minstrels of the English Royal Households," pp. 1–2.

30. See especially JoAnna Dutka, "Mysteries, Minstrels, and Music," *Comparative Drama*, 8 (1974), 112–24, and *Music in the English Mystery Plays*, Early Drama, Art, and Music, Reference Ser., 2 (Kalamazoo: Medieval Institute Publications, 1980), *passim.*

31. See especially Edmund A. Bowles, "Musical Instruments in Civic Processions during the Middle Ages," *Acta Musicologica*, 33 (1961), 147–61, and "Haut and Bas," pp. 115–40.

32. See especially the discussion in Edmund A. Bowles, "Musical Instruments at the Medieval Banquet," *Revue Belge de Musicologie*, 12 (1958), 41–51.

33. *Ludus Coventriae, or the Plaie Called Corpus Christi*, ed. K. S. Block, EETS, e.s. 120 (London: Oxford Univ. Press, 1922), p. 174.

34. For a description of the instruments, see Terence Ford and Andrew Green, *The Pierpont Morgan Library Medieval and Renaissance Manuscripts*, RIdIM/RCMI Inventory of Music Iconography, 3 (New York: Research Center for Musical Iconography, 1988), No. 1.

For another example of the feast of the prodigal son, see the woodcut used on the title page of a sixteenth-century playbook, below, p. 162 and fig. 139.

35. Ibid., No. 361. Loud instruments were not unusual; see the English court feast illustrated in Vienna, Österreichische Nationalbibliothek MS. 2534, fol. 165^{v}. Painted by a French artist in c.1470, the scene not only includes two loud instruments playing before the table while a course is being brought in, but also shows a fool in hood, coxcomb, and foolstick jesting in front of the musicians (Edmund A. Bowles, *La Pratique Musicale au Moyen Age* [Geneva: Minkoff and Lattès, 1983], Pl. 39).

36. See Zarnecki, *Early Sculpture of Ely Cathedral*, p. 50, figs. 87–92.

37. Remnant, *Catalogue of Misericords*, p. 35.

38. Remnant, *English Bowed Instruments*, pp. 64–65, figs. 150–51.

39. See *An Inventory of the Historical Monuments in the City of York* (Royal Commission on Historical Monuments, 1972), III, 9.

40. For a list of selected English bowed instruments, see Remnant, *English Bowed Instruments*, pp. 138–50.

41. Gwen and Jeremy Montagu, "Beverley Minster Reconsidered," *Early Music*, 6 (1978), 403. Uncritical use of illustrations of these minstrels is quite common; see, for example, Wickham, *Early English Stages*, III, Pl. VI, which reproduces eight minstrels, including the bagpiper, from Beverley Minster. One of Wickham's figures is eighteenth-century, and of the others only one, the psaltery player, is fully authentic.

42. Montagu, "Beverley Minster Reconsidered," p. 406.

VIII. ILLUSTRATIONS IN PRINTED PLAYBOOKS

1. Edward Hodnett, *English Woodcuts, 1480–1535* (London: Bibliographic Society, 1935), No. 2288; W. W. Greg, *A Bibliography of the English Printed Drama to the Restoration* (London: Bibliographic Society, 1939), Nos. 1–2.

2. See Robert Mullally, "The Source of the *Fulgens* Woodcut," *Theatre Notebook*, 30 (1976), 61–63, and also Alan Nelson, ed., *The Plays of Henry Medwall* (Cambridge: D. S. Brewer, 1980), p. 20.

3. Mullally, "The Source of the *Fulgens* Woodcut," pp. 63–64.

4. E. Gordon Duff, *A Century of the English Book Trade* (London: Bibliographical Society, 1948), p. 129.

5. See John M. Ward, "The Maner of dauncing," *Early Music*, 4 (1976), 129–30.

6. Greg, *A Bibliography*, No. 3(a).

7. Hodnett, *English Woodcuts*, No. 882.

8. Ibid., No. 877.

9. Ibid., pp. vii–viii.

10. Joseph Ames, William Herbert, and Thomas F. Dibdin, *Typographical Antiquities* (London: W. Miller, 1812), II, 335.

11. Alfred W. Pollard, "Some Notes on English Illustrated Books," *Transactions of the Bibliographical Society*, 6, Pt. 1 (1901), 38–51. The woodcut identified as Contemplation had first been used by an English printer in Pynson's *Kalender of Shepardys* (1506), sig. O4^{v}. For the character of Hick Scorner and its relation to a historical figure, Richard de la Pole, see Ian Lancashire, ed., *Two Tudor Interludes: The Interlude of Youth, Hick Scorner* (Manchester: Manchester Univ. Press, 1980), pp. 59–65.

12. Greg, *A Bibliography*, I, No. 3(c).

13. The earlier edition was probably from the 1520's. Skot was known to be active as a printer from 1521, when his first dated book was published, until the late 1530's; see Duff, *A Century of the English Book Trade*, p. 149, and Henry R. Plomer, *Wynkyn de Worde and His Contemporaries from the Death of Caxton to 1535* (London: Grafton, 1925), pp. 213–15. The later edition has a break in the left woodcut in the flower below the foot of Everyman; see Greg, *A Bibliography*, I, Nos. 4(c), 4(d).

14. For the first edition issued by Skot, see Greg, *A Bibliography*, I, No. 4(c), Pl. VIII; the title page is also illustrated in *Everyman*, ed. A. C. Cawley (Manchester: Manchester Univ. Press, 1961), frontispiece.

15. W. W. Greg, ed., *Everyman, from the Edition by John Skot, at Britwell Court*, Materialen zur Kunde des älteren Englischen Dramas, 4 (1904: rpt. Vaduz: Kraus, 1963), p. viii.

16. Hodnett, *English Woodcuts*, No. 961.

17. The woodcut is conveniently reproduced by Dietrich Briesemeister, *Bilder des Todes* (Unterschneidheim: Walter Uhl, 1970), fig. 126.

18. *Everyman*, ed. Cawley, p. 39.

19. See also Death with a dart in Julian Notary's edition of the *Kalendar of Shepardes* (c.1518), sig. G5^{v}.

20. These woodcuts are added in Skot's second edition but do not appear in his earlier edition.

21. Greg, *A Bibliography*, I, No. 20(a), Pl. XII. The woodcut, which previously had been used in Vérard's *Therence*, had also been used in Pynson's *Kalender of Shepardys*; see W. Bang and R. B. McKerrow, eds., *The Enterlude of Youth*, Materialen zur Kunde des älteren Englischen Dramas, 12 (1905; rpt. Vaduz: Kraus, 1963), p. 49.

22. Greg, *A Bibliography*, I, No. 20(b).

23. Ibid., I, No. 20(c), Pl. XIV.

24. Ibid., I, No. 21(a), Pl. XV.

25. The woodcut in another edition, Allde's quarto of 1569, may in fact be of more interest, though again it has nothing to do with the play itself; it contains two Death figures in procession and playing bapgpipes and a portative organ. See Greg, *A Bibliography*, I, No. 21(b), Pl. XVI.

26. Ibid., I, No. 30(b).

27. Ibid., I, No. 35(a).

28. Ibid., I, No. 35(b), Pl. XXII.

29. Ibid., I, No. 32(a).

30. Richard Southern, *The Staging of Plays before Shakespeare* (London: Faber and Faber, 1973), p. 96.

31. Greg, *A Bibliography*, I, No. 32(b).

32. Ibid., I, No. 5.

33. Ibid., I, No. 24(a), Pl. XVI.

34. On the sources of the *Three Laws*, see Peter Happé, ed., *The Complete Plays of John Bale* (Cambridge: D. S. Brewer, 1985), I, 13–14.

35. The printer may have been Dirik van den Straten of Wesel; see Robert Steele, "Notes on English Books Printed Abroad, 1525–48," *Transactions of the Bibliographical Society*, 11 (1912), 230–32.

36. Greg, *A Bibliography*, I, No. 26. Since the book was not entered in the Stationers' Register, the date likely was prior to 1557, while the earliest date would be about 1546, when Walley set up business as a stationer; see Duff, *A Century of the English Book Trade*, p. 164.

37. See "Day-Book of John Dorne," ed. F. Madan, *Collecteana*, 1st ser. (Oxford: Clarendon Press, 1885), as cited by W. W. Greg, ed., *The Interlude of Johan the Evangelist* (Oxford: Malone Society, 1907), p. vi.

38. For the iconography of St. John the Evangelist, see Réau, *Iconographie de l'art Chrétien*, III, Pt. 2, 708–20. A different version of the story of the attempted poisoning of the saint is told by Jacobus de Voragine, *The Golden Legend*, trans. Granger Ryan and Helmut Ripperger (1941; rpt. New York: Arno Press, 1969), p. 61.

39. Greg, *A Bibliography*, I, No. 35(c).

40. Duff, *A Century of the English Book Trade*, pp. 2–3.

41. Greg, *A Bibliography*, I, No. 71.

42. See especially Harold C. Gardiner, *Mysteries' End* (1946; rpt. Hamden, Conn.: Archon Books, 1967), pp. 65–93.

43. Frederick S. Boas, "*The Four Cardynal Vertues*: A Fragmentary Moral Interlude," *Theatre Notebook*, 5 (1950), 5–10; Southern, *Staging of Plays before Shakespeare*, pp. 349–51.

44. Boas, "*The Four Cardynal Vertues*," p. 5, only mentions the 1517 edition of Barclay's *Ship of Fools*; but see Barclay, *Shyppe of Fooles* (Wynkyn de Worde, 1509), sig. H8.

APPENDIX: EARLY ELIZABETHAN THEATERS AND THE ROSE

1. Chambers, *Elizabethan Stage*, II, 384; on the Curtain, apparently built in 1577, see ibid., II, 400–04.

2. See Berry, "The First Public Playhouses," pp. 133–48.

3. Ibid., p. 137.

4. Berry, "The First Public Playhouses," pp. 137–38.

5. Chambers, *Elizabethan Stage*, II, 384, 387.

6. Foakes, *Illustrations of the English Stage*, pp. 10–19.

7. *New York Times*, 30 Oct. 1989, pp. 13, 16.

8. See Foakes, *Illustrations of the Stage*, pp. 52–55.

9. See John B. Gleason, "The Dutch Humanist Origins of the DeWitt Drawing of the Swan Theatre," *Shakespeare Quarterly*, 32 (1981), 329–38.

10. This drawing has been used as evidence against the concept of an "inner stage," which nevertheless would have been quite theatrically ineffective on a stage like that of the Swan.

11. Limon and Limon, "An Interpretation of DeWitt's Drawing," pp. 233–42.

12. Chambers, *Elizabethan Stage*, II, 436–39, 466–68.

13. *Henslowe's Diary*, ed. R. A. Foakes and R. T. Rickert (Cambridge: Cambridge Univ. Press, 1961), pp. 16, 21.

14. Chambers, *Elizabethan Stage*, II, 408.

15. John Orrell and Andrew Gurr, "What the Rose Can Tell Us," *Antiquity*, 63 (1989), 421.

16. *Henslowe's Diary*, ed. Foakes and Rickert, pp. 6–7, 9–13.

17. Chambers, *Elizabethan Stage*, II, 409.

18. *Henslowe's Diary*, ed. Foakes and Rickert, p. 13.

19. Orrell and Gurr, "What the Rose Can Tell Us," pp. 423–25.

20. Ibid., p. 425.

21. Ibid., pp. 426–27.

22. Ibid., p. 428.

23. See the account by John Cox, "Rediscovering the Rose Theater," *Early Drama, Art, and Music Review*, 12 (1989), 5–9.

INDEX